Describing Electronic, Digital, and Other Media Using AACR2 and RDA

A How-To-Do-It Manual® and CD-ROM for Librarians

Mary Beth Weber
Fay Angela Austin

HOW-TO-DO-IT MANUALS®

NUMBER 168

Neal-Schuman Publishers, Inc.
New York London

Don't miss this book's companion website!

For updates on changes in *RDA* and other cataloging resources and practices; links to presentations, blog posts, and more; and to contact the authors with questions and feedback, visit:

http://www.neal-schuman.com/describingmedia

Published by Neal-Schuman Publishers, Inc.
100 William St., Suite 2004
New York, NY 10038

Printed and bound in the United States of America.

The paper used in this publication meets the minimum requirements of American National Standard for Information Sciences—Permanence of Paper for Printed Library Materials, ANSI Z39.48-1992.

Library of Congress Cataloging-in-Publication Data

Weber, Mary Beth.
Describing electronic, digital, and other media using AACR2 and RDA : a how-to-do-it manual and CD-ROM for librarians / Mary Beth Weber, Fay Angela Austin.
p. cm. — (How-to-do-it manuals ; no. 168)
Includes bibliographical references and index.
ISBN 978-1-55570-668-5 (alk. paper)
1. Cataloging of nonbook materials—Handbooks, manuals, etc. 2. Cataloging of audio-visual materials—Handbooks, manuals, etc. 3. Cataloging of electronic information resources—Handbooks, manuals, etc. 4. Descriptive cataloging—Standards. I. Austin, Fay Angela. II. Title.

Z695.66.W435 2011
025.3'4—dc22

2010042001

Contents

List of Figures

Preface

The goal of *Describing Electronic, Digital, and Other Media Using AACR2 and RDA: A How-To-Do-It Manual and CD-ROM for Librarians* is to provide a source of useful information and ideas for catalogers who are charged with creating descriptive records in the rapidly changing environment of resource description for digital and nontangible formats. With the publication of this manual, the authors aim to ease the transition from *Anglo-American Cataloguing Rules*, Second Edition (*AACR2*) to *Resource Description and Access* (*RDA*) as a practical, flexible tool by introducing the concepts behind the *Functional Requirements for Bibliographic Records* (*FRBR*) and by offering guided, step-by-step instructions for the creation of descriptive records based on its principles. Intended primarily for individuals who are familiar with resource description according to *Anglo-American Cataloguing Rules*, Second Revised Edition (*AACR2R*), integrated library systems (ILSs), and applying and interpreting Library of Congress Classification and Subject Headings, this manual is also appropriate for librarians, library assistants, and those individuals who are new to resource description but who may benefit from a cursory understanding of *AACR2* as an important link to *RDA*.

Scope

Describing Electronic, Digital, and Other Media Using AACR2 and RDA: A How-To-Do-It Manual and CD-ROM for Librarians covers a wide-ranging area of resources and topics. To reflect the shifts in trends, we do not include some standard categories of resources (e.g., printed music and globes) and focus instead on electronic, Internet, and other emerging resources, such as streaming audio and video. We do not cover classification in detail, because it varies by type of library, type of collection, and local practice. Institutions may choose not to classify nonbook materials or may selectively apply classification to some categories of these resources. The treatment of series is discussed briefly only when appropriate, because series are not as prevalent with nonprint resources as they are for monographs.

In this manual, we provide examples in MAchine-Readable Cataloging (MARC) format, Metadata for Object Description (MODS) schema, and Dublin Core (DC) to reflect different display formats that libraries may use to facilitate access to resources. Libraries may have separate modules for creating and providing access to MARC and non-MARC metadata collections, while other institutions provide federated searching that seamlessly enables access to both types of records, such as the University of Rochester's eXtensible Catalog (XC). We refer to all descriptive records in this manual as "metadata," regardless of whether they are described using MARC, MODS, or DC.

Many changes have taken place within the library and information field since the previous edition of this text, including the introduction of new material types (e.g., Blu-ray discs, streaming audio and video, and e-books) and the evolution of resource description standards (specifically, the development of *RDA*, addressed in more detail in "Introduction: The Future of Resource Description"). Catalogers need solutions for issues that arise during the course of their work; they seek assistance via listservs and blogs, by attending professional conferences and workshops, and through networking with colleagues. Still, a cataloger's best friend in deciphering how to catalog a nonprint resource is one that is easily accessible, quickly referenced, and available precisely when needed. *Describing Electronic, Digital, and Other Media Using AACR2 and RDA: A How-To-Do-It Manual and CD-ROM for Librarians* fulfills this need.

The title of this edition reflects current terminology and is more inclusive of the formats covered in the chapters. Although the terms *special formats cataloging* and *nonprint cataloging* are commonly used, we believe that the term *resource description* most accurately describes this manual and its mission. Because the terms *AV* and *audiovisual* are used to a lesser extent by the profession to describe these materials, we do not use them in this manual and instead use *electronic*, *digital*, and *media*.

This manual differs in content from the previous edition as follows:

- Chapter 3 provides a general overview of resource description for sound recordings. This chapter is designed for individuals who catalog these resources in addition to other nonbook formats, the "accidental cataloger," rather than the specialized music cataloger who may concentrate on a specific musical genre. For this reason, we do not include musical scores, which are a specialty and not appropriate to the scope of this text.
- Chapter 4's emphasis is on videorecording formats, including Blu-ray discs and streaming video. We do not address motion pictures in the text.
- We do not include continuing resources (formerly known as *serials*) and the Cooperative Online Serials (CONSER) Program documentation in this edition, as this is another area of specialty and frequently beyond the scope of the accidental cataloger who handles nonbook materials.
- We provide information in each chapter following the *FRBR* principles of description—work, manifestation, expression, and item—along with *RDA* and *AACR2* principles of resource description.
- With each chapter, we provide a list of resources for catalogers, such as electronic mailing lists, blogs, publications (print and electronic), professional organizations, and conferences.

- In keeping with emerging trends, we use the term *resource description* rather than *cataloging* to be inclusive of all work done to provide access to resources. We view the creation of MARC bibliographic records and non-MARC metadata as resource description and attempt in this manual to be inclusive of these concepts in the guidelines and examples.
- This edition includes a companion CD-ROM to supplement the main text and to serve as a reference guide for use as individuals are cataloging. The main text focuses on issues specifically related to the cataloging of nonbook resources while the CD guides users through the process of resource description and includes links to useful documentation and information. Note that the URLs provided for *RDA* in the companion CD are to the "RDA Constituency Review," and not the *RDA Toolkit*. We have taken this approach because all libraries will not transition to *RDA* right away. These links will direct users to something tangible as they begin working with *RDA*. There are minor inconsistencies in content, terminology, and some of the numbering of rules between the *RDA Toolkit* and the "RDA Constituency Review."

The authors acknowledge the difficulty of providing access to information that has the potential to become quickly outdated. For this reason, *Describing Electronic, Digital, and Other Media Using AACR2 and RDA: A How-To-Do-It Manual and CD-ROM for Librarians* includes a companion website (http://www.neal-schuman.com/describingmedia) that will provide a list of current resources about *RDA* and cataloging and will address changes to *RDA* as they emerge. We also provide a means for readers to contact us with questions and feedback.

Organization

The manual opens with "Introduction: The Future of Resource Description," which examines the impact of *FRBR* and emerging standards such as *RDA* on resource description.

Chapter 1, "Essential Background," provides an overview of resource description with discussion of the current initiatives and general considerations such as bibliographic description, subject access, added entries, and so forth.

Chapters 2 through 8 address carrier-specific resource description:

- Cartographic resources
- Sound recordings
- Videos
- Electronic resources
- Electronic integrating resources
- Microforms
- Multimedia kits and mixed materials

Each chapter begins with an overview of important considerations regarding specific media and carrier types, followed by an outline of the elements that may be included in resource description for the format. Examples of descriptive records that illustrate the points outlined in the chapters appear where the records are discussed rather than at the ends of the chapters as in the previous edition. This change provides information at point of need and reduces the time spent flipping through pages. The examples in this text are original, taken from the authors' work or work done by their respective staffs, and were not taken from bibliographic records submitted by other libraries to OCLC or from other institutions' ILSs. In the event that an example is similar to a record available in OCLC, the record submitted to the union databases postdates the record created for use in this text.

CD-ROM Contents

The companion CD-ROM is for catalogers to use as they create descriptive records. The organization of the CD follows that of the manual. It begins with an introduction that gives an overview of resource description, including a comparison of *AACR2* and *RDA*, and provides guidance on how to formulate core level description. It continues with seven sections that correspond to the carrier-specific resource description chapters. The CD will guide catalogers through the following procedures:

- creating descriptive records, beginning with selection of core elements for description;
- choosing preferred sources of information for each type of resource;
- identifying and assigning a title proper and variant titles;
- identifying and assigning publication details;
- creating a physical description through specific examples for each type of resource and carrier;
- providing a descriptive summary;
- providing subject access;
- adding additional access points;
- using both *AACR2* and *RDA*; and
- accessing live links to resources and examples.

Describing Electronic, Digital, and Other Media Using AACR2 and RDA: A How-To-Do-It Manual and CD-ROM for Librarians deciphers the challenges of resource description by guiding catalogers in how to:

- choose preferred access point to represent a work or expression based on the preferred source of information for each type of media;
- provide the descriptive treatment necessary for creating a basic metadata record;
- enter basic series information (the manual includes background information on changes to series treatment);
- formulate notes that are of special importance for nonprint resources, with an emphasis on notes specific to particular formats;
- formulate subject-added entries (personal, corporate, and topical) that are appropriate for each type of format; and

- provide preferred access points for creator and other responsible parties that are appropriate for each type of format.

Although an increasing amount of research is now conducted via the Internet and by consulting web publications and databases, the need still exists for organized guidelines and interpretations of them for catalogers to consult and apply in their work. When the first edition of this book, *Cataloging Nonbook Formats*, was published in 1993, standard sources provided excellent guidance in general principles of resource description but typically lacked information and examples covering the unique challenges posed by nonprint resources. The texts that were available at that time were often specific to one format (which is not helpful to individuals who handle several formats) and were rarely up-to-date regarding current standards, and sometimes successive editions to excellent texts were never published. The original text and its successor, *Cataloging Nonprint and Internet Resources* (2002), were written in response to the continuing need for the most clear, up-to-date guidance and examples for the resource description of nonprint resources. *Describing Electronic, Digital, and Other Media Using AACR2 and RDA: A How-To-Do-It Manual and CD-ROM for Librarians* continues this tradition.

Resources for Catalogers

Publications and Websites

Adamich, Tom. 2008. "*RDA* (*Resource Description and Access*): The New Way to Say, '*AACR2*.'" *Knowledge Quest* 36, no. 4: 64–69.

American Library Association, Canadian Library Association, and CILIP: Chartered Institute of Library and Information Professionals. 2010. *RDA Toolkit*. ALA, CLA, and CILIP. Accessed May 3. http://www.rdatoolkit.org/.

Joint Steering Committee for the Development of RDA. 2010. "Overview." JSC RDA. Last updated June 23. http://www.rda-jsc.org/.

Library of Congress. 2008. "Cataloging Principles and *RDA*: Resource Description and Access." Webcast featuring Barbara Tillett, Chief of the Cataloging Policy and Support Office, June 10. Library of Congress. http://www.loc.gov/today/cyberlc/feature_wdesc.php?rec=4327.

Library of Congress. 2008. "*Resource Description and Access*: Background/ Overview." Webcast featuring Barbara Tillett, Chief of the Cataloging Policy and Support Office, May 14. Library of Congress. http://www.loc.gov/today/cyberlc/feature_wdesc.php?rec=4320.

Library of Congress, Working Group on the Future of Bibliographic Control. 2010. "Testing Resource Description and Access (RDA)." Library of Congress. Accessed September 3. http://www.libraryofcongress.gov/bibliographic-future/rda.

Needleman, Mark. 2008. "The *Resource Description and Access* Standard." *Serials Review* 34, no. 3: 233–234.

Prather-Rodgers, Emily. 2010. "RDA Update Forum: [a Report from the 2010 American Library Association Midwinter Meeting, January 2010]." *ALCTS Newsletter Online*. American Library Association. http://www.ala.org/ala/mgrps/divs/alcts/resources/ano/v21/n1/event/fprog_rpt.cfm.

Electronic Mailing Lists

Autocat, devoted to the discussion of cataloging and standards, has approximately 4,600 subscribers in about 42 countries. See http://listserv.syr.edu/archives/autocat.html for information on how to join.

MLA-L, from the Music Library Association, is for those interested in music librarianship and is a forum for cataloging questions. See http://musiclibraryassoc.org/member.aspx?id=67 for information on how to subscribe.

MOUG-L, from the Music OCLC Users Group, is also open to subscribers who are not members of this group or OCLC users. See http://www.musicoclcusers.org/listserv.html for information on how to subscribe.

OCLC-CAT is primarily directed at catalogers who use the OCLC union database but also discusses updates to the MARC 21 Bibliographic Format and emerging trends within the profession. See http://www3.oclc.org/app/listserv for more information.

The *RDA Toolkit* mailing list, a way to keep current with developments regarding the Toolkit, became available in June 2010. See http://www.rda-toolkit.org/rdalist for information on how to subscribe.

RDA-L is devoted to the discussion of *RDA*. See http://www.rda-jsc.org/rdadiscuss.html for more information.

Cataloging Blogs and Websites

Catalogablog, maintained by David Bigwood, provides information on cataloging and classification, subject access, and other topics relevant to cataloging. See http://catalogablog.blogspot.com for more information.

Cataloging Aids, maintained by Lynne LeGrow, provides access to cataloging aids, reminders (such as changes to *Library of Congress Subject Headings*), and links to related resources. Visit http://cataids.wordpress.com.

Cataloging Futures, maintained by Christine Schwartz, discusses the future of cataloging and libraries. Visit http://www.catalogingfutures.com/cataloging futures.

The Online Audiovisual Catalogers (OLAC) website provides access to documents that address emerging standards. See http://www.olacinc.org/drupal/ for more information.

Conferences, Organizations, Etc.

The Association for Library Collections and Technical Services (ALCTS), a division of the American Library Association, consists of six sections, including a Cataloging and Classification section. See http://www.ala.org/ala/mgrps/divs/alcts/mgrps/ccs/index.cfm for information on the various groups within ALCTS. ALCTS hosts programs, forums, etc., at both the ALA Midwinter Meeting and the ALA Annual Conference. ALCTS also offers online courses.

Online Audiovisual Catalogers (OLAC), an organization for catalogers of non-print materials, holds conferences every two years. See http://www.olacinc.org/drupal for more information.

Acknowledgments

We acknowledge the contributions of our Rutgers colleagues Isaiah Beard, Chad Mills, and Jeanne Boyle. Isaiah and Chad helped with technical issues and Jeanne provided advice on legal matters and fair use.

The Future of Resource Description

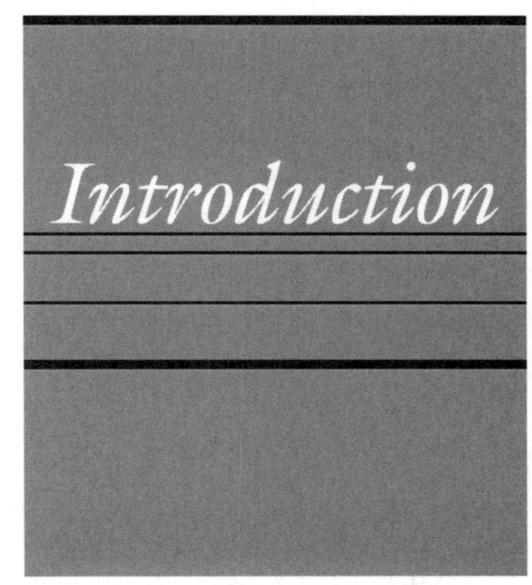

IN THIS CHAPTER:

Overview: Changes to the Resource Landscape

Technology has changed how libraries conduct business, how users access information, and how information professionals communicate. Flickr, Twitter, Facebook, and YouTube have dramatically altered how information is shared and disseminated. Sharing information is no longer a one-way mode of communicating; it is instead interactive, with readers being encouraged to post comments to presentations, blogs, and so on, a practice referred to as *self-tagging*. This practice culminated in early projects such as LibraryThing and the University of Pennsylvania's PennTags. Mobile devices also play an important role for library users, enabling them to search the catalog or download resources to their devices.

The concept of the library catalog has also changed dramatically, as has the terminology applied to this resource. Integrated library systems (ILSs), increasingly referred to as "next-generation" systems, provide access to a greater variety of information and services than their predecessors. Search interfaces such as Ex Libris's Primo and AquaBrowser and the University of Rochester's eXtensible Catalog (XC) provide many of the same services users enjoy on the web. Mellon's Project OLE (Open Library Environment) seeks to design and create a next-generation library automation environment. Federated searching enables users to seamlessly search an institution's MARC bibliographic and non-MARC metadata resources. Many libraries now have a presence on Facebook and take advantage of the applications offered by Web 2.0 technology. The introduction of OCLC's WorldCat local enabled libraries to provide a customizable interface as their online catalog.

The following timeline illustrates some of the changes that have taken place within the profession and that have had a significant impact on cataloging and classification.

- The Library of Congress startled the profession with its 2006 decision to discontinue creating series authority records. This move was prompted by the fact that indexing and keyword access enabled by ILSs offered the necessary access to series statements provided in the 490 field of the bibliographic record.[1]

- The 2006 merger of RLG (Research Libraries Group) and OCLC (Online Computer Library Center) ended the quandary among libraries regarding to which union catalog they contributed bibliographic records and used to obtain cataloging copy. The prevailing notion had been that RLG's records were more appropriate for academic libraries than those in the OCLC union database, despite lack of evidence to support such claims. RLG's RLIN product used the concept of "clusters," which showed every record contributed by member libraries, grouped under a specific edition or version of a resource. OCLC, in contrast, used the "master record" concept, which attached the holdings of all other libraries to a master record created by an authorized library, regardless of whether the record in the libraries' local catalogs might have been more fulsome. In 2008, OCLC struck a compromise by offering libraries the option of including institution records contributed by their specific institutions, attached to master records. This enabled viewing of records on the institution level. One benefit from the merger of RLG and OCLC is the creation of a stronger sense of community among libraries of all types.

A quote by Tony Gill, a former RLG employee, epitomizes the impact of this merger: "This merger is big news in the library world, at least in the world of academic/research libraries. Until now, they have always had a choice of two competing utilities, and two different union catalogues (and some used both). Now, 'there can be only one.'"

(*Source*: Hane, Paula J. 2006. "RLG to Merge with OCLC." *Information Today*. Posted on May 8. http://newsbreaks.infotoday.com/nbreader.asp?ArticleID=15851.)

- A 2008 MARBI decision made field 440 (Series Statement/Added Entry—Title) obsolete in the MARC 21 Bibliographic Format. MARC Proposal No. 2008-07 "proposes making field 440 obsolete in favor of using 490 (Series Statement) and the 8XX Series added entry fields for traced series. This simplifies practices and the need for systems to look multiple places in the records for the authorized series heading."[2] The implication of this proposal for libraries is that series procedures will need to be changed. Those libraries with automated authority control will need to work with their vendors to ensure that MARC 490 fields will not be flipped to 440s. Libraries will find it difficult to distinguish between the 490s they want indexed, because the Library of Congress has coded them as 490, and those they do not want to index, because they are traced differently in 8XX fields.
- Alternatives to OCLC for cataloging copy have emerged. Two alternatives are Biblios, an open source web-based resource description tool, and SkyRiver, a new bibliographic utility, launched in November 2009. Libraries are increasingly making use of vendor-supplied records or creating brief records for large record sets or serial collections. These choices impact workflow and the type and quality of resource description, which take on an added dimension in a shared environment.
- The emergence of institutional repositories is yet another change in how libraries collect resources and make them available.

> Libraries are creating access to locally produced content through a different set of standards (metadata) and face new challenges, including digital rights management, digital preservation, and digital curation.

The terms *cataloging* and *metadata* are used interchangeably. Vendors use *metadata* as their new buzzword; in many cases, their "metadata" is MARC records rather than those created in MODS or Dublin Core. The notion of metadata has become mainstream, and many cataloging and technical services operations are now known as "Cataloging and Metadata Services" or a variation of this wording. In some cases, the metadata and digital work have split off from cataloging and/or technical services. There is also a new "breed of librarians" (the Digital Services Librarian, Metadata Librarian, Emerging Technologies Librarian, etc.) who have responsibilities that extend beyond traditional technical services work.

Most important of all of these changes, *Resource Description and Access* (*RDA*), the new standard for describing resources and access to them, designed for the digital world,[3] is expected to replace the *Anglo-American Cataloguing Rules*, Second Revised Edition. The public release of the *RDA Toolkit* was in June 2010, followed by an open access period that ended in August 2010. A test period will run from June 2010 through April 2011, and a report is expected to be released to the library community at the conclusion of the test period.[4] The introduction of *RDA* has been an enormous undertaking, involving the Joint Steering Committee for the Revision of *AACR* (JSC) and its parent organization, the Committee of Principals (CoP). The decision to implement *RDA* stemmed from comments received during the revision of Part I of *AACR3*[5] when it became clear that a new approach was needed to accommodate the emerging digital environment, given that *AACR2* had been written when libraries still used the manual card catalog as their primary mechanism for inventory and access.

RDA states that descriptive records should include all of the core elements applicable to a particular resource that will enable users to *find*, *identify*, *select*, and *obtain* it. *RDA* is closely aligned with the principles of the *Functional Requirements of Bibliographic Records* (*FRBR*) and was designed to describe all types of metadata regardless of the schema used for the final description (MARC 21, MODS, Dublin Core [DC], etc.). *RDA* may be described as "schema agnostic" in this respect. In addition to core elements, other elements that are deemed necessary to distinguish a resource from similar resources may be included in the metadata.

RDA was developed using principles from the International Standard Bibliographic Description (ISBD) and the MARC 21 Formats for Bibliographic and Authority Data. The procedures in this manual are taken from *RDA* and incorporate concepts from *AACR2* when needed. This change is necessary to make this manual consistent with current and future resource description needs.

Implementation of *RDA* will have a major impact on how libraries work, and, in the spirit of the future, this introduction provides a preview

After concerns were raised by the Working Group on the Future of Bibliographic Control, the three U.S. national libraries (Library of Congress, National Agricultural Library, and National Library of Medicine) agreed to make a joint decision regarding *RDA* after testing *RDA* and a web product to ensure operational, technical, and economic feasibility.

(*Source:* Library of Congress, Working Group on the Future of Bibliographic Control. 2010. "Testing *Resource Description and Access* (RDA)." Accessed June 4. http://www.loc.gov/bibliographic-future/rda/.)

FOR MORE INFORMATION

To learn more about *RDA* testing, see http://www.rda-jsc.org/rdafaq.html #11 and http://www.loc.gov/ bibliographic-future/rda/test-partners.html.

More information on *RDA* and the *RDA Toolkit* is available at http://www .rdatoolkit.org/home, which provides archived access to a full draft of *RDA* (click on "Background"), with individual chapters as PDF documents and the complete draft available for download.

of *RDA*. The seven chapters included in this manual follow the *RDA* and *AACR2* guidelines for bibliographic description.

Functional Requirements for Bibliographic Records (FRBR)

FRBR, developed by the International Federation of Libraries and Associations (IFLA) in the 1990s, describes the relationships between user actions and retrieval of information and serves as the foundation for *RDA*. *FRBR*'s mantra has been "find, identify, select, and obtain."

FRBR defines three key areas of interest to users of metadata records:[6]

1. Products of intellectual or artistic endeavor
2. Entities responsible for the intellectual or artistic content, the physical production and dissemination, or the custodianship
3. Additional entities that serve as the subjects of intellectual or artistic endeavor

These areas of interest are referred to as "Group 1 entities," "Group 2 entities," and "Group 3 entities," respectively.

Group 1 entities describe the intellectual or artistic endeavor embodied in a metadata record and represent different aspects of user interest. They are defined as work, expression, manifestation, and item:[7]

- A **work** is an artistic or intellectual creation, such as a work of literature or an original musical composition. An example of a work is Dr. Seuss's concept of *The Cat in the Hat* character.
- An **expression** is the intellectual or artistic realization that a work takes each time it is "realized," through an intellectual or artistic creation. An expression is an idea and not a physical or digital resource. The manuscript for *The Cat in the Hat* is an example of an expression.
- A **manifestation** is a tangible product, the physical or digital form that an expression may take. Examples of manifestations include a Beginner's Book version of *The Cat in the Hat* and a game based on the book.
- An **item** is a single instance of a manifestation and is also a tangible physical or digital resource as compared to an idea or concept. An example of an item is a limited edition copy of the book or game.

Figure I.1 provides an overview of how Group 1 entities are related.

Group 2 entities record information about the individuals or corporate bodies responsible for the intellectual or artistic content, the physical production and dissemination, or the custodianship of the entities in Group 1.[8] Examples of Group 2 entities are authors, translators, editors, screenwriters (person), or publishers or manufacturers (corporate). These

Figure I.1. Group 1 Entities and Their Relationships

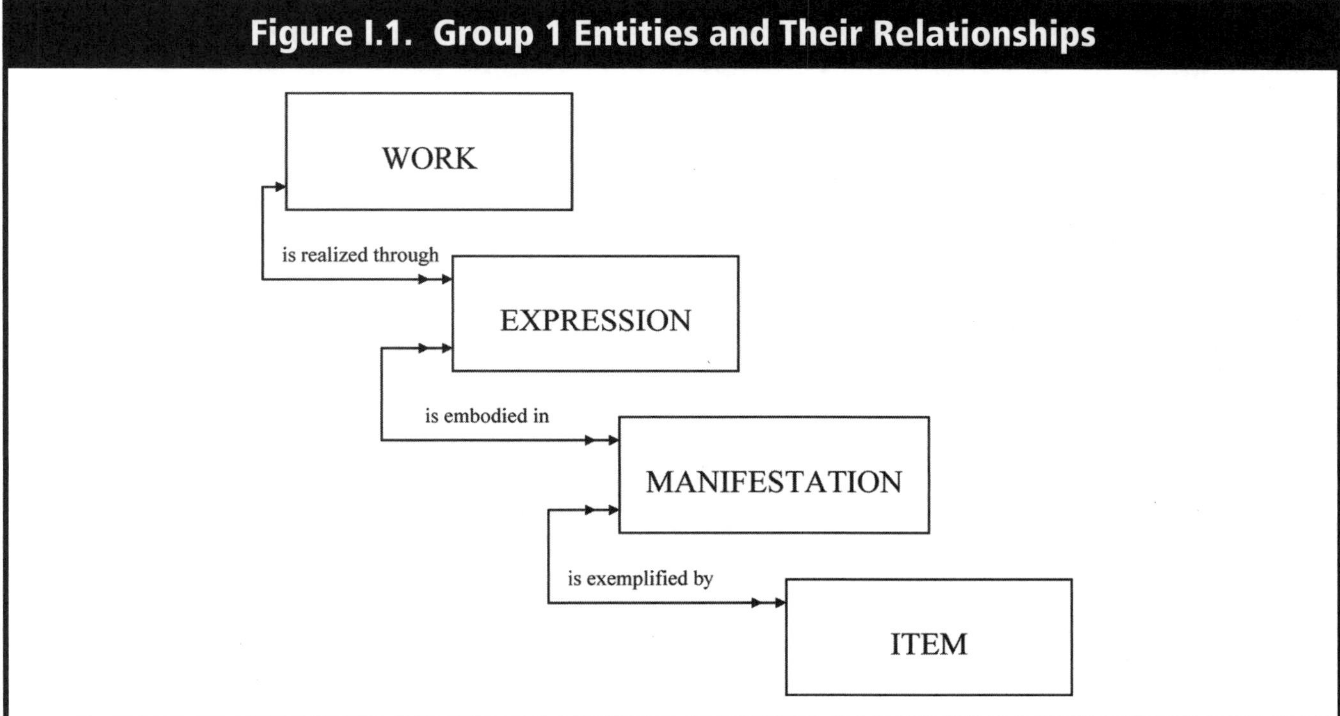

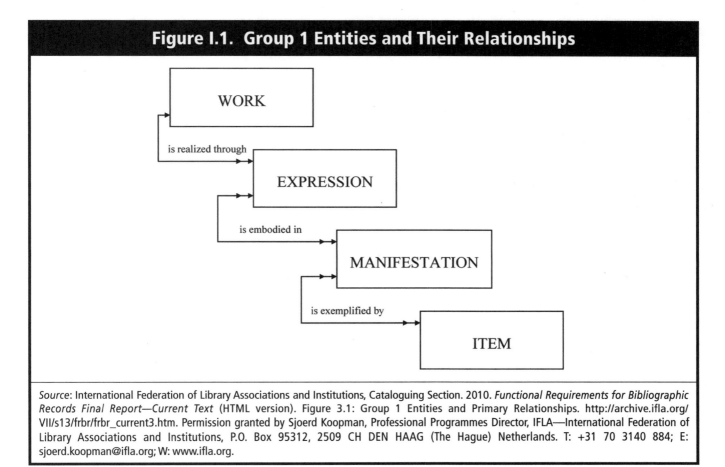

Source: International Federation of Library Associations and Institutions, Cataloguing Section. 2010. *Functional Requirements for Bibliographic Records Final Report—Current Text* (HTML version). Figure 3.1: Group 1 Entities and Primary Relationships. http://archive.ifla.org/VII/s13/frbr/frbr_current3.htm. Permission granted by Sjoerd Koopman, Professional Programmes Director, IFLA—International Federation of Library Associations and Institutions, P.O. Box 95312, 2509 CH DEN HAAG (The Hague) Netherlands. T: +31 70 3140 884; E: sjoerd.koopman@ifla.org; W: www.ifla.org.

entities include person and corporate body. Figure I.2 illustrates Group 2 entities and relationships.

Group 2 entities describe the relationships that may exist between Group 1 and Group 2 entities. For example, a work may be created by one individual or corporate body, it may be realized by another individual and/or corporate body, and a manifestation of that work may be produced by yet another individual or corporate body, culminating in an item that is owned by a specific individual and/or corporate body. This can be illustrated by the example of *The Cat in the Hat*. The book was originally written by Dr. Seuss in 1957. A *Cat in the Hat* game was later introduced by Wonder Forge (not the publisher of the original book). A motion picture based on the book was released in 2003 by Universal Pictures; widescreen and full screen editions were available on DVD in 2004.

Group 3 entities are the subject of Group 1's and Group 2's intellectual efforts and include **concept** (abstract ideas), **object** (a tangible physical objects), **event** (actions), and **place** (locations).[9] Figure I.3 demonstrates the relationship between Group 3 entities and Groups 1 and 2 entities and how this is manifested in subject relationships. Concepts may be represented by subject headings or other topical terms that reflect the ideas embodied in Group 1 entities. Objects are physical objects such as a

Figure I.2. Group 2 Entities and Their Relationships

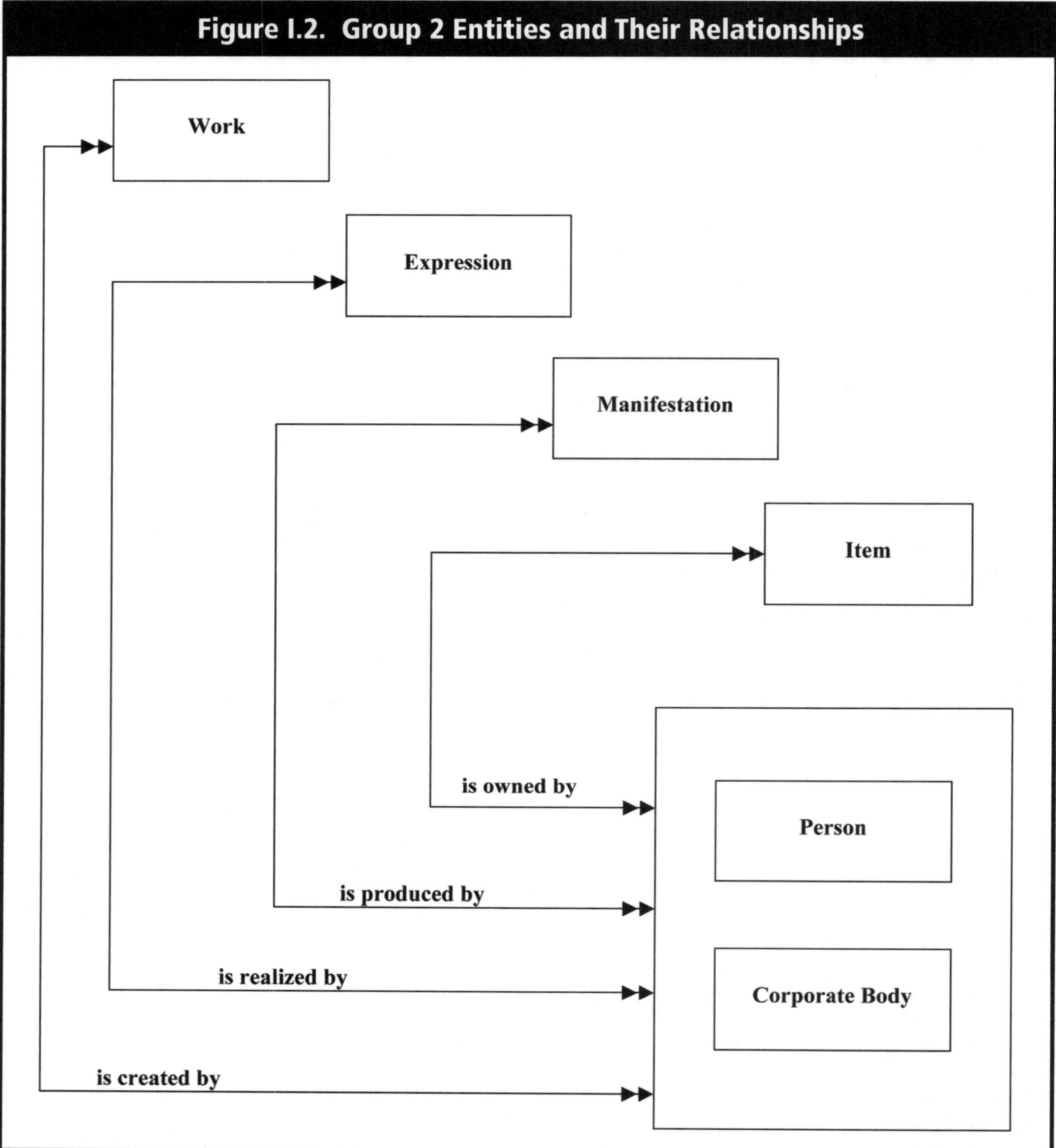

Source: International Federation of Library Associations and Institutions, Cataloguing Section. 2010. *Functional Requirements for Bibliographic Records Final Report—Current Text* (HTML version). Figure 3.2: Group 2 Entities and "Responsibility" Relationships. http://archive.ifla.org/VII/s13/frbr/frbr_current3.htm. Permission granted by Sjoerd Koopman, Professional Programmes Director, IFLA—International Federation of Library Associations and Institutions, P.O. Box 95312, 2509 CH DEN HAAG (The Hague) Netherlands. T: +31 70 3140 884; E: sjoerd.koopman@ifla.org; W: www.ifla.org.

Figure I.3. The Relationship between Group 3 Entities and Groups 1 and 2 Entities

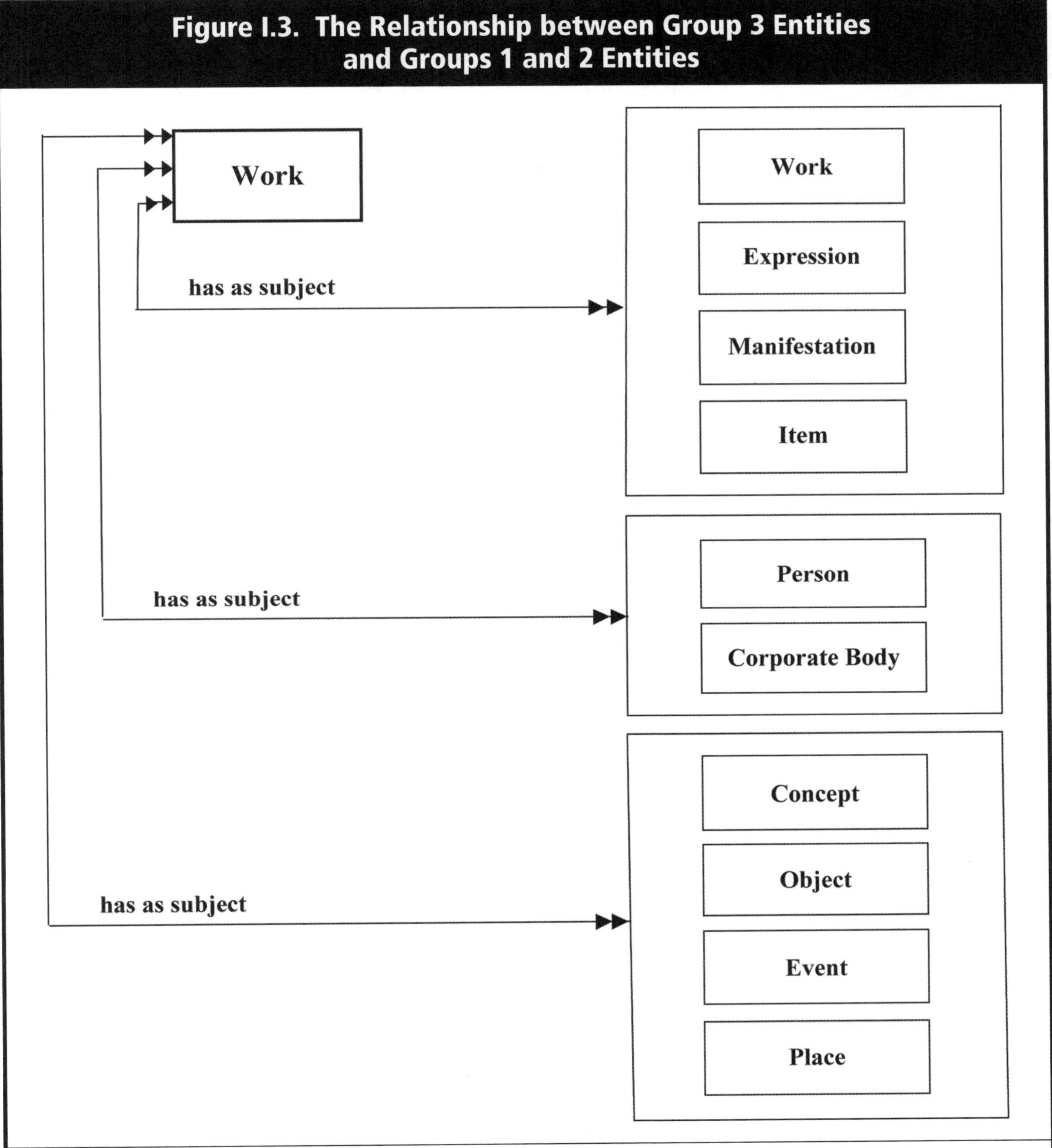

Source: International Federation of Library Associations and Institutions, Cataloguing Section. 2010. Functional Requirements for Bibliographic Records Final Report—Current Text (HTML version). Figure 3.3: Group 3 Entities and "Subject" Relationships. http://archive.ifla.org/VII/s13/frbr/frbr_current3.htm. Permission granted by Sjoerd Koopman, Professional Programmes Director, IFLA—International Federation of Library Associations and Institutions, P.O. Box 95312, 2509 CH DEN HAAG (The Hague) Netherlands. T: +31 70 3140 884; E: sjoerd.koopman@ifla.org; W: www.ifla.org.

printed book, a DVD, or a screenplay. Events are actions that take place at a given point in time. This enables catalogers to name and identify an event consistently and to relate resources about a given event (relate all resources on a given topic). Places are terrestrial or extraterrestrial, they may be historical or contemporary, and they may include geographic and/or political jurisdictions.[10]

In support of these *FRBR* requirements, *RDA* Rule 0.6.1 stipulates, "As a minimum, a record describing a resource should include all of the core elements applicable to that resource. The description should also include any additional elements required to differentiate the resource from any other similar resource."[11] Both the *FRBR* and *RDA* recommendations seemingly suggest that catalogers aim for specificity and differentiation rather than generalization when describing a resource.

Adherence to these *FRBR* principles must guide and inform the resource description. The user must be able to find any specific resource based on the descriptive metadata ascribed to it. In addition, users should be aware of the existence of all known related expressions and/or manifestations of the work. Having retrieved the descriptive record, users should be able to identify the resource sufficiently to distinguish it from any other resource. Finally, users must feel confident that the resources they have selected, based on their review of the resource description, are appropriate for their needs. In providing descriptive metadata, catalogers can either enhance or impede the resource discovery process. Enhancement should be the ultimate goal.

Conscious of our role as facilitators of resource discovery, catalogers must be wary of the implications of providing information that is misleading or unclear. The ability of those outside of the "known" user community to discover a resource via an external web query and the potential for discovery by the anonymous user suggest that catalogers should no longer presume to be cataloging for the immediate user community but should instead assume that the bibliographic record is being created as a public service for the global user community. As catalogers, we must be willing to take the courageous steps required to wear two hats—one as a user of resources and one as the cataloger, allowing both perspectives to guide and inform our work. Thinking outside the "familiar" box will encourage us to make smarter use of resources that already exist and to become more innovative and flexible in our selection, purchase, description, and use of these dynamic resources.

RDA Organization, Terminology, and Key Concepts

RDA is divided into ten sections that provide guidance on how to record attributes for the *FRBR* entities and relationships among these entities.[12] *RDA* emphasizes two main areas: recording attributes and recording relationships. The sections within *RDA* are as follows:[13]

Recording attributes

Section 1 Recording attributes of manifestation and item

Section 2 Recording attributes of work and expression

Section 3 Recording attributes of person, family, and corporate body

Section 4 Recording attributes of concept, object, event, and place

Recording primary relationships

Section 5 Recording primary relationships between work, expression, manifestation, and item

Section 6 Recording relationships to persons, families, and corporate bodies associated with a resource

Section 7 Recording subject relationships

Section 8 Recording relationships between works, expressions, manifestations, and items

Section 9 Recording relationships between persons, families, and corporate bodies

Section 10 Recording relationships between concepts, objects, events, and places

One significant change from *AACR2* to *RDA* is that *RDA* no longer requires the International Standard Bibliographic Description (ISBD), developed by IFLA to provide a standard description for resources. *RDA* is format neutral and does not require ISBD order or punctuation for resource description. In contrast, *AACR2* follows ISBD conventions for creating resource description. The value of using ISBD is to promote universal standards that facilitate information sharing and exchange. *RDA* does provide descriptive elements for creating metadata records in a manner similar to that used in *AACR2*.[14]

Chapter 1 of *RDA* provides general guidelines for recording attributes of manifestations and items. This section reviews these guidelines.

Types of Resources

Resource, as defined by *RDA*, refers to a work, expression, manifestation, or item. This term is not singular and applies to aggregates or components of a resource, such as a photograph in a collection, sheets that make up a map, or a DVD that is part of a multidisc set.[15]

Mode of issuance is a new concept introduced by *RDA*. It describes the manner in which a resource is made available, how it is updated, and its intended termination.[16] A single resource that is intended to be issued once, such as a monograph or a PDF file available on the web, is described as a *resource issued as a single unit*.[17]

A *multipart monograph* is a resource issued in two or more parts (successively or simultaneously) that is intended to contain a defined finite number of parts. Examples include a book series (e.g., a ten-volume set) or a trilogy of films (e.g., the *Matrix* series of movies).

An *integrating resource* is one that is continually changed or updated through the addition of parts that are integrated into the whole. Looseleaf manuals are the most commonly used example when describing this type of resource. However, websites or remote or direct access databases are also types of integrating resources.

Work, Expression, Manifestation, and Item

The terms *work*, *expression*, *manifestation*, and *item* (defined earlier in this chapter) are used in *RDA* to describe individual entities as well as the aggregates and parts of an entity.

Core Elements

Author's Note: Core elements for serials are included in *RDA* but not here because this text does not cover serials cataloging.

RDA outlines core elements that may be used to describe applications or resources. These core elements are similar in many ways to the Program for Cooperative Cataloging's (PCC's) core level standards for bibliographic records. The PCC core standard enables all types of libraries to create and exchange records that meet a minimum accepted set of standards.

The *RDA* core elements for a manifestation or work are as follows:[18]

- Title proper
- Statement of responsibility relating to title proper (only statement of responsibility relating to the title proper is required; if more than one, only the first recorded is required)
- Designation of edition
- Designation of a named revision of an edition
- Date of production (use for unpublished resources)
- Place of publication
- Publisher's name (if more than one, only the first recorded is required)
- Date of publication
- Place of distribution
- Distributor's name (if publisher is not identified; if more than one, only the first recorded is required)
- Date of distribution (if date of publication is not identified)
- Place of manufacture
- Manufacturer's name (if neither publisher nor distributor is identified; if more than one, only the first recorded is required)
- Date of manufacture (if neither date of publication, date of distribution, nor copyright date is identified)
- Copyright date (if neither date of publication nor date of distribution is identified)
- Title proper of series

- Numbering within series
- Title proper of subseries
- Numbering within subseries
- Identifier for the manifestation (if more than one, an internationally recognized identifier is preferred, if applicable)
- Carrier type
- Extent

RDA instructs catalogers to include additional elements when it is necessary to distinguish a given resource from others and to add any additional elements deemed necessary by the cataloging institution or by the cataloger's judgment.

Language and Script

RDA 1.4 provides a list of elements that should be recorded in the language and script in which they are provided, in or on the item being cataloged. This list is quite extensive and an abbreviated list of these elements follows:

- Title information (title proper, variants, key, etc.)
- Statement of responsibility
- Numeric/alphabetic/chronological designation of issues/parts
- Production information (place and producer name)
- Publication information (place, name, date)
- Distribution information (place, name, date)
- Manufacture information (place, name, date)
- Series information (title, statement of responsibility, numbering, subseries).

Levels of Description

RDA prescribes three types of description: comprehensive, analytical, and hierarchical. A comprehensive description describes the resource as a whole.[19] An analytical description describes a part of a larger resource,[20] such as a segment derived from a streaming video, data extracted from a data set, or part of a kit intended to be used as a unit. A hierarchical description combines a comprehensive description of the whole resource with analytical descriptions of one or more of its parts,[21] for example, an entire data set with separate descriptions of the specific data collections in the set.

Authors' Note: Hierarchical description is not covered in detail because it is beyond the scope of this manual.

When a New Description Is Required

There are times when a new metadata description is required for a resource. Some of the various instances outlined in *RDA* include the following:[22]

- **Multipart monographic resources**—A change in mode of issuance or change in media type for a multipart monographic resource.
- **Integrating resources**—A change in mode of issuance, change in media type, or re-basing of an integrating resource. Re-basing is when a new base set of volumes is issued for an integrating resource.

Dates

When the actual date of publication is known, record it as provided in or on the resource.

RDA refers to this as *Actual year known*. When a date is known to be one of two consecutive years, *RDA* instructs catalogers to record both dates and the word *or*. When a probable date can be determined, record this followed by a question mark. If a resource provides a probable range of years, the earliest probable date is recorded with the word *probably*, the last probable year, and a question mark. If a decade is known but not a specific date, the decade is recorded with the letter *s* (e.g., 1990s). A probable decade is recorded using the letter *s* and a question mark. A probable range of dates is described using the word *between*, the two dates separated by the word *and*, and a question mark. When the century is known, that date is provided followed by the letter *s*. A probable century is recorded using the probable date, followed by the letter *s* and a question mark. A probable range of centuries is recorded using the word *between*, the two dates separated by the word *and*, and a question mark. The earliest possible date for a resource is recorded using the words *Not before* and the date. The latest possible date is recorded using the words Not after and the date. If it is deemed necessary to record the earliest possible and latest possible dates for a resource, the word *between* precedes the dates and the two dates are linked by the word *and*. See the Quick Reference Chart for an example of how to record the different types of dates.

QUICK REFERENCE CHART: RECORDING DATES

Type of Date	How to Enter	Type of Date	How to Enter
Actual	2007	Century known	1900s
Consecutive years	2006 or 2007	Probable century	1900s?
Probable year	2005?	Probable range of centuries	Between 1900s and 2000s?
Probable range of years	Between 1999 and 2004?	Earliest possible date known	Not before August 16, 1920
Decade known	1980s	Latest possible date known	Not after November 11, 2001
Decade probable	1980s?	Earliest possible/latest possible date known	Between June 1, 1999 and October 10, 2004
Probable range of dates	Between 1950s and 1970s?		

Identifying Manifestations and Items

Chapter 2 of *RDA* provides guidance on identifying manifestations and items. This chapter also outlines how to provide comprehensive and analytical descriptions.

Comprehensive Description

Begin by choosing a source of information appropriate to the mode of issuance. Determine if the resource is a single unit, is issued in more than one part, or is an integrating resource. For single units, choose a source of information that identifies the resource as a whole.

RDA lists prescribed sources of information for describing resources issued in more than one part:[23]

- Information that identifies the first issue or part when the issues or parts are numbered sequentially
- Information that identifies the earliest issue or part if the issues/parts are not numbered or were not issued in the order of their sequential numbers
- Information that identifies the lowest numbered issue/part if the issues/parts are sequentially numbered and the first issue/part is not available
- Information that identifies the resource as a whole when the order of parts is not applicable

If the identification is not based on the first issue or part, the cataloger is instructed to note which issue/part was used for the purpose of identification.

Choosing a source of information to identify an integrating resource as a whole is slightly different. Ideally, a source of information that accurately identifies the current iteration of an integrating resource as a whole should be chosen. If this information is not available, sources of information that identify the current iteration of the contents as a collective source of information are consulted.

If there is no source of information identifying the current iteration of the integrating resource as a whole, treat the sources of information identifying the current iteration of its individual contents as a collective source of information for the current iteration as a whole.[24] Record the iteration consulted in a note.

Analytical Description

The guidelines for creating an analytical description also begin by choosing a source of information appropriate to the mode of issuance. When an analytical description is provided for a single part of a resource, *RDA* instructs catalogers to choose a source of information that identifies the specific part being described.

The guidelines for creating an analytical description for resources that consist of two or more parts instruct catalogers to use the same sources of information consulted for a comprehensive description of this type of resource.

RDA instructs catalogers providing an analytical description for a part or parts of an integrating resource to choose a source of information that identifies the most current iteration of the part or parts being described.

Sources of Information for Creating a Metadata Description

Choose a preferred source of information when creating a metadata description. *RDA* recommends using a source that forms part of the resource, such as storage medium and housing.[25] The selection of preferred source of information is driven by type of description (comprehensive or analytical) and the resource's presentation format (multipart, moving image, etc.). Accompanying materials of any type are treated as a part of the resource only when a comprehensive description is provided for a resource. In some cases, more than one source of information may be considered as a preferred source of information. *RDA* 2.2.3 provides specific instructions for this type of situation.

Multipart Resources

The preferred source of information for resources that consist of more than one part, such as multiple pages, sheets, or cards, or reproductions of images of multiple pages, sheets, or cards (may include microforms and digital images such as JPEGs and PDFs), is the title page, introductory sheet, or card. If this information is missing, *RDA* prescribes that a cover, caption, masthead, or colophon (or reproductions/images of these sources) may be used. In the absence of any of these sources of information, consult another source of information that forms part of the resource and give priority to sources that formally present information.[26]

Moving Images

The preferred source of information for moving image materials is the title frame(s) or title screen(s). Moving image resources include motion pictures, videorecordings, and video file formats. In the absence of title frames or screens, catalogers may consult title information printed or affixed to a physical container or textual metadata embedded in the resource. As stated in the previous section on multipart resources, in the absence of any of these sources of information, consult another source of information that forms part of the resource and give priority to sources that formally present information.

Other Resources

The preferred source of information for other resources (not multipart or moving images) is information printed or affixed to a physical container or textual metadata embedded in the resource. If these sources of information are lacking, consult another source of information that forms part of the resource and give priority to sources that formally present information.

Multiple Sources of Preferred Information

In cases when more than one source of information is appropriate to use as a preferred source of information, the *RDA* prescribes a hierarchy based on certain conditions:

- **Multiple languages**—When the preferred source of information is in different languages or scripts, follow this hierarchy:
  - choose the language or script that is most predominant in the resource;
  - choose the source in the language or script of translation when the resource has the same work in more than one language and the resource is known to be a translation;
  - choose the source in the original language or script if the resource contains the same content in multiple languages and the original language or script may be identified;
  - choose the first source that occurs.[27]

- **Different dates**—When resources that typically would not have multiple dates contain preferred sources of information that provide different dates, *RDA* advises catalogers to consult the preferred source of information with a later or latest date.

- **Reproductions**—If a reproduction provides preferred sources of information for the reproduction as well as the original, use the source of information for the reproduction.

Other Sources of Information

RDA prescribes other sources of information for catalogers to consult when information needed to identify a resource is available in sources that form part of the resource. Consult the following sources in the order provided:

- **Accompanying materials**—This ranges from accompanying printed matter, to websites that provide information on resources, to files (ReadMe or About files) that form part of a resource.
- **Containers**—In the absence of other sources of information, external containers that are not an essential part of the resource may be consulted. This includes extra packaging provided by manufacturers, such as that used to house computer software or videorecording sets. Examples are provided in Figure I.4.

- **Published descriptions of the resource**—This may be interpreted to include publisher's catalogs (both print and online) as well as websites and reviews.
- **Other available sources**—*RDA* defines this as reference sources. Again, this could be a print text or its online counterpart or a database.

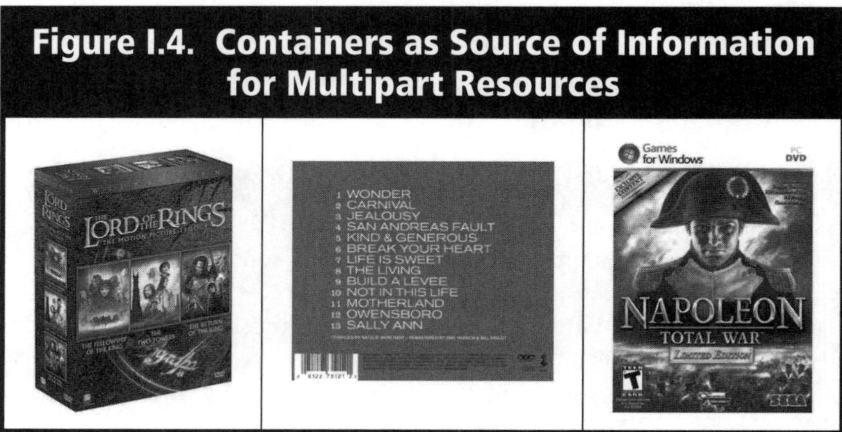

Figure I.4. Containers as Source of Information for Multipart Resources

In cases when an analytical description is provided for a multipart resource, *RDA* prescribes treating accompanying materials as a source external to the resource and not a component part. External containers that are purchased or made (such as archival preservation containers) are also considered as external sources.[28]

Document information taken from external sources in a note. This practice is very much the same treatment prescribed by *AACR2*. Document title information, statements of responsibility, edition information, production information, publication information, distribution information, manufacture information, and series information. A fuller list is available in *RDA* 2.2.4.

Selected Resources for Catalogers

American Library Association, Canadian Library Association, and CILIP: Chartered Institute of Library and Information Professionals. 2010. "RDA Toolkit." ALA, CLA, and CILIP. Accessed May 3. http://www.rdatoolkit.org.

Andrews, Sue. 2010. "Resource Description and Access . . . How Did We Get Here?" Presented at the British Columbia Library Association Conference, April 22. http://www.rda-jsc.org/docs/SueA_bcla2010.pdf.

Bowen, J. 2005. "FRBR: Coming Soon to Your Library?" *Library Resources & Technical Services* 49, no. 3: 175–188.

Hitchens, Alison, and Ellen Symons. 2009. "Preparing Catalogers for RDA Training." *Cataloging & Classification Quarterly* 47, no. 8, 691–707.

Joint Steering Committee for the Development of RDA. 2009. "RDA-FRBR Mapping." JSC RDA. http://www.rda-jsc.org/docs/5rda-rdafrbrmappingrev3.pdf.

Kincy, Chamya P., and Luiz H. Mendes. 2009. "Ready for RDA Implementation? . . . Help! The New Cataloging Code Is Coming!" Presented at the California Library Association Annual Conference, Pasadena, California, November 2. http://alcts.ala.org/crgwiki/images/1/10/RDA_CLA_Presentation.pdf.

Library of Congress, Working Group on the Future of Bibliographic Control. 2010. "RDA Train-the-Trainer Webcasts." Library of Congress. Accessed June 1. http://www.loc.gov/bibliographic-future/rda/trainthetrainer.html.

Maxwell, Robert L. 2008. *FRBR: A Guide for the Perplexed.* Chicago: American Library Association.

Oliver, Chris. 2010. "Tomorrow's Metadata: Improving Resource Discovery for the User." Presented at the Quebec Library Association Annual Conference, May 14. JSC RDA. http://www.rda-jsc.org/docs/ABQLA_RDA_tomorrow%27s_metadata.pdf.

Taylor, Arlene G. 2007. *Understanding FRBR: What It Is and How It Will Affect Our Retrieval Tools.* Santa Barbara, CA: Libraries Unlimited.

Notes

1. Winship, Douglass. 2006. "LC to Cease Providing Controlled Series Access." Posting forwarded from PCC list to the Autocat listserv of statement made by Beacher Wiggins, Director for Acquisitions and Bibliographic Access, April 20. Autocat Archives. http://listserv.syr.edu/archives/autocat.html (registration required).
2. Library of Congress. 2008. "MARC Standards: MARC Proposal No. 2008-07." Library of Congress. http://www.loc.gov/marc/marbi/2008/2008-07.html.
3. American Library Association, Canadian Library Association, and CILIP: Chartered Institute of Library and Information Professionals. 2010. *RDA Toolkit.* ALA, CLA, and CILIP. Accessed May 3. http://www.rdatoolkit.org/training.
4. OCLC Online Computer Library Center, Inc. 2010. "OCLC Policy Statement on RDA Cataloging in WorldCat for the U.S. Testing Period." OCLC. http://www.oclc.org/us/en/rda/policy.htm.
5. Joint Steering Committee for Development of *RDA.* 2010. "RDA: Frequently Asked Questions: 1. RDA Basics." JSC RDA. Last updated January 18. http://www.rda-jsc.org/rdafaq.html.
6. International Federation of Library Associations and Institutions. 2007. *Functional Requirements for Bibliographic Records Final Report: Current Text.* IFLA. Last revised December 27. http://www.ifla.org/VII/s13/frbr/frbr_current3.htm.
7. Ibid.
8. Ibid.
9. Ibid.
10. Ibid.
11. American Library Association, Canadian Library Association, and CILIP: Chartered Institute of Library and Information Professionals. 2010. *RDA Toolkit,* "Introduction, 0.6.1." ALA, CLA, and CILIP. Accessed May 3. http://www.rdatoolkit.org.
12. Ibid., Introduction, 0.5.
13. Ibid.

14. Joint Steering Committee for Development of *RDA*. "RDA: Frequently Asked Questions." Last updated January 18. JSC RDA. http://www.rda-jsc.org/rdafaq.html.
15. American Library Association, Canadian Library Association, and CILIP: Chartered Institute of Library and Information Professionals. 2010. *RDA Toolkit*, "Glossary." ALA, CLA, and CILIP. Accessed September 3. http://www.rdatoolkit.org.
16. Ibid.
17. Ibid., Chapter 2, 2.1.2.2.
18. Ibid., Chapter 5, 5.3.
19. Ibid., Chapter 1, 1.5.
20. Ibid., Chapter 1, 1.5.3.
21. Ibid., Chapter 1, 1.5.4.
22. Ibid., Chapter 1, 1.6.
23. Ibid., Chapter 2, 2.1.2.3.
24. Ibid., Chapter 2, 2.1.2.4.
25. Ibid., Chapter 2, 2.2.2.1.
26. Ibid., Chapter 2, 2.2.4.
27. Ibid., Chapter 2, 2.2.3.
28. Ibid., Chapter 2, 2.1.3.3.

Essential Background

Overview

This chapter examines the core elements of resource description for nonbook resources. Core elements are generally unique to the work and are essential to differentiation. To encourage catalogers to conceive of a work in a way that facilitates description, we grouped the core elements according to the *FRBR* entity groupings of work, expression, manifestation, and item. While this arrangement alters the strict numerical order of the MARC display format that catalogers have been trained to follow, it is more in keeping with the overarching goal of the new code, *RDA*, which can be used with any display format. *RDA* is "schema agnostic" in this respect. Moreover, the arrangement adopted in this text encourages the cataloger to identify with the user rather than with the display format. The user is interested in obtaining a particular work regardless of how the elements and characteristics of that work are displayed. MARC format employs a linear sequence, and other metadata schemes are defined by areas and use arrangements that aim to be logical rather than numerical.

RDA is currently being tested by the three American national libraries (Library of Congress, National Library of Medicine, and the National Agricultural Library) and by 26 independent testing partners. Information on the test plan and partner information is available at www.loc.gov/bibliographic-future/rda. "The goal of the test is to assure the operational, technical, and economic feasibility of *RDA*."[1] *RDA* was rolled out in June 2010; the American Library Association has made available the *RDA Toolkit*, a resource to help catalogers navigate from *AACR2* to *RDA*. Complimentary open access to the *RDA Toolkit* extended from June 2010 to August 31, 2010. Now that the open access period has concluded, catalogers seeking more information about the *RDA Toolkit* should go to http://www.rdatoolkit .org/openaccess. The *RDA Toolkit* is also available in Catalogers' Desktop as of June 2010. Additionally, ALA Publications has made the print copy available for sale in its online bookstore (see http://www.alastore.ala .org/SearchResult .aspx?CategoryID=252).

IN THIS CHAPTER:

RDA will have a major impact on how libraries work, and, in the spirit of the future, this introduction provides an overview of *RDA*. The chapters included in this manual provide guidelines on how to apply *RDA*, and in some cases they also provide *AACR2* guidelines for bibliographic description. In addition, the companion CD provides guidance in applying both *RDA* and *AACR2* guidelines for bibliographic description for the formats covered in this text.

In keeping with the *FRBR* principles and *RDA*, the user must be able to ***find***, ***identify***, ***select***, and ***obtain*** any work, and easily. It is the cataloger's obligation and responsibility to facilitate this process. As catalogers, our role is to create a resource description that serves as a surrogate for the resource. The description should be fulsome enough to enable users to discover information (find), know what they have found (identify), select among competing resources in search results list (select), and get the desired resources (obtain). The numbered examples given throughout this text illustrate three common display formats: MAchine-Readable Cataloging (MARC) format, Metadata for Object Description (MODS) schema (see Authors' Note on MODS), and Dublin Core (DC)—in this order.

Authors' Note on MODS: The MODS website provides the elements in the order in which they appear in MODS XML. However, the order provided in this manual parallels the order of elements as provided in the MARC checklist and follows the type of order libraries may use for their ILSs.

MARC format is the most mature of these display formats. It was developed by the late library pioneer Henriette Avram at the Library of Congress in the 1960s. MARC was developed to enable online displays of bibliographic description and uses the information that was previously printed on cards used in card catalogs. The MARC display and function mimic the order of elements that was provided in printed catalogs. MARC uses three types of elements: the record structure, the content designation, and the data content of the record.[2] The **record structure** conforms to two standards, Information Interchange Format (ANSI Z39.2) and Format for Information Exchange (ISO 2709), which are used to facilitate the exchange and sharing of data. **Content designation** is provided based on conventions that identify and characterize the data elements in a resource description and to support manipulation of that data.[3] **Data content** is defined by standards such as *AACR2*, *RDA*, *Library of Congress Subject Headings*, and so forth. MARC is complex and consists of over 200 elements that represent a variety of descriptive elements. The learning curve for MARC is steep, and it takes years for a cataloger to become proficient in MARC. Because there are so many elements in MARC, catalogers are typically more familiar with some elements than others, and this is driven by the types of materials they catalog. Some of the advantages of using MARC are that its data elements can provide rich detail, it can provide both simple and specialized description, and it constantly evolves to meet emerging needs.

Authors' Note on Spacing Conventions: The MARC examples provided in this text include spaces that precede and follow subfield codes. The spacing for subfield codes varies by system. OCLC uses such spacing, whereas one's ILS may require the spaces to be closed.

MODS, which is typically used to describe digital resources, is also maintained by the Library of Congress's Network Development and MARC Standards Office. It was developed in 2006 and retains standard bibliographic cataloging principles, making it easy for catalogers trained in MARC to make the transition. In contrast to MARC, MODS has 19 top level elements that describe title, resource type, names, language, physical description, notes, subjects, etc., in streamlined approach. The MODS top level elements and an overview are available at http://www

.loc.gov/standards/mods/v3/mods-userguide-generalapp.html#top_level. Some MODS elements have attributes that provide specificity, such as "type" (type of title, type of name, for example) or "authority" (which indicates from what authoritative source controlled vocabulary terms have been taken). In turn, many of the elements have subelements that further refine the element. For example, the MODS element **name** has the subelements **namePart** (to distinguish how a name should be parsed), **displayForm** (to show how a particular name should be displayed), **affiliation** (name of organization, etc., that the person or body in the name element was affiliated with when that particular form of the name was established), **role** (role the named person or body serves in relation to the resource), and **description** (description of the name when necessary for clarification or to distinguish it from similar names). All elements are optional and may be repeated as often as needed.

DC originated in 1994 at the 2nd International World Wide Web Conference.[4] The idea led to a brainstorming session at OCLC in Dublin, Ohio (which is the source of the name), where participants "discussed how a core set of semantics for Web-based resources would be extremely useful for categorizing the Web for easier search and retrieval."[5] DC consists of a core set of 15 broadly defined elements that include **Contributor** and **Creator** (rather than author or editor), **Description** (which may be free text or a table of contents, as compared to how MARC and MODS provide this information), **Identifier**, and **Rights**. In most cases, catalogers will use the set of 15 elements, which may be referred to as "unqualified DC." "Qualified DC" is defined as including "an additional element, **Audience**, as well as a group of element refinements (also called qualifiers) that refine the semantics of the elements in ways that may be useful in resource discovery."[6] All DC elements are optional and repeatable as needed.

Crosswalks for mapping among MARC, MODS, and DC are readily available. See Resources for Catalogers at the end of this chapter for more information. By including these display formats, we aim to provide examples for a wide cross-section of catalogers and to reflect the reality of the formats used in libraries and in digital projects.

Elements of Resource Description

Before examining the core elements of a description, it is important to recognize that each record contains technical elements that are important to but not an integral part of the work itself. While no technical elements are designated by *RDA* as core elements, they enable the various schemes to communicate with the appropriate technology and may be helpful in distinguishing among similar resources. Technical elements can also contain characteristics of the carrier and typically include information such as file type or file size (number of bytes). While the size of the file may be recorded in the technical area of the record, details about the extent of the work are considered mandatory and the extent is a designated core element.

Every descriptive record contains a section dedicated to machine-generated numeric data pertaining to record length, date of entry, file size and characteristics, and other technical details. There also may be several elements, not necessarily core, specific to the manifestation of a particular work. In some metadata schemes, this information may be entered in the Technical Metadata, which is separate from the descriptive record.

- Each resource or work contains essential characteristics that form the core elements of the resource. The first grouping of elements (Group 1 entities) relates to the work itself: the work, its expression, manifestation, and the item (a single exemplar of the work).
- Taken as a group, these entities can be subdivided into familiar characteristics such as those related to the **work**:
  - Title
    - Parallel title, Earlier title, Variant title (as appropriate)
  - Statement of responsibility
    - Responsible person(s)
    - Additional responsible person(s)
  - Date of creation
  - Subject of the work (content)
  - Related persons
- The second subgroup of entities relates to the **expression** of the work in whatever form it may be expressed:
  - Content type; genre
  - Extent
  - Edition
  - Publisher/place and date of publication
- The third subgroup of entities relates to the **manifestation** of the work (its physical representation):
  - Publisher (Name, Place, Date), because this may vary depending on the manifestation
  - Carrier type and media type; Extent (this may vary depending on the manifestation)
  - Series title/title proper of series
  - Numeric/Alpha-Numeric identifiers: ISBN, ISSN, DOI, URL, etc.
  - Designation of first issue for multipart works; numbering
- The final subgroup relates to the **item**: a single exemplar of the work such as a copy that may be available at the library. The characteristics of this final subgroup will relate to the location of the unique copy of the work.
- Within the grouping for the first level or Group 1 entities, second level or Group 2 entities are examined and discussed as they specify relationships of persons, organizations, and places to the work. Group 2 entities are those that define persons and/or corporate bodies (organizations) responsible for the

intellectual or artistic content, the physical production and dissemination, or the custodianship of such products.

- Finally, the *FRBR* Group 3 entities are the subjects of the work and are the intellectual or artistic endeavor. They describe an event, object, issue, and so forth.

These groupings will be illustrated using MARC, MODS, and DC.

MARC 21 Bibliographic Format enables coding for books, computer files/electronic resources, maps, mixed materials, music (sound recordings), continuing resources (more commonly known as *serials* or *periodicals*), and visual materials. The terminology used for these resources may sometimes differ from that provided in *AACR2* or *RDA* because they are content standards rather than display standards. MARC21 is an encoding standard as are MODS and DC.

In the MARC format, technical information about the record is entered in fields such as the Leader and in various numbered fixed fields (001, 006, 007, 008, etc.). Other fields that contain numerical information include the 010, 020–029, 040, 050 fields. These are variable fields that contain relevant information in numerical or alphabetic code form or in some combination of the two.

MARC 21 Bibliographic Format defines a Leader code for all bibliographic records that provide data elements in the form of numbers and/or coded values that define the parameters for processing the record. These parameters include record status, type of record (indicates the format of the resource), bibliographic level (monographic, serial, etc.), character coding scheme, encoding level (level of cataloging), descriptive cataloging code, etc. The Leader consists of 24 character positions and is used for machine processing of the records.

Some Leader codes are machine generated and include the following:

00–04	Logical record length
05	Record status
09	Character coding scheme
10	Indicator count
11	Subfield code count
12–16	Base address of data
19	Linked record requirement
20–23	Entry map

MODS and DC equivalents are provided in Figure 1.1 for quick reference.

The MARC 006–008 control fields contain controlled and coded information used for machine processing of bibliographic records.

The MARC 006 field Fixed-Length Data Elements—Additional Material consists of 18 character positions (positions 00–17) and is used to record special characteristics of resources that cannot be coded in the MARC 008 field Fixed-Length Data Elements. The 006 field records both multiple characteristics (mixed materials, multipart resources) and coded serial aspects of continuing resources in electronic form.

Information about the 006 field as it relates to the formats covered in this text will be provided in greater detail in the format-specific chapters.

Figure 1.1. MARC Leader Codes and MODS and DC Equivalents

MARC		MODS	DC
00–04	Record length	N/A	N/A
05	Record status	N/A	N/A
06	Type of record	<typeOfResource>	<Type>
07	Bibliographic level	<typeOfResource> with attribute "collection" for 07/code "c"	<Type>
08	Type of control	N/A	N/A
09	Character coding scheme	<originInfo> with encoding attribute	N/A
18	Descriptive cataloging form	N/A	N/A
19	Multipart resource record level	N/A	N/A

More information is available on the MARC 21 website at http://www.loc.gov/marc/bibliographic/concise/bd006.html. There are no MODS or DC equivalents for the MARC 006 field; information may be entered in MODS <note> and in the <Format> element in DC.

The MARC 007 field Physical Description Fixed Field contains alphabetic codes to indicate pertinent information that is technical or related to the physical characteristics of the carrier. The information recorded in the MARC 007 field can be provided in the MODS element <physicalDescription>. There is no direct equivalent in DC, and this information can be entered in the <Format> element.

The MARC 007 field begins with a letter that represents one of the various formats:

- c = electronic resource (direct and remote access electronic resources)
- e = cartographic materials (maps, atlases)
- h = microforms (microfiche, microfilm, etc.)
- m = motion picture (reel to reel films)
- o = kits
- s = sound recording (sound cassettes, vinyl discs, CDs, streaming audio)
- v = videorecordings (videocassettes, laser discs, DVDs, streaming video)

MODS codes the physical description information in the <physicalDescription> element and uses the subelement <form> with the attribute "authority" to provide the name of whatever authoritative list is used for controlled terms (see Example 1.1).

EXAMPLE 1.1

```
<physicalDescription>
    <form authority="marcsmd">map
    </form>
</physicalDescription>
```

The number of characters included in the MARC 007 field varies by format and ranges from 6 to 14. The characters provide information on color characteristics, sound characteristics, dimensions, etc. (see Example 1.2). The 007 field is covered in greater detail in the format-specific chapters. Consult the MARC 21 Bibliographic Format website (http://www.loc.gov/marc/bibliographic/concise/bd007.html) for additional information.

General information pertaining to details (language of the text, year of publication, type of resource, i.e., media type) is entered in the MARC 008 field. The first five positions are system related and provide the date when a resource was entered into a particular system; position 06 is for type of date/publication status; positions 07–10 record dates; positions 11–14 also record dates; positions 15–17 record information on place of publication, production, execution, etc.; positions 18–34 are format specific and describe characteristics of a given format; positions 35–37 provide language information; position 38 describes modified records; position 39 provides information on the cataloging source.

The MODS elements <genre>, <typeOfResource>, and <originInfo> can be used to indicate the information conveyed in the MARC 008. The MODS element selected depends on the type of information being described. This information can also be provided in the DC elements <Date> and <Language>.

EXAMPLE 1.2

Electronic resource

007 __ cr cn

c = electronic resource

r = remote (in this case, an Internet resource)

blank

c = multicolored

n = no sound (silent)

Microform

007 __ hc bfu bucu

h = microform

c = microfilm cassette

blank

b = negative

f = 35 mm.

u = reduction ratio unknown

Three blanks = reduction ratio; because unknown, spaces are left blank

b = black and white

u = emulsion on film unknown

c = service copy

u = base of film unknown

Technical Data and Numerical Identifiers

MARC fields that begin with zero (0) are reserved for numbers and codes. The following fields fall into this category.

Other Standard Identifier

Other standard identifiers (frequently numeric designations) are provided in the MARC 024 field, which is described in detail in the chapters on sound recordings and videorecordings.

Cataloging Source

Information on the origin of a bibliographic record, plus any institutions that have it, is provided in the MARC 040 field Cataloging Source, which is not repeatable. This information is also provided in the MODS element <recordInformation> modified with the subelement <recordContentSource>. This information is not readily accommodated in DC and could be entered in the element <Identifier>, which is used to provide a reference to a resource within a given context.

The following subfields are available for use in the MARC 040 field:

$a original cataloging agency

$c transcribing agency (which is typically the institution in $a)

$d modifying agency

Other subfields can be used in the 040; we limit discussion to those that are most predominantly used. No indicators are defined for the 040 field (see Example 1.3).

EXAMPLE 1.3

Original descriptive record created and transcribed by Rutgers University Libraries, modified by Library X (MARC example):

040 __ NjR$cNjR$dXyZ

Original descriptive record created and transcribed by Rutgers University Libraries (MODS example):

<recordInformation>

<recordContentSource authority="marcorg">NjR</recordContentSource>

</recordInformation>

Descriptive record from another institution (DC example):

<Identifier>XyZ</Identifier>

Language Code

Language codes provide information about the languages represented in a resource. This information is recorded in the MARC 041 field Language Code, which is not repeatable. Information is presented in alphabetic coded format and works in conjunction with the MARC 546 field Language Note. The 041 field is used when multiple languages are represented. This could take the form of a spoken word in one language and subtitles in another; another example is when a resource contains multiple languages. The MARC 041 field accommodates codes for a maximum of six languages. If more than six languages are present in the resource, the language for the title is coded as "mul" (multiple) to represent all the languages.

This information is provided in the MODS element <language> and the DC element <Language>. The MODS element is modified by the subelement <languageTerm> with the attribute "authority" to provide the authoritative list consulted for the character code used to represent language(s) (see Example 1.4). A list of codes that can be used, regardless of metadata schema, is available at http://www.loc.gov/marc/languages.

The MARC 041 field has the following subfields:

- $a language code for text, sound track, or separate title
- $b language code for summary or subtitle
- $d language code for sung or spoken text
- $e language code for librettos
- $g language code for accompanying materials other than librettos
- $h language code for original and/or intermediate translations of text

The initial indicator value used in the MARC 041 indicates whether a resource is or includes a translation. An initial indicator value of 0 indicates that the resource is not a translation and does not include a translation; a value of 1 indicates that the item is a translation or includes a translation (see Example 1.5).

EXAMPLE 1.4

041 0_ eng $a fre [Item is in English and French]

<language>
<languageTerm type="code" authority= "iso639-2b">pan </languageTerm>
</language>

<Language>sai</Language>

EXAMPLE 1.5

041 0_ $b eng
Silent with captions in English.

041 1_ $a freita $g engfreita
In French and Italian; program notes in English, French, and Italian

Geographic Information

Geographic information is conveyed using alphabetic coded information on the geographic area presented, described, covered, etc., by the resource. The MARC 043 field Geographic Area Code is used to record geographic information and can accommodate one to three codes, with multiple geographic codes separated by $a. Indicator values are not defined for the MARC 043 field.

This information is provided in the MODS element <subject> with the subelement <geographicCode> with the attribute "authority" to show the source of the code used. In DC, the element is <Coverage> (see Example 1.6). A full list of geographic area codes is available at www.loc.gov/marc/geoareas/gacs_name.html.

EXAMPLE 1.6

New Jersey, in the United States:
043 __ n-us-nj

Resource contains information pertaining to Spain and Mexico:

<subject>
<geographicCode authority= "marcgac"> n-cn-ab </geographicCode>
</subject>

Resource on Anhui Sheng (China):
<Coverage>a-cc-an</Coverage>

Library of Congress Classification Number

Library of Congress Classification Numbers can be given in the MARC 050 field Library of Congress Call Number when this type of classification is used for nonbook resources. Libraries can choose to use other classification schemes (Superintendent of Document Numbers (SuDocs, for example) or local schemes (shelved by title, accession numbers, or machine-generated generic numbers that are sequentially assigned).

Library of Congress Classification is provided in the MODS element <classification> with the attribute "authority." In DC, the element <Subject> is used.

These are the mostly commonly used subfields of the MARC 050 field:

$a classification number

$b item number

The $a is for the classification portion of the classification number and provides the class letter and numbers for a defined subject. This is sometimes referred to as a *stem* and is used for brief records or to facilitate broad subject searching. The $b is the item number of a classification number and contains the Cutter designation (typically for the author), dates, and other information to distinguish one item from another. Classification numbers are similar to addresses or URLs in that each is unique. The information provided in the MARC 050 $a and $b may also be represented in the MODS element <classification>, with the attribute "authority" to indicate the source of the classification code, and in the DC element <Subject>, as previously stated.

The initial indicator value used when creating a MARC 050 field indicates whether the item is in the Library of Congress's collection. An initial value of blank indicates that no information is provided and is used when libraries other than the Library of Congress provide classification numbers. The second indicator value indicates source of call number. Classification numbers provided by the Library of Congress have a second indicator value of 0; classification numbers provided by other libraries have a second indicator value of 4. This level of specificity is not provided in the MODS element <classification>. However, the MODS element <location> and the subelement <physicalLocation> can be used to specify the holdings institution and the physical location of a resource within the specified location (see Example 1.7). This information does not readily translate into DC but can be added in a named field if deemed important.

EXAMPLE 1.7

050 _0 HB1335 $b .M84
050 _4 GB1399.4.N51 $b F566 1971

<location>
<physicalLocation authority= "marcorg">NjR Media Services 2-152</physicalLocation>

Work

Title Proper

Each work is distinguished by its title. The title is generally considered to be the most important descriptive element. For items lacking a title, the cataloger can provide a title or some other means to identify a resource and to distinguish it from others.

The title proper is the title used when citing a resource, and it is entered in the MARC 245 field, the MODS <titleInfo> element with the subelement <title>, and the DC element <Title> (see Example 1.8).

EXAMPLE 1.8

245 00 Flight of the bumblebee

<titleInfo>
<title>Marriage certificate of Saros and Pappas</title>
</titleInfo>

<Title>House on the green</Title>

EXAMPLE 1.9

245 00 Powwow songs : $b music of the Plains Indians [subtitle/remainder of title information]

<titleInfo>
<title>Suzanne Fisher Staples </title>
<subTitle>the setting is the story </subTitle>
</titleInfo>

<Title>The real Wizard of Oz</Title>
<Title>The life and times of L. Frank Baum</Title>

EXAMPLE 1.10

245 03 L'Homme sur les quais = $b The man by the shore
[*Note*: parallel title is recorded in $b.]

EXAMPLE 1.11

245 10 My funny valentine $h [sound recording] / $c Chet Baker.

<titleInfo>
<title>Lovers of the Arctic Circle</title>
</titleInfo>
<name type="personal">
<namePart>Julio Medem </namePart>
<role>
<roleTerm type="text"> director</roleTerm>
</name>

<Title>Dances of India</Title>
<Creator>Shobhna Gupta</Creator>

EXAMPLE 1.12

245 10 Concerto in a-Moll für Flöte, Streicher und Basso continuo

<titleInfo>
<title>Piano concerto no. 2 in B-flat, op. 83</title>
</titleInfo>

<Title>Geology and resource assessment of the Venezuelan Guayana Shield at 1:500,000 scale</Title>

The title is taken from the preferred source for each specific format, which will be covered in the successive format-specific chapters.

RDA prescribes using information from reputable reference sources and suggests that catalogers consider how the title is represented in general usage when assigning a title proper. If the title is taken from a source other than the preferred source, or if the title was provided by the cataloger, this information must be stated in a note.

Title information other than the title proper may be related to the manifestation of a work rather than to the work itself, because a publisher may insert a parallel title in another language to describe a translation of an original work. A key title may also be supplied by a publisher to unify different manifestations of a work, etc.

MARC format provides subfields that describe various parts of a resource's title. The MODS element <titleInfo> has subelements, such as <subtitle>, to provide this information. The DC element <Title> can be repeated as often as needed to convey this type of information (see Example 1.9).

These are the MARC 245 subfields:

- $a title proper
- $b remainder of title (used for subtitles or other information that is not considered as part of the main title)
- $c statement of responsibility (use to record this first statement of responsibility)
- $h general material designation (GMD) (used to designate the type of resource)
- $n number of part/section (used to designate the part or section represented by the title
- $p name of part/section (used to designate the name of the part or section represented by the title)

The indicators used with the MARC 245 field support the indexing of the title. The second indicator specifies the number of characters to be ignored in indexing. The characters ignored represent the initial articles in all languages, any extraneous characters, plus one space (see Example 1.10).

The MARC 245 field, subfield $c, provides information on those persons, corporate bodies, or conferences/meetings with responsibility for the creation of the resource. This information is recorded in the MODS element <name> modified with the attribute "type" and would include the subelement <role> to indicate the role of the named person, corporate body, or conference to the resource. The information is placed in the DC element <Creator> (see Example 1.11).

Other elements can be included in a title proper. Examples are information that is integral to the work itself and/or information that is specific to the manifestation of the work being described, such as type of musical composition, medium of performance, and key (for musical works) and scale (cartographic works) (see Example 1.12).

Parallel Title

The parallel title is the title proper as provided in another language or script. Parallel titles are used when a resource is a translation or contains more than one language. Record this information in the $b of the MARC 245 field, the MODS element <titleInfo> with the subelement <subTitle>, and the DC element <Title>. If DC is used, titles can be repeated as necessary (see Example 1.13).

Parallel titles are formulated using information taken from within the resource. If a parallel title is taken from a source other than that used for the title proper, record this in a note if it is considered important to the resource description.

Other Title Information

Other title information includes subtitles, but it does not include information such as spine titles or other variations of the title. Record this information in the MARC 246 field, the MODS element <titleInfo> with the subelement <title> and the subelement <subTitle> if a subtitle is used or modified with the attribute "type" to identify type of title, and the DC element <Title> (see Example 1.14). Use the same source of preferred information used for a title proper when formulating another title.

Parallel Other Title Information

Parallel other title information is the foreign language counterpart for other title information and differs from the title proper. Supply this information if it no longer appears on the resource but is considered important for access and retrieval. Provide this information in the MARC 246 field, the MODS element <titleInfo> with the subelement <title> with type attribute="translated" for each parallel title, and the DC element <Title> (see Example 1.15).

The indicator values that are defined for the MARC 245 field indicate when a title added entry will be generated (first indicator) and the number of nonfiling characters (second indicator). A range of 0–9 nonfiling characters is defined for the second character.

A first indicator value of 0 (zero) indicates that there is no title added entry. The value is used when title main entry is chosen. A first indicator value of 1 is used when main entry is under author, corporate body, or conference and there will be a title added entry.

A second indicator value of 0 (zero) indicates that there are no nonfiling characters, such as initial articles or other characters to be skipped. Second indicator values of 1–9 indicate the number of nonfiling characters to be skipped in the title (see Example 1.16).

The MARC 246 field Varying Form of Title is used to record varying forms of the title or other title information not provided on or in the chief source of information but considered important for identification and/or access. This information is recorded in the MODS element <titleInfo> qualified by type "alternative" to specify a title variation and in the DC element <Title> with the qualifier "Alternative" (see Example 1.17, p. 30).

EXAMPLE 1.13

245 00 Bicycle thieves = $b Ladri di biciclette

<titleInfo>
  <title>Farewell my concubine</title>
  <subTitle>Pa-wang pieh chi</subTitle>
</titleInfo>

<Title>Red hat</Title>
<Title>Sombrero rojo</Title>

EXAMPLE 1.14

245 00 Farewell my concubine
246 31 Farewell to my concubine

<titleInfo>
  <title>Ascent of money</title>
  <subTitle>a financial history of the world</subTitle>
</titleInfo>

<titleInfo>
  <titleInfo type="translated" lang="eng">
<titleInfo type="translated" lang="eng">
  <title>Breathless</title>
</titleInfo>

<Title>Gender, culture, and the arts </Title>
<Title>Women, the arts, and society </Title>

EXAMPLE 1.15

245 00 Farewell my concubine
246 31 Pa-wang pieh chi

<titleInfo>
<titleInfo type="translated" lang="eng">
  <title>Breathless</title>
</titleInfo>

This level of specificity is not accommodated by DC; the element <Title> is repeated as often as needed.

EXAMPLE 1.16

245 00 Kyushu-Okinawa Summit 2000 official guide [title main entry, no filing indicators to be skipped]

245 14 The Highlands [title added entry; initial article "the" requires 4 nonfiling characters to be skipped]

EXAMPLE 1.17

```
<titleInfo>
  <title>Little Red Riding Hood</title>
  <title type=alternative>Petite
  chaperone rouge</title>
<Title>Red hat</Title>
<Title.Alternative>Sombrero rojo</Title>
```

EXAMPLE 1.18

```
246 1_ Title on container: $a Coping with
death and dying
<titleInfo>
<titleInfo type="alternative">
<title>Encyclopedia of Title nine and sports
</title>
</titleInfo>
<Title.Alternative>FHA Title I Loan Program
</Title>
```

The following subfields are available for use in the MARC 246 field (see Example 1.18):

- $a title
- $b remainder of title or parallel title
- $h medium to record the GMD (note that use of GMDs is no longer relevant when using *RDA*)
- $i display text (use for notes indicating source of title, placement of title, etc.)
- $n number of part/section of a work
- $p name of a part/section of a work

Additional subfields may be used with the MARC 246 field; we discuss and provide examples of the most predominantly used ones.

The initial indicator value in the MARC 246 field indicates note or added entry. The second indicator value provides information on type of title. A second indicator value of 0 (zero) indicates that a portion of the title is provided, and 1 is used for parallel titles. A complete list of indicators is available on the MARC 21 Bibliographic Format website at http://www.loc.gov/marc/bibliographic/bd246.html. Example 1.19 shows sample MARC 246 notes.

EXAMPLE 1.19

Portions of the main title

245 10 Federal Housing Administration : $b agency should assess the effects of proposed changes to the manufactured Home Loan program : report to congressional requesters

246 30 Agency should assess the effects of proposed changes to the manufactured Home Loan program

Remainder of title

245 00 Ocean steward : $b stewardship of the nation's marine protected species

246 30 Stewardship of the nation's marine protected species

Title on chief source and container differ

245 00 Rudaali

246 1_ Title on container: $a Rudalli, the mourner

245 04 Les liaisons dangereuses 1960 = $b Dangerous liaisons 1960

246 1_ Title on container and videocassette label: $a Liaisons dangereuses

Notes or added entries are addressed differently when using MODS and DC. Title variations are provided as needed, and less emphasis is placed on describing the source of title variation or type of title variation.

Variant Title

A variant title differs from the title proper, parallel title, and other title information. Variant titles may incorporate abbreviations or different representations of a spelling. Provide this information in the MARC 246 field, the MODS element <titleInfo> with the attribute "type" (abbreviated, translated, alternative, or uniform), and the DC element <Title> (see Example 1.20). Information can be taken from any source when formulating a variant title.

EXAMPLE 1.20

```
245 00 B2B
246 1_ B to B
246 1_ Business to business
<titleInfo>
<titleInfo type="abbreviated">
  <title>Annu. rev. nucl. part. sci.</title>
</titleInfo>
<Title>Business to business</Title>
<Title>B2B</Title>
```

Earlier Title Proper

An earlier variant title is a "title proper, parallel title, other title information, or parallel other title information appearing on an earlier iteration of an integrating resource that differs from that on the current iteration."[7] Supply this information if it no longer appears on the resource but is considered important for access and retrieval. Earlier variant titles are provided in the MARC 247 field Former Title, the MODS element <titleInfo> with the attribute type "alternative," and the DC element <Title> (see Example 1.21). Use the sources of information specified for the title proper, parallel title, other title information, or parallel other title information when formulating an earlier variant title.

Later Variant Title

A later variant title is a title proper, parallel title, other title, or parallel title information that appears on a later version of a multipart monograph that differs from what is provided on earlier versions. Later variant titles are best provided in the MARC 246 field Varying Form of Title, the MODS element <titleInfo> with the attribute type "alternative," and the DC element <Title> (see Example 1.22). Use the sources of information specified for the title proper, parallel title, other title information, or parallel other title information when formulating a later variant title.

Key Title

A key title is assigned by an ISSN registration agency. "ISSN national centers use field 222 for a unique title assigned to a continuing resource (serial or integrating resource) in conjunction with an International Standard Serial Number in field 022."[8] Record key titles in the MARC 222 field Key Title, the MODS element <titleInfo> with the attribute type "alternative," and the DC element <Title> (see Example 1.23). Information can be taken from any source when formulating a key title.

EXAMPLE 1.21

245 00 Early American studies
247 10 Explorations in early American culture

<titleInfo>
<titleInfo type="alternative">
<title>New era : an international review of new education</title>
</titleInfo>
[The title is New era in home and school.]

<Title>Early American studies</Title>
<Title>Explorations in early American culture</Title>

EXAMPLE 1.22

245 00 Tobacco outlook & situation
246 2_ Outlook and situation report. Tobacco

<titleInfo>
<titleInfo type="alternative">
<title>Soap and water and common sense </title>
</titleInfo>
[The title is Soap and water & common sense.]

Abbreviated Title

An abbreviated title is one that has been abbreviated for purposes of indexing or identification.[9] Provide this information in the MARC 210 field Abbreviated Title, the MODS element <titleInfo> with the attribute type "abbreviated" (which is equivalent to the MARC 210; see Example 1.24), and the DC element <Title>. Information can be taken from any source when formulating an abbreviated title.

Devised Title

A devised title is used when a resource lacks a title and must be supplied by the cataloger. Any source of information can be used to provide a devised title. The title should indicate the nature or content of the resource or the subject or a combination of the two.

Record devised titles in the MARC 245 field Title Proper, the MODS element

EXAMPLE 1.23

222 _0 JAMA, the journal of the American Medical Association
222 _0 Information technologies and international development $b (Online)

222 _0 Information technologies and international development $b (Online)
245 00 Information technologies and international development|h[electronic resource].

<titleInfo>
<titleInfo type="alternative">
<title>SIGICE bulletin</title>
</titleInfo>
[Title is SIGICE bulletin : monthly publication of the ACM Special Interest Group on Individual Computing Environments.]

EXAMPLE 1.24

210 0_ Inf. technol. int. dev.
245 00 Information technologies and international development $h [electronic resource]

<titleInfo>
<titleInfo type="abbreviated">
<title>Adv. at. mol. opt. phys.</title>
</titleInfo>
[Title is Advances in atomic, molecular, and optical physics.]

EXAMPLE 1.25

245 00 Sonata no. 2, op. 35

<titleInfo>

<title>Konzert, d-moll, für Flöte, Streicher und Continuo, Wq. 22 ; Konzert, G-dur, für Flöte, Streicher und Continuo, Wq. 169</title>

</titleInfo>

<Title>Their eyes were watching God </Title>

EXAMPLE 1.26

245 10 Utah recreation destinations and campgrounds

<titleInfo>

<title>Montana recreation guide</title>

</titleInfo>

<Title>Central Balkan region</Title>

EXAMPLE 1.27

245 00 Everyday stranger harassment : $b frequency and consequences / $c Kimberly M. Fairchild.

<titleInfo>Everyday stranger harassment: frequency and consequences

<name type="personal">

<namePart>Kimberly M. Fairchild </namePart>

<role>

<roleTerm type="text">author </roleTerm>

</role>

</name>

<Title>Everyday stranger harassment: frequency and consequences</Title>

<Creator>Kimberly M. Fairchild(author) </Creator>

EXAMPLE 1.28

245 00 Blade runner / $c Jerry Perenchio and Bud Yorkin present a Warner Bros. , Ladd Company release ; screenplay, Hampton Fancher and David Peoples ; producer, Michael Deeley ; director, Ridley Scott.

<titleInfo> with the subelement <title>, and the DC element <Title> (see Example 1.25). Additionally, note when the title has been devised. Example 1.25 indicates the departure from *AACR2*, which required catalogers to bracket this information. *RDA* does not require this information to be bracketed.

Devised titles used for music can include medium of performance, numeric designation (e.g., serial number, opus number), key, and/or another distinguishing characteristic if this information is deemed important for access and retrieval.[10]

Devised titles for cartographic resources must include the name or an identification of the area covered (see Example 1.26). The subject portrayed is included if it is applicable and deemed appropriate for access and retrieval.[11]

Statement of Responsibility

RDA defines statement of responsibility as a core element. The statement of responsibility provides names of corporate bodies and/or individuals responsible for production, creation, manufacture, etc., of a nonprint resource.

The statement of responsibility is provided in the MARC field 245 Title Proper in the $c statement of responsibility, the MODS element <name> with an attribute "type" to indicate type of name (personal, corporate, or conference), and the DC elements <Creator> or <Contributor>, depending on the role of the individual or corporate body. The MODS element <name> may be further refined using the subelements <namePart> to provide access to the various parts of a name and <role> to define the relationship of the name to the resource. *RDA* notes that statements of responsibility may occur in conjunction with a title, the designation of edition, the designation of a named revision of an edition, a series title, or a subseries title.[12]

ISBD punctuation prescribes recording each corporate body or individual presented in the statement of responsibility and separating those names by semicolons. This type of treatment is used in MARC records. MODS and DC elements for name and creator are repeated for each instance of a name. Additionally, MODS and DC provide title information and creator information separately.

In Example 1.27, the title *Everyday Stranger Harassment* by the author Kimberly M. Fairchild is represented in MARC, MODS, and DC.

The statement of responsibility is provided in the manner in which it appears in the preferred source of information. In Example 1.28, the statement of responsibility is formulated according to the order in which corporate and personal names are provided in the opening credits.

The film *Ghosts of the Pines*, which was produced by Bill Reed, is represented in Example 1.29 using MODS. The film *Aesthetics: Philosophy of the Arts*, produced by Lila Kononovich and directed by Pablo S. Garcia, is represented in Example 1.30 using DC. If the role of an individual or corporate body is not clear in the preferred source of information, *RDA* advises catalogers to note their role in brackets (see Example 1.31).

When a corporate body and the names of its members are provided in the preferred source of information, cite only the corporate body. If any of the members of the group making up that corporate body play a role of particular importance, include that individual (or individuals) in the statement of responsibility (see Example 1.32). *RDA* instructs catalogers to provide a statement of responsibility even when there is no named corporate body or individuals cited in the preferred source of information (see Example 1.33).

RDA 2.4.1.10.3 further instructs catalogers to record changes in the statement of responsibility for integrating resources. If the statement of responsibility for these resources has been changed or revised, it must be updated to reflect the current iteration of the integrating resource.

If a resource's statement of responsibility is provided in more than one language or script, *RDA* notes that the statement of responsibility should be recorded in the language or script of the title proper. In cases when this is not applicable, catalogers are instructed to then record the first statement of responsibility that is provided.

Responsible Persons/Organizations

The MARC 1XX fields (100 for personal name, 110 for corporate name, and 111 for meeting name) are used when the main entry is entered under a name. See "Choice of Main Entry" later in this chapter for a fuller explanation of the concept of main entry and how to apply it.

Name main entry information is provided in the MODS element <name> and can include the attributes <type> to specify if the name used is personal, corporate, or conference and <authority> to indicate when those names are part of a controlled authority file. The DC element <Creator> is used to provide personal, corporate, or conference names.

The MARC 100 field Main Entry—Personal Name has a number of subfields defined for use. These are the most commonly used:

- $a for personal name
- $c for titles or words associated with a personal name
- $d for dates associated with a name
- $q to provide the fuller form of a name

This information can be recorded in the MODS element <name> with the attribute <type> to indicate personal name. Catalogers using DC can qualify names with terms from the MARC list of relator terms. See http://lcweb2.loc.gov/diglib/loc.terms/relators/dc-relators.html. Example 1.34 shows a title associated with a given name.

The MODS User Guidelines, Version 3, defines the element <name> as "The name of a person, organization, or event (conference,

EXAMPLE 1.29

```
<titleInfo>
<title>Ghosts of the pines</title>
</titleInfo>
<name type="personal">
  <namePart>Reed, Bill</namePart>
  <displayForm>Bill Reed</displayForm>
<role>
<roleTerm type="text">producer</roleTerm>
</role>
</name>
```

EXAMPLE 1.30

```
<Title>Aesthetics : philosophy of the arts </Title>
<Contributor>Kononovich, Lila (Producer) </Contributor>
<Contributor>Garcia S., Pablo (Garcia Silva)(Director)
</Contributor>
```

EXAMPLE 1.31

245 00 Butterfly flight patterns / $c [produced by] Mitch Denda.

EXAMPLE 1.32

245 00 Map of Hunterdon County $[cartographic material] / $c prepared by the New Jersey Cartographic Society ; scale devised by Marc Edmonds.

EXAMPLE 1.33

245 00 Map of Hunterdon County / $c cartography provided by local surveyors.

```
<titleInfo>
  <title>School report card</title>
</titleInfo>
<name type="corporate">
  <namePart>Matawan Aberdeen School
  District </namePart>
</name>
```

EXAMPLE 1.34

100 1_ Sullivan, Arthur ,$c Sir, $d 1842-1900.

EXAMPLE 1.35

```
<name type="personal"
authority="naf">
  <namePart>Page, Penny Booth
  </namePart>
  <namePart type="date">1949-
  </namePart>
<name type="personal">
  <namePart type="given">Sullivan,
  Arthur</namePart>
  <namePart type="termsOfAddress">
  Sir</namePart>
  <namePart type="date">1842-1900.
  </namePart>
```

EXAMPLE 1.36

```
<Creator>Graham, Peter Scott</Creator>
```

EXAMPLE 1.37

110 1_ New York (State). $b Governor.

110 2_ United Nations. $b Open-ended Informal Consultative Process on Oceans and the Law of the Sea. $b Meeting $n (7th). $b 2006 : $c New York, N.Y.

EXAMPLE 1.38

```
<name type="corporate">
  <namePart>United States</namePart>
  <namePart>Court of Appeals (2nd
  Circuit)</namePart>
<name type="corporate">
<namePart>Museum of Arts and Design
(New York, N.Y.)</namePart>
</namePart>Simona and Jerome Chazen
Collection</namePart>
```

meeting, etc.) associated in some way with the resource."[13] The MODS element <name> has the attributes "type" (indicates personal, corporate, or conference name) and "authority" (cites the authoritative list consulted for the controlled vocabulary used). Additionally, this element has the subelements <namePart> (used for each part of the name that is parsed; see Example 1.35), <displayForm> (shows an unstructured form of the name), <affiliation> (provides the name of an organization or other corporate body associated with the name and may also include e-mail address, street address, job title), and <role> (relationship of the name to the resource being described). DC defines <Creator> as "An entity primarily responsible for making the resource" and <Contributor> as "An entity responsible for making contributions to the resource"[14] (see Example 1.36).

The MARC 110 field Main Entry—Corporate Name has a number of subfields defined for use (see Example 1.37). These are the most commonly used:

- $a corporate or jurisdiction name
- $b subordinate unit

The MODS element <name> has the attributes "type" (indicates personal, corporate, or conference name; see Example 1.38) and "authority" (cites the authoritative list consulted for the controlled vocabulary used). Additionally, this element has the subelements <namePart> (used for each part of the name that is parsed), <displayForm> (shows an unstructured form of the name), <affiliation> (provides the name of an organization or other corporate body associated with the name and may also include e-mail address, street address, job title), and <role> (relationship of the name to the resource being described). DC does not accommodate this level of specificity.

Additional Responsible Parties

Additional access points are provided using names (personal, corporate, conference) and/or titles having various relationships to a work.[15] These added entries can be further subdivided by form division (format of material), general subdivisions, chronological subdivisions, and geographic subdivisions. The MARC 7XX fields are used to provide additional access points. This information can be recorded in the MODS element <name> (which is equivalent to the MARC fields 700, 710, 711, and 730) and the DC element <Contributor> (which is equivalent to the MARC fields 700, 710, and 711). See the preceding section on statement of responsibility for more detail on names.

Personal Names

Personal names are included in a bibliographic record when additional access to the names of individuals not included in the statement of responsibility is necessary. Use the MARC 700 field Added Entry—Personal Name, the MODS element <name>, and the DC element <Creator> or <Contributor>, depending on the role, to provide this information.

This text focuses on the following subfields of the MARC 700 field:

- $a personal name
- $c titles associated with a name
- $d dates associated with a name
- $e relator term (a term that designates the relationship between a name and a work)
- $v form subdivision
- $x general subdivision
- $y chronological subdivision
- $z geographic subdivision
- $4 relator code (a MARC code that specifies the relationship between a name and a work)

The indicators defined for the MARC 700 field provide information on the type of personal name and the type of added entry (see Example 1.39). The first indicator has the following values: 0 (zero) indicates entry under a forename (single name); 1 indicates entry under a single surname (meaning that the name is not compound or hyphenated); 3 indicates a family name. A second indicator value of blank indicates that no information has been provided regarding type of added entry; a second indicator value of 2 is used for analytical entries.

EXAMPLE 1.39

```
700 1_ Bernard, Sheila Curran.

<name type="personal">
  <namePart type="given">Otto
  </namePart>
  <namePart type="family">Preminger
  </namePart>
  <role>
    <roleTerm type="code" authority=
    "marcrelator">drt</roleTerm>
    <roleTerm type="text" authority=
    "marcrelator">director</roleTerm>
  </role>
</name>

<Contributor>Chambers, Paul, 1935-1969
</Contributor>
```

Corporate Names

Corporate names are included in a descriptive record when additional access to corporate bodies not included in the statement of responsibility is necessary. Record added entries for corporate names in the MARC 710 field Added Entry—Corporate Name, the MODS element <name> with the attributes "type" for type of name and "authority" for the authoritative list that was consulted, and the DC element <Creator> or <Contributor>, depending on the role. This text focuses on the following subfields, which are defined for the MARC 710 field:

- $a corporate or jurisdiction name
- $b subordinate unit
- $n number of part/section/meeting
- $p name of part/section of a work
- $e relator term (a term that designates the relationship between a name and a work)
- $4 relator code (a MARC code that specifies the relationship between a name and a work)

The MODS element <name> has a subelement <role> to provide the same type of information as the MARC 710 field $e or $4. Roles may be defined in DC; consult the document *Relator Terms and Dublin Core Elements* (available at http://lcweb2.loc.gov/diglib/loc.terms/relators/dc-relators.html) for a list of terms to use with DC.

EXAMPLE 1.40

710 2_ Red Hot Peppers (Musical group) $4 prf

<name>

<name type="corporate">

<namePart> Newark (N.J.) </namePart>

<namePart>Public Information Office </namePart>

</name>

<Contributor> New Jersey. Office of Travel & Tourism</Contributor>

EXAMPLE 1.41

111 2_ International Conference on Advances in Product Development and Reliability $d (2008 : $c Chengdu, China)

111 2_ International Conference on Cancer Prevention $n (5th : $d 2008 : $c Saint Gall, Switzerland)

EXAMPLE 1.42

<name type="conference">

<namePart> International Conference on Research Reactors: Safe Management and Effective Utilization</namePart>

</name>

The indicators defined for the MARC 710 field provide information on the type of name and the type of added entry. The first indicator has the values 0 (zero) for an inverted name, 1 for name in jurisdiction order, and 2 for name in direct order. A second indicator value of blank indicates that no information has been provided regarding type of added entry; a second indicator value of 2 is used for analytical entries (see Example 1.40).

Meeting Names

Meeting names are included in a descriptive record when additional access to meeting names not included in the statement of responsibility is necessary. Use the MARC 111 field Main Entry—Meeting Name when a conference or meeting name is used as the main entry for a bibliographic record (see Example 1.41). The MARC 111 field has a number of subfields defined. These are the most common:

- $a for meeting or jurisdiction name
- $c for the location of the meeting or conference
- $d for the date of the meeting or conference
- $e for any units subordinate to the main meeting or conference name
- $n for the number of the part, section, meeting, etc.
- $p for the name of the part, section, meeting, etc.

The following MODS subelements may accompany the element <name>: <namePart>, which includes each part of the name to indicate dates associated with names or to specify parts of a personal name into family and given name; and <affiliation>, which provides the name of an organization or other corporate body associated with the name and may also include e-mail address, street address, etc. (see Example 1.42). DC does not accommodate this level of specificity.

Copyright Date

The date on which a work was copyrighted establishes ownership and rights and is specific to the work itself as intellectual property. The copyright date is a core element when neither the date of publication nor the date of distribution is provided. *RDA* defines copyright date as "a date associated with a claim of protection under copyright or a similar regime."[16]

Phonogram dates are considered as copyright dates. Copyright date and phonogram dates are preceded by the copyright symbol (©) and the phonogram symbol (℗). Catalogers are required to record only the latest copyright date when a resource has multiple copyright dates that relate to various aspects of the resource.

General Material Designation (GMD)

The GMD is traditionally used in MARC cataloging and ILSs to indicate the format of a resource. The resource described in an ILS may not be readily apparent to users even though the descriptive record provides a physical description that includes type of resource and its inherent characteristics. When separate descriptive records are used for each instantiation of a resource, it is believed that a GMD helps users to distinguish between different formats in which a title is available. For example, *Midnight Express* is the title of a book, as well as a motion picture, a motion picture sound track, and a videorecording. However, in an *FRBR*-based environment, GMDs are not as relevant because information on expressions, manifestations, and items are linked to works.

GMDs lack relevancy for institutions that use the single bibliographic record approach to represent multiple manifestations of a title (a paper and an electronic version of a title, for example). They are also not relevant in a MODS or DC environment. The single bibliographic record approach is becoming increasingly common, and groups such as CONSER and the Program for Cooperative Cataloging (PCC) provide documentation and guidance for catalogers who use it.

Notes

The MARC 505 Formatted Contents Note is a specialized note for a variety of nonprint materials. This information is recorded in the MODS element <tableOfContents> and the DC element <Description> with the qualifier <TableofContents> (see Example 1.43).

In this text we cover the MARC 505 Formatted Contents Note subfields $a formatted contents note, $r statement of responsibility, and $t title. Subfields $r and $t are used in enhanced contents notes. All of this information is placed in the MODS element <tableOfContents>, which accommodates the information that would be provided in the MARC 505 $a, $r, and $t subfields. The DC element <Description> with the qualifier <TableofContents> contains this information.

The indicators defined for the MARC 505 field indicate display constant and type of contents note. A first indicator value of 0 (zero) specifies contents; 1 is for incomplete contents (used when a resource is published on an ongoing basis or an institution has not purchased all parts of the resource); 2 is for partial contents. The second indicator value of blank indicates a basic contents note; a second indicator value of 0 (zero) indicates enhanced contents.

The MARC 520 Summary note is another specialized note that can be used for a variety of nonprint materials. This field describes the scope and general contents of the resource.[17] This information is recorded in the MODS element <abstract> and the DC element <Description> with the qualifier "Abstract."

Although a number of subfields are defined for use with the MARC 520 field, in this text we will focus on the $a summary. Only the first indicator is defined for the MARC 520 and provides information on the display constant. We will focus on the following indicator values: blank for a summary, 1 for a review, 3 for abstracts, and 4 for content advice. This level of specificity is not defined for the MODS element <abstract>. The DC element <Description> with the qualifier "Abstract" corresponds to the MARC 520 field with a first indicator of blank (summary) or 3 (abstract) (see Example 1.44).

EXAMPLE 1.43

505 0_ Dependency in development : where id was, there ego shall be -- Institutional politics and cultural intervention : they were killing their mothers -- Civilization and its contents : Buddhistic cyberspace in Kyoto -- Religion, cohesion and personal life : a homogeneous culture -- Mirrors of the other : why are you asking these questions?

<tableOfContents> 1. Slokam: Guru Brahma -- 2. Slokam: Manikya Veena -- 3. Pushpanjali -- 4. Alarippu -- 5. Jatiswaram -- 6. Varnam -- 7. Padam -- 8. Sabdam -- 9. Tillana -- 10. Mangalam. </tableOfContents>

<Description. TableofContents>Romeo and Juliet, fantasy overture -- The Tempest, symphonic fantasia, op. 18 -- Hamlet, fantasy overture, op. 67</Description>

EXAMPLE 1.44

520 __ The mission is to communicate, to a broad audience, the Laboratory's scientific and technological accomplishments particularly in the Laboratory's core mission areas—global security, energy and the environment, and bioscience and biotechnology. Includes summary of contents of each issue and lists of all recent patents.

```
<abstract>We compare the performance of an inexact Newton-multigrid method and Full Approximation Storage multigrid when solving radiation transport equations. We also present an adaptive refinement algorithm and explore its impact on the solution of such equations.</abstract>
```

<Description.Abstract>...summarizes research results for the programs that use the facilities at the NIST Center for Neutron Research (NCNR) for the period from Oct. 1996 through September 1997</Description>

EXAMPLE 1.45

546 __ French and English.

<language>In English, with Maori and sign language; English subtitles </language>

<Description>In Slovenian and English, with abstracts in the other language, 1994- ; English only, 1997-</Description>

The MARC 546 Language Note provides information on the languages contained in the resource, and it is recorded in a textual, not coded, form. We will focus on the subfield $a language note. This information is provided in the MODS element <language> and the DC element <Description> (see Example 1.45). No indicators are defined for the MARC 546 field.

The Language Note is used when more than one language is provided in a resource or to note languages (including sign language) when a resource is in a language that differs from what is predominantly used by the cataloging agency creating the metadata record. A list of MARC language codes, which are also used in MODS and DC, is available at http://www.loc.gov/marc/languages.

Subject Access

Subject headings are used to provide access to resources through personal names, corporate names, topical terms, or geographic names. Subject headings can be further divided into form subdivisions (format of material), general subdivisions, chronological subdivisions, and geographic subdivisions. We will not include meeting names and subject added entries for uniform titles in this text.

The MARC 6XX fields are used for subject access in general form. Subject access is recorded in the MODS element <subject> (which is equivalent to the MARC 600, 610, 611, 650, and 651) and the DC elements <Subject> qualified with LCSH (equivalent to the MARC 600, 610, 611, and 650) and <Coverage> (equivalent to the MARC 651).

Personal Names

Personal names are included in a bibliographic record when a resource is about an individual or individuals or when it contains a significant portion of information about an individual or individuals. Subject access to personal names is provided in the MARC 600 field, Subject Added Entry—Personal Name. This information is recorded in the MODS element <subject> with the subelement <name> and the DC element <Subject> with the qualifier <LCSH> (see Example 1.46). In this text we will focus on the following subfields defined for the MARC 600 field:

EXAMPLE 1.46

600 00 Björk.

<subject>

<name type="personal">

<namePart> Burton, Richard Francis </namePart>

<namePart type="termsOfAddress">Sir </namePart>

<namePart type="date">1821-1890 </namePart>

</subject>

<Subject.LCSH>Curie family</Subject>

$a personal name
$c titles associated with a name
$d dates associated with a name
$v form subdivision
$x general subdivision
$y chronological subdivision
$z geographic subdivision

The indicators defined for the MARC 600 field provide information on the type of personal name and the subject heading system or thesaurus consulted to provide the subject heading. The first indicator has values of 0 (zero) to indicate entry under a forename (single name) and 1 to indicate entry under a single surname (meaning that the name is not compound or hyphenated). A second indicator value of 0 (zero) indicates that a name is from the Library of Congress Name Authority file.

Corporate Names

Corporate names are included in a bibliographic record when the subject of a resource is a corporation or corporations or the resource contains a significant portion of information about a corporation or corporations. Subject access to corporate names is provided in the MARC 610 field Subject Added Entry—Corporate Name. We focus on the following subfields defined for the MARC 610 field:

- $a corporate or jurisdiction names
- $b subordinate units
- $v form subdivision
- $x general subdivision
- $y chronological subdivision
- $z geographic subdivision

This information is recorded in the MODS element <subject> with the subelement <name> and in the DC element <Subject> with the qualifier <LCSH>. The indicators defined for the MARC 610 field provide information on the type of personal name and the subject heading system or thesaurus consulted to provide the subject heading (see Example 1.47).

The initial indicator value indicates form of entry for names. An initial indicator value of 0 is for an inverted name; 1 is for jurisdiction name; and 2 is for a name in direct order. A second indicator value of 0 (zero) indicates that a name is from the Library of Congress Name Authority file.

EXAMPLE 1.47

610 10 United States. $b Dept. of Homeland Security [Jurisdiction name]

<name type="corporate">
<namePart> United States. Bureau of Labor Statistics</namePart>
</name> [Jurisdiction name]

<Subject.LCSH>Metro-Goldwyn-Mayer </Subject> [Name in direct order]

Conference Names

Meeting and conference names are included in a descriptive record when the subject of a resource is a meeting or a conference or the resource contains a significant portion of information about a meeting or conference. Subject access to meeting or conference names is provided in the MARC 611 field Subject Added Entry—Meeting Name. This information is recorded in the MODS element <subject> with the subelement <name> and in the DC element <Subject> with the qualifier <LCSH>. We will focus on the following subfields defined for the MARC 611 field:

- $a Meeting or jurisdiction name
- $c Location of meeting
- $d Date of meeting
- $e Subordinate unit
- $f Date of a work
- $l Language of a work

EXAMPLE 1.48

611 20 World Conference on Women $d (1995 : $c Beijing, China) [Name in direct order]

<name>
<name type="conference">
<namePart>Seminar on the Acquisition of Latin American Library Materials </namePart>
</name type="conference">
</name> [Name in direct order]

<Subject.LCSH>Conference on Security and Cooperation in Europe (1972 : Helsinki, Finland)</Subject>

EXAMPLE 1.49

650 _0 Papuans.

<subject authority="lcsh">
<topic>Silent films </topic>
</subject>

<Subject.LCSH>Foreign films</Subject>

$n Number of the part/section/meeting
$p Name of part/section of a work
$v Form subdivision
$x General subdivision
$y Chronological subdivision
$z Geographic subdivision

The indicators defined for the MARC 611 field provide information on the type of personal name and the subject heading system or thesaurus consulted to provide the subject heading. The initial indicator value indicates form of entry for names. An initial indicator value of 0 is for an inverted name; 1 is for jurisdiction name; and 2 is for a name in direct order. A second indicator value of 0 (zero) indicates that a name is from the Library of Congress Name Authority file (see Example 1.48).

Additional access points that consist of general subject terms, including names or events, are provided in the MARC 650 field Subject Added Entry—Topical Term.[18] This information is recorded in the MODS element <subject> with the attribute "authority" to note the authoritative list used and the subelement <topic> and in the DC element <Subject> with the qualifier <LCSH> (see Example 1.49).

In this text we will focus on the following subfields defined for the MARC 650 field:

$a Topical term or geographic name
$b Topical term following geographic name
$c Location of event
$v Form subdivision
$x General subdivision
$y Chronological subdivision
$z Geographic subdivision

The indicators defined for the MARC 650 field provide the information level of description and the subject heading system or thesaurus consulted to provide the subject heading. Four values are defined for the initial indicator, which provides level of subject: [blank], no information provided; 0, no level provided; 1, primary (for main focus or subject content of the resource); and 2, secondary (when the focus or subject content of the resource is of lesser importance).[19]

The second indicator value, as previously stated, provides the name of the subject heading system or thesaurus consulted to provide the subject heading. Eight indicator values are defined for the second indicator. A first indicator value of 0 (zero) is for *Library of Congress Subject Headings*; a value of 1 indicates Library of Congress terms for children's literature; a value of 2 indicates that a heading conforms to standards established for the National Library of Medicine; a value of 3 indicates that a heading conforms to standards established for the National Agricultural Library;

a value of 4 indicates that the source is unspecified; a value of 5 indicates that a heading conforms to standards established for Canadian Subject Headings, which is maintained by the Library and Archives Canada; a value of 6 indicates the term conforms to a list maintained by the Bibliothèque de l'Université Laval; a value of 7 indicates that the heading conforms for a specific set of subject heading system/thesaurus building rules.[20] Additional information on the MARC 650 field is available at http://www.loc.gov/marc/bibliographic/bd650.html.

The MODS element <subject> with the attribute "authority" is used to indicate which subject heading system or thesaurus was consulted to provide the subject heading. The DC element <Subject> qualified with LCSH, MeSH, or TGN (*Thesaurus of Geographic Names*) can be used in a limited fashion to indicate which subject heading system or thesaurus was consulted to provide the subject heading.

Geographic Names

The MARC 651 field Subject Added Entry—Geographic Name provides subject added entries by geographic name. This information is recorded in the MODS element <subject> with the subelement <geographic> or <hierarchicalGeographic> and in the DC element <Coverage> with the qualifier "Spatial." The MODS subelement <hierarchicalGeographic> is used to provide a hierarchical form of place name and contains the following subelements: <continent>, <country>, <province>, <region>, <state>, <territory>, <county>, <city>, <citySection>, <island>, <area>, and <extraterrestrialArea> (see Example 1.50).

We will focus on the following subfields defined for the MARC 651 field:

- $a Geographic name
- $v Form subdivision
- $x General subdivision
- $y Chronological subdivision
- $z Geographic subdivision

The first indicator is undefined for the MARC 651 field. The second indicator value provides the name of the subject heading system or thesaurus consulted to provide the subject heading. Eight indicator values are defined for the second indicator. The indicator values defined for the MARC 651 field are the same as those used for the MARC 650 field; see the preceding section or http://www.loc.gov/marc/bibliographic/bd651.html for more information.

EXAMPLE 1.50

```
651 _0 Korea $v Maps
<subject>
  <hierarchicalGeographic>
  <region> Barnegat Bay Region (N.J.)
  </region>
  </hierarchicalGeographic>
</subject>
<Coverage.Spatial>Roads--New Jersey
</Coverage>
```

Expression

Edition

An edition of a work represents a different expression. Designation of edition is an *RDA* core element and identifies the edition, version, etc., to which a resource belongs. An edition statement may include a statement

EXAMPLE 1.51

250 __ 6th edition, Ver. 7.4.

<originInfo>
<edition>Bertelsmann electronic edition</edition>
</originInfo>

<Description>1982 edition</Description>

EXAMPLE 1.52

250 __ [Version] 2.1

<originInfo>
<edition>11th ed.</edition>
</originInfo>

<Description>Revised 1952 version </Description>

EXAMPLE 1.53

250 __ March 2004 ed., Spanish version.

<originInfo>
<edition>11th ed.</edition>
<edition>New version</edition>
</originInfo>

<Description>Digital ed.</Description>

<Description>Spanish version </Description>

EXAMPLE 1.54

250 __ 2002 ed.

500 __ "TradeCAN 2002 edition programming was done by Ricardo Vasquez. Rudolf Buitelaar at UN-ECLAC prepared the user guide and the exercises available in a text file.

<originInfo>
<edition>9th ed.<edition>
</originInfo>

<note>[Edited by] Leslie Collier, Albert Balows, Max Sussman.</note>

<Description>The whole revised, corrected and improved / by George Morgan. </Description>

that it is a named revision of an edition. The edition statement may also include statement of responsibility information. Words or phrases that can be used to determine whether the resource being cataloged is an edition include "issue," "release," and "update."[21]

RDA prescribes consulting the same source of information used to transcribe the title to formulate an edition statement. This source should also be used for a statement of responsibility relating to the edition as well as for any named revisions to the edition being cataloged.

Edition statements are recorded in the form given in the preferred source of information. This information is recorded in the MARC 250 field Edition Statement, the MODS element <originInfo> with the subelement <edition>, and the DC element <Description> (see Example 1.51).

When a resource is issued in parts, or consists of parts, the statement of responsibility for the resource as a whole is recorded. If editions differ significantly between the parts of a multipart resource, this information is recorded in a note when this is deemed important for access and retrieval. *RDA* notes that statements indicating differences in content, geographic coverage, language or audience, or a different format or means of physical presentation, or a change in date associated with content may be interpreted as or used for edition statements.

Edition statements are formulated using the preferred sources of information for a specific format, using information provided within a resource, or using other sources of information as needed. If a designation of edition provides only brief information, such as letters or numbers, this information may be clarified or augmented by information in brackets supplied by the cataloger (see Example 1.52).

Catalogers may record more than one designation of edition. The MARC 250 Edition Statement is not repeatable, so information must be concatenated when more than one statement is present. While the same is not true for MODS or DC because elements may be repeated as needed, it may be preferable to string this information together in one statement for ease of use by patrons (see Example 1.53). *RDA* prescribes recording this information as dictated by sequence, layout, or typography of the resource.

Record statements that indicate regular revisions (as for integrating resources) as a frequency rather than as a designation of edition. Frequency is covered in detail in Chapter 6 of this manual.

Catalogers may choose to include information on a statement of responsibility related to the edition being cataloged. The statement of responsibility information for an edition is taken from the same sources of information that are used to record a designation of edition (see Example 1.54).

Catalogers may need to record a named revision of an edition. A named revision is indicated by a word or phrase or a group of characters that identify a particular revision of a named revision.[22] *RDA* specifies that designations of named revisions are taken from the same source of information used for the designation of the edition, a source from within the resource, or other sources of information as specified in *RDA* 2.2.4.

If the source of information contains a reference to a named revision of an edition, follow the instructions provided in *RDA* for recording edition information (see Example 1.55).

Record statements of responsibility related to named revisions of editions. Use the same source(s) of information consulted for a named revision of an edition.

Additional examples of a resource that is a new expression of a work include cases where the work was re-issued in a different genre or type, was edited by a different editor, or was supplemented with additional material. The translation of the work into a different language may also represent a new expression.

Manifestation

While *AACR2* stipulates that information about the carrier and the extent of the work are entered in a physical description (the MARC 300 field Physical Description, MODS element <physicalDescription>, or DC element <Format>), *RDA* introduces new 3xx fields to specify content type, media type, and carrier type. The MARC 300 field Physical Description is used to record extent, dimensions, and other physical details of an item being described. It is optional for electronic resources, streaming audio or video, and born digital resources. This information is recorded in the MODS element <physicalDescription> with the subelements <form> and <extent> and in the DC element <Format> qualified by "Extent" (see Examples 1.56 and 1.57).

The MARC 300 field has the following subfields:

- $a extent (includes specific material designation, number of parts, duration for sound and videorecordings)
- $b other physical details (sound and color characteristics, playing speed)
- $c dimensions (for size of physical resources)
- $e accompanying materials (for any supplementary or accompanying items regardless of format)

No indicators are defined for the MARC 300 Physical Description field.

Chapter 3 of *RDA* provides guidance on how to describe carriers of information. *RDA* instructs catalogers to base the description of the resource's carrier(s) on information presented by the resource or on accompanying materials or containers. Record this information in the MARC 300 field Physical Description, the MODS element <physical Description> with the subelement <extent>, and the DC element <Format>. The number and type(s) of carriers are recorded (see Example 1.58).

When a resource consists of more than one carrier type, the description of the carriers can be limited to carrier type and extent when a more detailed description is not required. Examples 1.59, 1.60, and 1.61 (see p. 44) are "format" agnostic and are intended to represent description in any of the three display formats used in this text.

EXAMPLE 1.55

250 __ 3rd ed. thoroughly corrected, revised, and expanded.

<originInfo>
<edition>2d ed. with additions, revised and corrected.</edition>
</originInfo>

<Description>entirely revised, corrected, edited, and annotated.</Description>

EXAMPLE 1.56

300 __ 1 videodisc (92 min.) : $b sd., col. ; $c 4 3/4 in.

<physicalDescription>
<form authority="marcform"> electronic</form>
<extent>1 streaming sound file (14 min.) </extent>
</physicalDescription>

<Format. Extent>2 maps on sheets 79 x 132 cm. and 97 x 107 cm.</Format>

EXAMPLE 1.57

300 __ 1 DVD : $b sd., col. ; $c 4 3/4 in.
300 __ 1 videodisc (88 min.) : $b sd., b&w ; $c 4 3/4 in. + $e 1 booklet (28 p. : ill. ; 18 cm.)

<physicalDescription>
<form authority="marcform"> videorecording</form>
<extent>1 videodisc (57 min.) : sd., col. ; $c 4 3/4 in. +1 clinician's manual (xi, 97 p.) </extent>
</physicalDescription>

<Format.Extent>1 map : $ col. ; 60 x 61 cm., on sheet 94 x 92 cm., folded in envelope 30 x 24 cm.</Format>

EXAMPLE 1.58

300 __ 1 map

<physicalDescription>
<extent>2 sound discs</extent>
</physicalDescription>

<Format>1 sheet</Format>

If carriers are housed in a container that is considered as an integral part of the resource, the dimensions of the external container should also be recorded (see Example 1.60).

If a detailed description of carrier(s) is preferred, *RDA* instructs catalogers to record other characteristics applicable to the carrier(s) (see Example 1.61).

When multiple heterogeneous carriers make up a resource, *RDA* instructs catalogers to record the predominant carrier type and the extent of the resource as a whole and to describe the units making up the resource as "pieces." If the number of component parts is not easily approximated, catalogers do not need to record the number of pieces (see Example 1.62).

EXAMPLE 1.59

1 videocassette, 1 sound cassette, 1 skills and strategies pamphlet

EXAMPLE 1.60

in container 25 x 30 cm.

EXAMPLE 1.61

A cartographic resource (map) would be described as:

1 map : both sides, col. ; 119 x 51 cm., on sheet 88 x 58 cm.

A sound disc would be described as:

1 sound disc : digital, audio ; 4 3/4 in.

EXAMPLE 1.62

various pieces in container (29 x 52 x 4 cm.)

Media Type

According to *RDA*, media type describes the "general type of intermediation device required to play, run, etc., the content of the resource."[23] Table 3.1 in Chapter 3 of *RDA* lists the media types. They are audio, computer, microform, microscopic, projected, stereographic, unmediated (resources that do not require playback equipment or other means), video, and other (used when a resource does not fit into the other categories).

Carrier Type

Carrier type is a core element and reflects the resource's storage medium, housing, and device(s) required to use it. Catalogers are instructed to describe the resource's content using one or more of these carrier types as appropriate. Examples of audio carriers are audio disc and audiocassette; microform carriers include microfiche and microform reels); computer carriers include computer disc and online resource; unmediated carriers include card and flipchart; and video carriers include videocassette. *RDA* 3.3.1.2 provides a complete list of carrier types.

Extent

Extent is a core element when a resource is complete or when the complete extent is known. Subunits are used when this information is readily available and considered important for identification and access. Extent is used to record the number and type of units or subunits that make up a resource. *RDA* describes a unit as "a physical or logical constituent of a resource."[24]

Extent is determined using information presented on or in the resource or on accompanying materials and/or the container. Include the number of units and the carrier term as listed in *RDA* 3.3.1.2. Record this information in the MARC 300 field Physical Description, the MODS element <physicalDescription> with the subelement <extent>, and the DC element <Format> qualified with "Extent" (see Example 1.63).

When a resource consists of a set of identical units, use the term "identical" to designate the type of unit (see Example 1.64).

The number of subunits making up a resource are recorded when this information is readily available and deemed important for identification and retrieval. Subunits are recorded in parentheses and follow the term used to designate the type of unit. If a computer file's subunits parallel a

EXAMPLE 1.63

300 __ 1 videodisc

<physicalDescription>

<extent>1 sound disc</extent>

</physicalDescription>

<Format>3 microfilm reels</Format>

EXAMPLE 1.64

8 identical review cards

print or graphic counterpart, the number of subunits are recorded following *RDA*'s instructions for recording the extent for cartographic resources (*RDA* 3.4.2), still images (*RDA* 3.4.4), or text (*RDA* 3.4.5) (see Example 1.65).

When describing other types of files, the number of files is specified using terms provided in *RDA* 3.19.2.3 to designate type of file.

EXAMPLE 1.65

1 computer disc (7 electronic remote sensing images)

Carrier Type and Dimensions of Carriers

Dimensions record the measure of the carrier(s) and/or a carrier's container. Measurement includes height, width, depth, length, gauge, and diameter.[25] *RDA* specifies that dimensions are typically recorded in centimeters and are rounded up to the next centimeter when necessary.

Publication Statement

The publication statement is an *RDA* core element and identifies the place of publication, publisher name(s), and the date(s) of publication. This information includes statements that pertain to the publication, release, or issuing of a resource. Consult the same source of information used for the title proper, other sources of information on or within the resource, or other sources of information as specified in *RDA* 2.2.4.

Record the place of publication and publisher name(s) in the forms given in the source of information. If the place of publication changes for an integrating resource, change it to reflect the current iteration of the resource. Record any information regarding an earlier place of publication if this information is deemed important for identification or access. The same applies to changes in publisher name.

Provide the local place name and larger jurisdiction if necessary for identification. Record this information in brackets. Provide this information in the MARC 260 field Publication, Distribution, etc. (Imprint); the MODS element <originInfo> with the subelement <place>, which has its own subelement <placeTerm>; and the DC element <Publisher>.

When there are multiple places of publication, *RDA* instructs catalogers to record the place names in the order indicated by the sequence, layout, or typography of the names provided in the source of information. When there are two or more publishers and two or more places associated with one or more of the publishers, record this information in the order indicated by the sequence, layout, or typography of the names provided in the source of information. If there is more than one language or script on the source of information consulted, use the language or script used for the title proper.

If the place of publication is not identified on or in the resource, the cataloger provides the place of publication or probable place. When a known or probable place of publication cannot be determined, *RDA* instructs catalogers to record "Place of publication not identified."

Provide the local place name and larger jurisdiction if this is necessary for identification. This information is recorded in brackets in the MARC 260 field Publication, Distribution, etc. (Imprint); the MODS element <originInfo> with the subelement <place>, which has its own subelement <placeTerm>; and the DC element <Publisher> (see Example 1.66).

EXAMPLE 1.66

260 __ [New Brunswick, N.J.]

```
<originInfo>
  <place>
    <placeTerm type="text">[Fairfield,
    Conn.]</placeTerm>
  </place>
</originInfo>
```

<Publisher>[Toronto, Ont.]<Publisher>

EXAMPLE 1.67

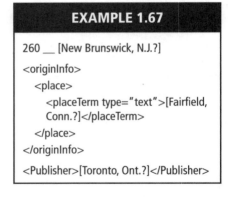

260 __ [New Brunswick, N.J.?]

<originInfo>
<place>
<placeTerm type="text">[Fairfield, Conn.?]</placeTerm>
</place>
</originInfo>

<Publisher>[Toronto, Ont.?]</Publisher>

EXAMPLE 1.68

260 __ [R.S.F.S.R.?]

<originInfo>
<place>
<placeTerm type="text">[Tas.?]</placeTerm>
</place>
</originInfo>

<Publisher>[Switzerland?]</Publisher>

EXAMPLE 1.69

260 __ Washington, D.C. : $b U.S. G.P.O.

<originInfo>
<publisher>HarperResource</publisher>
</originInfo>

<Publisher>FAA Distribution Division, NACO, AVN-530 </Publisher>

EXAMPLE 1.70

260 __ Wallingford, Oxon, UK : $b Published on behalf of the Nutrition Society by CAB International

<originInfo>
<publisher> Published for The Medieval Academy of America and SEENET by Boydell & Brewer </publisher>
</originInfo>

<Publisher>Penn Well Publication, published in cooperation with SPIE</Publisher>

Consult Appendix B, Table 1, in *RDA* for abbreviations used for countries, states, provinces, and territories. Do not abbreviate any names that are not listed in this table.

If a probable place of publication is used, provide the place name followed by the local jurisdiction if this information is necessary for identification. This information is followed by a question mark and enclosed in brackets (see Example 1.67).

If only the state or province, etc., is known, record this in brackets. In cases when this information is probable, follow it with a question mark (see Example 1.68).

Publisher's Name

The publisher's name is a core element and records the name of the person, family, or corporate body responsible for publishing, releasing, or issuing a resource.[26] The publisher's name is provided using the same source of information used for the title proper, other sources of information on or within the resource, or other sources of information as specified in *RDA* 2.2.4. Record this information in the MARC 260 field Publication, Distribution, etc. (Imprint), the MODS element <originInfo> with the subelement <publisher>, and the DC element <Publisher>. Record the publisher's name in the form in which it appears on or in the resource in hand (see Example 1.69).

Words or phrases that indicate the role the publisher has played in the production of the resource can be included. Record them as they appear on or in the source of information (see Example 1.70).

When a producer has not been identified or and cannot be determined, *RDA* instructs catalogers to use the note "Publisher not identified." Information is not recorded for this element for resources in an unpublished form.

Date of Publication

Date of publication is a core element that provides information on the date associated with the production, release, or issuing of a resource.[27] Consult the same source as used for the title proper, other sources of information on or within the resource, or other sources of information as specified in *RDA* 2.2.4 when providing a publication date. Record this information in the MARC 260 field Publication, Distribution, etc. (Imprint) $c, the MODS element <originInfo> with the subelement <dateIssued>, and the DC element <Date> (see Example 1.71).

When the first part or iteration of an integrating resource is known, record the publication date followed by a hyphen (see Example 1.72).

When the production of a resource has ceased or is complete, and the first and last iterations are available, include the ending date. Separate the beginning and ending dates with a hyphen (see Example 1.73).

When date(s) cannot be approximated, a date of publication is not recorded. When the date of publication cannot be identified, record the date of distribution, copyright date, or date of manufacture. If none of

EXAMPLE 1.71

260 __ Philadelphia : $b American Baptist Publication Society, $c 1917

<originInfo>
<dateIssued>1995<dateIssued>
</originInfo>

<Date>2008</Date>

EXAMPLE 1.72

260 __ Horsham, PA : $b LRP Publication, $c c1998-

<originInfo>
<dateIssued>2001-</dateIssued>
</originInfo>

<Date>2009-</Date>

EXAMPLE 1.73

260 __ Horsham, PA : $b LRP Publication, $c c1998-2006.

<originInfo>
<dateIssued>2001-2007</dateIssued>
</originInfo>

<Date>1999-2001.</Date>

these dates can be identified, *RDA* instructs catalogers to provide a date or approximate the date of publication. No date of publication is provided for resources in an unpublished form.

Distribution Statement

The distribution statement identifies the place(s) of distribution, distributor(s), and the date and place(s) of distribution. The distribution statement is a required element.

Consult the same source as used for the title proper, other sources of information on or within the resource, or other sources of information as specified in *RDA* 2.2.4 when providing a distribution statement. Record the distributor place and name in the forms provided in the source of information.

RDA states that the place of distribution should be changed for integrating resources for subsequent iterations. Changes in distributor name or subsequent additions of distributors should be changed or updated to reflect the current iteration in hand.

Provide the local place name and the name of the larger jurisdiction if this information is present in or on the resource. When more than one place of distribution is provided, record the place names in the order indicated by the sequence, layout, or typography of the names on the source of information. Record this information in the MARC 260 field Publication, Distribution, etc. (Imprint), the MODS element <originInfo> with the subelement <place> and its subelement <placeTerm>, and the DC element <Publisher> (see Example 1.74).

When there are two or more distributors, and two or more places associated with them, record the place names for each distributor in the order indicated by the sequence, layout, or typography of the names on the source of information. Record this information in the MARC 260 field Publication, Distribution, etc. (Imprint), the MODS element <originInfo> with the subelements <place> and <publisher>, and the DC element <Publisher> (see Example 1.75).

When the source of distribution is provided in more than one language or script, record this information in the script used for the title proper. If the place of distribution is not provided on or in the resource, *RDA* instructs catalogers to supply a place of distribution or to provide a probable place of distribution. When this information cannot be determined, catalogers may record "Place of distribution not identified."[28]

EXAMPLE 1.74

260 __ New York ; $a London : $b Springer

<originInfo>
<place>
<placeTerm>Berlin</placeTerm>
<placeTerm>London</placeTerm>
</place>
</originInfo>

<Publisher>Tokyo</Publisher>
<Publisher>Berlin</Publisher>

EXAMPLE 1.75

260 __ New York : $b Springer Science+ Business Media ; $a Austin, Tex. : $b Landes Bioscience

<originInfo>
<place>New York</place>
<publisher>Springer Science+Business Media</publisher>
</originInfo>

<originInfo>
<place>Austin, Tex.</place>
<publisher>Landes Bioscience </publisher>
</originInfo>

<Publisher>New York</Publisher>
<Publisher>Springer Science+Business Media</Publisher>
<Publisher>Austin, Tex.</Publisher>
<Publisher>Landes Bioscience</Publisher>

EXAMPLE 1.76

260 __ Zürich : $b JRP/Ringier ; $a [New York] : $b [Distributed in USA by] D.A.P./Distributed Art Publishers

<originInfo>
<publisher>Sole distributors for the U.S.A. and Canada</publisher>
</originInfo>

<Publisher>Distributed to the trade by Celestial Arts</Publisher>

EXAMPLE 1.77

260 __ New York : $b distributed by United Nations Development Programme, Bureau for Crisis Prevention and Recovery : $b distributed by United Nations Publications

<originInfo>
<publisher>Manohar Publishers & Distributors</publisher>
<publisher>Distributed in South Asia by Foundation Books </publisher>
</originInfo>

<Publisher>Mosaic Press [distributor] </Publisher>
<Publisher>Flatiron Book Distributors </Publisher>

Distributor's Name

The distributor's name is a core element when a publisher's name is not identified in or on the resource. *RDA* defines a distributor as a person, family, or corporate body responsible for distributing a resource. If there is more than one distributor name on or in a resource, catalogers are required to record only the first name. Recording any others is optional.

The distributor's name is taken from the same source as used for the title proper, other sources of information on or within the resource, or other sources of information as specified in *RDA* 2.2.4 when providing a distribution statement. Record any phrases or roles relating to the distributor's name that are given in the sources of information if these are deemed important or necessary for identification and access (see Example 1.76).

When there is more than one distributor name on or in the resource, record any additional names in the order indicated by the sequence, layout, or typography of the names on the source of information. Record this information in the MARC 260 field Publication, Distribution, etc. (Imprint), the MODS element <originInfo> with the subelement <publisher>, and the DC element <Publisher> (see Example 1.77).

If the distributor name is provided in more than one language or script, record the name in the script used for the title proper. If a distributor is not named on or in the resource and cannot be identified using sources as specified in *RDA* 2.2.4, catalogers may note "Distributor not identified."[29]

Date of Distribution

Date of distribution is a core element when the date of publication is not provided and cannot be identified. Consult the same source as used for the title proper, other sources of information on or within the resource, or other sources of information as specified in *RDA* 2.2.4 when providing the date of distribution.

When providing this information for integrating resources, use the beginning and/or ending date of distribution from the first and/or last iteration of the resource.[30] If only the first iteration of the resource is available, provide this date followed by a hyphen. When a cataloger knows that an integrating resource has ceased publication, the starting and ending dates of distribution should be supplied and separated by a hyphen.

Provide the date of distribution if it differs from the date of publication and this information is considered important for identification and access. If the date of distribution is not provided in or on the resource, the cataloger can provide it or an approximated date of distribution. When this information cannot be identified, catalogers may provide the note "Date of distribution not identified." This information is not provided for unpublished resources.

Manufacturer Statement

Manufacture statements identify place(s) of manufacture, manufacturer(s), and date(s) of manufacture. These statements reflect information about printing, duplication, etc.

The manufacturer's name is a core element only when the publisher and distributor are not identified. Likewise, the date of manufacture is a core element if the date of publication, date of distribution, and copyright date are not identified. *RDA* notes that the element "place of manufacture" is optional. Consult the same source as used for the title proper, other sources of information on or within the resource, or other sources of information as specified in *RDA* 2.2.4 when providing a manufacturer statement.

Manufacture statements are provided for unpublished resources. They are provided for published resources only when the publisher or distributor is not identified or when the date of publication or distribution is not identified.

If the place of manufacture changes on a subsequent iteration of an integrating resource, *RDA* instructs catalogers to update this information to reflect the information provided in the current iteration. Provide local place name when known, and record it in brackets. Provide the name of the larger jurisdiction when it is necessary for identification. When the place of manufacture is uncertain, provide the probable local place of manufacture and follow it with a question mark. Record the manufacture statement in the MARC 260 field Publication, Distribution, etc. (Imprint), the MODS element <originInfo> with the subelement <publisher>, and the DC element <Publisher>. Examples 1.78 and 1.79 are display-format agnostic.

When the country, state, province, etc. (but not the local place name), of manufacture is known, provide this information in brackets. When this information is not certain, follow it with a question mark.

EXAMPLE 1.78

[New Brunswick, N.J.] [known place of manufacture]

[Lima, Ohio?] [probable place of manufacture]

EXAMPLE 1.79

[Latvia] [known place of manufacture]

[U.K.?] [probable place of manufacture]

Manufacturer's Name

Manufacturer's name is a core element when a publisher or distributor has not been identified. The manufacturer is the person, family, or corporate body responsible for duplicating, casting, etc., a resource in its published form.[31] Catalogers are required to provide only the first name when more than one manufacturer name is given.

Consult the same source as used for the title proper, other sources of information on or within the resource, or other sources of information as specified in *RDA* 2.2.4 when providing a manufacturer's name. Record this information in the MARC 260 field Publication, Distribution, etc. (Imprint), the MODS element <originInfo> with the subelement <publisher>, and the DC element <Publisher>. Record any functions noted by the manufacturer when they are included in or on the source of information (see Example 1.80).

When more than one manufacturer is provided in or on the resource, *RDA* instructs catalogers to record them in the order indicated by the sequence, layout, or typography of the names on the source of information. When no manufacturer information is provided, catalogers may note "Manufacturer not identified," per *RDA*.

EXAMPLE 1.80

260 __ New York, N.Y. : $b Manufactured for and marketed by PolyGram Video

<originInfo>
<publisher>Manufactured and distributed by Pacific Arts </publisher>
</originInfo>

<Publisher>Manufactured by the Werner Co.</Publisher>

Date of Manufacture

RDA specifies that the date of manufacture is treated as a core element when no date of publication, date of distribution, or copyright date is provided on or in the resource. The date of manufacture is the date provided for the printing, duplicating, casting, etc., of a resource in its published form.[32] This information can be taken from any available source and is recorded in the MARC 260 field Publication, Distribution, etc. (Imprint) $c, the MODS element <originInfo> with the subelement <dateIssued>, and the DC element <Date>.

When the first part of an integrating resource is available, record the date of manufacture for the current iteration. Follow the date with a hyphen to indicate the resource is ongoing. If manufacture of the resource ceases or is complete and the first and last iterations of the resource are available, record the dates, separated by a hyphen.

If the date of manufacture cannot be identified, *RDA* instructs catalogers to supply or approximate a date. If an approximated date cannot be determined, catalogers can note "Date of manufacture not identified."

Series Statement

RDA defines a series as "A group of separate resources related to one another by the fact that each resource bears, in addition to its own title proper, a collective title applying to the group as a whole."[33] The MARC 8XX fields are used to provide series added entry information for a series associated with a title.[34] An 8XX field is used when the form of the series recorded in the 490 field cannot be used as a series added entry (see Example 1.81).

EXAMPLE 1.81

```
490 1_ Map and chart series ; $v MCH093
<relatedItem type="series">
  <titleInfo>
    <title>Geologic investigations series
    ; I-2791</title>
  </titleInfo>
</relatedItem>
```

The MARC 490 field Series Statement is used to record series titles. It is not used to create title added entries for series statements as a means of access and retrieval. In October 2008, MARBI Proposal 2008-07 to make the MARC 440 field Series Statement/Added Entry—Title obsolete in the MARC 21 Bibliographic Format was approved.[35] When catalogers wish to provided a series title added entry, they must now include both a MARC 490 and a related 8XX Series Added Entry field. Record series statements in the MODS element <relatedItem> with the attribute "type," which can be used to specify series, and the DC element <Relation> qualified with "IsPartOf" (see Example 1.82)

EXAMPLE 1.82

```
490 0_ Collectors series
<relatedItem type="series">
  <titleInfo>
    <title>Collection africaine</title>
  </titleInfo>
</relatedItem>
<Relation.IsPartOf>Stereo treasury series
</Relation>
```

Seven subfields are defined for use in the MARC 490 field. In this text, we will limit discussion to the $a series statement (to record series title) and the $v Volume/sequential designation (to record volume number or sequential designation used for the series statement). The MODS element <relatedItem> applies only when the series is not traced and is equivalent only to MARC 490 $a and $v. DC does not provide this level of specificity.

Only the first indicator value is defined for use in the MARC 490 field. An initial indicator value of 0 (zero) indicates that the series is not traced; a value of 1 is used when the series is traced differently. The traced series is provided in the appropriate MARC 8XX field.

Series: Personal Names

A personal name series records an author and title series added entry using an author's personal name. Record an author/title series added entry in the MARC 800 field, the MODS element <relatedItem> with attribute type "series" and subelement <name>, and the DC element <Relation> with the qualifier <IsPartOf> (see Example 1.83). In this text, we focus on these MARC 800 subfields:

$a personal name
$b numeration
$c titles and other words associated with a name
$d dates associated with a name
$e relator term
$f date of a work
$n number of part/section of a work
$p name of part/section of a work
$q fuller form of name
$t title of a work
$4 relator code

The indicators defined for the MARC 800 field provide information on type of personal name. The first indicator has the values of 0 (zero) for forename, 1 for surname, and 3 for family name. The second indicator is undefined.

Series: Corporate Names

A corporate name series records a corporate body and title series added entry using the corporate body name. Record an author/title series added entry in the MARC 810 field, the MODS element <relatedItem> with the attribute "series" and the subelement <name>, and the DC element <Relation> with the qualifier <IsPartOf> (see Example 1.84). We focus on these MARC 810 subfields:

$a corporate or jurisdiction name
$b subordinate unit
$c location of meeting
$e relator term
$f date of a work
$l language of a work
$n number of part/section of a work
$p name of part/section of a work
$t title of a work
$4 relator code

The first indicator is defined for the MARC 810 field and provides information on type of corporate name. Its values are 0 (zero) for inverted form of name, 1 for names provided in jurisdiction order, and 2 for names in direct order. The second indicator is undefined.

EXAMPLE 1.83

800 1_ Joyce, James, $d 1882-1941. $t James Joyce archive.

```
<relatedItem>
  <titleInfo>
    <title>British theatre</title>
  </titleInfo>
<name type="personal">
  <namePart type="given">John
  </namePart>
    <namePart type="family">Bell
    </namePart>
</name>
</relatedItem>

<relatedItem type="series">
  <titleInfo>
    <title>British theatre</title>
  </titleInfo>
<name type="personal">
    <namePart type="given">John
    </namePart>
    <namePart type="family">Bell
    </namePart>
</name>
</relatedItem>

<Relation>Wesley, Valerie Wilson </Relation>
<Relation.IsPartOf>Tamara Hayle mystery
series </Relation>
```

EXAMPLE 1.84

810 2_ Kimbell Art Museum. $t Kimbell masterpiece series.

```
<relatedItem type="series">
  <titleInfo>
    <title>Sackler Colloquium series</title>
  </titleInfo>
  <name type="conference">
  <namePart> Arthur M. Sackler Colloquia of
  the National Academy of Sciences
</namePart>
  </name>
</relatedItem>

<Relation.IsPartOf>International SAMPE
Metals and Metals Processing Conference.
International SAMPE Metals and Metals
Processing Conference series ; v. 3</Relation>
```

EXAMPLE 1.85

811 2_ Columbia University Bicentennial Conference. $t Columbia University Bicentennial Conference series.

```
<relatedItem type="series">
  <titleInfo>
    <title>Northeast Conference reports
    </title>
  </titleInfo>
  <name type="conference">
    <namePart>Northeast Conference
    on the Teaching of Foreign Languages
    </namePart>
  </name>
</relatedItem>
```

<Relation.IsPartOf>European Conference on Advanced Materials and Processes 6th : 1999 Munich, Germany). EUROMAT 99 ; v. 12</Relation>

Series: Meeting Names

A meeting name series records a meeting name and title series added entry using the meeting name. Record a conference or meeting name series added entry in the MARC 811 field, the MODS element <relatedItem> with the attribute "series" and the subelement <name>, and the DC element <Relation> with the qualifier <IsPartOf> (see Example 1.85). We focus on these MARC 811 subfields:

$a meeting or jurisdiction name
$c location of meeting
$e subordinate unit
$f date of a work
$j relator term
$l language of a work
$n number of part/section of a work
$p name of part/section of a work
$t title of a work
$4 relator code

The first indicator is defined for the MARC 811 field and provides information on type of corporate name. The first indicator's values are 0 (zero) for inverted form of name, 1 for names provided in jurisdiction order, and 2 for names in direct order. The second indicator is undefined.

Item

Details pertaining to a specific manifestation of the work include location details such as the Universal Resource Locator (URL) and Digital Object Identifier (DOI).

Electronic Location and Access

Electronic location and access provide information on where a resource is located and how it can be accessed, including any user or access restrictions, and it can accommodate more than one mode of access (FTP, HTTP, etc.). Record this information in the MARC 856 field Electronic Location and Access, the MODS element <identifier> with the attribute "type" for URI, and the DC element <Identifier> with the qualifier <URI>. Although not all nonprint and electronic resources will include a MARC 856 field or URI in their description, this element has significantly impacted access and retrieval and is therefore included in this overall description of essential resources that should be included in metadata records. We will focus on these subfields defined for the MARC 856 field:

$a host name
$u Uniform Resource Identifier
$z public note

Note that, while an extensive number of subfields are defined for the MARC 856 field, librarians actually use relatively few of them. The complete range of subfields is available at http://www.loc.gov/marc/bibliographic/bd856.html.

The first indicator defined for the MARC 856 field describes the method(s) used to access the resource. The most commonly used values are 0 (zero) for e-mail, 1 for FTP, 2 for remote login (Telnet), 3 for dial-up, and 4 for HTTP. Of these methods, HTTP is by far the most commonly used. A few sites/resources still permit FTP access. Telnet and dial-up access are rare.

The second indicator describes the relationship of the resource cited in the URI to the resource described in the metadata record. The values defined for this indicator are 0 (zero) for resource, 1 for version of resource, and 2 for related resource (see Example 1.86).

EXAMPLE 1.86

856 11 $u ftp://ftp.fao.org/docrep/fao/011/i0137e/i0137e.pdf

856 11 $u ftp://ftp.fao.org/docrep/fao/011/i0459e/i0459e00.pdf $z Connect to online version

<identifier type="uri">http://www.census.gov/econ/census02/guide/g02zip.htm </identifier>

<Identifier.URI>http://vnweb.hwwilsonweb.com/hww/jumpstart.jhtml?prod=SS Access from campus or login via Rutgers account</Identifier>

Resources for Catalogers

Dublin Core Metadata Initiative. 2010. "DCMI Home." DCMI. Last updated September 10. http://dublincore.org.

Joint Steering Committee for Development of *RDA*. 2007. "RDA-FRBR Mapping." June 14. http://www.rda-jsc.org/docs/5rda-frbrmapping.pdf.

Library of Congress, Network Development and MARC Standards Office. 2005. "MODS to Dublin Core Metadata Element Set Mapping Version 3." Library of Congress. http://www.loc.gov/standards/mods/mods-dcsimple.html.

Library of Congress, Network Development and MARC Standards Office. 2008. "MARC to Dublin Core Crosswalk." Library of Congress. http://www.loc .gov/marc/marc2dc.html.

Library of Congress, Network Development and MARC Standards Office. 2008. "MARC to MODS Mapping: Version 3.3." Library of Congress. http://www.loc.gov/standards/mods/mods-mapping.html.

Library of Congress, Network Development and MARC Standards Office. 2009. "Draft RDA to MODS Mapping." Excel file accessed via MODS News link. Library of Congress. http://www.loc.gov/standards/mods/.

Library of Congress, Network Development and MARC Standards Office. 2010. "MODS: Metadata Object Description Schema: Official Website." Library of Congress. http://www.loc.gov/standards/mods.

Notes

1. Library of Congress, Working Group on the Future of Bibliographic Control. 2010. "Testing Resource Description and Access (RDA)." Library of Congress. Accessed June 22. http://www.loc.gov/bibliographic-future/rda.
2. MARBI, American Library Association's ALCTS/LITA/RUSA Machine-Readable Bibliographic Information Committee, in conjunction with the Network Development and MARC Standards Office, Library of Congress. 1996. "The MARC 21 Formats: Background and Principles." Library of Congress. http://www.loc.gov/marc/96principl.html.
3. Ibid.
4. Dublin Core Metadata Initiative. 2010. "DCMI History." DCMI. Accessed June 22. http://dublincore.org/about/history.

5. Ibid.
6. Dublin Core Metadata Initiative. 2010. "DCMI Glossary." DCMI. Accessed June 22. http://dublincore.org/documents/usageguide/glossary.shtml#Q.
7. American Library Association, Canadian Library Association, and CILIP: Chartered Institute of Library and Information Professionals. 2010. *RDA Toolkit*, Chapter 2, 2.3.7. ALA, CLA, and CILIP. Accessed September 3. http://www.rdatoolkit.org.
8. OCLC. 2010. "OCLC Bibliographic Formats and Standards: 222 Key Title." OCLC. Accessed June 22. http://www.oclc.org/bibformats/en/2xx/222.shtm.
9. American Library Association, Canadian Library Association, and CILIP: Chartered Institute of Library and Information Professionals. 2010. *RDA Toolkit*, Chapter 2, 2.3.10. ALA, CLA, and CILIP. Accessed September 3. http://www.rdatoolkit.org.
10. Ibid., Chapter 2, 2.3.11.1.
11. Ibid., Chapter 2, 2.3.11.2.
12. Ibid., Chapter 2, 2.4.1.
13. Library of Congress. 2010. "MODS User Guidelines Version 3." Accessed September 7. Library of Congress. http://www.loc.gov/standards/mods/v3/mods-userguide.html.
14. Dublin Core Metadata Initiative. 2008. "Dublin Core Metadata Element Set, Version 1.1." DCMI. Last updated June 9. http://dublincore.org/documents/dces.
15. Library of Congress, Network Development and MARC Standards Office. 2007. "MARC 21 Format for Bibliographic Data: 70X–75X: Added Entry Fields—General Information." Library of Congress. http://www.loc.gov/marc/bibliographic/bd70x75x.html.
16. American Library Association, Canadian Library Association, and CILIP: Chartered Institute of Library and Information Professionals. 2010. *RDA Toolkit*, Chapter 2, 2.11.1.1." ALA, CLA, and CILIP. Accessed September 7. http://www.rdatoolkit.org.
17. Library of Congress, Network Development and MARC Standards Office. 2007. "MARC 21 Format for Bibliographic Data: 520: Summary, Etc. (R)." Library of Congress. http://www.loc.gov/marc/bibliographic/bd520.html.
18. Ibid., "650: Subject Added Entry—Topical Term (R)." http://www.loc.gov/marc/bibliographic/bd650.html.
19. Ibid.
20. Ibid.
21. American Library Association, Canadian Library Association, and CILIP: Chartered Institute of Library and Information Professionals. 2010. *RDA Toolkit*, Chapter 2, 2.5.2.1. ALA, CLA, and CILIP. Accessed September 3. http://www.rdatoolkit.org.
22. Ibid., Chapter 2, 2.5.6.1.
23. Ibid., Chapter 3, 3.2.1.1.
24. Ibid., Chapter 3, 3.4.1.3.
25. Ibid., Chapter 3, 3.5.1.
26. Ibid., Chapter 2, 2.8.4.1.
27. Ibid., Chapter 2, 2.8.6.1.
28. Ibid., Chapter 2, 2.9.2.6.
29. Ibid., Chapter 2, 2.9.4.7.
30. Ibid., Chapter 2, 2.9.6.5.

31. Ibid., Chapter 2, 2.10.4.3.
32. Ibid., Chapter 2, 2.10.6.
33. Ibid., Glossary.
34. Library of Congress, Network Development and MARC Standards Office. 1999. "MARC 21 Format for Bibliographic Data: 80X–83X: Series Added Entry Fields." Library of Congress. http://www.loc.gov/marc/bibliographic/bd80x83x.html.
35. Library of Congress, Network Development and MARC Standards Office. 2008. "MARC Proposal No. 2008-06." Library of Congress. http://www.loc.gov/marc/marbi/2008/2008-06.html.

Cartographic Resources

IN THIS CHAPTER:

Overview

Cartographic resources, more commonly known as *maps*, are an important part of many libraries' collections. Some specialized libraries have collections that consist primarily of cartographic resources, with staff teams who devote their time exclusively to cataloging these materials. The level of description provided for cartographic resources depends on such factors as the extent of a library's collection, the available staff, and the importance of these resources to the library's holdings and institutional mission.

Important Considerations

RDA's glossary defines cartographic resources as "cartographic content" and describes them as having "Content that represents the whole or part of the Earth, any celestial body, or imaginary place at any scale."[1] *AACR2* notes that cartographic resources represent the entire Earth as a whole or any celestial body.[2] Cartographic resources may consist of sheet maps (single or multiple sheets) or atlases and can also be available in a digital format.

Cartographic resources may be historical (maps or atlases for a given point in time), may geographically represent a particular topic (railroads, cancer mortality worldwide), may be government documents, may provide special characteristics (contours, shading), or may manifest themselves as a special format (a game, wall map, or manuscript, for example). Cartographic resources that are maps may be issued as single or multiple sheets, and the sheets that make up a map can be double sided or include multiple-scale statements, informational insets, etc. This chapter addresses cataloging of print maps and atlases. Globes, views, and remote sensing images are not included. *RDA* notes that the description of the carrier should be based on evidence presented by the actual resource as well as on any accompanying materials or containers (which might include envelopes, slipcases, etc.).[3] *RDA* also notes that further information can be taken from any additional sources, which can be interpreted as websites or documentation prepared by the publisher, granting agency, and so forth.

As noted in Chapter 1, we organize our discussion of resources by work, expression, manifestation, and item. *RDA* instructs catalogers to use preferred sources of information, which are described in the Introduction. Preferred sources of information consist of a source that forms part of the resource and is appropriate to the type of description (see the preceding section) and to the resource's presentation format.[4] *RDA* Chapters 3 and 7 discuss how to describe a cartographic resource's carrier and content. Carriers can be described using information from the resource itself, external packaging, accompanying materials, or any other sources deemed appropriate. Content is described using information from the resource and from any other source.

Resource Description

Work

FRBR defines *work* as a "distinct intellectual or artistic creation." A work is realized through expressions of that particular work. Works are represented by a resource description. Description is based on the cartographic resource and the information provided on or in it.

Preliminary questions about the work include the following:

- What type of resource is being described? Is it a map or an atlas?
- How does the resource present itself? What is its title?
- Is the resource primarily a map, or does it include text and accompanying illustrations, etc.? The type of resource must be clearly stated in the description.
- What subject matter is discussed, and what is the creator trying to communicate?
- Can the creator be readily identified?

Elements that relate to a work are the following:

- Title (earlier title and variant title as appropriate)
- Form of work
- Coordinates
- Equinox
- Subject

Title

Title Proper

The concept of main entry dates back to the era of printed catalogs. This concept persists in the online environment. *RDA* 17.1.3 describes construction of a main entry as a preferred access point, meaning that it is a standardized access point that represents a particular entity. It is constructed using the preferred title for a resource, which is preceded by the preferred access point for a person, family, or corporate body that is responsible for the work.

The main entry can be the cartographer or the corporate body responsible for the content of the cartographic resource. This decision is generally driven by a library's local policies. A library can choose to describe all of its nonbook resources with title main entry. Government and other agencies are typical main entries for cartographic resources (e.g., New Jersey Department of Transportation, Bureau of Geographic Information Systems, Geological Society of America, or Geographia Map Company).

Choice of main entry is driven by who did what rather than by prominence of information. Per *AACR2* Rule 21.1B2f, a corporate body that is selected as a main entry for a cartographic resource must specifically be designated as a map-making entity. Title main entry may be chosen when cartographic resources are the work of many individuals and/or corporate bodies and it is not possible to attribute authorship to a particular individual or corporate body. A cartographer must provide more than a drawing to be cited as a main entry, and a corporate body must be a map-making body to be given main entry. Lack of a statement of responsibility is another reason to choose title main entry for maps and atlases.

In MARC format, title information includes main title, remainder of the title (typically referred to as a subtitle), and statement of responsibility, provided in the MARC 245 field. In MODS, this information is provided in the element <titleInfo>, which is defined as "A word, phrase, character, or group of characters, normally appearing in a resource, that names it or the work contained in it."[5] Figure 2.1 shows an example of source of title on the resource. The type attribute of this element identifies the type of title: abbreviated, translated, alternative, or uniform.[6] The MODS <titleInfo> element also has the subelements title (main title), subTitle, partNumber, and partName. The element <Title> is used in DC (see Example 2.1). Chapter 1 provides detailed information on title.

Figure 2.1. Source of Title for a Cartographic Resource

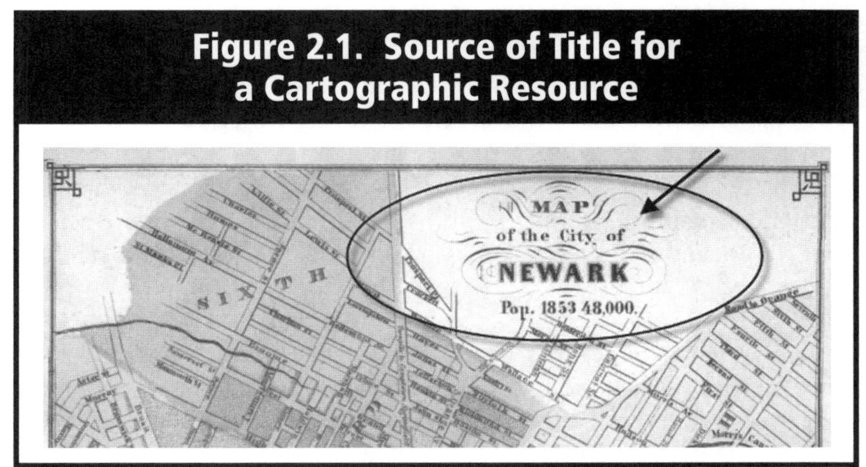

EXAMPLE 2.1

245 00 Jersey Shore vacation map

<titleInfo>
<title>Map of Monmouth County </title>
</titleInfo>

<Title>Cumberland County, New Jersey </Title>

EXAMPLE 2.2

245 00 Atlas of world railroads

<titleInfo>
<title>Atlas of world railroads</title>
</titleInfo>

<Title>Atlas of world railroads</Title>

RDA defines title as a core element; other types of titles are optional.[7] Consult the preferred source of information for formulating a title proper (see Example 2.2) (for guidelines, see *RDA* 2.2.2). The preferred source will form part of the resource and is appropriate for the *type* of description and *presentation format*.[8] If the title of a cartographic resource includes a statement of scale, *RDA* 2.3.2.8.2 instructs catalogers to include this information in the title statement.

When using the MARC format, provide title information in the MARC 245 field Title Statement. These subfields are available for the 245 field:

- $a title
- $b remainder of title
- $c statement of responsibility
- $h General Material Designation (GMD)
- $n number of part/section
- $p name of part/section.

When using MODS, provide title information in <titleInfo> with the subelement <title>. MODS includes attributes that reflect the type of title and subelements to provide number and part of title. For DC, record this information in the <Title> element.

Devised Title

When there is no discernible title on a cartographic resource, *RDA* 2.3.11.5 states that catalogers may provide a *devised* title. Use a devised title when there is no discernible title on the resource, accompanying materials, or other sources. *AACR2* states that a title supplied by a cataloger must be bracketed and the source of the title recorded in a general note.

Rule 3.1B2, *AACR2*, notes that statements of scale that appear as part of the title proper should be included in the transcription of the title statement. *RDA* 2.3.2.8.2 states that when the title of a cartographic resource contains a statement of scale, the cataloger should include the scale in the title transcription (see Example 2.3).[9]

EXAMPLE 2.3

245 10 Fotomapa 1:1 000 000

<titleInfo>
<title>1:50,000, the West Indies</title>
</titleInfo>

<Title>Suomen maaperä 1:1 000 000 </Title>

Remainder of Title

Record remainder of title information in MARC 245 $b, which is not repeatable. Provide this information in the MODS element <titleInfo> with the subelement <subTitle>, which the MODS documentation describes as "A word, phrase, character, or group of characters that contains the remainder of the title information after the title proper."[10] Record remainder of title in the DC element <Title> (see Example 2.4).

EXAMPLE 2.4

245 00 Land of the Maya : $b a traveler's map

<titleInfo>
<title>Jersey Shore vacation map </title>
<subTitle>northern Ocean-Monmouth </subTitle>
</titleInfo>

<Title>The Highlands</Title>

<Title>Water, beauty, life</Title>

Variant Title

Cartographic resources may include insets with unique titles, and sheet maps may include additional maps on the verso. Envelopes or containers for cartographic resources may provide a title that differs from that on the chief source of information. In such a case, make a note stating this difference, and include an added title entry for the variant title. Variant titles are covered in *AACR2* Rule 1.7B4 and *RDA* 2.3.1. *AACR2* instructs catalogers to create variant titles only when they are significant or when a resource is more commonly known by such a title. *RDA* instructs catalogers to create variant titles when they are considered important for identification or access.[11]

Record title variations in the MARC 246 field Varying Form of Title (which is repeatable), the MODS element <titleInfo> with the types "alternative" and <displayLabel> (used to provide additional text), and the DC element <Title> qualified by <Alternative>.

Title variations provide other titles by which a resource may be known. This includes abbreviations or acronyms, parallel titles in another language, or when one title appears on external packaging and another title is given in the chief source of information. Providing access to title variations permits users to search for a resource in multiple ways (see Example 2.5). Chapter 1 gives detailed information on providing variant title information.

Form of Work

FRBR specifies that the form of work is the class of resources to which the work belongs. Form of work is a core element in *RDA* that catalogers can use to distinguish a work from another resource with the same title or name. *RDA* 6.3.1 notes that form of work is the class or genre to which a resource belongs. For the purposes of this text, we define form of work as map or atlas.

Coordinates

The glossary in *Cartographic Materials* defines coordinates as measures of latitude and longitude.[12] Record coordinates in the following order: westernmost extent of area covered (longitude); easternmost extent of area covered (longitude); northernmost extent of area covered (latitude); southernmost extent of area covered (latitude).

Provide information on cartographic mathematical data, including scale, projection, and/or coordinates, in coded form in the MARC 034 field Coded Cartographic Mathematic Data (which is repeatable); the MODS element <subject> with the subelement <cartographics>, which has a subelement <coordinates> that provides a statement of coordinates covered by the resource; and the DC element <Coverage>. Cartographic mathematical data is not mandatory, and the decision to include it is left to the cataloger's judgment.

RDA 7.4 provides guidance on recording coordinates of cartographic content. Information can be taken from any source within the resource; when this is not possible, information can be taken from any other source.[13] Follow the same rules, as outlined in *RDA* 7.4.2.2., when recording latitude and longitude (see Example 2.6).

The following subfields are defined for the MARC 034 field:

$d coordinates—westernmost longitude

$e coordinates—easternmost longitude

EXAMPLE 2.5

Title on chief source and external envelope differ:

245 00 Land of the Maya : $b a traveler's map

246 _1 $i Title on envelope: $a Ancient Maya world

Portion of the main title:

245 00 Metro road map of Philadelphia and vicinity

246 30 Metro road map of Philadelphia

246 30 Road map of Philadelphia and vicinity

Title on chief source and variant title provided within map border:

```
<titleInfo>
  <title>Southern New Jersey zip code road map</title>
<titleInfo type="alternative" display Label="title within map border:">
  <title>Franklin's southern New Jersey zip code road map</title>
</titleInfo>
```

Title on chief source and variant title provided within map border:

```
<Title>Southern New Jersey zip code road map</Title>
<Title.Alternative>Franklin's southern New Jersey zip code road map</Title>
```

See Also . . .

Work—Title proper (Chapter 1, pp. 27–32)

EXAMPLE 2.6

034 1_ 43600

```
<subject>
  <cartographics>
    <coordinates>37200</coordinates>
  </cartographics>
</subject>
<Coverage>54109440</Coverage>
<Coverage>W1800000</Coverage>
<Coverage>E1800000</Coverage>
<Coverage>N0900000</Coverage>
<Coverage>S0800000</Coverage>
```

$f coordinates—northernmost latitude

$g coordinates—southernmost latitude

The MARC21 Bibliographic Format website (http://www.loc.gov/marc/bibliographic/bd034.html) provides additional information on the 034 field and indicator values.

Equinox

Cartographic Materials defines equinox as "One of two points of intersection of the ecliptic and the celestial equator, occupied by the sun when its declination is 0°."[14] *RDA* defines equinox in less lofty terms, and *RDA* 7.5.1.1 refers to it as "one of two points of intersection of the ecliptic and the celestial equator, occupied by the sun when its declination is 0°."[15]

Information on equinox can be taken from any source. When coordinates are provided for a celestial chart, equinox is also recorded. Equinox is recorded by year and sometimes includes month. Record this information in the MARC 034 field, $p, Coded Cartographic Mathematic Data (which is repeatable), the MODS element <subject> with the subelement <cartographics>, and the DC element <Coverage> (see Example 2.7). Equinox is not required for cartographic resources cataloging.

EXAMPLE 2.7

```
034 1_ b $p 2001
<subject>
   <cartographics>2001</cartographics>
</subject>
<Coverage>2001</Coverage>
```

Subject

Consult the *Library of Congress Subject Headings* (*LCSH*), the *Library of Congress Subject Cataloging Manual* (*SCM*), and the *Library of Congress Map Cataloging Manual* (*MCM*) when formulating subject headings for cartographic resources. The *SCM* states that the first subject heading provided in a bibliographic record should correspond most closely to the classification number used. *MCM* also states that, with the exception of the heading that most closely corresponds to the class number, there is no set order for presenting topics provided by the map or atlas.

Maps or atlases of an identifiable place must be assigned a subject heading for that area. Peripheral areas can be ignored. For example, a map for one place might include small portions of surrounding states, and these areas can be disregarded in most cases.

Analyze the content of the map, and assign subject headings that are appropriate to what the item is rather than how the publisher describes the item. For example, a road map and tourist map are not the same thing, and the subject heading should accurately represent the content of the map. In the case of atlases, map subject headings may be assigned to all atlases. Use the subject heading Atlases for world atlases published in the United States. For atlases published in other countries, use the subject heading Atlas, followed by the name of the country of publication.

See Also...

Topical Terms (Chapter 1, pp. 40–41)

Geographic Terms (Chapter 1, p. 41)

Subject Added Entries (Chapter 1, pp. 38–40)

Expression

FRBR defines *expression* as the intellectual or artistic *realization* of a work. When various expressions of a work have been identified, each description must highlight the elements that distinguish it from the other. Cartographic resources are not as likely to be reinterpreted as other resources, but they may be abridged, summarized, or annotated (this is more likely for atlases). Use "version," "revision," or any other term authorized by *AACR2* or *RDA* in the description. Record information about the edition or version of a work in the MARC 250 field (which is not repeatable), the MODS element <edition>, and the DC element <Description>. Additional information about the version of the resource can be recorded in notes.

Other important elements related to the expression of a work include the language of the text, genre, and extent of content. Language is a core element of description that must be recorded in the fixed field of the MARC record and in the appropriate areas of MODS and DC. Record additional details about language, such as the availability of the resource in other languages, in the MARC 530 field reserved for information about other available versions or formats. Record details related to the language of the resource in the MARC 546 field and in the language area specified for MODS and DC.

All known differences must be recorded, and catalogers should remain alert to the fact that significant differences can signal that the different expression is actually an entirely new work. Elements that relate to an Expression are the following:

- Form of expression
- Scale
- Projection
- Relief

Form of Expression

The *FRBR* website notes that "The form of expression is the means by which the work is realized (e.g., through alpha-numeric notation, musical notation, spoken word, musical sound, cartographic image, photographic image, sculpture, dance, mime, etc.)."[16] In the case of cartographic resources, this would be cartographic content, cartographic image, or as an atlas.[17] Record this information in the first type positions of the MARC 006 field, which notes form of material; cartographic resources are coded as **e** for "cartographic material," meaning nonmanuscript cartographic material. Record this information in the MODS element <genre> using the term "map" or "atlas" and in the DC element <Type>.

Coded Cartographic Mathematical Data

Record information on cartographic mathematical data (including scale, projection, and/or coordinates) in coded form in the MARC 034 field Coded Cartographic Mathematical Data, which is repeatable; the MODS element <subject> with the subelement <cartographics>, which has the subelement <coordinates> to provide a statement of coordinates covered by the resource; and the DC element <Coverage>. This information is mandatory.

RDA 7.4 provides guidance on recording coordinates of cartographic content. Information may be taken from any source within the resource;

when this is not possible, it can be taken from any other source.[18] Follow the same rules, as outlined in *RDA* 7.4.2.2, when recording latitude and longitude. The following subfields are defined for the MARC 034 field:

$a category of scale, with three code values: a—linear scale, b—angular scale, and z—other type of scale
$b constant ratio linear horizontal scale
$c constant ratio linear vertical scale
$d coordinates—westernmost longitude
$e coordinates—easternmost longitude
$f coordinates—northernmost latitude
$g coordinates—southernmost latitude
$h angular scale
$j declination—northern limit
$k declination—southern limit
$m right ascension—eastern limit
$n right ascension—western limit
$p equinox
$s G-ring latitude
$t G-ring longitude

The first indicator value specifies type of scale. An initial indicator value of 0 indicates that scale is indeterminable or that no scale information is recorded; a value of 1 indicates the presence of a single horizontal scale; a value of 3 indicates that there is a range of scales.

The second indicator value specifies type of ring for digital cartographic resources. A second indicator value of blank indicates that information on type of ring is not applicable (meaning that the item is not a digital cartographic resource). The MARC21 Bibliographic Format website (http://www.loc.gov/marc/bibliographic/bd034.html) provides additional information on the MARC 034 field and indicator values.

Scale

RDA states that scale is a core element only for cartographic resources. Scale information can be taken from any source on the resource; it is recorded as a representative fraction expressed as a ratio.[19] *AACR2* Rule 3.3B1 instructs catalogers to provide scale as a representative fraction expressed as a ratio. The ratio by is preceded by the term "Scale." Scale is recorded even when this information is also given in the title statement. Statements of scale can apply to horizontal, angular, or other measurements provided in the resources.

Scale is sometimes given as a statement rather than as a ratio. Convert the information into numerical form. A rule of thumb is that there are 63,360 inches in a mile. If the cartographic material states "1 inch 4 miles," multiply 63,360 × 4 253,440. Record as: Scale [1:253,440]. If the scale is approximated, use the abbreviation "ca." in the scale statement. If a scale is not recorded as a fraction, record it as a representative fraction.

Scale can also be estimated based on a bar scale or grid that appears on the resource. Use the phrase "Scale not given" when a scale statement cannot be determined or estimated based on the information provided or because of lack of information. The Bureau of Economic Geology provides an online scale calculator at http://www.beg.utexas.edu/GIS/tools/scale2.htm.

Provide scale information in the MARC 255 field Cartographic Mathematical Data, which is repeatable. It has the following subfields:

$a statement of scale
$b statement of projection
$c statement of coordinates
$d statement of zone
$e statement of equinox

No indicators are defined for the MARC 255 field.

Record scale in the MODS element <subject> with the <subelement> <cartographics>, which has its own subelements <coordinates>, <scale>, and <projection>. Record this information in the DC element <Coverage> with the qualifier "Spatial" (see Examples 2.8 and 2.9). Figures 2.2 and 2.3 illustrate statements of scale on cartographic resources.

If a resource contains more than one scale, or if a multipart item contains more than one scale, a separate statement may be provided for each scale. When more than one scale is present, catalogers are given the option of providing multiple statements or using the note "Scales

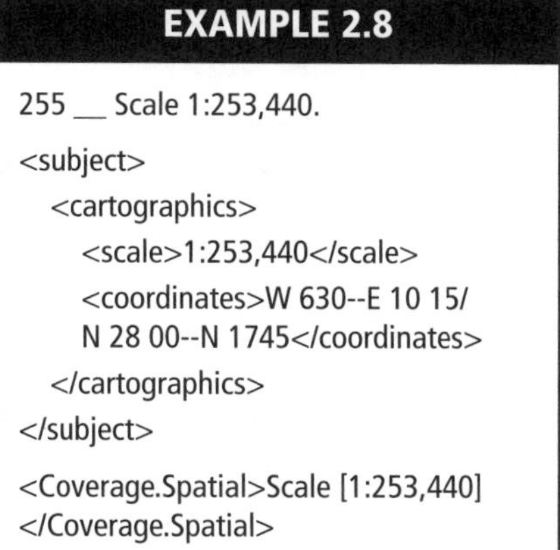

EXAMPLE 2.8

255 __ Scale 1:253,440.

<subject>
<cartographics>
<scale>1:253,440</scale>
<coordinates>W 630--E 10 15/ N 28 00--N 1745</coordinates>
</cartographics>
</subject>

<Coverage.Spatial>Scale [1:253,440] </Coverage.Spatial>

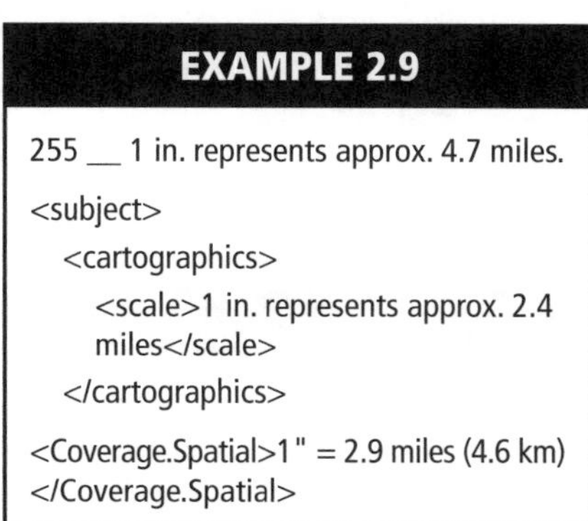

EXAMPLE 2.9

255 __ 1 in. represents approx. 4.7 miles.

<subject>
<cartographics>
<scale>1 in. represents approx. 2.4 miles</scale>
</cartographics>

<Coverage.Spatial>1" = 2.9 miles (4.6 km) </Coverage.Spatial>

Figure 2.2. Scale Statement for a Cartographic Resource: Example 1

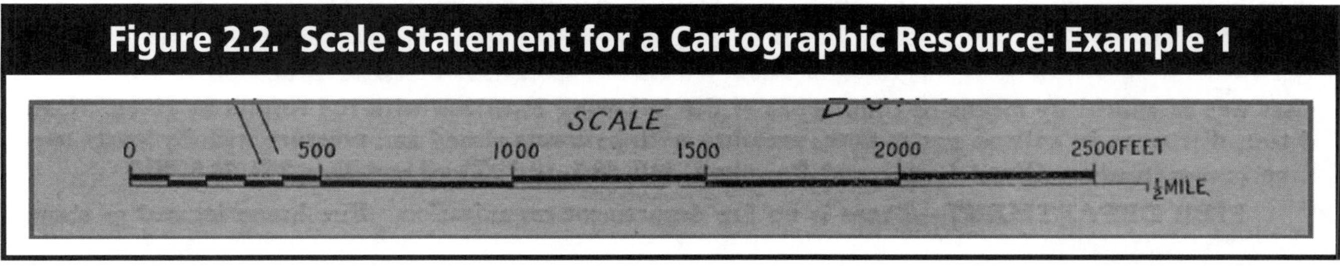

Figure 2.3. Scale Statement for a Cartographic Resource: Example 2

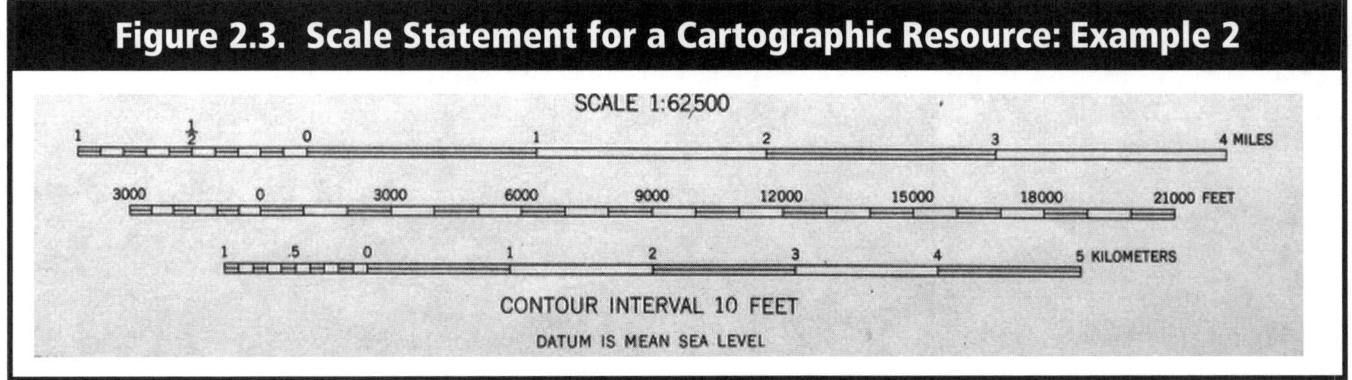

differ." If a resource is not drawn to scale, *RDA* 7.25.3.3 instructs catalogers to use the note "Not drawn to scale."

Supplemental information can be recorded as additional scale information. This information pertains to comparative measures or limitation of the scale to particular parts of the content.[20] Take this information from any source within the resource. Enclose additional scale information in brackets if it presents unusual information that cannot be verified, when a direct quotation is more precise than a statement in conventional form, or when the statement is incorrect or contains errors.[21]

Projection

Projection is the means or system used to represent Earth's surface. *RDA* classifies projection as other details of cartographic content. Providing projection is optional and only if readily available. Consult any source of information.

Record projection (abbreviated as "proj.") after the statement of scale in the MARC 255 field Cartographic Mathematical Data. Record projection in the MODS element <subject> with the subelement <cartographics>, which has the subelement <projection>, and in the DC element <Coverage> with the qualifier "Spatial" (see Example 2.10).

MCM instructs catalogers to record projection statements in English regardless of language in which the resource is written. The manual also states that the first word and any proper names in a projection statement should be capitalized. Figure 2.4 shows an example of a projection statement.

Coordinates

Geographic coordinates use degrees of latitude and longitude to describe a location on the Earth's surface.[22] *RDA* states that coordinate information can be taken from any source within the resource; if information is not available, it can then be taken from any source.

Rule 3.3D1 of *AACR2* states that information on coordinates can also be included and is expressed in degrees (°), minutes ('), and seconds ("). If appropriate, each coordinate is preceded by W, E, N, or S (see Example 2.11).

Relief

Relief is reflected through contours, form lines, satellite imagery, shading, etc. Record this information in the MARC 500 field General Note, which is repeatable; the MODS element <note>; and the DC element <Description> (see Example 2.12).

Figure 2.4. Projection Statement for a Cartographic Resource

Lambert Azimuthal Equal-Area Projection
(Map center point: Equator, 160°W).

EXAMPLE 2.10

255 __ Scale 1:23,000,000 ; $b Azimuthal equal-area proj.

<subject>
<cartographics>
<scale>1:1,609,000</scale>
<projection>Conic proj., standard parallels</projection>
</cartographics>
</subject>

<Coverage.Spatial>Scale [1:253,440] </Coverage>

<Coverage.Spatial>Azimuthal equal-area proj.</Coverage>

EXAMPLE 2.11

255 __ Scale [ca. 1:50,000,000] ; $b Spherical Mercator proj. $c (W 170°--W 170°/N 80°--S 65°).

<subject>
<cartographics>
<scale>1:50,000</scale>
<coordinates> E 89°30'--E 89°45'/ N 28°50'--N 28°25'</coordinates>
</cartographics>
</subject>

<Coverage.Spatial>Scale 1:50,000 </Coverage>

<Coverage.Spatial>(E 89°30'--E 89°45'/ N 28°50'--N 28°25</Coverage>

EXAMPLE 2.12

500 __ Depths and relief shown by hypsometric tints and contours (in uncorrected meters).

<note>Relief shown by hachures and spot heights.</note>

<Description>Relief shown by contours. </Description>

Manifestation

AACR2, Rule 1.1C states that use of a General Material Designation (GMD) is optional. GMDs are replaced in *RDA* with three different elements: content type, media type, and carrier type. Record these elements the MARC 336, 337, and 338 fields. The MARC 21 Format for Bibliographic Data defines them as:

336 "The form of communication through which a work is expressed."

337 ". . . reflects the general type of intermediation device required to view, play, run, etc., the content of a resource." The 337 can be used in addition to or instead of the coding for media type in the MARC 007 field.

338 ". . . reflects the format of the storage medium and housing of a carrier in combination with the media type."[23]

RDA Chapter 3 provides instruction on how to describe carriers of content. *RDA* Chapter 7 provides guidance on how to describe content of resources. Carriers can be described using information from the resource itself, from external packaging, or from accompanying materials.

Content Type

The MODS element <typeOfResource> is equivalent to the MARC 336 field. See www.loc.gov/standards/mods/v3/mods-userguide-elements.html#titleinfo for a list of values defined for this element. The value "cartographic" is used for cartographic resources. The DC element <type>, which describes the nature or genre of a resource, is roughly equivalent to the MARC 336 field.

The *RDA* list for content types contains the terms that catalogers consulting *RDA* use for cartographic resources (available at http://www.loc.gov/standards/valuelist/rdacontent.html). Terms used to describe cartographic resources include "cartographic image" or "cartographic tactile image."

Media Type

The MARC code list for *RDA* media types (http://www.loc.gov/standards/valuelist/rdamedia.html) lists the terms used in the MARC 337 field. The terms will not be applied to cartographic resources unless some type of equipment is required to view or use them. This information is recorded in the MODS element <note>. There is no DC equivalent.

Carrier

The term and code list for *RDA* carrier types (http://www.loc.gov/standards/valuelist/rdacarrier.html) lists the terms used in the MARC 338 field. Cartographic resources most frequently fall under the category "unmediated carriers," and the carrier term "sheet" is used to populate the 338 field.

Extent

Extent is a core element for cartographic resources when the resource is complete or the total extent is known. Rules for describing the extent of cartographic resources are outlined in *RDA* 3.4.2.2. The number of units and a term from the list provided in *RDA* 3.4.2.2 are recorded; the list includes the terms "atlas" and "map." According to *RDA* 3.4.2.5, atlases are described by specifying the number of volumes and pages.

Record this information in the MARC 300 field Physical Description, the MODS element <physicalDescription> with the subelement <extent>, and the DC element <Format> with the qualifier "Extent."

Dimensions

RDA 3.5 contains basic instructions for recording dimensions. Provide information on size, width, etc., as appropriate. Record this information in the MARC 300 field Physical Description, $c (which is not repeatable), the MODS element <physicalDescription> with the subelement <extent>, and the DC element <Format> qualified by "Extent."

Dimensions for cartographic resources measure the height times the width between the neat lines (see Figure 2.5), which are the lines or borders that enclose a map rather than the actual size of the sheet(s) used for the maps. The dimensions of the sheet(s) can be given if neat lines are lacking, when it is difficult to determine the actual area covered, or when one or more borders are lacking. Record dimensions in centimeters and abbreviate as "cm." Record height in centimeters for atlases.

If the height or width of a map is less than half the measurement of the same dimension of the sheet on which it is presented, or when there is substantial additional information on the sheet (e.g., text), record the dimensions of the map, etc., followed by the dimensions of the sheet.[24] Separate the measurements by a comma, and cite the dimensions of the sheet using the word "on" (see Example 2.13). Take information from the resource itself or from any additional sources as needed.

EXAMPLE 2.13

300 __ 1 map : $b col. ; $c 40 x 63 cm., on sheet 82 x 67 cm.

300 __ 1 atlas (100 p.) : $b 100 col. maps ; $c 29 cm.

<physicalDescription>
<extent>1 map : col., mounted on wooden rods ; 99 x 158 cm.</extent>
</physicalDescription>

<physicalDescription>
<extent>1 atlas (1 v. (various pagings)) : col. ill., col. maps ; 23 x 38 cm.</extent>
</physicalDescription>

<Format.Extent>1 map : col. ; 78 x 108 cm.</Format>

<Format.Extent>1 atlas (128 p.) : col. ill., col. maps ; 25 cm.</Format>

Figure 2.5. Neat Lines on a Cartographic Resource

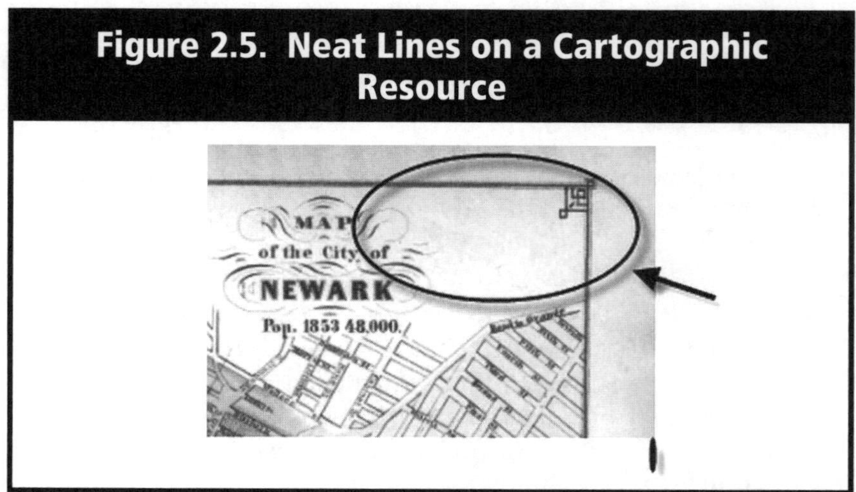

EXAMPLE 2.14

300 __ 1 map on 7 sheets : $b col. ; $c 140 x 196 cm., on sheets 82 x 108 cm.

<physicalDescription>
<extent>1 map : col. ; on 2 sheets 85 x 108 cm., folded to 27 x 22 cm.
</extent>
</physicalDescription>

<Format.Extent>2 maps in 1 portfolio : col., mounted on linen ; 78 x 99 cm., on sheets 82 x 104 cm., folded in separate covers 22 x 16 cm., in 1 portfolio 22 x 17 cm.</Format>

300 __ 1 atlas (128 p.)

<physicalDescription>
<extent>1 atlas (1 v. (various pagings))
</extent>
</physicalDescription>

<Format.Extent>1 atlas (xiv, 450 p.) </Format>

If a map is in sheets of two sizes, record both sets of dimensions. *RDA* 3.5.2.3 states that when cartographic resources are on sheets of more than two different sizes, record the greatest height and width and "or smaller."

When a map is presented in an outer cover, such as a portfolio, and is intended to be folded, record both the dimensions of the map and the dimensions of the map when it is folded. Precede the second set of dimensions by a comma, and any dimensions that refer to a folded map include the wording "folded to" (see Example 2.14). See *RDA* 3.5.2.6 for more information.

If the extent cannot be determined, estimate the number. Then include the term "approximately" in the extent statement (see Example 2.15).

When a cartographic resource consists of more than one sheet, *RDA* 3.4.2.3 instructs catalogers to record the number of cartographic units and sheets (see Example 2.16). *RDA* 3.4.2.3 states that when a cartographic resource is issued in more than one part and is intended to function as one unit, record the number of units and the word "in" to specify how the units are represented (see Example 2.17). Figures 2.6 and 2.7 show MARC format resource descriptions for a map and an atlas.

Layout

According to *RDA*, record information for cartographic resources (excluding atlases) that provide images on both sides and at the same scale as "both sides" (see *RDA* 3.11.2.3 for further details). Record this information in the MARC 300 field Physical Description, the MODS element <physicalDescription> with the subelement <extent>, and the DC element <Format> qualified by "Extent" (see Example 2.18)

EXAMPLE 2.15

300 __ approximately 50 maps

<physicalDescription>
<extent>Approximately 500 maps </extent>
</physicalDescription>

<Format.Extent>Approximately 80 maps</Format>

EXAMPLE 2.16

300 __ 3 maps on 1 sheet

<physicalDescription>
<extent>2 maps on 1 sheet</extent>
</physicalDescription>

<Format.Extent>2 maps on 1 sheet </Format>

EXAMPLE 2.17

300 __ 8 diagrams on 2 sheets

<physicalDescription>
<extent>1 map on 2 sheets and 1 data sheet
</extent>
</physicalDescription>

<Format.Extent>1 map on 3 sheets </Format>

EXAMPLE 2.18

300 __ 8 diagrams on 2 sheets : $b both sides

<physicalDescription>
<extent>1 map on 2 sheets and 1 data sheet : both sides</extent>
</physicalDescription>

<Format.Extent>1 map on 3 sheets : both sides
</Format>

Figure 2.6. Sample MARC Descriptive Record for a Cartographic Resource

```
007:     : aj canzn
008:     : 030715s2002 nju a s 0 eng d
034: 1   : a|b255000
035:     : (OCoLC)ocm51390155
040:     : NjR|cNjR
043:     : n-us-nj
050: 4   : G3811.F7 2002|b.N4
052:     : 3811
110: 1   : New Jersey.|bDept. of Transportation.|bBureau of Geographic Information Systems.
245: 10  : Legislative districts & representatives|h[cartographic material] /|cmapping
           by the New Jersey Department of Transportation, Division of Information
           Technology ; Graphic Information Systems in cooperation with U.S. Department
           of Transportation, Fedral Highway Administration.
246: 3   : Legislative districts and representatives|h[cartographic material]
255:     : Scale [ca. 1:255,000].
300:     : 1 map :|bcol. ;|c107 x 60 cm., on sheet 110 x 61 cm.
500:     : At lower left: Legislative Services.
500:     : Includes names of members of New Jersey Legislature keyed by number to
           district numbers on map.
596:     : 2
610: 10  : New Jersey.|bLegislature|xElection districts|vMaps.
610: 10  : New Jersey.|bLegislature|vDirectories.
650: 0   : Election districts|zNew Jersey|vMaps.
650: 0   : Legislators|zNew Jersey|vRegisters.
651: 0   : New Jersey|vMaps.
710: 1   : New Jersey.|bOffice of Legislative Services.
710: 1   : New Jersey.|bBureau of Geographic Information Systems.
710: 1   : United States.|bFederal Highway Administration.
```

Book Special Request

Article Delivery

Mark

Report Error

EXAMPLE 2.19

300 __ 1 atlas (100 p.) : $b 100 col. maps

300 __ 1 map : $b col.

<physicalDescription>

<extent>3 maps on 1 sheet ; $b col. </extent>

</physicalDescription>

<Format.Extent>2 maps on 1 sheet : $b both sides, col.</Format>

Color Content

Color content is an optional element in *RDA*. Include color content when it is considered important for identification and selection. Take information from the resource or additional information from any source.

Record this information in the MARC 300 field Physical Description, $b, which is not repeatable. Record it in the MODS element <physical Description> with the subelement <extent> and in the DC element <Format> with the qualifier "Extent" (see Example 2.19).

Base Material

RDA 3.6.1 provides information on base materials, which are defined as "the underlying physical material on which the content of a resource is stored."[25] Base material is not a core element. Take information from the resource, accompanying materials, or container. *RDA* 3.6.1.3 provides a list of base materials that should be used, including vellum and plastic. Catalogers consulting *AACR2* are instructed to follow Rule 3.5C4, which states that information on the material on which the item may be recorded if it is available and considered to be important.

Figure 2.7. Sample MARC Descriptive Record for an Atlas

MARC Fixed Field	Record type: e Bibliographic level: m
006	e m
007	a $b d $d c $e a $f n $g z $h n
008	Desc: a Dat_TP: s Date 1: 2006 Date 2: Ctry: ii Relief: Base: Map_Type: e GovtPub: i Form: ndx:1 Spec_Fmt: Lang: eng Source: d
040	NjR$cNjR
050 _4	G2281.P2 $b T83 2006
052 __	7651
110 2_	TTK Healthcare Limited. $b Printing Division.
245 10	TTK road atlas of India / $c designed, compiled, cartographed . . . by TTK Healthcare Limited, Printing Division ; edited by S. Ravi ; text by Georgina.
246 30	Road atlas of India
255	Scales differ.
260	Chennai, India : $b TTK Healthcare Ltd., Printing Division, $c c2006.
300	1 atlas (79 p.) : $ col. ill., col. maps ; $c 25 cm.
500	Includes tourist information.
505 0_	India -- States -- Union territories -- Cities -- Route maps -- Miscellaneous.
650 _0	Roads $z India $v Maps.
651 _0	India $v Guidebooks.
700 1_	Ravi, S. $q (Swaminathan), $d 1947-
700 0_	Georgina.

Record this information in the 300 MARC field Physical Description, $b, which is not repeatable. Record it in the MODS element <physical Description> with the subelement <extent> and in the DC element <Format> qualified by "Extent" (see Example 2.20).

Mounting

RDA 3.8.1.3 instructs catalogers to record the material used to mount maps if this information is readily available. Take information on mounting from the resource or additional information from other sources. *RDA* 3.6.1.3 lists the terms to use.

Record this information in the MARC 300 field Physical Description, $b, which is not repeatable. Record it in the MODS element <physical

EXAMPLE 2.20

300 1 map : $b vellum

<physicalDescription>
<extent>1 map : plastic</extent>
</physicalDescription>

<Format.Extent>1 map : vellum
</Format>

EXAMPLE 2.21

300 __ 1 map : $b col., mounted on cloth

<physicalDescription>
<extent>1 map : col., mounted on wooden rods</extent>
</physicalDescription>

<Format.Extent>2 maps in 1 portfolio : col., mounted on linen</Format>

EXAMPLE 2.22

245 00 Map of Hunterdon County $h [cartographic material] / $c prepared by the New Jersey Cartographic Society; scale devised by Marc Edmonds.

<name>
<name type="corporate">New Jersey. Dept. of Transportation. Bureau of Geographic Information Systems </name type>
</name>

<Contributor>Geological Society of America</Contributor>

EXAMPLE 2.23

250 __ 4th large scale ed.

<originInfo>
<edition>New census</edition>
</originInfo>

<Description>Summer 2002</Description>

See Also...

Place of Publication/Distribution (Chapter 1, pp. 45–46)
Manufacturer (Chapter 1, pp. 48–50)
Series (Chapter 1, pp. 50–52)

Description> with the subelement <extent> and in the DC element <Format> qualified by "Extent" (see Example 2.21).

Statement of Responsibility

RDA Chapter 11 describes how to choose and construct preferred names for corporate bodies. *RDA* 11.2 describes how to record corporate body names. Corporate names can be preferred or variant forms of the name. A preferred name is a core element and forms the basis for the preferred access point that presents that particular body.[26] According to *RDA* 11.2.2.2, determine the preferred name form for a corporate body by consulting the following sources in order of preference: "a) the preferred sources of information (see 2.2.2) in resources associated with the corporate body; b) other formal statements appearing in resources associated with the corporate body; c) other sources (including reference sources)."[27] Use the name by which a corporate body is commonly known as the preferred name. Record corporate names following the general instructions in *RDA* 8.5. Formulate the preferred corporate name after consulting preferred sources of information in resources that are associated with the corporate body, statements about other formats that are provided in resources associated with the corporate body, and other sources including reference works.[28]

Enter the statement of responsibility in the MARC 245 field Title Statement, $c. The MODS User Guidelines, Version 3, defines the element <name> as "The name of a person, organization, or event (conference, meeting, etc.) associated in some way with the resource."[29] DC defines <Creator> as "An entity primarily responsible for making the resource" and <Contributor> as "An entity responsible for making contributions to the resource."[30] The choice of DC element will depend on the role and contributions of the person or corporate body provided in the main entry (see Example 2.22).

Edition

Record edition information for cartographic resources in the MARC 250 field Edition Statement, the MODS element <originInfo> with the subelement <edition>, and the DC element <Description> (see Example 2.23). *RDA* 2.5.2 provides information on designation of editions.

Resource Identifiers

The relevant fixed fields for cartographic resources are the Leader and the MARC fields 006, 007, and 008. The MARC 006 field for cartographic resources describes the form of the material, relief, projection, type of cartographic resource, form of item, and special format characteristics. Cartographic resources are coded "e" for printed cartographic resources. The MODS element <typeOfResource> specifies a resource's characteristics, and general type of content of the resource is equivalent to the MARC 006 field.[31] The DC element <Type> is equivalent to the MARC 006 field in that it describes a resource's nature or genre.

The MARC 007 field provides information about a resource's special characteristics. It is coded "a" for maps and "r" for remote sensing images. A print atlas is coded "a" for maps. Digital atlases may include two 007 fields, one for the map characteristics (coded "a") and a second to reflect the resource's electronic characteristics (coded "c") (see Example 2.24). There are no subfields or indicators defined for the 007 field. The field's selected values are the following:

Position 00	Category of material; is always a for "map"
Position 01	SMD; d (atlas); j (map); y (view); z (other)
Position 02	Undefined; leave blank
Position 03	Color; a (one color); c (multicolored)
Position 04	Physical medium; a (paper); g (textile); u (unknown); z (other)
Position 05	Type of reproduction; f (facsimile); n (not applicable); u (unknown); z (other)
Position 06	Production/reproduction details; b (photocopy); d (film); u (unknown); z (other)
Position 07	Positive/negative aspects; a (positive); b (negative); m (mixed polarity); n (not applicable)

A full list of values for the 007 field is available on the MARC 21 Bibliographic Format website at http://www.loc.gov/marc/bibliographic/bd007.html.

The MODS element <physicalDescription> qualified with <form authority="marc category">map</form> or <form authority="marc category">remote sensing image</form> is equivalent to the MARC 007 field for cartographic resources. The DC element <Type> is roughly equivalent to the MARC 007 field.

The MARC 008 field provides coded information that describes special bibliographic aspects of the item being cataloged. The MODS element <genre> qualified by <genre authority="marcgt"> map, <genre><genre authority="marcgt">atlas are equivalent to the MARC 008/position 25 codes a, b, c, and e respectively. The MODS elements <genre>, <typeOf Resource>, and <originInfo> can be used to indicate the information conveyed in the MARC 008 field. The MODS element used depends on the type of information being described. This information is provided in the DC elements <Date> and <Language>.

The values in this field, from positions 18 to 34, are the same as those in the 006 field positions 1 to 17. The character positions 00 to 17 are the same for all resources and contains information on publication status, date of publication, etc. Positions 00 to 05 are for the date when an item was entered on file. Position 06 is for the type of date used to describe the resource and publication status. Positions 07 to 10 are for the first date associated with a resource; positions 11 and 14 are for the second date associated with a resource. Positions 15 to 17 are for the place of publication, production, or execution.

The 008 field for maps includes relief (positions 18 to 21), projection (positions 22 and 23), type of cartographic resource (position 25), form of item (position 29), and special format characteristics (positions 33

EXAMPLE 2.24

007 ad aanzn
- a = map
- d = atlas
- blank
- a = one color
- a = paper
- n = type of reproduction not applicable
- z = other production/reproduction details
- n = positive/negative aspect not applicable

aj cgnzn
- a = map
- j = map
- blank
- c = multicolored
- g = textile
- n = type of reproduction not applicable
- z = other production/reproduction details
- n = positive/negative aspect not applicable

EXAMPLE 2.25

008 940714s1993 dcu ac a f 0 eng d

and 34). Remote sensing data and digital atlases can be coded in the 008 as computer files. Unlike the 007 field, the 008 field is not repeatable. It is important to ensure that all of the relevant values are entered in this field (see Example 2.25).

The 008 field and values for cartographic resources (described as maps) are fully described on the MARC 21 Bibliographic Format website at http://www.loc.gov/marc/bibliographic/bd008.html.

Publication, Production, Distribution, Etc., Area

The publication statement is a core element in *RDA* and basic instructions are addressed in 2.8.1.1. The general rule 3.4B in *AACR2* covers publication, distribution, etc., details. Enter details about the publication, such as the name of the publisher and date and place of publication, in the MARC 260 field. Enter this information in the MODS element <originInfo> qualified by the subelements <place>, <publisher>, and <copyrightDate>. For DC, enter this information as <dcterm><Publisher>, and use the label <date> for the date information recorded in the YYYY-MM-DD format. More information is provided in greater detail on pages 45–50 in Chapter 1.

Item

Item Identifier

Library of Congress Call Number

If Library of Congress Classification is used for maps and atlases, the G schedule is used. Call number construction for atlases consists of three parts: area number (may be a major area or a subarea atlas), Cutter number (may be for authority responsible for the atlas or subarea Cutter plus Cutter for authority responsible for the atlas), and date of publication. Call numbers for maps consist of three or four parts: area number (may be a major area), subject area of the map (geographic area, map of a subject, region or feature, political division, city or town), date of publication, and Cutter for authority responsible for the map (see Example 2.26).

EXAMPLE 2.26

Atlas

050 _4 G1796.S6 $b J65 1820

<classification authority="lcc"> G1046.E1 S4 2009</classification>

<Subject.LCC>G3301.E1 2009.B37 </Subject>

Map

050 _4 G3913.L5C5 2002 $b .S4

<classification authority="lcc"> G3811.P2 1999.H3 </classification>

<Subject.LCC>G3813.O2P2 1999.H3 </Subject>

Provide a Library of Congress Call Number (if applicable according to the cataloging agency's policies and procedures for nonprint resources) in the MARC 050 field Library of Congress Call Number, which is repeatable, the MODS element <classification> with the attribute "authority," and the DC element <Subject> qualified by the classification scheme (LCC in this case) (see Example 2.27).

EXAMPLE 2.27

050 00 G1782.M4C5 $b T7 2004

<classification authority="lcc">JK609.M2 </classification>

<Subject.LCC>G3812.C6E635 2003 $b .J4 </Subject.LCC>

The subfields of the MARC 050 field are $a classification number and $b item number. The initial indicator value indicates that an item is in Library of Congress's collection. An initial value of blank is used when libraries other than the Library of Congress provide classification numbers. The second indicator value indicates the source of the call number. Classification numbers provided by Library of Congress have a second indicator value of zero; classification numbers provided by other libraries have a second indicator value of 4 (see Example 2.28).

EXAMPLE 2.28

050 _0 G2165.1-111 $b U5 1998

050 _4 G3813.M4 1999 $b .H3

MCM provides detailed instructions on how to classify maps using the Library of Congress Classification (LCC). It is available in print or online via Cataloger's Desktop (accessible by subscription only) at http://desktop.loc.gov.

Maps classed according to LCC follow the G schedule, which covers geography, anthropology, and recreation. The G schedule assigns each geographic entity a five-number sequence to describe subareas that range from general to specific. The Library of Congress's document *Special Instructions and Tables of Subdivisions for Cartographic Materials* (http://www.loc.gov/catdir/cpso/class_g.pdf) describes these subareas:

0 or 5 for a general geographic area; used to classify general atlases or maps

1 or 6 to classify maps or atlases by subject; further subarrangements are listed in the G schedule

2 or 7 to classify maps or atlases by region, natural features, etc., and alphabetically

3 or 8 to classify maps or atlases by major political divisions such as counties, states, provinces, etc., and alphabetically

4 or 9 to classify maps or atlases by city or town, and alphabetically[32]

Geographic Classification

Provide information on geographic classification that represents the cartographic resource's geographic area and (if appropriate) geographic subarea and populated place name covered by the resource. Record it in the MARC 052 field Geographic Classification, which is repeatable. Record it in the MODS element <classification>, which can be qualified with the attribute "authority" to indicate authoritative source for the classification, such as "lcc" for "Library of Congress Classification"; and in the DC element <Subject>. Note that this is not an exact fit for either DC, because <Subject> typically applies to the MARC fields 050 (Library of Congress Classification), 060 (National Library of Medicine Call Number), 080 (Universal Decimal Classification Number), and 082 (Dewey Decimal Classification Number), or MODS.

The MARC format for geographic classification has two indicator values. The first indicator value provides information on source of code. A first indicator value of blank indicates that the source of the geographic code is the Library of Congress Classification; a value of zero indicates that the source of the code is the U.S. Department of Defense Classification. The second indicator is undefined (see Example 2.29).

The following subfields are available for the MARC 052 field:

$a geographic classification area code

$b geographic classification subarea code; repeatable and may be strung together following $a when subareas fall within a main area for the same code[33]

$d populated place name [rarely used; no example is provided for this reason]

The subfields work in conjunction with the MARC 651 field Subject Added Entry—Geographic Name (see Example 2.30).

EXAMPLE 2.29

052 __ 2165

<classification authority="lcc">4362 M4 </classification>

<Classification.LCC>3201</Classification>

EXAMPLE 2.30

052 __ 3813

651 _0 Jersey City (N.J.) $v Maps.

052 __ 3814$bJ5

052 __ 3814$bJ5$bH9$bU6$bW3$bW4 $bG9$bN6$bB3

<classification authority="lcc">3913L5 </classification>

<Classification.LCC>4582N48>3201 </Classification>

EXAMPLE 2.31

020 __ 3540221816
020 __ 9783540221816

International Standard Book Number

Monographic resources are often assigned an International Standard Book Number (ISBN). In 2007, the publishing industry switched from a 10-digit ISBN to a 13-digit ISBN. This change was prompted by a need to expand the numbering capacity of the ISBN system and to align the numbering system for books with the global EAN.UCC identification system. The new ISBNs are preceded by a three-digit prefix 978, to be succeeded by a 979 prefix (see Example 2.31). The 979 prefix will not be implemented until all 978 prefixes have been assigned.

Resources can have both a 10- and a 13-digit ISBN, and libraries can enter both in their bibliographic records. If this practice is followed, the 13-digit ISBN is entered first. Older materials may bear only a 10-digit ISBN. If an ISBN ends with the character "x," the letter is entered in uppercase.

A free online ISBN tool that converts 10-digit ISBNs to their 13-digit counterparts is available at www.isbn.org/converterpub.asp. Provide this information in the MARC 020 field International Standard Book Number, which is repeatable, the MODS element <identifier>, and the DC element <Identifier> (see Example 2.32). This information can be helpful in identifying specific versions of a resource.

No indicators are defined for the MARC 020 field. Consult the MARC 21 Bibliographic Format Web site (www.loc.gov/marc/bibliographic/concise/bd020.html) for more information.

EXAMPLE 2.32

020 __ 1929377150
<identifier>1570840687</identifier>
<Identifier>0875303072</Identifier>

Related Items

RDA refers to accompanying materials as "related items." According to Chapter 24, *RDA*, "The term related item refers to an item related to the item being described (e.g., an item used as the basis for a microform reproduction)."[34] This type of information is not a core element in *RDA*. Chapter 24 also explains its relationship designators, and Appendix J.2.5 provides terminology for these relationships. The relationship is described when it is considered to be important. The list includes the terms "augmented by" (used when a related item adds to the content of the resource being described) and "guide" (used when a related item is intended to guide users through the main resource being described).

Catalogers using *RDA* may want to use an unstructured description to describe related resources. *RDA* defines an unstructured description as "A full or partial description of a resource written as a sentence or paragraph."[35] This is a departure from *AACR2*-prescribed treatment, which offers the option of describing related resources as part of the larger physical description.

Record this information in the MARC 500 field General Note, the MODS element <note>, which provides general information in text form, and the DC element <Description> (see Example 2.33).

EXAMPLE 2.33

300 __ 1 map : $b col. ; $c 58 x 96 cm., on sheet 92 x 147 cm., folded in envelope 31 x 23 cm.
500 __ Augmented by 1 pamphlet (32 p. : ill. ; 28 cm.).

<physicalDescription>
<extent>1 map ; 100 x 53 cm., on sheet 132 x 87 cm., folded in envelope 31 x 23 cm.</extent>
<note>Augmented by 1 explanatory text (8 p. : ill., maps ; 28 cm.)</note>
</physicalDescription>

<Format.Extent>1 map on 2 sheets : col. ; $c 95 x 190 cm., on sheets 99 x 71 cm. and 99 x 97 cm.</Format>
<Description>Augmented by 1 legend sheet (1 leaf : 2 col. maps ; 26 cm. diameters on sheet 99 x 40 cm.) </Description>

Notes

Notes provide a variety of information to further describe and facilitate access to resources. They supplement other elements and are typically used when an element (physical description, for example) cannot accommodate certain types of information.

Nature of Content

"The nature of the content is the specific character of the content of a resource. . . ."[36] *RDA* specifies that information may be taken from any source. Record this information in the MARC 500 field General Note (which is repeatable), the MODS element <note>, and the DC element <Description>, which is used for a free-text description of resources (see Example 2.34). Figures 2.8 through 2.11 illustrate resource description using MODS and DC.

History of the Work

RDA prescribes using history of the work to provide information relating to the history of a resource. Record this information in the MARC 500 field General Note, which is repeatable and differs from the MARC 250 field. Record it in the MODS element <note>, because <originInfo> with the subelement <edition> is equivalent to the MARC 250 Edition Statement. Use the DC element <Description> to record this information, as this element is used to provide a free-text account of resources (see Example 2.35).

Mathematical and Other Cartographic Data

RDA 7.27.1 instructs catalogers to provide mathematical data in addition to or that elaborates on the information recorded in statements

Figure 2.8. Sample DC Descriptive Record for a Map

<Title>Map of the City of Newark, Essex County, N.J.</Title>

<Description>Map from the State Atlas of New Jersey. Based on State Geological Suvery and from additional surveys. By and under the direction of F.W. Beers. Published by Beers, Comstock and Cline, 36 Vesey Street, New York. 1872.</Description>

<Contributor>Beers, F.W. (cartographer)</Contributor>

<Date>1872</Date>

<Type>StillImage</Type>

<Type>cartographic materials</Type>

<Format>image/tiff (tiff)</Format>

<Identifier>http://hdl.rutgers.edu/1782.3/SPCOL.Map.973</Identifier>

<Identifier>rutgers-lib:3982</Identifier>

<Language>English</Language>

<Relation>RU Special Collections</Relation>

<Relation>SPCOL</Relation>

<Coverage>New Jersey--Newark</Coverage>

<Rights>This object may be copyright-protected. Contact the owner or rights holder for permission to reproduce.</Rights>

EXAMPLE 2.34

500 __ Shows plats, section by section, lot dimensions, named streets and railroad lines, surrounding areas and bodies of water, and restrictions contained in all deeds of conveyance.

<note>Includes 3 inset maps, user information, legend, and note containing biodiversity priorities.</note>

<Description>Plastic coated map is described as "easy to handle, easy to fold, durable--won't tear, and write on-wipe off."</Description>

See Also . . .

Language of Content (Chapter 1, pp. 25, 26)

EXAMPLE 2.35

500 __ Originally published as the New York Times atlas of the world.

<note>Reissued with corrections and new additions.</note>

<Description>Reproduction. Originally published: 1932.</Description>

EXAMPLE 2.36

500 __ Depths and relief shown by hypsometric tints and contours (in uncorrected meters).

<note>Relief shown by hachures and spot heights.</note>

<Description>Relief shown by contours.</Description>

Figure 2.9. Sample MODS Descriptive Record for a Map

```
<titleInfo>
<title>Map of Berkeley Heights, 1962</title>
<titleInfo>
<name type="personal">
   <namePart type="given">Charles</namePart>
   <namePart type="family">Van Beuschoten</namePart>
   <description>Berkeley Heights Township Engineer</description>
</name>
<role>
<roleTerm type="text"> associated name</roleTerm>
</role>
<typeOfResource>Still image</typeOfResource>
<genre type="aat">map</genre>
<genre type="aat">cartographic materials</genre>
<originInfo>
   <dateCreated>1962</dateCreated>
<language>
<languageTerm type="text"> English<languageTerm>
</language>
<abstract>Map of Berkeley Heights, New Jersey, from 1962. Free Acres is located in Grid B6 in the lower left-hand section of
the map.</abstract >
<subject>
<topic>Immigrants</topic>
<geographic>New Jersey</geographic>
<geographic>New Jersey—Berkeley Heights Free Acres</geographic>
<identifier type="local">SPCO</identifier
<identifier type=hdl>http://hdl.rutgers.edu/1782.3/SPCOL.Map.963</identifier>
<location>
   <physicalLocation>Physical Location (Rutgers University. Libraries. Special Collections and University Archives
   </physicalLocation>
```

EXAMPLE 2.37

500 __ Distributor information taken from label affixed to jacket.

<note>Previously distributed by Maparama, Inc. </note>

<Description>Distributed to depositories in paper (1 map : col. ; 54 x 38 cm., on sheet 87 x 109 cm., folded to 22 x 28 cm., in envelope 24 x 30 cm.), shipping list no.: 2008-0440-P.</Description>

of scale, projection, and coordinates.[37] Record this information in the MARC 500 field General Note, which is repeatable, the MODS element <note>, and the DC element <Description> (see Example 2.36, p. 77).

Publication, Distribution, Etc., Information

Per *RDA* 2.20.7, provide notes on publication, distribution, etc., details not included in the publication, distribution, etc., area but are considered to be important. Provide this information in the MARC 500 field General Note, which is repeatable, the MODS element <note>, and the DC element <Description> (see Example 2.37).

Figure 2.10. Sample MODS Descriptive Record for an Atlas

```
<titleInfo>
   <title>Atlas of Bergen County, New Jersey</title>
   <subTitle>made from actual surveys of each township and village, and from historical facts, arranged specifically for this
   work</subTitle>
<name type="corporate">Building Materials and Technology Promotion Council (India)</name>
<typeOfResource>cartographic</typeOfResource>
<originInfo>
   <place>New Delhi</place>
<physicalDescription>
   <extent>1 atlas (ca. 750 p.) : col. ill., col. maps (chiefly folded) ; 31 cm.</extent>
</physicalDescription>
<classification authority="lcc">G1258.B4G48 2006.W35</classification>
<note>Reprint. Originally published: Reading, Pa. : C.C. Pease, successor to A.H. Walker, [1876]</note>
<subject>
   <scale>Scales differ.</scale>
<subject authority="lcsh">
<topic>Real property—New Jersey—Bergen County--Maps</topic>
<genre>Bergen County (N.J.)--Maps</genre>
<topic>Bergen County (N.J.)--History</topic>
<genre>Bergen County (N.J.)--Directories</genre>
```

Figure 2.11. Sample DC Descriptive Record for an Atlas

```
<Creator>Building Materials and Technology Promotion Council (India)</Creator>
<Coverage.Spatial>a-ii---</Coverage>
<Coverage.Spatial>Scales differ</Coverage>
<Date>2006</Date>
<Description>Includes statistical charts showing housing materials and level of damage risk from natural disasters.</Description>
<Format.Extent>1 atlas (ca. 750 p.)</Format>
<Identifier>8186930132</Identifier>
<Identifier>9788186930137</Identifier>
<Publisher>Building Materials & Technology Promotion Council, Ministry of Housing & Urban Poverty Alleviation, Govt. of
India</Publisher>
<Subject.LCC>G2281.C1 B6 2006</Subject>
<Subject.LCSH>Natural disasters--India--Maps</Subject>
<Subject.LCSH>Dwellings--Protection--India--Statistics</Subject>
<Title>Vulnerability atlas of India, first revision</Title>
<Title.Alternative>Earthquake, windstorm and flood hazard maps and damage risk to housing</Title>
<Type>atlas</Type>
```

EXAMPLE 2.38

530 __ Also issued separately as part of World factbook, Reference map appendix, 1999-

<note type="additional physical form"> Also available as paper map and pamphlet. </note>

<Relation.HasFormat>Available also through the Library of Congress Web site as a raster image. </Relation>

EXAMPLE 2.39

590 __ Use restricted to Special Collections Reading Room.

<note>Library's copy 1 lacks accompanying guide. </note>

<Description>Library's copy imperfect. </Description>

590 __ Atlases are noncirculating.

EXAMPLE 2.40

500 __ With: Mineral resources map of Mongolia.

740 0_ Mineral resources map of Mongolia $h [map].

<titleInfo>
<title>Six Flags [cartographic material] </title>
<subtitle>Great Adventure Theme Park </subtitle>

<relatedItem>With (on verso): Pictorial drive thru map of Six Flags Wild Safari Animal Park.</relatedItem>

<Title>Davy Crockett National Forest [cartographic material]</Title>

<Relation>Map of "Four C National Recreation Trail" on verso.</Relation>

EXAMPLE 2.41

245 00 Hagstrom street map of Ocean County, New Jersey $h [map].

740 0_ Map of Ocean County, New Jersey $h [map].

<titleInfo>
<title>Six Flags [cartographic material]</title>
<subtitle>Great Adventure Theme Park</subtitle>

<relatedItem>With (on verso): Pictorial drive thru map of Six Flags Wild Safari Animal Park.</relatedItem>

<Title>Davy Crockett National Forest [cartographic material]</Title>

<Relation>Map of "Four C National Recreation Trail" on verso.</Relation>

Other Formats

RDA 3.1.2 describes how to record information when manifestations of a resource are available in other formats. Record this information in the MARC 530 field Additional Physical Form Available Note (which is repeatable), the MODS element <note> with the type attribute "additional physical form," and the DC element <Relation> with the qualifier "HasFormat" (see Example 2.38).

Local Notes

Provide descriptive or copy-specific information about maps or atlases in the MARC 59X field Local Note (which is repeatable), the MODS element <note>, and the DC element <Description> (see Example 2.39). These notes can include information to identify a local copy of a resource or to describe local restrictions on access.

Referencing Related Works

RDA allows catalogers to describe related works that are provided with the resource being described. *RDA* 25.1.1.3 discusses how to describe related works.

Record this information in the MARC 500 field General Note, which is repeatable, the MODS element <relatedItem>, and the DC element <Relation>. In MARC, the information given in this type of note can also be used as the basis for a 740 field, Added Entry—Uncontrolled Related/Analytical Title (see Example 2.40).

Related Titles

RDA allows catalogers to describe related works that are provided with the resource being described. *RDA* 25.1.1.3 discusses how to describe related works.

Record this information in the MARC 740 field Added Entry—Uncontrolled Related/Analytical Title, the MODS element <relatedItem>, and the DC element <Relation>. The MARC 740 field has these subfields:

- $a uncontrolled related/analytical title
- $h medium
- $n number of part/section of a work
- $p name of part/section of a work

The initial indicator value indicates number of nonfiling characters (0–9). The second indicator value indicates type of added entry. A blank second indicator value indicates that no information is provided; a second indicator value of 2 indicates an analytical entry and means the item in the bibliographic record contains the work represented by the added entry (see Example 2.41). Additional information is available on the MARC 21 website (http://www.loc.gov/marc/bibliographic/bd740.html).

Resource Description (MARC, MODS, FISO) Checklists

The following checklists have been provided as a handy reference guide to the fields and/or areas most frequently used when creating descriptive records for cartographic materials. They are intended as guidelines and reminders. Cataloging treatment and choice of access points may vary by library, level of cataloging, and so forth. Always remember that you are the best judge when deciding which fields and/or areas are appropriate to describe the resource you have in hand, *distinctly* and *sufficiently*.

MARC CHECKLIST

For additional information about the MARC fields required by BIBCO (the Monographic Bibliographic Record Program), see http://www.loc.gov/catdir/pcc/bibco/coresr.html.

Type of Record: Use **e** for cartographic resource.

Bibliographic Level: This is usually **m** for monographic.

006: Only the first value is coded in this field: **e** for cartographic material. This value determines the specific 008 field to be used for the resource. The other values for this type of resource are coded in the 008 field for visual materials.

007: Use for maps (this applies to atlases).

Example:
$a a $b j $c [blank] $d c $e a $f n $g u $h m [007 for a map]
$a a $b d $c [blank] $d c $e a $f u $g u $h n [007 for an atlas]

008: Use for visual materials:

Relief: Type of relief indicated

Projection: Type of projection indicated

Type of cartographic material: Indicate if it is a single map, map series, or atlas.

Lang: eng

Date 1: Date of publication

Date 2: Use when multiple dates are available, such as in multipart resources. Other positions in this field relate to all types of resources.

020: **ISBN**: Monographic resources are often assigned an International Standard Book Number, which must be entered as it appears on the resource.

034: **Coded Cartographic Mathematical Data**: Record information on cartographic mathematical data (including scale, projection, and/or coordinates) in coded form.

050: **Library of Congress Call Number**: Assign a classification number according to the G schedule.

052: **Geographic Classification**: Provide information on geographic classification that represents the cartographic resource's geographic area and (if appropriate) geographic subarea and populated place name covered by the resource.

100: Author: Choice of main entry is driven by who did what rather than by prominence of information.
A corporate body selected as a main entry for a cartographic resource must specifically by designated as a map-making entity.

(Cont'd.)

MARC CHECKLIST *(Continued)*

245: Title: Title main entry may be chosen when cartographic resources are the work of many individuals and/or corporate bodies and it is not possible to attribute authorship to a particular individual or corporate body. Take the title from the cartographic resource.

250: Edition Statement: Record statements containing terms such as "edition" or that imply a given time period such as "Summer 2000". The edition statement is not repeatable; concatenate as needed.

255: Cartographic Mathematical Data: Record statement of scale.

260: Publication Details: $a Place of publication : $b Publisher, and $c date of publication or distribution.

300: Extent of Item: Record the number of units that comprise the resource in the first subfield ($a). Also give additional information about the resource, such as color (in subfield $b) and size (subfield $c).

400: Series Statement: Provide if applicable.

500: Note Field: Use for a variety of information, especially information deemed important by the cataloger but for which no MARC field has been specified. This field is also used for the mandatory "Source of title note" when the title has been supplied by the cataloger.

520: Note (Summary): Use to provide a summary of the resource's content.

530: Additional Physical Form Available Note: Use when manifestations of a resource are available in other formats; this field is repeatable.

650 and 655: Subject and Genre: Enter subject terms in the 650 field and genre headings in the 655 field.

MODS CHECKLIST

<typeOfResource> specifies type of resource being cataloged; in this case it will be "cartographic."

Example:
<typeOfResource>cartographic</typeOfResource>

<genre> provides information on a style, form, or content expressed in the resource.

Example:
<genre>atlas</genre>
<genre>map</genre>

<identifier> with the attribute " type" provides standard identifiers, such as the ISBN.

Example:
<identifier type="isbn">9783540221814</identifier>

<subject> with the subelement <cartographics> modified by its own subelement <coordinates> provides a statement of coordinates for the cartographic resource.

<recordInfo> with the subelement <recordContentSource> and the attribute "authority" provides the code or name of the organization that created or modified the original resource description.

Example:
<recordInfo>
<recordContentSource>Rutgers University Libraries</recordContentSource>
</recordInfo>

(Cont'd.)

MODS CHECKLIST *(Continued)*

<languageTerm> has the type="code" and authority="iso639-2b" (several codes may be used in "authority"; see http://www.loc.gov/standards/mods/v3/mods-userguide-elements.html#language for additional information).

Example:

```
<language>
  <languageTerm type="code" authority="iso639-2b">eng</languageTerm>
</language>
```

<classification> with the attribute "authority" indicates the type of classification scheme used to provide subject access to the resource.

Example:

```
<classification authority="lcc">G1796.S6$bJ65 1820</classification>
```

<name> provides information on name of a person, organization, or event (conference, meeting, etc.) associated with the resource. This element has a "type" attribute to specify the type of name (personal, corporate, or conference) and an "authority" attribute to enable catalogers to specify what authoritative source was consulted to provide the authorized form of the name. This element also has a subelement <role> to specify the role of the named person, corporate body, or conference in relation to the resource.

Example:

```
<name type="personal">
  <role>
    <roleTerm type="text">cartographer</roleTerm>
  </role>

<name type="corporate">
  <namePart>Rand-McNally Press</namePart>
</name>
```

<titleInfo> conveys the title or name of a resource. When the main portion of the title is referenced as core, there is only one core subelement, <title>.

Example:

```
<titleInfo>
<title>Jersey shore vacation map</title>
</titleInfo>
```

Use <titleInfo> with the type="alternative" and the subelement <title> to convey title variations.

Example:

```
</titleInfo><titleInfo type="alternative">
<title>Shadowlands</title>
</titleInfo>
```

<originInfo> with the subelement <edition> describes the version or edition of the resource being described.

Example:

```
<originInfo>
  <edition>7th ed.</edition>
</originInfo>
```

<originInfo> with the subelement <place> and its subelement <placeTerm> with type="text," the subelement <publisher>, and the subelement <dateIssued> provides information on publication, distribution, etc.

(Cont'd.)

MODS CHECKLIST *(Continued)*

<physicalDescription> with the subelements <form> and <extent> provides descriptive information about the resource. In this text the authoritative source for <form> (used to describe the resource's physical description) is MARC format and is documented in the subelement; see the following example. The subelement <extent> describes the number and types of units that make up a resource.

Example:

```
<physicalDescription>
  <form authority="marcform">map</form>
  <extent>2 sheets</extent>
</physicalDescription>
<physicalDescription>
  <form authority="marcform">map</form>
  <extent>400 pages : ill. ; 32 cm.</extent>
</physicalDescription>
```

<relatedItem> with the attribute type "series" provides information on the series to which a cartographic resource belongs.

Example:

```
<relatedItem type="series">
  <titleInfo>
    <title>Collection africaine</title>
  </titleInfo>
</relatedItem>
```

<note> provides general information about the cartographic resource.

Example:

```
<note>Shows plats, section by section, lot dimensions, named streets and railroad lines, surrounding areas and bodies of water, and restrictions contained in all deeds of conveyance.</note>

<note>Plastic coated map is described as "easy to handle, easy to fold, durable--won't tear, and write on-wipe off."</note>
```

<subject> with the attribute type "authority" and the subelement <name> with the attribute " type" (personal, corporate, conference) provides information on the primary topics of the resource.

Example:

```
<subject>
<name type="personal">
<namePart>Burton, Richard Francis</namePart>
<namePart type="termsOfAddress">Sir</namePart>
<namePart type="date">1821-1890</namePart>
</subject>

<name type="corporate">
  <namePart>United States. Bureau of Labor Statistics</namePart>
</name>
```

FISO CHECKLIST

Having constructed the descriptive record, the cataloger may find it appropriate to review the description based on the *FRBR* principles: *find*, *identify*, *select*, *obtain*:

F—The potential user has to *find* the material.

I—The user should be able to *identify* the resource, distinguishing it from any similar item.

S—The user should be able to retrieve and *select* the material as the appropriate one for a specific purpose or task.

O—The record should help the user to *obtain* the material by giving information about its location and availability and any requirements for and/or conditions of use.

The following questions are helpful in rating the completed product:

- ❑ Does the description represent the resource accurately? Comprehensive resource description can be time-consuming, but it is worth the effort.
- ❑ Have all possible access points been made available?
- ❑ Have all variant titles been recorded?
- ❑ Have the names of cartographers, publishers, and others who have had some responsibility for compiling or preparing the resource been verified in established authority databases?
- ❑ Can any element or attribute benefit from additional exposure (such as being given title access or an explanatory note)?

Resources for Catalogers

Andrew, Paige G. 2003. *Cataloging Sheet Maps: The Basics.* Binghamton, NY: The Haworth Information Press.

Andrew, Paige, Susan Moore, Elizabeth Unger Mangan, Velma Parker, and Grace Welch. 2002. *Map Cataloging: Learning to Describe Cartographic Materials.* Chicago: Association for Library Collections & Technical Service (ALCTS).

Bertuca, David J. 2010. "Map Catalogers' Tool Box." State University of New York at Buffalo, University of Buffalo Libraries. Last updated April 6. http://library.buffalo.edu/maps/mapresources/map_cat_tools.php.

Moore, Susan M., and Lucinda M. Hall. 2001. "Map Cataloging: Learning the Basics." University of Northern Iowa. http://www.stonybrook.edu/libmap/basics.pdf.

Notes

1. American Library Association, Canadian Library Association, and CILIP: Chartered Institute of Library and Information Professionals. 2010. *RDA Toolkit*, "RDA Constituency Review," Glossary. ALA, CLA, and CILIP. Accessed June 22. http://www.rdatoolkit.org/constituencyreview.
2. American Library Association. 2005. *Anglo-American Cataloguing Rules*, 2nd ed. (2002 Revision with 2005 Update). Chicago: American Library Association. Accessed via Cataloger's Desktop April 28, 2010.
3. American Library Association, Canadian Library Association, and CILIP: Chartered Institute of Library and Information Professionals. 2010. *RDA Toolkit*, "RDA Constituency Review," Chapter 3, 3.5.2. ALA, CLA, and CILIP. Accessed June 22. http://www.rdatoolkit.org/constituencyreview.
4. Ibid., Chapter 2, 2.2.2.

5. Library of Congress. 2010. "MODS User Guidelines, Version 3: Detailed Description of MODS Elements." Library of Congress. Accessed June 22. http://www.loc.gov/standards/mods/v3/mods-userguide-elements.html#recordinfo.
6. Ibid.
7. American Library Association, Canadian Library Association, and CILIP: Chartered Institute of Library and Information Professionals. 2010. *RDA Toolkit*, "RDA Constituency Review," Chapter 2, 2.3. ALA, CLA, and CILIP. Accessed June 22. http://www.rdatoolkit.org/constituencyreview.
8. Ibid., Chapter 2, 2.2.2.1.
9. Ibid., Chapter 2, 2.3.2.8.2.
10. Library of Congress. 2010. "MODS User Guidelines, Version 3: Detailed Description of MODS Elements." Library of Congress. Accessed June 22. http://www.loc.gov/standards/mods/v3/mods-userguide-elements.html.
11. American Library Association, Canadian Library Association, and CILIP: Chartered Institute of Library and Information Professionals. 2010. *RDA Toolkit*, "RDA Constituency Review," Chapter 2, 2.3.6.3. ALA, CLA, and CILIP. Accessed June 22. http://www.rdatoolkit.org/constituencyreview.
12. Mangan, Elizabeth Unger. 2003. *Cartographic Materials: A Manual of Interpretation for AACR2*. 2002 revision. Chicago: American Library Association. Accessed via Cataloger's Desktop May 6, 2010.
13. American Library Association, Canadian Library Association, and CILIP: Chartered Institute of Library and Information Professionals. 2010. *RDA Toolkit*, "RDA Constituency Review," Chapter 7, 7.4.1.2. ALA, CLA, and CILIP. Accessed June 22. http://www.rdatoolkit.org/constituencyreview.
14. Mangan, Elizabeth Unger. 2003. *Cartographic Materials: A Manual of Interpretation for AACR2*. 2002 revision. Chicago: American Library Association. Accessed via Cataloger's Desktop May 6, 2010.
15. American Library Association, Canadian Library Association, and CILIP: Chartered Institute of Library and Information Professionals. 2010. *RDA Toolkit*, "RDA Constituency Review," Chapter 7, 7.5.1.1. ALA, CLA, and CILIP. Accessed June 22. http://www.rdatoolkit.org/constituencyreview.
16. International Federation of Library Associations and Institutions. 1997. *Functional Requirements for Bibliographic Records: Final Report* (as amended and corrected through February 2009), "4.3.2 Form of Expression." IFLA. http://www.ifla.org/files/cataloguing/frbr/frbr_2008.pdf.
17. American Library Association, Canadian Library Association, and CILIP: Chartered Institute of Library and Information Professionals. 2010. *RDA Toolkit*, "RDA Constituency Review," Chapter 6, 6.10.1.3. ALA, CLA, and CILIP. Accessed June 22. http://www.rdatoolkit.org/constituencyreview.
18. Ibid., Chapter 7, 7.4.
19. Ibid., Chapter 7, 7.25.
20. Ibid., Chapter 7, 7.25.5.1.
21. Ibid., Chapter 7, 7.25.5.3.
22. Reister, Jim. 2008. *Introduction to Topographic Maps*. Geospatial Training and Analysis Cooperative. http://geology.isu.edu/geostac/Field_Exercise/topomaps/grid_assign.htm.
23. Library of Congress, Network Development and MARC Standards Office. 2010. "MARC 21 Format for Bibliographic Data: 3XX: Physical Description, Etc. Fields—General Information." Library of Congress. http://www.loc.gov/marc/bibliographic/bd3xx.html.
24. American Library Association, Canadian Library Association, and CILIP: Chartered Institute of Library and Information Professionals. 2010. *RDA*

Toolkit, "RDA Constituency Review," Chapter 3, 3.5.2.5. ALA, CLA, and CILIP. Accessed June 22. http://www.rdatoolkit.org/constituencyreview.
25. Ibid., Chapter 3, 3.6.1.
26. Ibid., Chapter 11, 11.2.2.1.
27. Ibid., Chapter 11, 11.2.2.2.
28. Ibid., Chapter 11, 11.2.2.4.
29. Library of Congress. 2010. "MODS User Guidelines, Version 3: Detailed Description of MODS Elements." Library of Congress. Accessed June 22. http://www.loc.gov/standards/mods/v3/mods-userguide-elements.html#recordinfo.
30. Dublin Core Metadata Initiative. 2008. "Dublin Core Metadata Element Set, Version 1.1." DCMI. http://dublincore.org/documents/dces.
31. Library of Congress. 2010. "MODS User Guidelines, Version 3: Detailed Description of MODS Elements." Library of Congress. Accessed June 22. http://www.loc.gov/standards/mods/v3/mods-userguide-elements.html#recordinfo.
32. Library of Congress. 2000. "Subclass G (Cartographic Materials)—Special Instructions and Tables of Subdivisions." Library of Congress. http://www.loc.gov/catdir/cpso/class_g.html.
33. Library of Congress, Network Development and MARC Standards Office. 2010. "MARC 21 Format for Bibliographic Data: 052—Geographic Classification." Available: http://www.loc.gov/marc/bibliographic/bd052.html.
34. American Library Association, Canadian Library Association, and CILIP: Chartered Institute of Library and Information Professionals. 2010. *RDA Toolkit*, "RDA Constituency Review," Chapter 24, 24.1.3. ALA, CLA, and CILIP. Accessed June 22. http://www.rdatoolkit.org/constituencyreview.
35. Ibid., Chapter 25.
36. Ibid., Chapter 7, 7.2.1.1.
37. Ibid., Chapter 7, 7.27.1.

Sound Recordings

IN THIS CHAPTER:

Overview

The variety of carriers on which sound recordings are now available was inconceivable when the first edition of this manual was published. Sound recordings, both musical and nonmusical, can now be downloaded from the Internet onto portable electronic devices or carriers capable of storing vast amounts of data.

The miniaturization of electronic carriers makes it possible for almost everyone to have a portable music library that can be carried in a pocket or around the neck. Both options are not only possible but seem to be preferred by many people as the popularity of MP3 players and other such devices continues to increase. The embrace of portability does not mean that all music buffs have abandoned the familiar discs: CDs *and* vinyl LPs are still collected and treasured and show no signs of imminent demise. Many purists remain convinced that nothing rivals the quality and integrity of sound produced by high-end stereophonic and/or digital playback equipment, and music copyright issues have had an impact on the freedom with which downloadable music from sites such as iTunes and Napster is available. Nevertheless, for the most mundane uses, downloadable music has found its way into the mainstream and is extremely popular, particularly with the younger generation. Although downloadable music is available for free via websites such as the Creative Commons and Wikipedia Music, to name a few, limitations imposed by digital rights management (DRM) have converted some former "downloaders" into listeners and/or borrowers, and a growing number of libraries now provide access to downloadable audio either independently or through a vendor, such as OverDrive.

The hybrid CD/DVD carrier, gaining in popularity with publishers and users alike, presents new challenges for the cataloger faced with describing resources published via these carriers. Another hybrid carrier, the Playaway, made its debut in 2005 and has revolutionized the audiobooks industry, irrevocably bonding content and carrier and eliminating concerns about proprietary readers and file compatibility. Because the

Playaway is considered both an audiobook and an electronic resource, its description must reflect its hybrid nature.

In addition, recorded books, known popularly as *audiobooks*, have evolved into recordings suitable for playback on MP3 players, iPods, iPhones, and similar devices that require specific file formats such as MP3 and Windows Media Audiofile (WMA) technology for playback, making compatibility a critical factor in the selection of these resources. Along with downloadable music and recorded books, some libraries offer connections to websites where patrons can listen to music in real time or to recorded conference proceedings and speeches via streaming audio in the library or on a home computer. It is also anticipated that many libraries will continue to add locally produced audio recordings such as taped oral histories and recorded speeches to their collections.

The description of a sound recording should answer, with the same clarity as that of textual resources, any questions that a user may have when trying to determine the identity and validity of the resource. The potential user should be able to *find*, *identify*, *select*, and *obtain* the resource with the least amount of frustration and inconvenience, and the caliber of the resource description is critical to the success of this endeavor. The most common types of sound recording likely to be encountered in today's libraries are examined in detail in this chapter, and the elements and/or characteristics that are unique to specific types of sound recordings are highlighted in the annotated examples. Descriptive elements that are common to all types of resources are reviewed in Chapter 1 of this manual.

Important Considerations

Access

As libraries face the reality of dwindling budgets, the acquisition of resources is usually the first area to experience detailed scrutiny. Librarians continue to debate the cost-effectiveness and wisdom of acquiring resources that are freely available outside of the library. Sound recordings present special challenges regarding the appropriateness of limits and boundaries of content delivery, while concerns about the restrictions imposed by Digital Rights Management (DRM)[1] and the Digital Millennium Copyright Act (DMCA)[2] further complicate the acquisition and accessibility of sound recordings and other digital and online media.

Though providing sound recordings for patrons is not a new phenomenon for most libraries, the current environment is such that the proliferation of content, the miniaturization of carriers, the ease and facility with which content can be copied and/or downloaded onto personal electronic devices, and the speed with which all of this can be accomplished have introduced a new sense of urgency and distrust within the community of stakeholders regarding rights, royalties, and compliance.

Digital Rights Management

Working with sound recordings, particularly those that can be downloaded from the Internet, requires some understanding of DRM, which refers to software that is designed to control or limit how a file can be played, copied, downloaded, shared, or accessed. Such information may be displayed on the resource itself and, if present, must be displayed in the resource description so that the user can comply with the terms of the agreement. Digital rights information can be entered as a note in each record, or it can be posted alongside the record or in a prominent area of the library's website. Figure 3.1, a screen print taken from the

Figure 3.1. Examples of Digital Rights Information Records

OverDrive Music		
This title can be played during the lending period.		
Collaborative play of this title is not allowed.		
This title cannot be burned to CD.		
This title can be transferred to a portable device during the lending period.		
All copies of this title, including those transferred to portable devices and other media, must be deleted/destroyed at the end of the lending period.		
eNYPL Music		
Transfer to Device:	Allowed	
Burn to CD:	Not allowed by publisher	
Playing Rights:	Can be played on a PC for duration of lending period	
Collaborative Play:	Not allowed by publisher	
All copies of this title, including those transferred to portable devices and other media, must be deleted/destroyed at the end of the lending period		
Excerpt:	Friday night (WMA format)	
Copies available:	1	
Copies owned:	1	
Lending period:	21 days	
File size:	18994 KB	**Plays on:**
Number of parts:	1	PC Mac
Duration:	40 minutes	
Software version:	OverDrive Media Console 1.0 or later	Burn to CD WMA
ISBN:		
Release date:	Jan 22, 2008	iPod MP3

New York Public Library's website, provides a good example of individual postings for each record. As shown, each record includes a chart containing the rights owner's name and indicates, through the use of universal symbols, the type of equipment required for playback.

In response to market demand, the availability of DRM-free audio is gaining in popularity among music and audiobook publishers. However, a few words of caution are appropriate here. DRM-free does not mean copyright-free,[3] and, in the current environment where the conversation about ownership, rights, and protection is becoming increasingly louder, it is expected that the inclusion of rights information will eventually become mandatory for resource description. Based on the current BIBCO Core Record standards (located at http://www.loc.gov/catdir/pcc/bibco/coresr.html), the inclusion of such information is not mandatory. Similarly, rights information is not regarded as a core element of description in *RDA* even though this information can be accommodated in MARC, MODS, and DC at the present time. In the MARC format, rights information may be recorded in the MARC fields 542 (Information Relating to Copyright Status), 540 (Terms Governing Use and Reproduction Note), and 038 (Record Content Licensor). Rights information is often already included for most resources in metadata schemes such as MODS, where it is provided in the respective MODS elements <originInfo> (copyright information), <accessCondition> qualified by "type="useAndReproduction," and <name> qualified by "type" personal and the subelement "role" with the term "licensor." Rights information is provided in the DC element <Rights>.

Musical versus Nonmusical

Determining whether a resource is a musical or nonmusical sound recording is the first step the cataloger takes toward selecting appropriate descriptive metadata. In the current multimedia environment primary content is not always easily discernible and nonmusical sound recordings can include musical interludes, as in the case of poetry read to or interspersed with light background music. All aspects of the content must be revealed in the resource description.

Reproductions

Resource description for sound recordings requires a thorough understanding of the concepts of *version* and *interpretation*. Each sound recording begins as an original work or composition, but, in almost every category of music, reproductions abound. Newer renditions, interpretations, and rearrangements of original works by various composers and/or performers are commonplace. Re-mastered recordings and re-recordings of classical and popular compositions, particularly those in the public domain, are also categorized as musical reproductions. The concepts of version and interpretation assume some relationship between an original work and its various expressions and manifestations. Delineating the relationship between a specific work and other expressions and/or manifestations of the work is vitally important to resource discovery. When the cataloger has determined that the resource in hand is a different expression or manifestation of an existing work, this recognition should trigger a number of steps dedicated to the capture of critical elements of description and differentiation. In the absence of an "FRBRized" catalog,[4] the inclusion of information about other expressions and/or manifestations of the work should be integral to resource description, as related resources often provide valuable supplementary information.

Based on current trends, noted especially in public libraries, some argue that full cataloging for certain types of downloadable books and music is unnecessary. Today, libraries can contract with vendors to provide access to these types of resources either through A–Z lists or by accepting descriptive records from the vendor for load into the library's ILS. The quality of the vendor-supplied records should be reviewed and options for MARC and non-MARC metadata explored. It is also important to consider and anticipate the needs and overall preference of users and potential users and to use this information prudently. One also has to recognize the impact of such decisions on staff time and the requirement for cataloging expertise if the library opts to provide in-house cataloging (resource description). Answers to the following questions can help to guide a library's decision regarding the description and use of sound recordings:

- Is the resource restricted by a license?
- Is access to the content free for every user?
- With regard to tangible resources, should the library own the equipment required for playback? Or is the collection meant exclusively for external circulation?
- Should the library provide access to downloadable content that is readily available elsewhere? DRM and/or licensing agreements may prohibit or limit downloads.
- Should the library consider providing access to audio recordings via a consortium to eliminate maintenance of the descriptive records?
- Who is the typical user of the resource? Can this user gain ready access to the resource outside of the library?

Once the decision has been made to acquire sound recordings, catalogers must be prepared to invest the time required to provide detailed resource description. Providing appropriate access to these resources generally becomes the overarching issue for catalogers, and careful attention to detail will ensure that a seemingly minor detail is recorded because it may be *the* critical piece of information that distinguishes one version of a work from the other. Recording the information as it appears on the resource, with careful attention to spelling, is especially important because poetic license is more readily embraced in the artistic community. Names of performers and the titles of their works are particularly vulnerable. Ample resources are available via the Internet where catalogers can obtain and/or verify information about practically any recording and/or those responsible for its production. Most publishers maintain websites through which they advertise and/or review the works they publish or produce. Commercial websites such as Allmusic.com and Amazon.com also contain helpful information.

RDA gives catalogers more freedom to add or omit information when constructing the descriptive record, based on their judgment. It is hoped that, given this freedom, catalogers will take into account the needs and expectations of users and potential users. In the effort to enhance resource description, some libraries now attach colorful images (images of the dust jacket of books or images of the containers for audio recordings, for example) to the descriptive record. When a library's resources include musical sound recordings, this practice can be taken a step further by adding links to publishers' or vendors' websites where the user can listen to samples of specific tunes and soundtracks, if desired. Such websites usually include the option to purchase and download a single soundtrack or an entire album for immediate use. Providing access to such options enhances the resource discovery experience for the user.

Specialized music libraries or libraries that serve music programs in colleges and universities will most likely face additional challenges based on the nature of their clientele and collections, factors that will have a definite impact on the level and detail of description given to this category of resources. This chapter is not directed toward the specialized music cataloger but seeks instead to offer guidance to the cataloger who occasionally creates descriptive records for sound recordings.

Resource Description

Resource description for sound recordings can be a rewarding activity that becomes less challenging for catalogers who take the time to understand and, when necessary, research the information found on the resource so that they can present it accurately. The newer hybrid resources may initially present a challenge; however, it is easier to capture and describe all essential elements of hybrids by viewing them as two distinct components that comprise the whole.

Work

A work is represented by its description. Representation is achieved through packaging, publicity, publishers' notes, etc. As catalogers, we also represent (re-present) the work by our description, our choice of descriptive metadata, our choice of access points, and the information to which we give prominence in the notes we construct. Re-presenting the work seeks to introduce it, afresh, to the user or potential user who may be unaware of its existence but who may discover the work because of the cataloger's skillful use of metadata. In representing the work, the cataloger must give appropriate credit to those responsible for creating the work and must accurately record its title and describe the physical characteristics and manifestation of the work sufficiently so that a potential user can readily identify it. Preliminary questions about the work include:

- What type of resource is being described? A musical composition or performed music?
- How does the resource present itself? What is its title?
- Does the resource consist primarily of sound or spoken words? Or is it a combination of spoken words and sound or musical notes? The type of resource must be clearly stated in the description.
- What subject matter is discussed, and what is the creator trying to communicate?
- Can the creator be readily identified?

Although most musical recordings are collaborative productions, *RDA* 18.3 requires recording only the creator having principal responsibility for the work as the access point for the work and in the statement of responsibility:

> When recording relationships between a resource and persons, families, and corporate bodies associated with that resource, include as a minimum all of the following elements listed below that are applicable and readily ascertainable.
>
> - Creator (if more than one, only the creator having principal responsibility named first in resources embodying the work or in reference sources is required; if principal responsibility is not indicated, only the first-named creator is required)
> - Other person, family or corporate body associated with a work

Optionally, other persons/organizations that have contributed significantly to the content or creative aspects of the work may be recorded in the statement of responsibility or notes area and as additional access points, which should include the appropriate relationship designators to specify relationship to the work.

Access points can be personal, corporate, or title depending on the nature of the work. A preferred access point is constructed using the preferred (authorized) name of the responsible person or persons and/or the preferred title of the work. The preferred title of a musical work is a core element of description and is addressed in *RDA* 6.14.2. The individual or entity responsible for the artistic or intellectual content of the work is referred to as the personal/corporate author and is considered the main entry in *AACR2*. *RDA* has opted for the term "creator," a very important access point for any type of work.

Using *AACR2*, the selection of "main entry" for sound recordings is not as clear-cut as it may seem. The main entry may be the performer rather than the creator, as is often the case for pop music and music albums. *RDA* and *AACR2* both require the cataloger to establish a preferred access point representing the creator of the work, though *RDA* further suggests that the first named on the resource is the only name required both for preferred access and in the statement of responsibility.

EXAMPLE 3.1

Amadei, Filippo, flourished 1690–1730
Bononcini, Antonio Maria, 1677–1726
Handel, George Frideric, 1685–1759

Preferred access points representing the creators for:

The most favorite songs in the opera of Muzio Scaevola / compos'd by three famous masters. The composers are Amadei, Bononcini, and Handel.

Note: Based on *RDA* 19.2.1.3 (Recording creators), the three composers are all listed as preferred access points representing the creator(s) because the work was "compos'd by three famous masters."

QUICK TIP

All names used in the descriptive record must be authorized and should reflect the preferred names of those responsible for or associated with the work.

The essential difference between *AACR2* and *RDA* regarding access points for the work is that the former requires the cataloger to think in terms of a single "main entry" and added entries. *AACR2* also requires a title "main entry" when the number of responsible persons exceeds the "rule of three." The selection process has been simplified in *RDA*. Although the cataloger must still determine who bears principal responsibility for the work, all who have made significant contributions to the work may be recorded both in the statement of responsibility and as access points (where use of the appropriate relationship designator is required). *RDA* does not require a single main entry but does require the cataloger to select the responsible person or persons based on the extent of creative contribution and other established criteria, allowing that there may be several persons, each of whom is equally responsible for the creation of the work (see Example 3.1, from *RDA* 19.2.1.3: Recording creators).[5]

Depending on the level of resource description and at the cataloger's discretion all responsible persons, including co-creators and/or others bearing primary responsibility for the work, may be recorded in the statement of responsibility, where use of the abbreviation "et al." is prohibited. *RDA* allows for an unlimited number of personal access points for the work provided that those named share principal responsibility for the work (these are listed as preferred access points) and/or that they are recorded in the statement of responsibility (which may include other responsible persons who may be selected as additional access points). The appropriate relationship designators must be used for all parties and must be selected from *RDA* Appendix I.

RDA Chapter 6 (Identifying Works and Expressions) describes every aspect of the identification process that is designed to reveal the unique nature of the work, its title, and its content type (as defined in *RDA* 6.10.1.3, Table 6.1) and can be consulted for additional information regarding access points. See *RDA* Chapter 19 for additional information about the identification of responsible persons or corporate bodies associated with a work and *RDA* 18.5.1 for basic instructions on recording relationship designators.

Preferred Title

One of the important tasks of the cataloger is to decide on the preferred title of the work. Unlike tangible resources, whose contents can be visually inspected, sound recording contents cannot. The cataloger must rely on the title, generally found on the label of the work, and on other information found on the resource and/or in accompanying material such as program notes and/or summaries.

When choosing the preferred title, the *AACR2* rules for the description of sound recordings (Chapter 6.0B1) make it clear that textual data affixed to the resource or its carrier is preferred. The resource itself, including the carrier and any affixed label, is the chief source of information. If both of these fail to present a clearly identifiable title for the entire work, use accompanying textual data, giving preference to textual information rather than that acquired orally.[6] *RDA* supports these requirements (*RDA* 2.2.2.1; 2.2.2.4) but also stipulates that the preferred title can be taken from *any* source, specifically resources embodying the work or reference sources.[7]

If the work consists of a collection of multiple discs without a collective title, or when each disc has a distinctive title, data from accompanying material may be used to construct a title when appropriate language suggestive of a title is found on the resource. In both cases, prefer to use the collective title on the container if there is one. Alternatively, for resources lacking a collective title the cataloger may list each title separately and provide additional access points for the individual titles in the resource description (*RDA* 2.3.2.9 and *AACR2* Chapter 6.1G2).

Rule 1.1B1 in *AACR2* instructs catalogers to transcribe the "title proper" exactly as to wording, order, and spelling but not necessarily as to capitalization and punctuation. *RDA* requires the cataloger to record information exactly as presented on the resource, in the language of its content, and prohibits the use of abbreviations unless found on the resource (see *RDA* 6.2.1 and *RDA* Appendix B for additional information).

Enter the preferred title in the MARC 245 field, subfield $a, which is not repeatable. Record it in the MODS element <title> and the DC element <Title>.

As with all resources, it is important to record the title accurately because it is one of the resource's primary access points.

Variant Title

Variant titles may be found on the resource or in the accompanying material. When an alternate title, or information that can be construed as an alternate title, is found on the resource the cataloger must provide this alternate or variant title in the descriptive record. Enter variant titles in the MARC 246 field, the MODS element <title> with the attribute type "alternative," and the DC element <Title>. *AACR2* requires providing access to variant or other titles, but *RDA* does not consider the variant title to be a core element.[8]

Although not mandatory for sound recordings, a cataloger may prefer to use a "source of title" note if the preferred title is taken from any source other than the resource itself. "When choosing a preferred source of information, treat both the storage medium (e.g., paper, tape, or film) and any housing (e.g., a cassette or cartridge) that is integral to the resource as part of the resource itself."[9] If information for the title is taken from any source other than the resource itself, or if constructed by the cataloger, a "source of title note" should be entered in the MARC 500 field (for general notes) or in the MODS element <note>, and the DC element <Description>.

The content and type of content (genre or form of work) are both essential elements of the work that facilitate the assignment of the appropriate subject terms, which should be taken from an authorized thesaurus or list. *RDA* Chapter 6, Table 6.1, identifies the content types for sound recordings as "performed music," "sounds," and "spoken word," and catalogers are encouraged to use as many types as necessary to describe the resource sufficiently. If the content type of the resource cannot be readily ascertained, *RDA* instructs the cataloger to record "unspecified." Use "other" when *RDA* Table 6.1 does not provide an appropriate content type (*RDA* 6.9.1.3). *RDA* 6.3.1.3 addresses the form of the work.

Performed Music

With regard to performed music, the guidelines found in *AACR2* are more precise that those given in *RDA*. *AACR2* Chapter 21.23C1 specifies, "If a sound recording containing works by different persons or bodies has a collective title, enter it under the heading for the person or body represented as principal performer." Popular music albums fall into this category because they are generally compilations of works by different composers produced under a collective title.

Alternatively, a performer whose role is strictly limited to the *performance* of a single work or a collection of works by a single composer cannot be considered the creator principally responsible for the work, which must be ascribed to the composer. A sound recording that consists of a single work must be entered under the heading appropriate to that work, generally the heading for the creator (*AACR2* Chapter 21.23A1).

AACR2 Rule 6.1F1 instructs catalogers to enter a person or entity named in the chief or preferred source of information in the statement of responsibility "if the participation of the person(s) or body (bodies) named in a statement found in the chief source of information goes beyond that of performance, execution, or interpretation of a work." This rule continues by stating, "if participation is confined to performance, execution or interpretation (as is commonly the case with 'serious' or classical music and recorded speech), give the statement of contribution in the note area." This last instruction requires the cataloger to determine the extent and significance of the contributions of those responsible for the creation of the work. Moreover, the performer or interpreter, if well known and/or popular, may be prominently mentioned on the resource although limited in responsibility to that of performer. In such cases, the cataloger may use "cataloger's judgment" to record the performer in the statement of responsibility, clearly identifying his or her role as that of performer. The cataloger may also create an authorized access point under this name, with the addition of the appropriate relationship designator.

Simply put, *AACR2* mandates the following:

- Select the composer as the creator of a single work. Record the composer in the statement of responsibility area and provide the appropriate authorized access point. Performers can be referenced in the statement of responsibility and recorded in the note area and as additional access points, when appropriate.
- Select the performer as the "main entry" when the performance is that of a compilation of works by different composers and/or writers produced under a single title. The performer takes

precedence as the vocalist/performer responsible for the expression of the work. This is particularly applicable to popular music (rock, rhythm and blues albums, etc.) where miscellaneous works are compiled, performed, and produced under a collective title.

RDA supports these requirements (*RDA* 6.28.1.2 and 20.2.1.3) but allows all co-creators and persons bearing primary responsibility for the work to be acknowledged as access points.

Additionally, *RDA* 7.23.1.3 echoes the basic rule regarding performers (*AACR2* Chapter 6.1F1) and requires the cataloger to record "the names of performers, narrators, and/or presenters, if they are considered to be important. For performers of music, indicate the medium in which each performs." *RDA* 19.2.1.1 further suggests that the performer be acknowledged as a co-creator in a collaborative work between two or more persons performing different roles, as shown in Example 3.2 (from *RDA* 19.2.1.1).

Both *AACR2*[10] and *RDA*[11] have established the composer as the individual bearing principal responsibility for a musical work except in cases of compilations including works by various composers and in cases where miscellaneous musical selections, with or without a collective title, are performed by one or more persons.

Alternatively, a performance can include a variety of compositions by different composers and/or include various singers and/or musicians. If no single performer or composer can be identified as the person responsible for the work, the performers, singers, and/or musicians who perform together may be listed in the statement of responsibility if they are prominently mentioned on the resource. They can also be recorded in the performer notes area in the order that they are listed on the resource, depending on the extent and significance of their contribution to the work. It is also possible to record the name of a musical group as the preferred responsible party if the group performance is significant. Appropriately, the composers responsible for the work must be given credit as songwriters and should be listed as additional access points and in the notes area of the record.[12]

A general rule of thumb, therefore, is to select the performer or performers as primarily responsible for the creation/production of a work that includes musical selections, by various composers, performed by a single individual, a group, or individuals performing different tasks, as shown in Example 3.2.

A good example of performed music where the performer is selected as the primary responsible person is the album *Music Box* by Mariah Carey (see Example 3.3). The album includes miscellaneous musical selections composed by various composers but sung by a single performer. Mariah Carey is prominently identified as the principal performer and is given credit as such. Mariah Carey is important to this work primarily because the sound recording contains works by different composers, under a collective title (*AACR2*

EXAMPLE 3.2

Elling, Kurt
Hobgood, Laurence
Amster, Rob
Raynor, Michael

Authorized access points representing the creators for:

Live in Chicago / Kurt Elling. -- Kurt Elling, vocals; Laurence Hobgood, piano; Rob Amster, bass; Michael Raynor, drums, percussion. Jazz performances of songs by various composers.

QUICK TIP

Catalogers using the MARC format are required to select a "main entry" which is entered in the MARC 1XX field or, when appropriate, in the MARC 245 field as the "title main entry." Co-creators and persons equally responsible for the creation or production of the work must be entered in the MARC 7XX fields for "added entries." *RDA* does not require the cataloger to choose a single "main entry." Catalogers using various metadata schemas may enter as many creators as required in the appropriate field used for creators. All co-creators and persons bearing primary responsibility for the work may be acknowledged as access points for the work.

EXAMPLE 3.3

```
100 1_ Carey, Mariah. $e Performer $2 rda.
245 10 Music box / $c by Mariah Carey.

<name type="personal">
  <namePart>Carey, Mariah</namePart>
  <displayForm>Mariah Carey
</displayForm>
  <role>
    <roleTerm
type="text">performer</roleTerm>
  </role>
</name>
<titleInfo>
  <title>Music box</title>
</titleInfo>

<Contributor>Carey, Mariah</Contributor>
<Title>Music box</Title>
```

Chapter 21.23C1), sung primarily by Maria Carey who is the featured singer in each selection on the album.

Mariah Carey was selected as the responsible person, and the appropriate "relator code" was entered after her name. The preferred form of her name (authorized form) was recorded in the MARC 100 field and in the statement of responsibility. A list of relator codes is available at http://www.loc.gov/marc/relators/relaterm.html and also in *RDA* Appendix I.

Note: Entry under popular name or pseudonym has been authorized in *RDA* 9.2.2.3, a change that was influenced by the argument that users will generally use the popular name of performers in search queries. Performers are known for using stage names, and this is especially true for performers in popular, jazz, and rap music, etc. An authority record taken from the Library of Congress Authority File is shown in Example 3.4. The MARC format is used for this entry. The performer is widely known as *Babyface*, the name that is used on all of his albums. Recording this name as the preferred name for this performer guarantees that his fans will find all records composed or performed by him.

EXAMPLE 3.4

100 0_ $a Babyface $c (Musician)
400 1_ $a Edmonds, Kenneth
400 0_ $a Baby Face $c (Musician)
400 1_ $a Edmonds, Kenny
670 __ $a His Tender lover [SR] p1989: $b label (Babyface)

Interpreted Music

The *Nutcracker Suite* was not originally written as a jazz score. However, the version of the work illustrated in Example 3.5 is still recognizable as Tchaikovsky's work, and as such Tchaikovsky must be given credit as the creator of the work.

This work was rearranged by Duke Ellington, a well-known jazz artist who "altered" the work in his unique way and who is prominently listed on the resource. Ellington therefore deserves recognition in the statement of responsibility for his significant role in the production of this particular version of the work and must also be entered as an additional access point for the work. Example 3.5 also illustrates the use of the preferred title in unifying different versions of a work.

EXAMPLE 3.5

Preferred access point: Tchaikovsky, Peter Ilich, 1840-1893.

Preferred title: Shchelkunchik. Selections; arr.

Title and statement of responsibility: The nutcracker suite / Duke Ellington.

Additional access point: Ellington, Duke.

The Harlem Nutcracker, another work that is based on Tchaikovsky's *Nutcracker*, in which Duke Ellington collaborated with others, is an example of a work that has been considerably altered, thus requiring that it be considered a new work. *The Harlem Nutcracker* is *based* on Tchaikovsky's *Nutcracker Suite* but has largely been rescored and retitled by Duke Ellington, Billy Strayhorn, and David Berger, who are the creators of the "new" work (see Example 3.6).

EXAMPLE 3.6

Preferred access points: Ellington, Duke; Strayhorn, Billy; Berger, David.

Preferred title: The Harlem Nutcracker

Statement of responsibility: Duke Ellington, Billy Strayhorn, David Berger; based on themes by Peter Illyich Tchaikovsky.

Additional access point: Tchaikovsky, Peter Ilich, 1840-1893. Shchelkunchik. Suite. Selections; arr.

Based on the significant alteration of the content, the work must be considered an adapted work and as such Duke Ellington, Billy Strayhorn, and David Berger are considered the creators/composers of the new work and are the preferred access points for the work according to *RDA* 6.28.1.5.2 (Adaptations).

Composed Music

For musical compositions, the composer or songwriter is generally considered the primary person responsible for the intellectual work. The performance of the work, by an orchestra or pianist, requires access under the composer as creator (principal responsible person) with additional access points for the orchestra and/or other performer(s) (see Example 3.7).

The same concept generally applies for sound recordings that are primarily opera and musicals. The music was written to be performed, and the composer is generally the creator, although sometimes assisted by others. Musicals and/or selections of musicals are also entered under the songwriter or creator responsible for the musical, and principal performers are given credit as performers, singers, etc. For example, Verdi is credited as the creator responsible for the composition of his operas and is the primary and preferred access point for his work. Performers are treated as additional access points for his work.

Exception: Miscellaneous works by various composers performed by an orchestra must be entered under the name of the orchestra in the absence of a single composer responsible for the work. The names of the various composers may be entered as additional access points for the work and/or in the notes or listing of the contents, at the discretion of the cataloger. The same applies to selections from various operas sung by a performer. The performer must be entered as the responsible person, the primary and preferred access point for the work.

As a general rule, whoever is important enough to be conspicuously mentioned on the resource should be considered an important contributor to the work. *AACR2* (21.6B1) instructs catalogers to "transcribe statements of responsibility relating to those persons or bodies credited with a major role in creating the intellectual content of the sound recording (e.g., as writers of spoken words, composers of performed music, producers having artistic and/or intellectual responsibility) as instructed in 1.1F." Typography can also be used in determining which name(s) to record in the statement of responsibility (*AACR2*, 21.6B1). *RDA* suggests that persons bearing equal responsibility for the creation of the work may be listed in the statement of responsibility at the cataloger's discretion. Only the first named is required. All others related to the work can be given credit if deemed important access points.

Record the statement of responsibility in subfield $c of the MARC 245 field. List all others, including additional performers and producers, etc., in the notes area of the record with specific mention as to their roles (performer, vocalist, etc.) in the production of the work. Record this information in the MODS element <name> with the attribute "type" to specify personal name and the subelement <role> to specify the role of the person in relation to the resource. In DC, use the element <Contributor> to signal that the added personal names are of people who made some contribution to the creation of the resource.

Expression

When various expressions of a work have been identified, the description of each expression must highlight the elements that distinguish it from the others. Different versions of a work are considered different expressions of the work if the content or form has been altered. The concept of "version" was discussed earlier in this chapter, and its importance as

EXAMPLE 3.7

Creator (preferred access point): Chopin, Frédéric, 1810-1849.

Role term: composer.

Title: Chopin: the complete preludes

Statement of responsibility: performed by Rafał Blechacz.

Additional access point: Blechacz, Rafał.

Role term: performer.

an element of distinction was emphasized. Differentiation is an essential *FRBR* requirement.[13]

Sound recordings are particularly susceptible to interpretation by several different performers and singers. Audiobooks, although not as susceptible to artistic reinterpretation, can be abridged, summarized, or annotated. Alternatively, one version may contain additional intonation, may be read by more than one person, and/or may be read for a special occasion. The audio recording or its accompanying material may contain an edition or version statement that generally signals differences in the contents of the resource. Information about the edition or version of a work must be recorded in the MARC 250 field, which is not repeatable, using "version," "revision," or any other term authorized in *AACR2* and/or *RDA* in the description. This type of information is entered in the "version" or edition area of the various metadata schemes. Additional information about the version of the resource can be recorded in the general notes area.

See Also...
Edition (Chapter 1, pp. 41–43)

The terms "expression" and "version" merit definitions here because they are often used interchangeably in library literature. Chapter 3.2.2 (pp. 19–21) in the *FRBR* document (www.ifla.org/publications/functional-requirements-for-bibliographic-records) clarifies that an "expression" of a specific work *excludes variations in physical form*: "The boundaries of the entity *expression* are defined, however, so as to exclude aspects of physical form, such as typeface and page layout, that are not integral to the intellectual or artistic realization of the *work* as such." "Expression" as a term used in resource description originated in the *FRBR* document that has been adopted by, and has provided the basis for, *RDA*.[14]

"Version" has been used liberally by publishers over the years to describe a different "run" or production of a specific work and is generally ascribed to expressions of a specific work not necessarily in the same genre or format. In *RDA*'s glossary "version" refers the user to the following explanation: "A characteristic other than content type, language of expression, or date of expression that serves to differentiate an expression from another expression of the same work." Both definition and explanation may be interpreted to mean that the term "version" may also be used to refer to or include differences in physical manifestation.

A different version or expression of a work may include adaptations, enhancements, or abridgements or may distinguish between a live recording that includes audience participation and the studio recording of the same work, all of which indicate variations in the content of the work. For sound recordings, the reissue or reproduction of a specific work by a different publisher or performer or in a different recording format (digital rather than analog, for example) constitutes a different manifestation of the work if the content has not been altered. A good rule of thumb is to associate an "expression" of a work with its content. When the term "version" is used, the cataloger must be wary since "version" may be applied to both differences in content (expression) and physical manifestation, the physical embodiment of the work generally via its carrier (the audio disc or Internet in the case of sound recordings).

Another term that requires careful analysis is the word "interpretation." Used in relation to musical recordings the word "Interpreted" or "Interpretation" connotes the understanding or perception that artists or performers have of their own or others' work—the intellectual content of the work. Generally, in undertaking the interpretation of a work, artists or performers have determined that the content of a specific work needs to be viewed or heard in a particular way to be appreciated and/or understood, or they simply want to challenge the user to acknowledge another viewpoint. The "interpreted" work reflects the way in which the "interpreter" wants listeners to perceive or be influenced by the work. Depending on the extent of interpretation and/or improvisation, the interpreted work may be considered a different expression of the work (where the creator of the original work is still considered the creator) or an entirely *new* work requiring the cataloger to name the person or performer responsible for the interpretation as the creator of the new work. It is important to note that the role of the interpreter and the identification of the individual with "principal responsibility" for the work are issues that stakeholders within the library community continue to closely review. They have acknowledged the need for more precise guidelines regarding this area because it generally presents several challenges for the occasional music cataloger faced with different expressions or versions of a work. During the period of public comment for *RDA*, The Association for Recorded Sound Collections, in a letter to the Joint Committee responsible for *RDA* (available at http://www.libraries.psu.edu/tas/jca/ccda/docs/arsc2 .doc), sought to influence the proposed *RDA* treatment of sound recordings, suggesting the ambiguity of some rules and examples and requesting specific guidelines and examples pertaining to interpretation and improvisation. Two of the most troubling areas identified in the letter include reproductions (altered work versus "new" work) and choice of preferred/principal responsible person, specifically the role of performers.

RDA 19.2.1.1, "Basic Instructions on Recording Creators," addresses how to determine whether the resource being cataloged is a "new" work: "A person, family, or corporate body responsible for modifying a previously existing work in a way that substantially changes the nature or content of the original is considered to be a creator of the new work." The cataloger is required to judge whether the content has been "substantially changed." In this context, "content" refers to the "intellectual" content, the essential core of the work.

RDA 6.28.1.6 provides additional instructions regarding adaptations of musical works. When confronted with such decisions, catalogers must be prepared to use judgment when determining the creator(s) with principal responsibility for the work. See *RDA* 19.2.1.3 for examples that illustrate the choice of preferred responsible persons.

Other important elements related to the expression of a work include language of the text, genre, and the type and extent of the content. Language is a core element of description and must be recorded in the fixed field of the MARC record and in the appropriate areas of MODS and DC. Record details related to the language of the resource in the

MARC 546 field, the MODS element <note> with the attribute type "language," and in the DC element <Language>. Record additional details about language, such as the availability of the resource in other languages, in the MARC 530 field reserved for information about other available versions or formats. Record this information in the MODS element <note> with the attribute type "additional physical form" and in the DC element <Relation> with the qualifier "HasFormat." All known differences must be recorded, so remain alert to the fact that significant differences may signal that an expression is actually an entirely new work.

Music Box by Mariah Carey illustrates the decisions catalogers face when working with different versions of a work. *Music Box* was originally produced in 1993 on CD in the United States. It was also produced in the same year in Europe on CD, with a bonus soundtrack. Although also expressed as a musical recording, the minor variation (the addition of soundtrack number 11) signaled a new expression of the work, thus requiring a new descriptive record.

Figures 3.2 through 3.4 represent images of the 1993 European edition of the CD *Music Box.* Note the addition of the bonus soundtrack (No. 11), shown on the CD itself and on the container's label. The image of the back cover (see Figure 3.3) displays the publisher's number, the International Standard Music Number (ISMN), and the double D symbol signifying special playback characteristics (Dolby Digital). The songs contained in the album are also listed along with the copyright statement.

The duration of the album is not listed on the disc or anywhere in the accompanying material. However, a web search located information on

Figure 3.2. Image of the CD *Music Box*

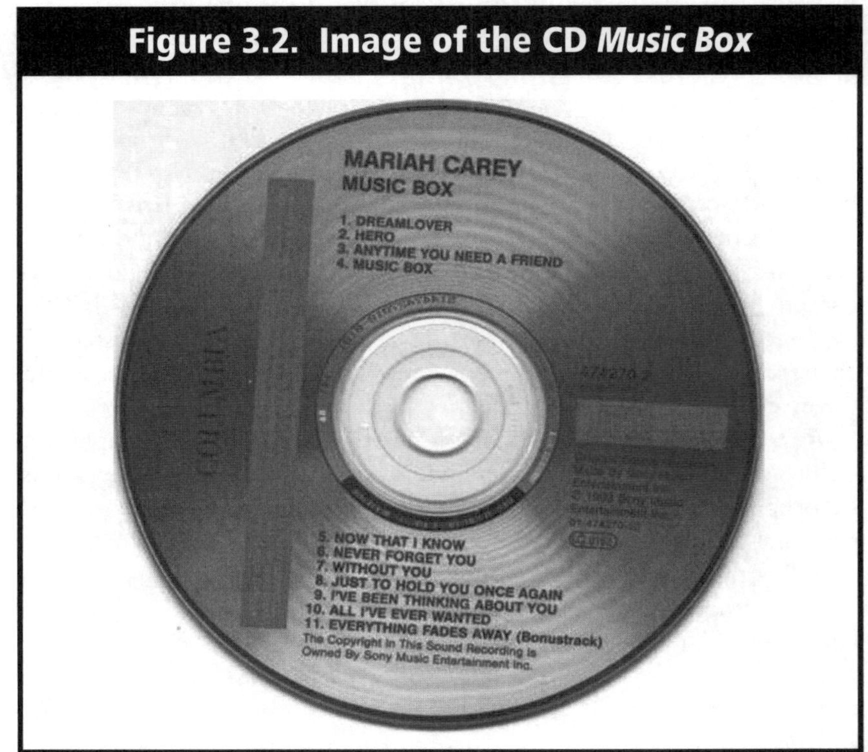

Figure 3.3. Image of the Back Cover of the Container of the CD *Music Box*

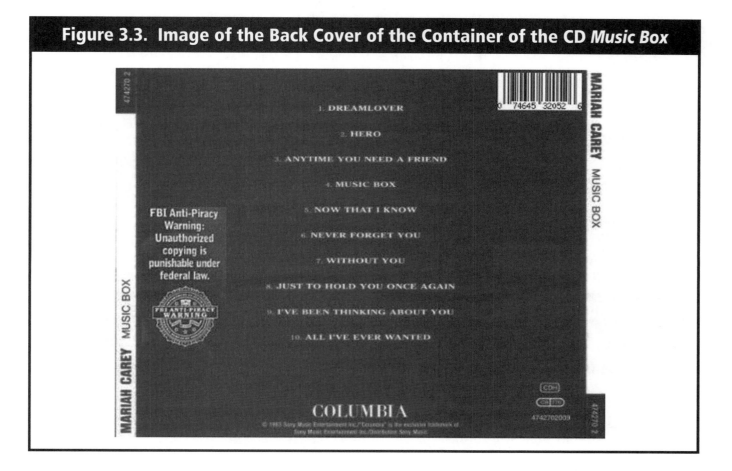

Figure 3.4. Front Cover of the CD *Music Box* with Extra Bonus Track Label

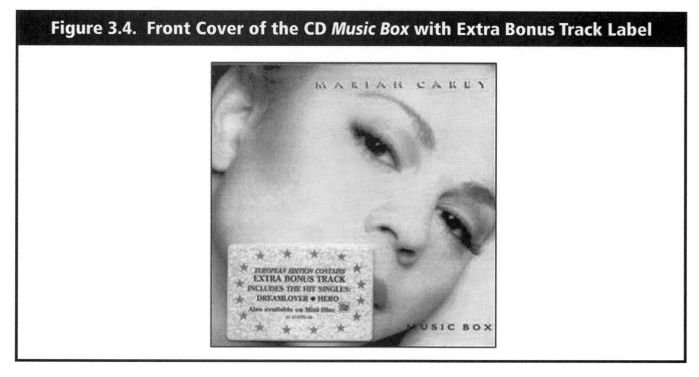

the original ten-track production, including the duration of the album and of each soundtrack on the album, and the cataloger can use this information to enhance the record as recommended in *RDA* 7.22.1.3 (see Figure 3.5). The information also includes the release dates of other versions of the work and alerts us of the existence of a bonus track edition (see "Other Editions" in the screenshot). Clicking on the information for the bonus track retrieved the screenshot shown in Figure 3.6.

The bonus track edition represents both a different expression and a different manifestation of the work. The descriptive record shown in Figure 3.7 reflects this.

Manifestation

The discussion of the term "expression" in the previous section related to the content of the CD. "Manifestation" relates to the physical

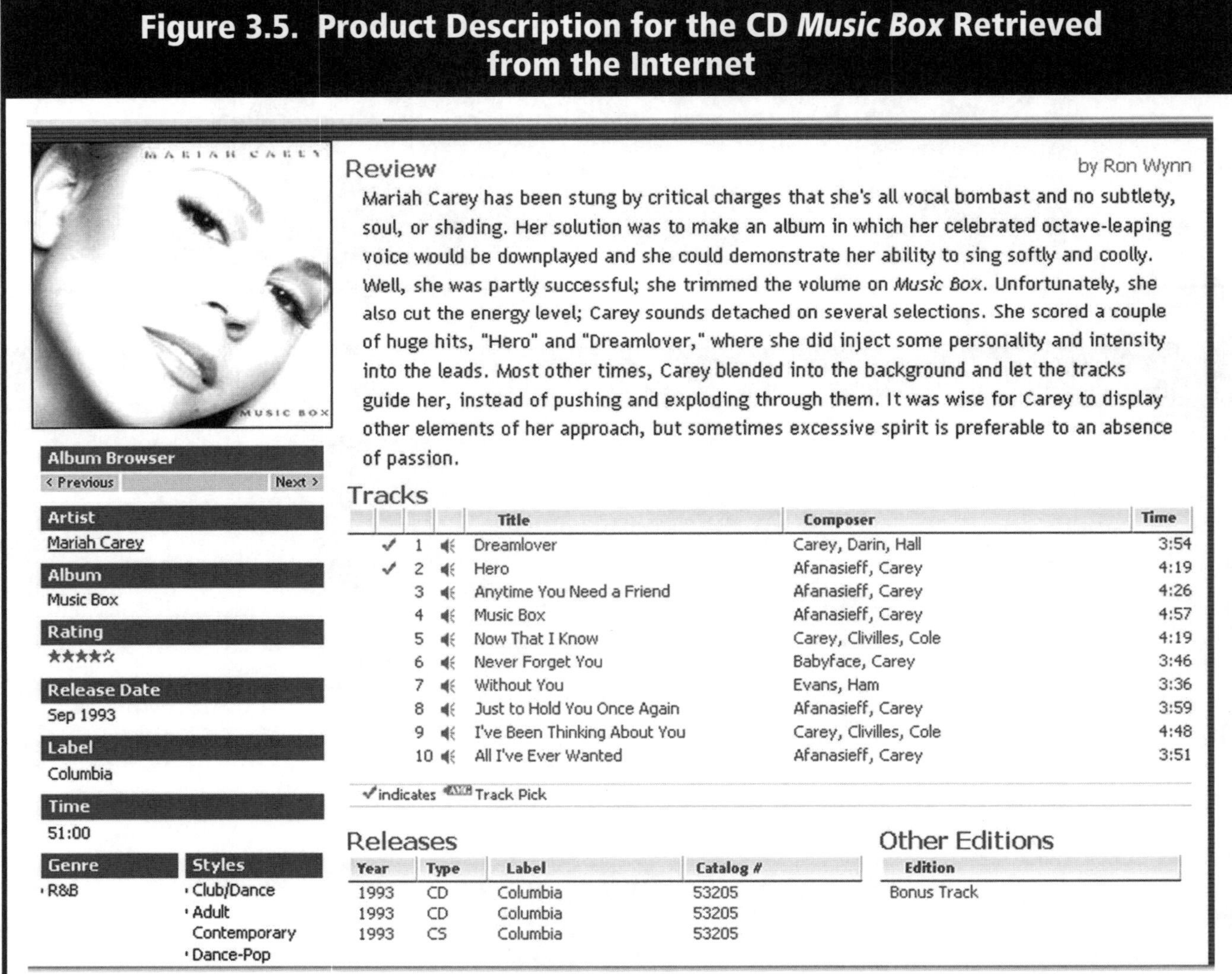
MARIAH CAREY
MUSIC BOX
Review
by Ron Wynn
Mariah Carey has been stung by critical charges that she's all vocal bombast and no subtlety, soul, or shading. Her solution was to make an album in which her celebrated octave-leaping voice would be downplayed and she could demonstrate her ability to sing softly and coolly. Well, she was partly successful; she trimmed the volume on *Music Box*. Unfortunately, she also cut the energy level; Carey sounds detached on several selections. She scored a couple of huge hits, "Hero" and "Dreamlover," where she did inject some personality and intensity into the leads. Most other times, Carey blended into the background and let the tracks guide her, instead of pushing and exploding through them. It was wise for Carey to display other elements of her approach, but sometimes excessive spirit is preferable to an absence of passion.
Album Browser
‹ Previous
Next ›
Artist
Mariah Carey
Album
Music Box
Rating
★★★★☆
Release Date
Sep 1993
Label
Columbia
Time
51:00
Genre
R&B
Styles
Club/Dance
Adult Contemporary
Dance-Pop
Tracks
✓indicates Track Pick
Releases
Other Editions

	#	Title	Composer	Time
✓	1	Dreamlover	Carey, Darin, Hall	3:54
✓	2	Hero	Afanasieff, Carey	4:19
	3	Anytime You Need a Friend	Afanasieff, Carey	4:26
	4	Music Box	Afanasieff, Carey	4:57
	5	Now That I Know	Carey, Clivilles, Cole	4:19
	6	Never Forget You	Babyface, Carey	3:46
	7	Without You	Evans, Ham	3:36
	8	Just to Hold You Once Again	Afanasieff, Carey	3:59
	9	I've Been Thinking About You	Carey, Clivilles, Cole	4:48
	10	All I've Ever Wanted	Afanasieff, Carey	3:51

Year	Type	Label	Catalog #
1993	CD	Columbia	53205
1993	CD	Columbia	53205
1993	CS	Columbia	53205

Edition
Bonus Track

Figure 3.5. Product Description for the CD *Music Box* Retrieved from the Internet

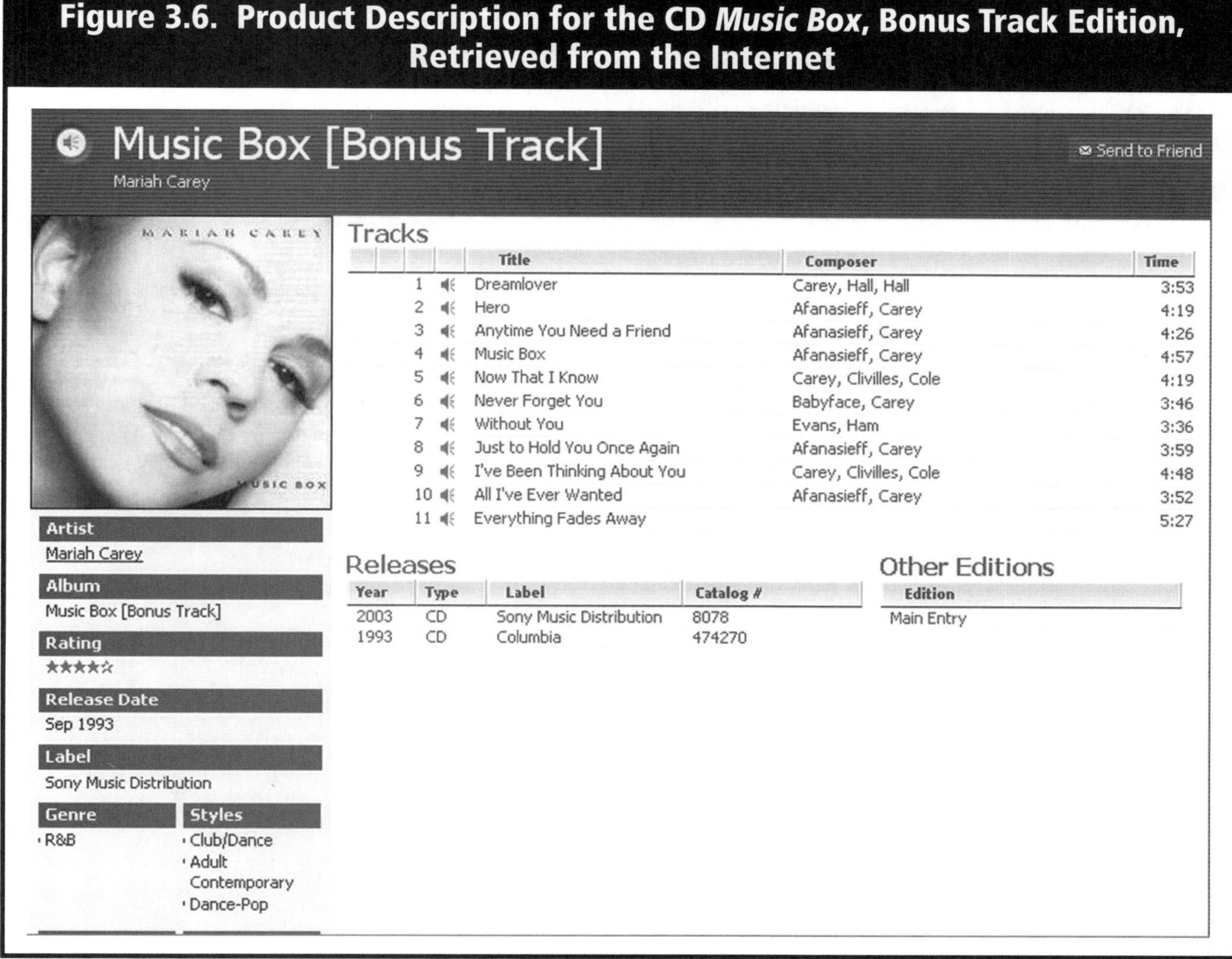

Figure 3.6. Product Description for the CD *Music Box*, Bonus Track Edition, Retrieved from the Internet

representation of the resource via its carrier. An examination of the cases and covers of the CDs gave no indication that the European version was different from the U.S. version except for a label affixed to the front cover of the European version stating that a bonus soundtrack was included. The original U.S. production contained 10 songs, and the European reissue contained 11. Both discs included the statement that the original sound recording was issued in 1993.

The most significant difference between the two manifestations of *Music Box*, however, was indicated by the publisher's number. On tangible resources, the publisher's number is a unique alphanumeric identifier assigned by the publisher that is embedded in or etched on the disc or printed on a label affixed to the disc or container. A difference in the publisher's number signals the requirement for a new descriptive record. Based on the variation in content and the difference in publishers' numbers, the U.S. and European productions of *Music Box* require separate descriptive records, both to highlight the differences in content

Figure 3.7. Descriptive Record for the European Bonus Track Production of the CD *Music Box*	
Leader Positions	Position 06 (record Type): j [musical sound recording] Position 07 (Bibliographic Level): m [monograph; single part issue]
007 Musical sound recording	$a s $b d $c (undefined) $d f $e s $f (blank) $g g $h (blank) $i (blank) $j m $k m $l (blank) $m e $n (blank) [The codes in the 007 field above show that the item is: • "s" a sound recording • "d" sound disc • "f" speed of 1.4 m per sec • "s" stereophonic configuration • "g" of dimension (4 3/4in. = 12 cm) • "m" a mass-produced disc • "m" material is plastic with metal • "e" special playback (digital recording) No attempt has been made to code the following subfields, which are left blank: $f, $h, $i and $l are applicable to tapes rather than discs. Subfield $n (capture and storage techniques) is also left blank because this information was not readily available. Position 3 ($c) is undefined.]
008	Lang: eng Ctry: nyu Aud: Time: Form of composition: pp [popular music] Accompanying material: d [accompanying material contains lyrics] Date typ: s Date 1: 1993 [date of release in US and UK]
028 02	4742702 $b Columbia
100 1_	Carey, Mariah, $d 1970-
245 10	Music box $h [sound recording] / $c Mariah Carey.
260 __	$b Columbia, $c p1993.
300 __	1 audio disc. : $b digital, stereo ; $c 12 cm
500 __	Copyright held by Sony Music.
508 __	Produced and arranged by Walter Afanasieff and Mariah Carey.
505 0_	1. Dreamlover / M. Carey, D. Hall -- 2. Hero / M. Carey, W. Afanasleff -- 3. Anytime you need a friend / M. Carey, W. Afanasleff / -- 4. Music box / M. Carey, W. Afanasleff -- 5. Now that I know / M. Carey, R. Clivilles, D. Cole -- 6. Never forget you / M. Carey, Babyface --7. Without you / W.P. Ham, T. Evans -- 8. Just to hold you once again / M. Carey, W. Afanasleff -- 9. I've been thinking about you / M. Carey, R. Clivilles, D. Cole -- 10. All I've ever wanted. / M. Carey, W. Afanasleff -- 11. Everything fades away.
500 __	Lyrics ([8] p. ; ports.) inserted in container.
500 __	Compact disc.
500 __	Also released in 1993 in North America. The version produced, released and distributed in the United States does not contain the bonus soundtrack "Everything fades away".
650 _0	Popular music.
710 2_	Columbia Records.
710 2_	Sony Music.

(expression) and in physical representation, as exemplified by the difference in publishers' numbers and in such physical characteristics as additional text and a new label (signaling a different manifestation).

Publishers' numbers must be recorded in the MARC 028 field (reserved for publisher's number) and/or in the MODS element <identifier> with the attribute type "music publisher," and/or in the DC element <Identifier>. The identifier found on Mariah Carey's CD *Music Box* is shown in Example 3.8.

Both CDs also contain ISBNs, printed on the accompanying program notes leaflet. ISBNs must be recorded in the MARC 020 field, the MODS element <identifier> with the attribute type "isbn" and the DC element <Identifier>.

URLs (web addresses) on accompanying materials offer additional points of uniqueness by providing specific locations for supplementary information related to the work being described. Notably for information on the Internet, the URL is less constant than an embedded number and presents its own unique challenges to librarians and researchers alike. Record such information in the MARC 776 field, the MODS element <relatedItem> with the attribute type "otherFormat," and the DC element <Relation> with the qualifier "HasFormat."

The physical manifestation of the work is realized in its carrier. The identification of the media and carrier types and the corresponding technical details are essential to resource description. Technical details are generally recorded in the MARC 006, 007, and 300 fields. MODS has no equivalent for the MARC 006 field. Information conveyed in the MARC 007 and 300 fields is recorded in MODS element <physical Description> with various subelements. DC has no equivalents for the MARC 006 and 007 fields; the DC element <Format> with the qualifier "Extent" is equivalent to the MARC 300 field. Example 3.9 shows the MARC 007 fixed field, which is mandatory for sound recordings. Additional information about the valid codes for this field is available at http://www.oclc.org/bibformats/en/0xx/007sound.shtm.

Additional fields (MARC 337 for media and MARC 338 for carrier) facilitate a more precise description of the carrier using terms selected from the appropriate *RDA* tables (Table 3.1: Media type and Table 3.3.1.3: Carrier type). The content type (though related to the expression or the resource rather than to its manifestation) also provides valuable information about the resource and is included here merely as an example. The appropriate terms for Mariah Carey's CD *Music Box* follow:

MARC 336 (Content Type): performed music $2 rdacontent

MARC 337 (Media Type): audio $2 rdamedia

MARC 338 (Carrier Type): audio disc $2 rdacarrier

Used in conjunction with the MARC 006 and 007 fields, the MARC 336, 337, and 338 fields provide the specificity lacking in the General Material Designations (GMDs) they have replaced and are indexed to allow for easy retrieval by specific type of content, media, and/or carrier. Although the GMD has been discontinued in *RDA*, it may still be

EXAMPLE 3.8

CK 53205: Columbia.

EXAMPLE 3.9

007 __ $a s $b d $d f $e s $f n $g g $h n $i n $j m $m e $n d

Position 00: $a: Category of material (use **s** for all sound recordings)

Position 01: $b: Special material designator (**d** for CDs; **z** for streaming audio)

Position 03: $c: Undefined

Position 04: $d: Speed (**f** for CDs)

Position 05: $e: Configuration of playback (**s** for stereophonic)

Position 06: $f: Groove width, pitch

Position 07: $g: Dimensions (**g** for CDs : 4¾ in. or 12 cm)

Position 08: $h: Tape width: **n** not applicable for discs

Position 09: $i: Tape configuration: **n** not applicable for discs

Position 10: $j: Kind of disc: **m** for mass produced

Position 11: $k: Kind of material

Position 12: $l: Kind of cutting

Position 13: $m: Special playback characteristics (**e** for digital recordings)

Position 14: $n: Capture and storage technique (**d** for digital)

See Also . . .

MARC 337 (Chapter 1, p. 44)
MARC 338 (Chapter 1, p. 44)

EXAMPLE 3.10

245 00 Music box $h [sound recording] / $c Mariah Carey.
245 00 Prelude in E minor $n pt. 1 $h [sound recording].
245 00 Pianoworks for kids. $n Volume 2, $p Just imagine, concentration and affirmation $h [sound recording] / $c [Ken Johnson].

required for records contributed to some cataloging utilities. The GMD has been relevant only to MARC-based description and the term "sound recording" has been used for all types of audio recordings except streaming audio and downloadable music, which are considered online resources. The GMD is not repeatable and is recorded in the delimiter $h of the MARC 245 field, enclosed in square brackets immediately after the title in the $a subfield and preceding the subtitle. For musical sound recordings where the title contains a number or part that is integral to the identification of the work, the GMD is recorded after the number or part of the work (see Example 3.10).

Title information can also be recorded in the MODS element <title> and in the DC element <Title>.

For additional help in constructing the MARC 245 field, consult OCLC's guidelines at http://www.oclc.org/bibformats/en/2xx/245.shtm. One need not be an OCLC user to consult the guidelines, which provide clear instruction and information. Instructions for use of the MARC 245 field can also be found at http://www.loc.gov/marc/bibliographic/bd245.html.

Publication details provide important information related both to the expression of a work (date of creation) and to a specific manifestation of a work. Information about the publisher and/or distributor is generally written on the carrier or in the accompanying material and must be recorded as it appears.

For the publisher use the form of name found on the record label rather than the established corporate name. If there is a recognizable logo or record label, use this as publisher.

When the role of the publisher is significant, such as when the publisher is responsible for the creation of a particular version of a work, record the publisher in the "additional responsible persons" area of the resource description. Record this information in the MARC 710 field to provide an additional access point, in the MODS element <name> qualified by type of name (corporate) and the subelement <role>, and in the DC element <Contributor>.

Information about the distributor, when found on the resource, is deemed important enough to record, most notably in the absence of an identifiable publisher. In this case, record the information in the $b subfield of the MARC 260 field preceded by the term "distributed by." Record distributor information in the MODS element <originInfo> and in the DC element <Publisher>.

If the resource and/or the printed accompanying material includes several dates, make every attempt to discern the correct date of production. It is important to recognize a date of reissue because the presence of such a date requires that the cataloger record the original date of production, if known. Reissued works also require the code **r** in the "type of date" area of the MARC 008 fixed field. Record this information in the MODS element <originInfo> with the subelement <dateIssued> and in the DC element <Date> with the qualifier "Issue."

When the date of production and the date of issue are identical and one is preceded by "c" and the other by "p," interpret the resource as an original production (as in Example 3.11, from Mariah Carey's CD *Music Box*). If the dates are different, record the date preceded by "p" as the date of production.

There may be several different dates on the disc or on the carrier. Use the phonogram/publication date if present rather than the copyright date. Do not use the copyright symbol in the date field for sound recordings. Generally the copyright date on the container relates to the artwork and printed material, not to the recording. The copyright date of the artwork should not be misconstrued as the date on which the work was produced. If the only date on the item is found on the packaging, do not record this as a copyright date even if it is recorded as such. Record the date in square brackets and omit the copyright symbol (©).

The MARC 300 field contains the number of discs or pieces that comprise the resource and technical details related to the carrier, such as whether the sound is stereophonic. The MARC 300 field complements the MARC 007 field, and information that is recorded in coded form in the MARC 007 field is repeated, in text, in the MARC 300 field. Provide extent in the MODS element <physicalDescription> with the subelements <form> and <extent> and in the DC element <Format> with the qualifier "Extent" (see Example 3.12).

Note: *RDA* currently recommends the use of centimeters (cm.) in the MARC 300 field, but optionally local cataloging authorities may instruct otherwise. Per *RDA* 3.5.1.3: "Unless instructed otherwise, record dimensions in centimeters to the next whole centimeter up, using the metric symbol cm." Catalogers using *RDA* guidelines must use cm. in the $e subfield of the MARC 300 field and in the MODS element <physicalDescription> with the subelement <Extent>. DC has no equivalent of MARC 300 $c. Record the duration of the album in the MARC 306 field; this information is optional for core level cataloging. Neither MODS nor DC has an equivalent of the MARC 306 field, but duration may be recorded in the physical description or general notes area.

Note: It may be more useful to the patron if information about the duration of each title on the soundtrack is recorded in the contents area immediately following the title as generally displayed on the disc or in the accompanying published material.

The website http://www.allmusic.com is a good resource for supplementary information about popular sound recordings. However, the cataloger must ensure that the correct version of the recording has been located before using descriptive elements found on the Internet. The publisher's number and/or the ISBN must be identical to the resource being described when using supplementary information found outside of the resource itself.

Downloadable Music

Music Box is also available for download to an MP3 player either as an album or as individual soundtracks or songs. The description for the downloadable version of the album, which is considered both an electronic or online resource and audio, requires two carrier types described as follows:

EXAMPLE 3.11

c1993 Sony Music Entertainment Inc. /
p1993 Sony Music Entertainment Inc.

EXAMPLE 3.12

```
300 __ 1 audio disc. : $b digital, stereo. ;
$c 12 cm.

<physicalDescription>
   <form authority="marcform">sound
   </form>
   <extent>1 audio disc</extent>
</physicalDescription>

<Format.Extent>1 audio disc. : digital,
stereo.</Format>
```

MARC 336 (Content Type): performed music $2 rdacontent

MARC 337 (Media Type): audio $2 rdamedia

MARC 338 (Carrier Type): audio disc $2 rdacarrier

MARC 338 (Carrier Type): online resource $2 rdacarrier

Figure 3.8 shows a MARC descriptive record for the MP3 downloadable version of the album. However, a library may opt not to catalog downloadable music but may provide the appropriate "other format" note in the MARC 530 field and the URL of the website where the product is available for download or purchase in the 856 field of the MARC record for the sound disc. Such information can also be added to the appropriate MODS record in the MODS element <location> with the subelement <URL> and in the DC element <Identifier> for the CD or DualDisc.

Figure 3.8. Descriptive Record for MP3 Downloadable Version of the CD *Music Box*

Leader 06 Leader 07	j [musical sound recording] m [monograph; single part issue]
006 [electronic]	m [electronic] h[sound]
007 [sound recording]	$a s $e s $m e [The codes in the 007 field above show that the item is: • "s" a sound recording • "s" stereophonic configuration • "e" special playback (digital recording) No attempt has been made to code the other subfields, which are not relevant to this type of hybrid media and are not represented in this example.]
007 [electronic]	$a c [electronic resource] $b r [remote] $f a [sound on medium]
008	Lang: eng Ctry: nyu Aud: Time: Date typ: r [reproduction] Date 1: 2008 Date 2: 1993 [date of original recording]
100 1_	Carey, Mariah, $d 1970-
245 10	Music box $h [electronic resource] / $c Mariah Carey.
260 __	New York : $b Columbia, $c p1993.
300 __	1 streaming audio file : $b digital, MP 3 (256 kbps)
508 __	Produced and arranged by Walter Afanasieff and Mariah Carey.
505 0_	1. Dreamlover / M. Carey, D. Hall -- 2. Hero / M. Carey, W. Afanasleff -- 3. Anytime you need a friend / M. Carey, W. Afanasleff -- 4. Music box / M. Carey, W. Afanasleff -- 5. Now that I know / M. Carey, R. Clivilles, D. Cole -- 6. Never forget you / M. Carey, Babyface -- 7. Without you / W.P. Ham, T. Evans -- 8. Just to hold you once again / M. Carey, W. Afanasleff -- 9. I've been thinking about you / M. Carey, R. Clivilles, D. Cole -- 10. All I've ever wanted. / M. Carey, W. Afanasleff -- 11. Everything fades away.

(Cont'd.)

Figure 3.8. Descriptive Record for MP3 Downloadable Version of the CD *Music Box (Continued)*

538 __ 538 __	Mode of access: World Wide Web Web browser; iPod(r), MP3 player, or Realplayer on a computer.
500 __ 530 __	Sold by SONY BMG Music Entertainment Downloads LLC. Also available on CD and on cassette.
500 __	Originally released on August 31, 1993.
650 _0	Popular music.
710 2_	Columbia Records.
710 2_	Sony Music.
856 40	http://downloads.myplaydigital.com/Album.aspx?id=68817

Audiobooks

Nonmusical sound recordings include audiobooks and recorded sound. An essential difference in the description of these resources compared with musical recordings is that the content type (MARC 336) is "spoken word" or "sound." This type or form of the work is also generally coded "i" in the Leader 06 position of the MARC record.

Audiobooks are generally "expressions and manifestations" of works that were previously expressed textually or in the printed form. One advantage of describing such audiobooks or recorded books, which will probably change in the near future as more content is published originally as digital media, is that there may be a known author and title since the printed resource is generally published first. The author or creator is the person responsible for the work and must be selected as the preferred or main "access point." The reader or narrator, who must be added to the description as an essential contributor, provides an additional access point for the work.

The image in Figure 3.9 represents the audiobook cataloged in Figure 3.10. The container (visible in Figure 3.9) provides important information that must be included in the resource description. The container houses five audio discs, each of which contains identical information except for the number of the disc. The title is taken from the resource itself (the container and the discs).

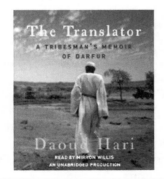

Figure 3.9. Front Cover and Basic Product Details for the Audiobook *The Translator*

AUDIO-BOOK:

Product Details

- **Audio CD**
- **Publisher:** Random House Audio; Unabridged edition (March 18, 2008)
- **Language:** English
- **ISBN-10:** 0739368583
- **ISBN-13:** 978-0739368589

Figure 3.10. MARC Descriptive Record for the Audiobook *The Translator*

Leader field	Position 06: i [spoken words] Position 07: m [monograph] Position 19: a [multipart resource]
006	Generally the codes for this field are entered in the 008 field below.
007	$a s $b d $c [undefined] $d f $e s $f [blank] $g g $h [blank]) $m e $n d
008	Lang: eng Date: 2008 Type of date "s" [single] Country: nyu Form of music: n [not applicable for spoken word sound recording] Form of item: q [direct electronic] Literary text: am [a=autobiographical; m=memoirs]
020 __ 028 02	9780739368589 RHCD 2321 $b Random House
100 1_	Hari, Daoud.
245 14	The translator [sound recording] : $b a tribesman's memoir of Darfur / $c Daoud Hari ; read by Mirron Willis.
246 30	Tribesman's memoir of Darfur
250 __	An unabridged production.
260 __	New York : $b Random House Audio, $c c2008.
300 __	5 audio discs (6 hours) : $b digital ; $c 12 cm.
490 0_	Random House Audio & Listening Library
500 __	Originally published in print by Random House, 2008.
500 __	Subtitle from container.
511 0_	Narrator: Mirron Willlis.
520 __	The story of a young man who came face to face with genocide- time and again risking his own life to fight injustice and save his people.
546 __	In English.
600 1_	Hari, Daoud.
650 _0	Translators $z Sudan $z Darfur $v Biography.
655 _0	Audiobooks
700 1_	Willis, Mirron, E. (Mirron Edward) $d 1965 $e narrator.
856 41	$u http://www.randomhouseaudio.com

It is clearly stated on the container that this is an unabridged version. What is not immediately visible on the container (shown in Figure 3.9) is the stated duration, the publisher number, the ISBN, the summary information, and the category or type of recording (five compact discs). This information was found upon close examination of the resource itself, including the carrier.

The Playaway

More publishers are taking advantage of the new technology to publish combined media. The Playaway is described as a "self-playing digital audiobook" that contains a preloaded audio file in a proprietary format called ACELP. *AACR2* Chapters 6 (on sound recordings) and 9 (on electronic resources) are both used when cataloging this type of hybrid material. Figure 3.11 shows product details for a playaway title and Figure 3.12 shows the MARC fields that are unique to the description for Playaways.

The DualDisc

The DualDisc is a CD on one side and a DVD on the other side that also enables the user to connect to a related online resource. The DualDisc is a popular double-sided optical disc increasingly found in musical publishing, as more music publishers take advantage of this new format, which enables them to produce the soundtrack of the production on the CD side and the music video of the performance on the DVD flip side.

System requirements are an essential component of the resource description, as specifications frequently vary and special equipment may be required. Figures 3.13, 3.14, and 3.15 illustrate resource description for a popular DualDisc.

Catalogers who have struggled with describing this hybrid resource will welcome the enhancements introduced in *RDA*, such as the introduction of repeatable MARC fields that contain content and media types. Catalogers using non-MARC displays in many cases have already taken advantage of the unrestricted free-text areas of the various metadata schemes.

The MARC 538 system requirements note is not required for audio recordings because the type of information provided in the 300 field (the specific medium designator) is usually sufficient to alert the user to

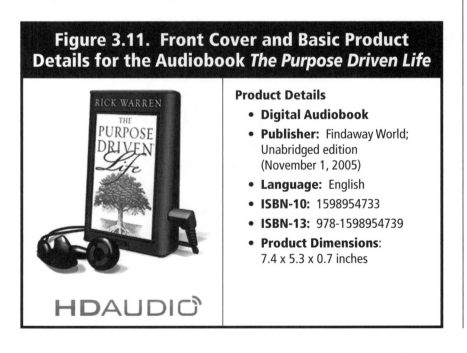

FOR MORE INFORMATION

Please consult the following OLAC documents for additional information related to resource description for playaways:

"Guide to Cataloging Playaway Devices Based on *AACR2* Chapters 6 and 9": http://www.olacinc.org/drupal/capc_files/playawaysPDF.pdf

"Playaways and RDA": http://www.olacinc.org/drupal/capc_files/PlayawaysAndRDA.pdf

Figure 3.11. Front Cover and Basic Product Details for the Audiobook *The Purpose Driven Life*

Product Details

- **Digital Audiobook**
- **Publisher:** Findaway World; Unabridged edition (November 1, 2005)
- **Language:** English
- **ISBN-10:** 1598954733
- **ISBN-13:** 978-1598954739
- **Product Dimensions:** 7.4 x 5.3 x 0.7 inches

Figure 3.12. MARC Descriptive Record for the Audiobook *The Purpose Driven Life*	
Leader 06 Leader 07	i [non-musical sound recording] m [monograph; single issue]
006	m [electronic]
007 [sound] 007 [electronic]	$a s $b z $c [undefined] $d z $e u $f n $g z $h n $j m $k z $m e $n u $a c [electronic resource] $b z $d n $e z $f a [sound on medium]
008 020 028 00	Lang: eng Date 1: 2006 Date 2: 2002 Type of date "r" [previously published] Ctry: ohu 9781598954739 LP1332 $b Playaway Digital Audio
100 1_	Warren, Richard, $d 1954-
245 14	The purpose-driven life $h [electronic resource] / $c Rick Warren.
250 __ 260 __	Unabridged. [Chagrin Falls, Ohio] : $b Findaway World, $c 2006.
300 __	1 sound media player (ca 9 hr.) : $b digital ; $c 7.4 x 5 .3 in.
500 __ 511 0_	Packaged with 1 set of earphones + 1 AAA battery. Narrated by the author; Rick Warren.
538 __	Playaway Digital Audio.
500 __	Issued on Playaway, a dedicated audio media player.
520 __	"This book will help you understand why you are alive and God's amazing plan for you—both here and now, and for eternity."—Container.
650 _0	Christian life.
710 2_	Findaway World, LLC.
856 42	[This field may be used to add a link to the publisher's website for supplementary information related to the resource. Since the resource is self-contained, this field is not used for the resource.]

Figure 3.13. MARC Descriptive Record Using *AACR2* for the CD/DVD Hybrid DualDisc *Devils & Dust*	
Leader Positions	Position 06 (record Type): j [musical recording] Position 07 (Bibliographic Level): m [monograph]
006	[The 006 field values not accommodated in the 008 field are entered here if applicable. No values are required in this case and the field is not created for this record.]
	(Cont'd.)

Figure 3.13. MARC Descriptive Record Using *AACR2* for the CD/DVD Hybrid DualDisc *Devils & Dust (Continued)*

007 Sound recording	s $b d $d f $e s $g g $j m $k m $m e $n [blank] [The codes in the 007 field show the following about the carrier: • "d" speed of 1.4 m per sec • "f" stereophonic configuration • "g" of dimension (4 3/4 in. = 12 cm) • "m" a mass-produced disc that is made of plastic with metal • "m" (a mass-produced CD) • "e" special playback (digital recording) No attempt has been made to code for capture and storage techniques in $n, which is left blank.]
007 DVD Video	v $b d $c # $d c $e v $f a $g i $h z $i s [The codes in the 007 field show the following about the carrier: • "v" a videorecording • "d" a videodisc • # blank (undefined position) • "c" multicolored • "v" DVD format • "a" containing sound on medium • "i" the sound is on the videodisc • "z" the currently listed dimensions are inappropriate for this medium • "s" with the playback configured as stereophonic.]
008	Lang: eng Form of composition: rc [rock music] Ctry: nyu Desc: a Date 1: 2005 Date 2:
028 02	CN 93900 $b Columbia.
100 1_	Springsteen, Bruce. $4 prf
245 10	Devils & dust $h [sound recording] / $c Bruce Springsteen.
246 13	Devils and dust
260 __	New York, NY : $b Columbia, $c p2005.
300 __	1 DualDisc : $b digital, dolby 5.1 surround ; $c 4 3/4 in. [Note: There is no mention on the disc or container of the duration of the album or of individual selections. This information must be omitted.]
538 __	DualDisc. Side A: CD. Side B: dolby digital with surround sound and PCM stereo. "The audio side of this disc does not conform to CD [i.e. 'Red Book CD'] specifications and therefore not all DVD and CD players will play the audio side of this disc" --Container.
505 0_	Side A (CD): 1. Devils & dust -- 2. All the way home -- 3. Reno -- 4. Long time comin' -- 5. Black cowboys. -- 6. Maria's bed -- 7. Silver Palomino -- 8. Jesus was an only son -- 9. Leah -- 10. The hitter -- 11. All I'm thinkin' about -- 12. Matamoros Banks. Side B (DVD): All 12 songs plus filmed acoustic performances of Devils & Dust; Long time comin'; Reno; All I'm thinkin' about; Matamoros Banks.
518 __	DVD "performances filmed in New Jersey, in February 2005" -- Container
650 _0	Popular music.
700 1_	O'Brien, Brendan, $4 prod.
856 42	http://www.brucespringsteen.net/albums/devils.html
856 4_	http://www.amazon.com/Devils-Dust-Bruce-Springsteen/dp/B0007WF1WS/ref=sr_1_1?ie=UTF8&s=music&qid=1242750933&sr=8-1

Figure 3.14. MODS Descriptive Record for the CD/DVD Hybrid DualDisc *Devils & Dust*

Descriptive Area	
<titleInfo>: <titleInfo type="alternative">	Devils & dust Devils and dust
<typeof Resource>:	Sound recording. Videorecording
<name>:	Springsteen, Bruce. Performer.
<genre>:	Rock music
<origin Info>: Place: Publisher: Date:	New York Columbia 2005
<physicalDescription>: (form, extent, Internet media type, digital origin, etc.)	1 DualDisc digital, dolby 5.1 surround Dual disc DVD Contains DVD on one side and CD on the other.
<abstract>:	[May be entered as appropriate.]
<tableOfContents>:	Side A (CD): Contains: 1. Devils & dust -- 2. All the way home -- 3. Reno -- 4. Long time comin' -- 5. Black cowboys -- 6. Maria's bed -- 7. Silver Palomino -- 8. Jesus was an only son -- 9. Leah -- 10. The hitter -- 11. All I'm thinkin' about -- 12. Matamoros Banks. Side B (DVD): All 12 songs plus filmed acoustic performances of: Devils & Dust; Long time comin'; Reno; All I'm thinkin' about; Matamoros Banks.
<note>: <credits> Artistic and/or technical credits	For mature audiences. O'Brien, Brendan, Producer.
<subject>:	Popular music. Rock music.
<classification>:	[Optional. Insert if required.]
<identifiers>: (hdl)	CN 93900 $b Columbia.
Related names	O'Brien, Brendan, Producer.
<physicalLocation>:	[Use as appropriate.]

the type of playback equipment required. However, detailed information about the way in which the resource can be accessed is required in this field when providing resource description for hybrids and streaming audio. System requirements information is recorded in the MODS element <note> with the attribute type "system details" and in the DC

Figure 3.15. MARC Descriptive Record Using *RDA* for the CD/DVD DualDisc *Devils & Dust*

Leader Positions	Leader 06 [Type of record]: j [musical sound recording] Leader 07 [Bibliographic level]: m [monograph; single issue]
006	g [projected medium] v [video] l [live action]
007 Audio	$a s $b d $c (undefined) $d f $e s $f (blank) $g g $h (blank) $i (blank) $j m $k m $l (blank) $m e $n (blank) [The codes in the 007 field show the following about the item: • "s" a sound recording • "d" sound disc • "f" speed of 1.4 m per sec • "s" stereophonic configuration • "g" of dimension(43/4 in. =12 cm) • "m" a mass-produced disc • "m" material is plastic with metal • "e" special playback (digital recording) No attempt has been made to code the following subfields, which are left blank: $f, $h, $i and $l are applicable to tapes rather than discs. $n (capture and storage techniques) is also left blank because this information was not readily available. Position 3 ($c) is undefined.]
007 DVD Video	v $b d $c # $d c $e v $f a $g i $h z $i s [The codes in the 007 field show the following about the item: • "v" a videorecording • "d" a videodisc • # blank [undefined position] • "c" multicolored • "v" DVD format • "f" containing sound on medium • "i" the sound is on the videodisc • "z" the currently listed dimensions are inappropriate for this medium • "s" with the playback configured as stereophonic.]
008	Lang: eng Form of composition: rc [rock music] Ctry: nyu Desc: i Date 1: 2005 Date 2: [Combined 006 and 008 values for all types of material.]
028 02	CN 93900 $b Columbia.
040 __	NjR $c NjR $e rda [Resource description conforms to *RDA*.]
100 1_	Springsteen, Bruce. $e performer
245 10	Devils & dust / $c Bruce Springsteen.
246 13	Devils and dust
260 __	New York, NY : $b Columbia, $c p2005.
300 __	1 DualDisc : $b digital ; $c 12 cm. [Note: There is no mention of duration of the album or of individual selections. This information must be omitted if it cannot be verified.]
336 __ 337 __ 338 __	$a Performed music $2 rdacontent $a Audio $a video $2 rdamedia $a Audio disc $a videodisc $2 rdacarrier
538 __	DualDisc. Side A: CD. Side B: DVD. dolby digital with surround sound and PCM stereo.
500 __	Lyrics on insert in container

(Cont'd.)

Figure 3.15. MARC Descriptive Record Using *RDA* for the CD/DVD DualDisc *Devils & Dust (Continued)*	
505 0_	Side A (CD): Contains: 1. Devils & dust -- 2. All the way home -- 3. Reno -- 4. Long time comin' -- 5. Black cowboys -- 6. Maria's bed -- 7. Silver Palomino -- 8. Jesus was an only son -- 9. Leah -- 10. The hitter -- 11. All I'm thinkin' about -- 12. Matamoros Banks. Side B (DVD): All 12 songs plus filmed acoustic performances of: Devils & Dust; Long time comin'; Reno; All I'm thinkin' about; Matamoros Banks.
508 __	Produced by Brendan O'Brien, Bruce Springsteen, and Chuck Plotkin.
511 0_	Bruce Springsteen and other musicians.
518 __	DVD: "performances filmed in New Jersey, in February 2005" -- Container
538 __	DualDisc: CD (side A), DVD (side B) (Region 1) ; Dolby Digital 5.1 surround sound and PCM stereo.
650 _0	Rock music.
650 _0	Popular music.
700 1_	O'Brien, Brendan, $e producer.
856 42	http://www.brucespringsteen.net/albums/devils.html
856 4_	http://www.amazon.com/Devils-Dust-Bruce-Springsteen/dp/B0007WF1WS/ref=sr_1_1?ie=UTF8&s=music&qid=1242750933&sr=8-1

element <Relation> with the qualifier "Requires." The example of Bruce Springsteen's work *Devils & Dust* (in Figure 3.13) shows this type of note in the MARC 538 field where the cataloger has added information from the container insert specifying that "the audio side of this disc does not conform to CD specifications."

Streaming Audio

Considered more of an electronic resource, streaming audio is also a hybrid resource. The audio elements must comply with the rules and guidelines for the description of spoken word recordings, and the online aspects must be treated as such (see Figure 3.16). Online audio resources present the same problems as all online resources. They are subject to change at any time, and the library has no control over these remote access files. The importance of the URL suggests that the library should make every attempt to ensure permanency of the link, and the cataloger is required to include the date on which the file was viewed on the Internet. Enter this information in the MARC 500 field, the MODS element <note>, and the DC element <Description>. Also ensure that the file is really streaming audio, as downloadable audio may also be nonstreaming, for example, when the entire file is downloaded to the user's desktop or player.

Note: In the example in Figure 3.16 the file duration (playing time) is listed in the 300 field where it is immediately useful to the user rather

Figure 3.16. MARC Descriptive Record for the Streaming Audio File "The National Security Constitution in an Age of Globalization"

Leader 06 Leader 07	i [Spoken word] m [Monograph]
006 [Electronic resource]	m h s
007 [Sound] 007 [Electronic resource]	$a s $b z $d z $e z $f n $g n $h n $k z $m e $n d $a c $b r $e n $f a
008	Lang: eng Form: s Type of date "s" [single] Ctry: pau Date: 2008
040	NjR $c NjR
100 1_	Koh, Harold Hongju, $d 1954-
245 14	The National Security Constitution in an age of globalization $h [electronic resource] / $c Harold Koh.
260 __	Philadelphia, Pa. : $b National Constitution Center; $b Univ. of Pa Law School, $c 2008.
300 __	1 streaming audio file (01:24:06) : $b digital, MP 3 format.
490 1_	Owen J. Roberts memorial lecture
530 __	Also available as a streaming video file from the University of Pennsylvania Law School's website at: http://www.law.upenn.edu/cf/newsroom/videoaudio/theNationalSecurityConstitution.html
520 __	The National Constitution Center and the University of Pennsylvania Law School welcome Harold Koh, the Dean of Yale Law School and Gerard C. and Bernice Latrobe Smith Professor of International Law, to deliver the 51st Annual Owen J. Roberts Memorial Lecture
518 __	Program recorded on 09/15/08 at the National Constitution Center, Philadelphia, Pennsylvania.
500 __	Title from webpage (viewed on April 1, 2009).
500 __	15th Owen J. Roberts memorial lecture, delivered at the National Constitution Center, Philadelphia, Pa.
650 _0	Separation of powers $z United States.
710 1_	University of Pennsylvania. $b Law School.
830 00	Owen J. Roberts Memorial Lecture.
856 40	http://hancock.constitutioncenter.org/media/owen_roberts_lecture/owen_roberts_lecture_harold_koh_9-15-08_(64).mp3

than in the 306 field, which can also be used to convey the duration. Consult http://www.loc.gov/marc/bibliographic/bd306.html for additional information about the MARC 306 field.

Locally Produced Sound Recordings

Locally recorded music or spoken words are not considered published resources. However, if the locally made recording is a copy/reproduction of a published work, the description of the original must form the basis of the resource description.

If the recording is a unique local recording, all requirements for description of the resource mimic those of published resources in all areas except for the publication details area. Although the cataloger may have information about the recording organization or person responsible for the recording, these are not considered publishers of the resource. The cataloger must specify in the general resource description, in the note area, that the recording was locally produced and may enter a date on which the recording was made if this is readily available.

Information about the recording must contain sufficient information for the user to find it and distinguish it from any other work. If the recording is related to another resource in or outside of the library, this information should be made available to the user by recording it in a general note field and as a "related resource." The MARC 776 field, the MODS element <relatedItem>, and the Dublin Core element <relation> are used for this purpose.

Item

Enter copy-specific information in the appropriate vendor-identified local fields or areas of the various metadata schemes reserved for local or copy-specific information. Copy information can include a shelf locator, call number, or information about the condition of the resource.

Notes

This area is important for sound recordings and is relevant to all areas of description. Certain types of notes relate to the work, while some add detail to the expression, manifestation, or item. For sound recordings, particularly musical recordings, contents notes and the performer notes provide essential information for the user. In the latter, performers and others who are credited with the creation and/or production of the work may be recorded whether or not they are selected as additional access points. Some relevant notes follow:

- Performer notes record those individuals or corporate bodies who have contributed, artistically or stylistically, to a particular work but who are not selected as the creator or main entry. *AACR2* and *RDA* require catalogers to provide additional access points for those who have contributed significantly to a work. Enter this information in the MARC 511 field Participant or Performer Note, the MODS element <note> with the attribute type "performers," and the DC element <Note> (there is no DC equivalent to the MARC 511 field).
- Notes on other available formats record the presence of other formats (manifestations) of the work. For example, record the existence of a cassette version when the CD is being cataloged. For audiobooks that are reproductions of print books, the

existence of the print version should be recorded. Provide this information in the MARC 530 field Other Available Formats, the MODS element <note> with the attribute type "additional physical form," and the DC element <Description> with the qualifier "Relation."

- Details about the date, place, and circumstances under which the recording was made may be documented. Examples include notes specifying the date on which the recording was made, as appropriate for a live recording. Record this in the MARC 518 field Date, Time, Place of Event/Recording; the MODS element <note> with the attribute type "venue"; and the DC element <Note>.
- Composers, musicians, and producers not listed in the statement of responsibility may be acknowledged in a separate note. Record this information in the MARC 508 field Credits Note, the MODS element <note> with the attribute type "creation/production credits," and the DC element <Contributor>.
- Many sound recordings are accompanied by some type of printed material. Record the presence of accompanying material or program notes in the MARC 500 field and/or the $e subfield (accompanying material) of the MARC 300 field Physical Description. Record this information in the MODS element <note> and the DC element <Description> (see Example 3.13).
- Enter information about the language of the recording in the MARC 546 field Language Note, when appropriate, particularly for operas that are sung in languages other than English. The MARC 546 field also highlights the presence of more than one language in the resource (see Example 3.14). The language of the content is also recorded in the MARC fixed field area and the MARC 041 field. For additional information about the language note, consult http://www.loc.gov/marc/bibliographic/bd546.html. This information may also be included in the MODS element <note> with the attribute type "language" and in the DC element <Language>.
- A brief summary of the contents and/or purpose of the resource can be helpful for the user. Provide this information in the MARC 520 field Summary, the MODS element <abstract>, and the DC element <Description> with the qualifier "Abstract." In addition, including a URL in the summary gives the cataloger the option of providing a link to external websites for information about the resource.
- Providing a contents note is highly recommended. The contents of sound recordings are generally most important to the user. The duration of each soundtrack and any other resource-specific information can provide critical elements of distinction among versions of the same work. Inclusion of the URL linking to the publisher's website or other appropriate content found on the

EXAMPLE 3.13

500 __ Lyrics ([8] p. ; ports.) inserted in container.

<note>Program notes in container.
</note>

<Description>Lyrics in container.
</Description>

EXAMPLE 3.14

546 __ Program notes by Alan Newcombe, Richard Osborne, Klaus Bennert, and Francis Drosel; in English, German, and French, with Italian and Spanish translations.

Internet adds to the value of the resource discovery experience. Record this information in the MARC 505 field Contents Area, the MODS element <tableOfContents>, and the DC element <Description> with the qualifier "Table OfContents."

Resource Description (MARC, MODS, FISO) Checklists

The following checklists have been provided as a handy reference guide to the fields and/or areas most frequently used when creating descriptive records for sound recordings. They are intended as guidelines and reminders. Cataloging treatment and choice of access points may vary by library, level of cataloging, and so forth. Always remember that you are the best judge when deciding which fields and/or areas are appropriate to describe the resource you have in hand, *distinctly* and *sufficiently*.

MARC CHECKLIST

For additional information about the MARC fields required by BIBCO (the Monographic Bibliographic Record Program), see http://www.loc.gov/catdir/pcc/bibco/coresr.html.

Leader 06: **Type of record**: Use **i** for nonmusical sound recordings and **j** for musical sound recordings.

Leader 07: **Bibliographic level**: This is usually **m** for monographic.

006: Use the same codes for this field as those listed later for the MARC 008 field. The Playaway requires a MARC 006 field for electronic resources. Record the audio aspect in the Leader 06 field and the electronic resource aspects in the MARC 006 field.

007: This field is mandatory for all sound recordings. BIBCO core level cataloging standards require that the following positions be coded:

- **Position 00**: Category of material (**s** for all sound recordings)
- **Position 01**: Special material designator (**d** for CDs; **z** for streaming audio)
- **Position 03**: Speed (**f** for CDs)
- **Position 04**: Configuration of playback channels
- **Position 05**: Groove width/groove pitch
- **Position 06**: Dimensions (**g** for CDs)
- **Position 07**: Tape width (when appropriate)
- **Position 08**: Tape configuration (when appropriate)
- **Position 12**: Special playback characteristics (e for digital recordings)
- **Position 13**: Capture and storage technique

For additional information about the valid codes for the 007 field, see http://www.oclc.org/bibformats/en/0xx/007sound.shtm. The Playaway requires an additional MARC 007 field to describe its unique electronic characteristics.

008: This field contains codes about the work, some of which may be repeated elsewhere in the descriptive record, such as in the 006 field. Enter characteristics such as language, the type of audio recording, the target audience, and the dates of publication in this field. Use lowercase letters. The Playaway requires **s** for form in position 23. For detailed information about this field, see http://www.loc.gov/marc/bibliographic/bd008m.html.

(Cont'd.)

MARC CHECKLIST *(Continued)*

024: **International Standard Recording Number**: This is generally found on the printed material accompanying a CD or cassette and is a unique resource identifier that is mandatory if available.

028: **Publisher Number**: Most discs and cassettes will have a publisher number, which is generally preceded by the alphabetic code for the publisher. This is another unique identifier for the resource, and it must be added to the descriptive record if available.

Example:
09026-63706-2 $b RCA.

100: Enter the author, creator, or person responsible for the intellectual content of the work in this field.

245: **Title**: Enter the preferred title of the resource.

246: **Variant Title**: Record this information if appropriate.

GMD: Now obsolete. Use it in the $h subfield of the MARC 245 field only if required by the local cataloging authorities. Enter the appropriate term in $h of the 245 field, enclosed in square brackets: [Sound recording].

If used, the GMD for the Playaway and for streaming audio is [electronic resource].

The following MARC fields may be used in lieu of the GMD for the Playaway:

MARC 336: spoken word $2 rdacontent
MARC 337: audio $2 rdamedia
MARC 338: other audio carrier $2 rdacarrier

For streaming audio:

MARC 336: spoken word $2 rdacontent
or
MARC 336: sounds $2 rdacontent
MARC 337: computer $2 rdamedia
MARC 338: online resource $2 rdacarrier

260: **Publisher Information**: $a [Place] : $b [Publisher], $c [Date]. Remember, pay attention to the dates on the resource because most recorded books and Playaways are reproductions of original works. Record the date of the original work, if known.

Example:
$c 2006, p2002. (The original of the work was produced in 2002.)

300: **Extent of Resource**: $a [extent] : $b [other characteristics] ; $c [dimensions].
For electronic resources, record information about the specific file format and duration in this field.

SMD: Record in the $a subfield of the MARC 300 field. Use for CDs, DVDs, MP3s, SACDs, DVD-audio sound media players, online resources, and streaming audio files. Use as instructed by local cataloging authorities.

Examples:
4 audio discs (*RDA* has authorized the use of audio discs in this field)
1 streaming audio file (size/duration); or 1 online resource (*RDA* term)
336 (Content Type), insert authorized codes or terms
337 (Media Type), insert authorized codes or terms
338 (Carrier Type), insert authorized codes or terms

336: Content Type (spoken word $2 rdacontent)
337: Media Type (audio $2 rdamedia)
338: Carrier Type (other) $2 rdacarrier

Sample 300 field for the playaway:
1 sound media player (ca. 4 hr.) : $b digital ; $c 3 3/8 x 2 1/8 in.

See http://www.loc.gov/standards/valuelist/ for other appropriate values.

(Cont'd.)

MARC CHECKLIST *(Continued)*

306: Duration (playing time).

Notes: Source of Title Note (MARC 500): This is mandatory for Playaways and other hybrid resources that require the use of computerized devices.

Example:
Title from Playaway label.

The following MARC note fields have been approved for use when describing Playaways.

500: Playback requirements must be recorded for the Playaway and other hybrid electronic resources. Record this information as a general note.

Examples:
"Requires one set of earphones and one AAA battery for playback."
"In container (21 x 13 x 3 cm.) with earphones and AAA battery."

511: Performer Notes.

Examples:
Read by: Mary Smith.
Narrated by: John Majors.

520: **Summary**: Use this field whenever possible to enhance the utility of the descriptive record.

530: **Other Formats Note**: Information about the existence of a print copy of the work is appropriate in this field.

650: **Subject Term**: At least one subject must be assigned.

655: **Genre Heading**: Audiobooks.

856: **Electronic Location and Access**: Use if appropriate to link to the publisher's website or other important information.

For additional information about cataloging streaming audio, see http://ublib.buffalo.edu/libraries/units/cts/olac/capc/streamingmedia.html.

MODS CHECKLIST

For additional information about constructing a descriptive record for sound recordings using MODS, see http://www.loc.gov/standards/mods/v3/mods94759273.xml

<typeOfResource> To specify type of resource being cataloged; in this case it will be "sound recording."

Example:
<typeOfResource>sound recording</typeOfResource>

<genre> Provides information on a style, form, or content expressed in the resource.

Example:
<genre>jazz</genre>

<identifier> with the attribute " type" is used to provide standard identifiers, such as the ISBN.

Example:
<identifier type="isbn">9783540221814</identifier>

(Cont'd.)

MODS CHECKLIST *(Continued)*

<recordInfo> with the subelement <recordContentSource> with the attribute "authority" is used to provide the code or name of the organization that created or modified the original resource description.

Example:

```
<recordInfo>
   <recordContentSource>Rutgers University Libraries</recordContentSource>
</recordInfo>
```

<languageTerm> with the type="code" and authority="iso639-2b" (several codes may be used in authority; see http://www.loc.gov/standards/mods/v3/mods-userguide-elements.html#language for additional information).

Example:

```
<language>
   <languageTerm type="code" authority="iso639-2b">eng</languageTerm>
</language>
```

<classification> with the attribute "authority" is used to indicate the type of classification scheme used to provide subject access to the resource.

Example:

```
<classification authority="lcc">ML1.S6J65 2005</classification>
```

<name> Use to provide information on name of a person, organization, or event (conference, meeting, etc.) associated with the resource. This element has a <type> attribute to specify the type of name (personal, corporate, or conference) and an authority attribute (<authority>) to enable catalogers to specify what authoritative source was consulted to provide the authorized form of the name. This element also has a subelement <role> which is used to specify the role of the named person, corporate body, or conference in relation to the resource.

Example:

```
<name type="personal">
   <role>
      <roleTerm type="text">Performer</roleTerm>
   </role>
<name type="corporate">
   <namePart>Sony Music</namePart>
</name>
```

<titleInfo> is used to convey the title or name of a resource. When the main portion of the title is referenced as core, there is only one core subelement, <title>.

Example:

```
<titleInfo>
<title>Music box</title>
</titleInfo>
```

Use <titleInfo> with the type="alternative" and the subelement <title> to convey title variations.

Example:

```
</titleInfo> <titleInfo type="alternative">
<title>Songs from the nutcracker suite</title>
</titleInfo>
```

(Cont'd.)

MODS CHECKLIST *(Continued)*

<originInfo> with the subelement <edition> is used to describe the version or edition of the resource being described.

Example:
```
<originInfo>
  <edition>7th ed.</edition>
</originInfo>
```

<originInfo> with the subelement <place> and its subelement <placeTerm> with type="text", the subelement <publisher>, and the subelement <dateIssued> is used to provide information on publication, distribution, etc.

<physicalDescription> with the subelements <form> and <extent> provide descriptive information about the resource. In this text the authoritative source for <form> (used to describe the resource's physical description) is the MARC format. The subelement <extent> describes the number and types of units that make up a resource.

Example:
```
<physicalDescription>
  <form authority="marcform">sound disc</form><extent>1</extent>
</physicalDescription>
```

<tableOfContents> Use for the contents of sound recordings when this information is supplied by the publisher.

Example:
```
<tableOfContents>
Overture -- Attack of the ghouls -- Midnight stroll -- Snowflake joys.
</tableOfContents>
```

<relatedItem> with the attribute type "series" is used to provide information on the series when appropriate.

Example:
```
<relatedItem type="series">
  <titleInfo>
    <title>Classics collection</title>
  </titleInfo>
</relatedItem>
```

<note> is used to provide general information about the resource.

Example:
```
<note>Based on the play by William Shakespeare.</note>
```

<subject> with the attribute type "authority" and the subelement <name> with the attribute " type" (personal, corporate, conference) provides information on persons and organizations that are subjects of the resource. Use subelement <topic> for the resource's primary topics. The descriptive record should contain at least one subject term.

Example:
```
<subject>
  <name type="personal">
<namePart> Burton, Richard Francis</namePart>
<namePart type="termsOfAddress">Sir</namePart>
<namePart type="date">1821-1890</namePart>
</subject>
<subject authority="lcsh">
  <topic> Water.</topic>
</subject>
```

FISO CHECKLIST

Having constructed the descriptive record, the cataloger may find it appropriate to review the description based on the *FRBR* principles: *find, identify, select, obtain*:

F—The potential user has to find the material.

I—The user should be able to identify the resource, distinguishing it from any similar item.

S—The user should be able to retrieve and select the material as the appropriate one for a specific purpose or task.

O—The record should help the user to obtain the material by giving information about its location and availability and any requirements for and/or conditions of use.

The following questions are helpful in rating the completed product:

- ❑ Does the description represent the resource accurately? Comprehensive resource description may be time-consuming, but it is worth the effort.
- ❑ Have all possible access points been made available?
- ❑ Have all variant titles been recorded?
- ❑ Have the names of performers, creators, contributors, and publishers been verified in established authority databases? And have they been recorded giving the appropriate level of credit to those who are responsible for the intellectual content of the work? Remember: musical recordings require distinction between creator and performer.
- ❑ Does the description make it quite clear that specialized equipment is required to use specific component parts of the resource?
- ❑ Can any element or attribute benefit from additional exposure (such as being used as an additional access point or requiring an explanatory note)?

Resources for Catalogers

Allmusic. 2010. Rovi Corporation. Accessed August 4. http://www.allmusic.com.

Cole, Richard, and Ed Schwartz. 1996–2009. *Virginia Tech Multimedia Music Dictionary*. Virigina Polytechnic Institute and State University. http://www.music.vt.edu/musicdictionary.

Coyle, Karen. 2003. "The Technology of Rights: Digital Rights Management." Karen Coyle. http://www.kcoyle.net/drm_basics1.html.

Layton, Julia. 2010. "How Digital Rights Management Works." HowStuffWorks, Inc. Accessed August 4. http://computer.howstuffworks.com/drm.htm/printable.

LiLI: Libraries Linking Idaho. 2010. "Cataloging Music Sound Recordings." Idaho Commission for Libraries. Accessed August 4. http://www.lili.org/forlibs/ce/sable/course4/sec2-cataloging-music-7.htm.

OLAC, Online Audiovisual Catalogers. 2010. "Playaways and RDA." OLAC. Accessed August 24. http://www.olacinc.org/drupal/capc_files/PlayawaysAndRDA.pdf.

Playaway Cataloging Joint Task Force. 2008. "Guide to Cataloging Playaway Devices Based on AACR2 Chapters 6 and 9." OLAC. http://www.olacinc.org/drupal/capc_files/playawaysPDF.pdf.

Sony Music Entertainment. 2001. *Essentials of Music Online Glossary*. Sony Music Entertainment. http://www.essentialsofmusic.com/glossary/glossary.html.

Notes

1. American Library Association. 2010. "Digital Rights Management (DRM) and Libraries." American Library Association. Accessed June 4. http://www.ala.org/ala/issuesadvocacy/copyright/digitalrights/index.cfm.
2. U.S. Copyright Office. 1998. "The Digital Millennium Copyright Act of 1998: U.S. Copyright Office Summary." U.S. Copyright Office. http://www.copyright.gov/legislation/dmca.pdf.
3. Lee, Timothy. 2008. "DRM-Free Doesn't Mean Copyright-Free." Techdirt. http://www.techdirt.com/articles/20080303/141855416.shtml.
4. Dickey, Timothy J. 2008. "FRBRization of a Library Catalog: Better Collocation of Records, Leading to Enhanced Search, Retrieval and Display." *Functional Requirements for Bibliographic Records* Report. *Information Technology and Libraries*, March 1.
5. American Library Association, Canadian Library Association, and CILIP: Chartered Institute of Library and Information Professionals. 2010. *RDA Toolkit*, Chapter 19.2.1.3. ALA, CLA, and CILIP. Accessed August 21. http://www.rdatoolkit.org/.
6. American Library Association. 1998. *Anglo-American Cataloguing Rules*, 2nd ed. rev. Chicago: American Library Association.
7. American Library Association, Canadian Library Association, and CILIP: Chartered Institute of Library and Information Professionals. 2010. *RDA Toolkit*, Chapter 6.2.1.2 and 6.2.2.2. ALA, CLA, and CILIP. Accessed August 4. http://www.rdatoolkit.org/.
8. Ibid., Chapter 1.3.
9. Ibid., Chapter 6.2.1.2, 6.15.1.2, and 6.15.2.2.
10. American Library Association. 1998. *Anglo-American Cataloguing Rules.* 2nd ed. rev., Chapter 21.23C1. Chicago: American Library Association.
11. American Library Association, Canadian Library Association, and CILIP: Chartered Institute of Library and Information Professionals. 2010. *RDA Toolkit*, Chapters 6.28.1.2 and 20.2.1.3. Accessed August 4. http://www.rdatoolkit.org/.
12. Ibid., Chapter 19.2.1.
13. International Federation of Library Associations and Institutions, Cataloguing Section. 2009. *Functional Requirements for Bibliographic Records* (6.2.2). IFLA. http://archive.ifla.org/VII/s13/frbr.
14. Kiorgaard, Deirdre. 2008. "RDA Core Elements and FRBR User Tasks." JSC RDA. http://www.rda-jsc.org/docs/5chair15.pdf.

Videos

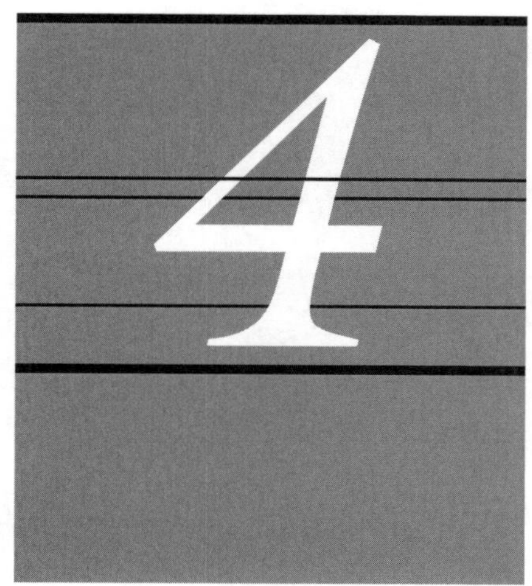

Overview

The video continues to be an enduring resource for libraries. The technology has undergone many transformations, from its revolutionary beginning as U-matic technology, then the evolution to DVDs, and now the current trend in streaming videos available via third party providers or from one's library via a service such as MyLibraryDV for a virtual loan period. Video on demand and streaming video provide libraries with attractive new options for delivering content, and the new formats will continue to influence decisions about the acquisition, description, and storage of these types of resources.

As libraries explore new options for resource description, the leading entities within the profession continue to devise and revise guidelines for video resources. Lacking the expertise and the will, some libraries have opted for minimum level cataloging for the video-on-demand resources that they do not own and/or accept the brief vendor-supplied descriptive records provided as an option with purchase or subscription packages for load into their integrated library systems (ILSs). Alternatively, other libraries employ the technology that enables users to link seamlessly to the vendor's website to conduct a search of resources available there, preferring not to create descriptive records for streaming video at all. A brief description of the resource (usually the title, publisher, and date of publication) to which the URL is added is generally placed on the library's website rather than in the ILS to alert users to its availability. In addition, some libraries are taking advantage of options that allow vendors to host the ILS, or specific aspects of it, thereby providing libraries with the services they need when the staff expertise is lacking. An example of this is the Software as a Service (SaaS) option where a vendor hosts the FRBRized catalog of a library's resources. Whatever methods are employed to provide access to resources delivered via these newer carriers, the next few years are likely to see libraries of all types making increased use of streaming video and audio, a decision that may be driven in part by the economy realized in reduced storage and maintenance requirements for libraries.

IN THIS CHAPTER:

A review of the library literature and a cursory survey of current practices in academic libraries in the United States, Europe, and selected other countries reveal that several variations and combinations of data storage methods and service delivery are currently being used. While there is some evidence that descriptive records for the newer electronic formats are not being routinely added to the library's ILS because of the limitations of most ILS systems and the incompatibility of formats, the flexibility and accommodations offered with *RDA* and *FRBR* are expected to effect change in this area as system vendors respond with appropriate adjustments and new capabilities.

RDA facilitates the most detailed description of the newer electronic resources. The areas of change that potentially have the greatest impact on the description of video resources include the following:

- **Concept**—The work (content) is conceived of as distinct from the carrier (video, in this case). Although not a totally new concept, perceiving the intellectual content apart from the carrier requires a change in orientation for most catalogers.
- **Description**—The rules provide options regarding the level and extent of description while placing more emphasis on specifying relationships between the work and its various expressions and manifestations. The use of relationship designators is strongly recommended in *RDA*.
- **Specificity**—There is a renewed emphasis on specificity in resource description, especially as related to carriers. It is now possible to use multiple terms to describe hybrid resources, allowing for a level of description not previously accommodated in the MARC display format or in MARC-based systems.

Important Considerations

Most works produced on video are collaborative efforts, and, in an exception to the general rule for collaborative works, the title of the video resource is mandated as the preferred access point representing the work.[1] Nevertheless, the choice of additional access points, from among those who have created or performed the work, requires an understanding of the rules associated with the selection of preferred and additional access points (which are covered in detail in *RDA* Chapter 19).

The influence of globalization means that videos can be produced and distributed anywhere in the world. Unlike the printed resource for which language may be the only barrier, videos require special equipment for playback, and this single factor limits access to some types of videos in some parts of the world. Catalogers need to be aware of region codes and regional restrictions, because technical specifications can vary according to country of origin or region. Copyright restrictions, which are generally stated in or on the resource, and licensing agreements must both be reviewed so that pertinent information can be noted in the descriptive record when appropriate.

AACR2 (Appendix D-9: Glossary) defines *videorecording* as "[a] recording on which visual images, usually in motion and accompanied by sound, have been registered; designed for playback by means of a television set." *RDA* has supplanted the term *videorecording* with *video* and in its glossary provides a more up-to-date and appropriate description that includes media used to store digital images, inherently accommodating streaming video in this description. *RDA*'s glossary defines *video* as "Media used to store moving or still images, designed for use with a playback device such as a videocassette player or DVD player. Includes media used to store digitally encoded as well as analog images." The examples in this manual use the term *video*.

The DVD format has replaced half-inch VHS videotapes as the predominant type of video collected by libraries. In addition, dual-layer and double-sided discs are quite common today. Dual-layer discs contain two distinct layers of data and two serial numbers on the same side of the disc, are typically gold in color, and include a menu indicating the content on each layer.[2] Double-sided discs contain information on both the front and back sides of the disc and often contain different versions of the same film (e.g., widescreen and full-screen versions) to accommodate user preferences.

For catalogers familiar with *AACR2* and MARC 21, *RDA* requires a reorientation in thinking about video description. The focus on the carrier has been such a major part of our cataloging experience that we may have sometimes failed to give the work the attention it deserves. *RDA* requires catalogers to view the work as the essential core of resource description. Content trumps carrier. Description of the carrier, while it may receive secondary focus, is nevertheless still important, as there is a direct relationship between carrier specifications and access to content.

The ability to "FRBRize"[3] descriptive records opens up another option for libraries seeking to provide access to all expressions and/or manifestations of a work available in or through the library. The online catalog equipped with FRBR-based functionality enables linking of separate descriptive records to a main record that fully describes a single expression or manifestation of a work, generally the first manifestation received. Future manifestations of the same work require only a brief record listing specific physical elements related to the carrier and publication history, obviating the need for full resource description for each expression or manifestation of a work.

Resource Description

The work and its video carrier must be described sufficiently and accurately. A good rule of thumb is to consider any information that the publisher has noted on the disc and/or on the container as information worthy of inclusion in the descriptive record. The elements that help to identify the work and distinguish it from any other will help users feel confident enough to select the work as appropriate for their needs. Selection can be enhanced by links to reviews, trailers, and other supplementary information about the video that may be available on the web.

Figure 4.1 shows a decision chart that may be familiar to most catalogers. It represents the old concept of video description when emphasis was placed on the carrier type and on the selection of the MARC workform and codes required for this type of resource. The chart presents the common MARC fixed field values for the most popular video formats found in libraries. Each type of video represented in categories A through E is associated with the medium designator "Videorecording," the authorized General Material Designation (GMD) for all video types represented in the chart.

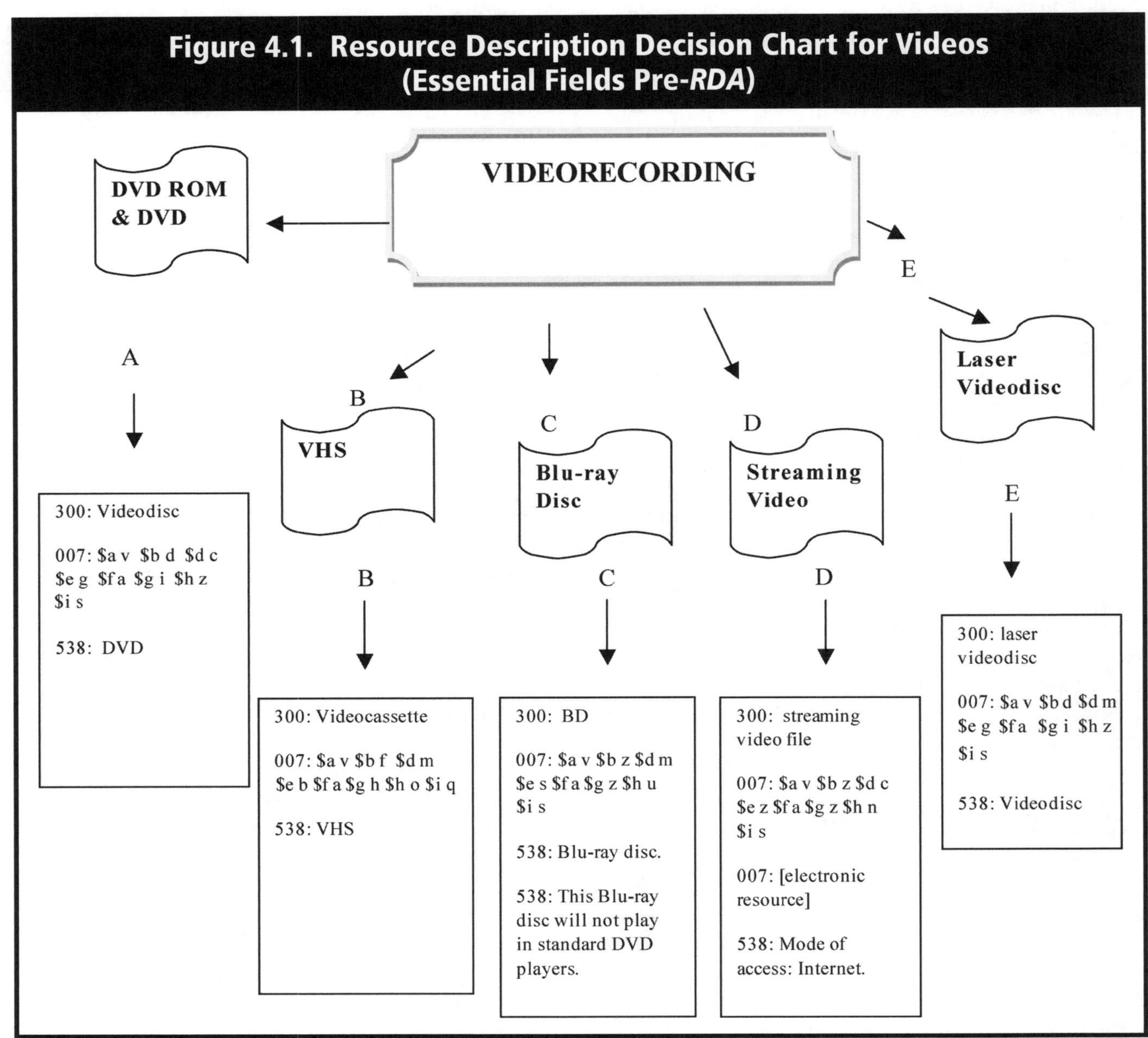

Figure 4.1. Resource Description Decision Chart for Videos (Essential Fields Pre-*RDA*)

The chart in Figure 4.2 illustrates a new way of thinking about resource description. Emphasis is placed on the description of the work, reinforcing the caveat that neither the carrier nor the display format

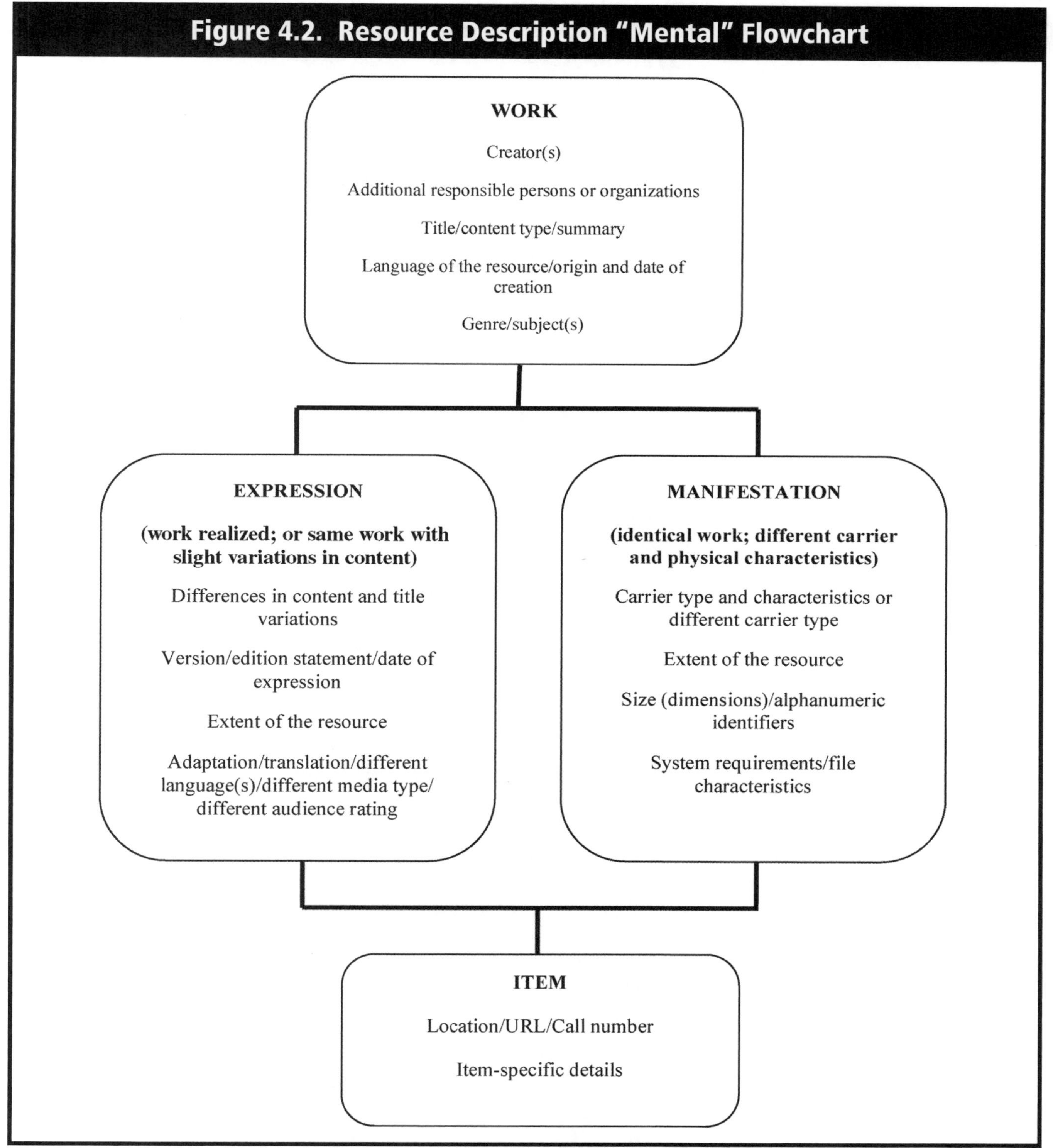

should limit the description of the resource. The discussions in this chapter have been influenced by the second chart.

Work

Elements related to the intellectual content of a resource include the title, the creator and persons/organizations responsible for its creation, and the subject matter covered. The preferred source of information for videos is the resource itself, and, when selecting the preferred title, catalogers are instructed to take the title from the title frame, item itself, or accompanying material in the order suggested below.

RDA 2.2.2.3 stipulates that "If the resource consists of moving images (e.g., a film reel, a videodisc, a video game, or an MPEG video file), use the title frame or frames, or title screen or screens, as the preferred source of information." The title frame is the preferred source for the preferred title of the resource and for any supplementary title information. *RDA* 6.2.1.2 instructs catalogers to take the title or titles from any source if the preferred sources are absent or do not offer an identifiable title. If attempts to locate the title from acceptable other sources are unsuccessful, the cataloger may supply a title. The devised title must be enclosed in square brackets, and the source of title must be documented in a general note area such as in the MARC 500 field. *RDA* 6.2.2.4 further instructs that "For works created after 1500, choose as the preferred title the title in the original language by which the work has become known through use in resources embodying the work or in reference sources."

AACR2 Rule 21.1C1 states that a resource should be entered under title proper (or preferred title) when personal authorship is unknown or is shared by a large number of individuals and authorship cannot be attributed to one particular individual. Entry under title is also recommended when a resource is not issued by a corporate body or when a resource is a collection of works by different individuals or corporate bodies. Catalogers are further instructed in Rule 1.1B1to transcribe the title proper exactly as to wording, order, and spelling, but not necessarily to capitalization and punctuation.

RDA, however, goes a step further and, in an exception to the general rule for collaborative works, in 6.27.1.3 (Exceptions), instructs the cataloger to enter videos, games, etc., under the title. The title must be recorded as it appears on the resource, and the use of abbreviations that do not appear on the resource is prohibited.

Record title information in MARC 245 Title Statement, which is not repeatable. Indicator values here control additional access to the title when it is not used as the preferred access point or main entry. When using the MODS scheme, record the preferred title of the resource in the <title> area. Use the DC element <Title> for this information.

AACR2 Rule 7.7B3 stipulates that a note indicating the source of title must be used if the title is taken from any source other than the prescribed sources of information or if it has been supplied by the cataloger. *RDA* 2.2.4 supports this instruction with the following guideline:

"If information taken from a source outside the resource itself is supplied in any of the elements listed below, indicate that fact either by means of a note or by some other means (e.g., through coding or the use of square brackets)." Such elements include the title proper, other title information, statement of responsibility, etc.

The source of title note and other such notes are entered in the MARC 500 field General Note, which is repeatable (see Example 4.1). MODS and DC also provide respective note fields (<note> and <Note>).

A note specifying the source of the preferred title may also be placed in the general note area of any metadata scheme or as a cataloger's note as recommended in *RDA* Chapter 2.2.4.

A note indicating that the title was taken from the container must be used if the cataloger has not viewed the title screen. Time restraints may prevent the cataloger from viewing each video for which he or she prepares a descriptive record, and this is acceptable, especially because pertinent information about the specific video can often be found on the publisher's website. However, a word of caution is warranted here. The cataloger must be absolutely sure that the information retrieved online is for the identical version being described and when doubtful must omit information that cannot be verified.

All variations of the title should be recorded, because they offer important access points for the resource. Record variant titles in the MARC 246 field Varying Form of Title, which is repeatable. Variant titles include abbreviated versions of the title as found on the resource and may also include parallel titles in other languages or the title that appears on external packaging or accompanying materials when different from the preferred title. Providing access to all variations of a title allows users to search for a resource in multiple ways. Example 4.2 shows the layout of a typical MARC 246 field. Use of indicators 1 and 3 instruct the computer to create a note for the other title and the print constant "Other title" may be generated for public display. Appropriate subfield codes can be used as required. For detailed information regarding the use of subfield codes in the title and variant title areas of the MARC record, see http://www.loc.gov/marc/bibliographic/bd20x24x.html.

Variant title information is entered in the title area of various metadata schemes and can be defined according to the type of title, as shown in Example 4.3, which illustrates the parallel or alternate title in a different language, using MODS.

For additional information regarding the selection and transcription of the preferred and variant titles, consult *RDA* Chapter 2 and Chapter 6.2–6.2.3.5. *RDA* 2.3.4.6 also provides special instructions regarding the titles on trailers that are produced in advance of the published resource.

RDA rules for description are not based on the identification of a "main entry" and/or "added entries." These concepts have been replaced by "preferred access point for the resource," "creator," "preferred responsible persons," and "additional access points." The preferred title is preceded by the preferred creator, when appropriate, and the preferred name of the creator is entered in the MARC 1XX fields, in the MODS <creator> area, or the DC <Creator> element.

EXAMPLE 4.1

500 __ Title supplied by cataloger.
500 __ Title taken from accompanying printed documentation.
500 __ Title from container.

QUICK TIP

Catalogers who submit descriptive records to OCLC should insert the encoding level "K" in the fixed field of the record to indicate that the cataloging is less than full level and is incomplete.

EXAMPLE 4.2

246 13 $a variant title, $n number of part/section, $p name of part/section

EXAMPLE 4.3

<titleInfo>
<title>Little red riding hood</title>
<title type=alternative>Petite chaperone rouge</title>

The statement of responsibility naming the individual or individuals responsible for the creation or production of the resource follows the title and can include the names of individuals such as directors, producers, screenwriters, production companies, and/or organizations responsible for producing the video. Others associated with the work or production may be recorded in the descriptive record, depending on the level of description selected. Rule 7.1F1 in *AACR2* instructs catalogers to include in the statement of responsibility individuals or organizations with a major role in creating a film. In addition, the Library of Congress Rule Interpretation (LCRI) for Rule 7.1F1 states that catalogers should include the names of those who bear some degree of overall responsibility for the work in the statement of responsibility in the order in which they appear on the resource. If recorded, these names can be used to create additional access points for the resource.

The names of other individuals or groups who participate or perform in the production of the video can also be entered in the MARC 511 field, which is repeatable. This field is not limited to performers or actors and may include hosts, narrators, interviewees, etc. The names of characters portrayed by performers can also be included in this field.

Use of the first indicator value of 1 instructs the system to generate the word "Cast:" preceding the information contained in the field. If the cataloger selects the first indicator of 0, this prevents the insertion of "Cast:" and allows the cataloger to control the display of the text in this field, allowing for the insertion of any term or heading the cataloger selects for display with the text (e.g., "narrator" or "hosted by"). The cataloger can also choose to omit the heading (see Example 4.4).

EXAMPLE 4.4

511 0_ Narrator, Howard James.
511 1_ Cast: Kim Basinger, Alec Baldwin, Michael Madsen, Jennifer Tilly.
511 0_ Hosted by Bill Moyers.

Catalogers are also required to specify the role or function of those responsible for the production of the video. This information is recorded in the MARC 508 field Creation/Production Credits Note, which is not repeatable, and can also be entered in separate 7XX fields for additional persons and/or organizations associated with or responsible for the work or its production. The decision to create additional access points for persons or organizations responsible for the production of the video is subject to local practices and may depend on the cataloger's judgment regarding the significance of the contribution. *AACR2* Rule 7.7B6 and *RDA* 7.24.1.3 instruct catalogers not to include assistants, associates, or others who have made minor contributions to the production.

The LCRI for Rule 7.7B6 also instructs catalogers to list individuals or corporate bodies in this order: photographers; camera; cameraman/men; cinematographer; animator(s); artist(s) illustrator(s); graphics; film editor(s); photo editor(s); narrator(s); voice(s); music; consultant(s); adviser(s). Furthermore, the LCRI for this rule stipulates that the following individuals or corporate bodies should not be provided in credits information: assistants or associates; production supervisors or coordinators; project or executive directors; technical advisers or consultants; audio or sound engineers; writers of discussion or program; others who have made minor or purely technical contributions. Indicator values are undefined for the 508 field (see Example 4.5).

EXAMPLE 4.5

508 __ Script, Wayne Wang, Terrel Seltzer, Isaac Cronin ; cinematography, Michael Chin ; editor, Wayne Wang ; music, Robert Kikuchi.
508 __ Screenplay, Ray Goldrup; edited by Stephen L. Johnson, Janice Hampton, Peter McCrea; music, Merrill Jensen.

Information regarding those who have made a significant contribution to a production can be quite lengthy and may contain references to corporate entities associated with the work (see Example 4.6).

Access points can be created for any leading performers and/or narrators and those with ancillary yet important roles, such as supporting actor/actress. These names must be entered in the MARC 7XX fields followed by an appropriate relator code that is entered in either subfield $4 (relator code) or subfield $e (relator term) to specify the role played by the person or organization named therein. Relator terms and codes provide searchable access points. Terms are preferred when using *RDA* as the basis for description, because the use of abbreviations is discouraged. Additional information about the 7XX fields is given at http://www.loc.gov/marc/bibliographic/bd70x75x.html. The list of approved relator codes is available at http://www.loc.gov/marc/relators/relacode.html. *RDA* Appendix I lists the approved *RDA* relationship designators.

The language of a resource is a required core element of description and insertion of a language code, indicating the primary language used in the video, is mandatory in the fixed field of the MARC record. When the code used in the fixed field is insufficient to represent the languages used in or associated with a resource, such as when multilingual resources are being described, the MARC 041 field and the 546 Language Note field are used in conjunction with the language code in the fixed field to represent the different languages contained in the resource. The MARC 546 note area also accommodates information about subtitles, the language of accompanying printed material and about closed-captioning for the hearing impaired and is generally not used when the resource is confined to a single language and lacks subtitles and/or closed-captions. The symbol CC on the external packaging indicates closed-captioning which is recorded in the general note area (MARC 500 field).

A summary of the content of the resource can help the user to determine the importance of the resource for his or her specific need. Summaries are entered in the MARC 520 field and should be limited to two to three sentences unless more information is warranted. Information can be taken from the container; supplied by the cataloger; or taken from a website such as the Internet Movie Database, the publisher's website, or, in some cases, a website established by the actors or performers in the video. The source of information used to create the note should be acknowledged. Alternatively, catalogers may reference a summary provided in an external source in the MARC 520 note and provide the link to the summary by including the appropriate URL.

In MARC records the first indicator value provides an introductory phrase for the 520 field. A blank first indicator value generates the display "Summary" in the public display version of the descriptive record. Other first indicator values that can be used are 1 for "Review" and 4 for "Content Advice." The second indicator value is undefined and must be left blank (see Example 4.7). For additional information on indicator values for the MARC 520 field, see http://www.loc.gov/marc/bibliographic/bd520.html. Enter summaries in the appropriate designated areas of the MODS and DC records.

EXAMPLE 4.6

508 __ Katowice: Produced by UNCHS (Habitat) ; director, Sharad Shankardass. A tale of four cities: Producers, Eleanor Cody, Sharad Shankardass ; director/script, Sharad Shankardass.

QUICK TIP

An optional track designed for the hearing impaired is not considered closed-captioning. This information must be recorded in a MARC 500 general note.

EXAMPLE 4.7

520 __ "A unique exploration of the maligned mother figure in Jewish twentieth century culture"-- Container.

520 1_ The Last Time I Saw Paris is an engrossing romantic drama that tells a good story with fine performances and an overall honesty of dramatic purpose."-- Variety (http://www.variety.com/review/VE1117792489.html?categoryid=31&cs=1&p=0)

520 4_ Space Chimps "includes mild sexual innuendo and toilet humor." $u http://www.sun-sentinel.com/entertainment/movies/sfl-

At a minimum, the cataloger must provide some indication of the subject matter or topics that are represented in the work. Subject terms are an important element of resource description specifically provided for the convenience of users and potential users. The subject matter can be conveyed either by using a summary in conjunction with subject terms or by adding at least one subject term to the description of the resource. Use of a subject term is required as a core element of description in *RDA*, as specified in *RDA* 0.6.7. The subject term is entered in the MARC 6XX fields and is generally taken from an approved list such as the *Library of Congress Subject Headings* (*LCSH*).

Genre or form headings provide access to categories within moving images, a useful feature that enhances the resource discovery experience for researchers and film buffs. They provide useful information about the work itself and can serve to distinguish between different works or versions of a work. The Library of Congress has developed a genre/form thesaurus to be used in conjunction with the *LCSH* manual and has reiterated that genre headings apply to the content of the resource, not to the carrier. Hence, the abbreviation "DVD" is not used as a genre heading. For additional information about the Library of Congress project, see http://www.loc.gov/catdir/cpso/genreformgeneral.html.

The approved list of genre headings for moving images (films, television programs, and videorecordings) is available on the Cataloger's Desktop (available at http://www.loc.gov/cds/desktop/; subscription required) and at http://www.hahnlibrary.net/libraries/formgenre.html. Some of the commonly used headings for videos include "Videorecordings for the hearing impaired," "Music videos," and "Musical films." The genre heading is added in the 655 field of the MARC record and cannot be subdivided geographically, topically, chronologically, or by form (see Example 4.8).

EXAMPLE 4.8

655 _0 Survival television programs.
655 _0 Musical films.

The indexing capabilities of the current library systems, specifically, keyword indexing, enable individual terms within the descriptive record to serve as points of access to the record and its contents. Now, more than ever, the cataloger's role is to look critically at the item in hand and describe it in ways that maximize chances for resource discovery.

Two popular feature films have been selected for examination: *Must Love Dogs / You've Got Mail* and *The Bourne Trilogy*. The MARC format is the display vehicle for the descriptive records.

The cataloger may begin by asking the essential questions: What is the work? What is the creator trying to communicate? What is the title of the work? The first work *Must Love Dogs / You've Got Mail* is billed as a "romance double feature," and this is prominently noted on the container. The way in which a resource represents itself often gives clues to its content and may influence the description of the resource.

Figure 4.3 contains publisher information and the image of the container for *Must Love Dogs / You've Got Mail*. The information on the container and/or accompanying materials is generally selective and may not provide all of the information required for comprehensive description. The publisher's information in Figure 4.3 alludes to the main cast members, the stars of the feature film. However, on closer

Figure 4.3. Publisher Information and Container Image for *Must Love Dogs / You've Got Mail*

 	**Product Details** • **Actors:** Tom Hanks, Meg Ryan (Romance Double Feature) • **Format:** Closed-captioned, Color, DVD-Video, Widescreen, NTSC • **Language:** English • **Region:** Region 1 (U.S. and Canada only. Read more about DVD formats.) • **Aspect Ratio:** 1.33:1 • **Number of discs:** 1 • **Rating:** PG-13 • **Studio:** Warner Home Video • **DVD Release Date:** January 2, 2007 • **Run Time:** 218 minutes • One disc containing recordings on side A and side B.
Product Details • UPC: 085391126362 • Source: WARNER HOME VIDEO • Region Code: 1 • Language: English • Time: 3:38:00 • Sales Rank: 1,454	**This set contains DVDs which may be available separately:** • *Must Love Dogs* • *You've Got Mail* **Features:** Must Love Dogs: Full-screen version; Additional scenes; Pass the Beef gag reel; Theatrical trailer; Languages: English & Français (dubbed in Quebec); Subtitles: English, Français & Español (feature film only); You've Got Mail: Widescreen [16 x 9 1.85:1] version; HBO First Look: a conversation with Nora Ephron; Interactive Discover New York's Upper West Side map tour; Commentary by director/co-writer Nora Ephron and producer Lauren Shuler Donner; Music-only audio track; Extensive enhanced features for your DVD-ROM PC; Theatrical trailer gallery; Subtitles: English & Français (feature film only)

examination (in the finer print on the discs and in the accompanying material) other important cast members are noted. Members of the cast are essential to the production of the film, and their names should be entered in the MARC 511 field (as shown earlier in Example 4.4). If their roles are significant, additional access points (added entry) should be created inserting the preferred names of the performers and/or contributors in separate MARC 700 fields or in the appropriate area of the MODS and DC records.

The producer also plays an important role in the production of the feature film and should be cited in the statement of responsibility. The producer also merits recognition as an additional access point for the resource. Personal and/or corporate names must be verified in the Library of Congress Authorities file, or in any other authorized source, for accuracy and appropriateness before they are added to descriptive records. In addition, appropriate relationship designators must be added to the names to specify the type of relationship to the resource being described. The use of abbreviations has been discontinued, and relationship is conveyed by the use of approved terms and phrases (e.g., "film producer"). The delimiter $e subfield precedes the relationship designator term and is repeatable, as shown in the MARC 700 field in Figure 4.4, which reflects the two distinct roles played by the contributor named in that field. The use of DVD-video, instead of DVD, reflects *RDA* terminology used to describe this category of commercially produced videos. As we continue to examine the pertinent fields in a descriptive record for a DVD-video, it will be helpful to refer to the descriptive record in Figure 4.4.

The title of the resource in Figure 4.4 comprises two distinct titles for two separate productions, and each title must be accessible to the potential user. Although the title must be recorded in the title field as it appears on the resource, the second title must also be used as an additional access point for the resource because either title can be used in a search query. The second title "You've got mail" has been entered in the MARC 246 field Alternate Title, as shown in Figure 4.4. Additional or alternate titles are recorded in the appropriate title field of the MODS and DC core record, generally accompanied by a term specifying the type of title (see Example 4.9).

EXAMPLE 4.9

```
<titleInfo> <titleInfo type="alternative">
   <title>You've got mail</title>
</titleInfo>
```

Expression

The DVD-video described in Figures 4.3 and 4.4 is a double-sided disc containing two different feature films—one on side A and one on side B. Both films must be fully and accurately described regarding the content, version, specific features, and requirements. The first-named film on the container must be recorded first in the $a of the MARC 245 field Title as the *preferred title*, because this is the title by which the resource is first represented. The title of the second film must be recorded in the subfield b (other title information) of the same field and must also be entered in the MARC 246 field Variant Title to provide an additional access point for the resource.

Edition and/or version statements alert the cataloger and the user to the possibility that the resource exists in another physical form or version. Edition statements must be recorded as they appear on the resource. Consider words such as "edition," "version," and "issue" as edition statements. Statements that note differences from other editions, as well as named reissues, can also be recorded in the edition statement area of the record (the MARC 250 field Edition Statement). This field may not be repeated, though it is possible to concatenate information in an edition statement. Catalogers using *AACR2* must ensure that any abbreviations used in the edition statement have been authorized in *AACR2* Appendix B; forms of numerals should be taken from *AACR2* Appendix C.

An examination of the features described in Figure 4.3 (see p. 141) reveals that the film *You've Got Mail* is distributed in the widescreen version and *Must Love Dogs* is the full-screen version, information that is critical for the user. Version is an essential element of resource description that is prevalent among commercially produced videos. Version also gives an indication of the extent of the work and other features such as a

Figure 4.4. Annotated MARC Resource Description for Cataloging the *Must Love Dogs / You've Got Mail* DVD-Video

Leader Positions	Position 06 [Type of Record]: g [projected medium] Position 07 [Bibliographic Level]: m [monograph]
006	Form of material "g" [projected material]
007	$a v $b d $c [blank] $d c $e v $f a $g i $h z $i s
008	Time: 218 Type of material: v Tech: "l" (Live action) Lang: eng Ctry: cau Date: 2007
020 __ 028 42 028 42 041 1_	085391126362 112636A $b Warner Home Video 112636B $b Warner Home Video $a eng $a fre $j eng $j fre $j spa [Note: The language code in $a is also the code used in the fixed field for language of the resource. $j is used to indicate the language of subtitles. Both $a and $j are repeatable. Corresponding information about language is entered in the 546 field (see below). The languages in $a indicate that the film is available for viewing in either of the languages selected (English or French). Spanish is only available through subtitles.]
100	[Not applicable since most DVDs are a cooperative effort of many individuals.]
245 00	Must love dogs $h [videorecording] : $b You've got mail [Note: The GMD, when used, is recorded after the first portion of the title.]
246 13	You've got mail [The second title is entered in the 246 to provide access to the second title.]
250 __	[This field has not been used for the edition statement since two statements would be required. The edition statement entered in the 250 field must pertain to the entire work. Since one statement cannot reflect the editions for both films, the 500 note field must be used instead.]
260 __	$a Burbank, CA : $b Warner Home Video, $c p2007
300 __	1 DVD-video (98 min. ; 120 min.) : $b sd., col. ; $c 4 3/4 in. [The duration listed in parentheses represents the duration for each video, separately.]
490 1_	Romance double feature [Note: The 490 field is used to coincide with the recent PCC decision requiring the use of 490 in field for all series. The series to which this video belongs has been verified in the Library of Congress Authorities database. Note the use of the corresponding 830 field below.]
538 __ System details	DVD video, NTSC; double-sided; Dolby digital surround stereo; surround 5.1; Region 1. Aspect ratio 1:33.1 Requires computer with DVD-Rom drive to access extensive enhanced features in "You've got mail".
511 0_	Must love dogs: Diane Lane; John Cusack. You've got mail: Tom Hanks; Meg Ryan.

(Cont'd.)

Figure 4.4. Annotated MARC Resource Description for Cataloging the *Must Love Dogs / You've Got Mail* DVD-Video *(Continued)*	
508 __	"Must love dogs": produced by Polly Cohen, Brad Hall and Ronald G. Smith. "You've got mail": produced by Nora Ephron and Lauren Schuler Donner.
500 __	Special features: Must love dogs: Fullscreen version, ... etc. "You've got mail": widescreen version; . . . . etc.
505 0_	Side A. Must love dogs. -- Side B: You've got mail.
520 __	"Must love dogs" is [include summary here] "You've got mail": the story of a mega bookstore owner and the owner of a small family owned book store who unwittingly fall in love, via email, while the mega bookstore owner, Tom Hanks, is trying to buyout the small family owned bookstore (owned by Meg Ryan).
546 __	"Must love dogs" : In English and French with English, French and Spanish subtitles. "You've got mail": In English with French and Spanish subtitles.
650 _0	Feature films.
655 _0	Feature films.
700 1_	Lane, Diane, $e actor.
700 1_	Cusack, John $e actor.
700 1_	Hanks, Tom, $e actor.
700 1_	Ryan, Meg, $e actor.
700 1_	Ephron, Nora, $e screenwriter, $e director.
700 1_	Donner, Lauren Schuler, $e film producer.
710 2_	Warner Studios.
830 0_	Romance double feature.
856 42	A URL may be added in this field to provide a link to reviews or to additional information from the publisher.
Note: All personal names must be verified in Library of Congress Name Authority file or other appropriate authority.	

film that has been edited for viewing by children or from which offensive language has been removed. A specific version of a film may also prevent its use by a certain category of users, such as if it has not been closed-captioned for the hearing impaired. A work expressed in a different genre, works that include additional content such as trailers, a translation of the work or film into another language and/or the uncut version of a film when an edited version exists—all require separate descriptive records.

As noted in the example in Figure 4.4 (see p. 143), the MARC 250 field Edition/Version was not used. The statement in the 250 field must refer to the entire resource. It is possible to construct a combined edition statement, but the cataloger in this example preferred to give the statement about the version of both films in a general note field. Example 4.10 shows additional examples of edition/version statements generally found on videos.

The original language of the film in Figure 4.4 is English, but it contains subtitles and/or additional footage in several languages. The descriptive record in Figure 4.4 demonstrates the use of the various fields required to describe multilingual works. Variations in language or the inclusion or exclusion of subtitles or assistive listening devices can generally be considered evidence that the resource in hand is a different version of an existing work. The inclusion of sign language in one version when absent in another requires the cataloger to create separate descriptive records for the un-captioned and captioned versions. Previously, such differences were attributed to a lack of uniform publication standards and/or to a lack of the cataloger's knowledge about motion picture and videorecording formats. Information regarding the language of the film and the presence or absence of subtitles and/or closed-captioning is important and must be recorded. Example 4.11 provides additional examples of the language fields used to describe multilingual and close-captioned works. Additional information on closed-captioning is available from the National Captioning Institute at http://www.ncicap.org.

Information about the geographic area covered by the resource can be entered in the MARC 043 field Geographic Area Code, which contains no indicator values and is not repeatable (see Example 4.12). The 043 field can accommodate one to three alphabetic codes, and multiple geographic codes are separated by $a. Additional information about this field is available at www.loc.gov/marc/bibliographic/bd043.html.

Manifestation

The content of the video is not visible to the naked eye, except when the appropriate equipment is used. The cataloger must therefore rely on the carrier and any accompanying material to supply the information needed for resource description. The level of specificity recommended by *RDA* facilitates differentiation between similar resources, including those of the same carrier type. An accurate description of the carrier is extremely important for differentiation and to provide advance notification of playback equipment required to view the resource.

"Carrier" is defined in the *RDA* Glossary as "A physical medium in which data, sound, images, etc., are stored. For certain types of resources, the carrier may consist of a storage medium (e.g., tape, film) sometimes encased in a plastic, metal, etc., housing (e.g., cassette, cartridge) that is an integral part of the resource." The video is one of many media carriers, and the term "videorecording" is currently used and may continue to exist in older records as the GMD for a variety of video types, including DVDs, VHS tapes, Blu-ray discs (BD). The specific type of video carrier determines the codes used in the MARC fixed field of the bibliographic record, and verification of the type of video carrier can generally be achieved quite easily by a close examination of the physical carrier, by

EXAMPLE 4.10

250 __ Director's cut.
250 __ Deluxe letterbox ed.; 25th anniversary ed.
250 — Newly transferred restored version.
250 __ Blu-ray version.
250 __ High definition, 2-disc unrated edition.

QUICK TIP

RDA prohibits catalogers from using abbreviations that do not appear on the resource being described.

EXAMPLE 4.11

Fixed Field code: spa
041 1_ spa $j eng
546 __ Spanish dialogue with English subtitles.

Fixed field code: eng
041 __ eng $a fre $a spa
546 __ Dialogue in English, French, and Spanish.

Fixed field code: eng
546 __ Closed-captioned for the hearing impaired.

EXAMPLE 4.12

043 __ n-us---
[North America, United States]

043 __ a-kr---
[Asia, Korea]

the declaration on the resource itself, or by the system requirements (as is the case for streaming video and video on demand) stipulated for using the resource.

Specific elements relating to the carrier and to the resource's use are considered technical elements. This type of information suggests and specifies the type of equipment needed to view the resource. In the MARC format, provide the description of the carrier in both the fixed fields and in the 300 field Physical Description. The 007 field Physical Description Fixed Field accommodates information about the resource and its carrier in alphabetic coded form. Information not coded or represented in the 007 field can be reflected in the 300 Physical Description field of the MARC record. Both fields are discussed in detail in the following section, and a full list of values for the 007 field for videos is available at http://www.loc.gov/marc/bibliographic/bd007v.html. The coded information in the 007 field in Example 4.13 defines specific elements of the carrier.

EXAMPLE 4.13

v	d	blank	c	g	a	i	z	s

007 __ vd cgaizs
v = a video
d = a disc
c = recorded in color
g = a laser optical videodisc
a = containing sound on the medium
i = the sound is on the videodisc
z = with dimensions not represented in the list of supplied dimensions
s = in stereo

EXAMPLE 4.14

300 __ 1 videodisc (30 min.) : $b sd., col. ; $c 4 3/4 in.

Some types of information are repeated in the 300 field, which is a variable field that contains additional information about the resource, such as the duration or running time. The 300 field, as shown in Example 4.14, includes the SMD (Specific Material Designation), extent of the resource, and other physical attributes.

The 007 fixed field and the 300 variable field complement each other. Both contain descriptive elements pertaining to the technical characteristics of the video. Information not included in the 007 field is often recorded in the 300 field, as in Examples 4.13 and 4.14. The running time of the videodisc was not recorded in the 007 field, but it is clearly stated in the 300 field. Running time is also recorded in the MARC 008 field (for those using OCLC, this field is located in the fixed field area of the record).

RDA retains the use of the *AACR2*-authorized SMDs for each type of video, and the chart in Figure 4.1 (see p. 134) provides corresponding MARC fixed and variable field values for the specific video types. These values describe some of the physical attributes typically associated with the specific type of video. For those using other vehicles for bibliographic display, such as MODS and DC, the information illustrated in Figure 4.1 is recorded in the specific named areas of those schemes.

Essential information not directly related to the intellectual content of the resource is entered in the areas specified for characteristics of the carrier or media type. This information can be entered in a header or in a separate technical record that also contains system generated data. Technical elements are entered in the MARC fixed fields as shown in Figure 4.4 (see pp. 143–144) or in the technical record or technical details area of other display schemes.

The manifestation of the work relates to its physical representation, and as such descriptive elements related to the carrier are a major focus of the description. Catalogers are instructed to provide the total number of physical items comprising the resource and the appropriate SMD per Rule 7.5B1 in *AACR2.* The SMD is not identical to the GMD. Rather, it is used to specify type, while the GMD describes the broad category of carriers into which a resource may fall.

DVD

As shown in Figure 4.4 (pp. 143–144) MARC descriptive records for the DVD-video are quite comprehensive. *RDA* descriptive records for the same resource will be practically identical, except for the addition of the MARC fields 336, 337, and 338:

MARC 336: Content Type: [Two-dimensional moving image]

MARC 337: Media Type: [Video]

MARC 338: Carrier Type: [DVD-video]

The following MARC fields have replaced the use of the GMD in *RDA*:

336: Content Type—This field accommodates information about the *type* of content, not the specific contents of the resource (e.g., two-dimensional moving image).

337: Media Type—This field contains the specific media type (e.g., video).

338: Carrier Type—This field contains information about the specific carrier (e.g., video disc, videocassette).

For additional information on these codes and the subfield codes authorized for use, see http://www.loc.gov/marc/formatchanges-RDA.html.

Record the extent of the resource (number of discs, file size, etc.) in the $a subfield of the MARC 300 field, which is not repeatable. Other information to include in the 300 field relates to the playing time of the video, sound and color characteristics, and dimensions (when applicable) (see Example 4.15). Enter information about accompanying material such as program notes or booklets in the $e subfield of this field.

Additional attributes of the video resource can be recorded in the general 500 note field of the MARC record when this information cannot be accommodated elsewhere in the descriptive record.

QUICK TIP

The MARC 006 and 008 fields also contain information that may relate to the technical aspects of a video. While the 006 field is used to complement the 008 field, in some systems the 008 and 006 fields are combined with the Leader fields into one general fixed field area.

Authors' Note: The insertion of the authors' notes in some fields in the examples and figures in this manual is intended to clarify or emphasize specific areas of the description and are included for illustration only. They are not intended as part of the descriptive record.

EXAMPLE 4.15

300 __ 2 videocassettes

300 __ 1 videodisc [It is also acceptable to use "DVD" instead of "videodisc." *RDA* requires the use of "DVD-video" in this field.]

300 __ 2 Blu-ray discs + $e program guide.

300 __ streaming video file [description for streaming video per *AACR2*]

300 __ 1 online resource (30 min.) : $b digital [description for streaming video per *RDA*]

AND

500 __ Streaming video file

EXAMPLE 4.16

020 __ 0774701919
020 __ 1417200871
020 __ 9781417200870
[10- and 13-digit ISBNs recorded in the same descriptive record]

The ISBN is a unique numeric identifier, one of many numbers that may be associated with a specific video production. Enter unique numerical data used to identify a specific manifestation of a work or resource in the MARC 02X fields or in the <resourceIndentifier> area of the various metadata schemes (see Example 4.16). Such identifiers serve to distinguish between different versions of a resource.

Older items are more likely to have a 10-digit ISBN, whereas the newer videos will contain a 13-digit ISBN or both. Thirteen-digit ISBNs begin with the prefix of 978 or 979. The ISBN is recorded in the MARC 020 field International Standard Book Number, which is repeatable. Do not enter more than one ISBN in a single 020 field except when specifying invalid or incorrect numbers, an occurrence that requires the use of a valid subfield code. The MARC 020 field has the subfields $a for ISBN, $c for terms of availability (price), and $z for canceled or invalid ISBN/ISSN number. The 020 field does not contain indicators. Additional information on the MARC 020 is available at www.loc.gov/marc/bibliographic/bd020.html. Detailed information about the 13-digit ISBN and guidelines on how to enter multiple ISBNs is available in OCLC's Bibliographic Formats and Standards at http://www.oclc.org/bibformats/en/0xx/020.shtm.

Miscellaneous numbers associated with a video can be entered in the MARC 024 field Other Standard Identifier when deemed important. For example, the 024 field is used to record Universal Product Code (UPC), barcode, etc., and is repeatable. Two indicators are defined for the 024 field. The first indicator is for type of standard number. A first indicator value of 1 (UPC) is used for videos. A second indicator notes a difference between a scanned number or code and the same number or code in eye-readable form. Three values are defined for the second indicator:

Blank = No information provided

0 = No difference

1 = A difference exists between the scanned and eye-readable versions of a number or code.

EXAMPLE 4.17

024 11 741952307198 [UPC Code]
024 1_ 0121390579 [Barcode from container]

If a second indicator value of 1 is used, provide both versions of the UPC in separate 024 fields (see Example 4.17).

Enter a formatted publisher number in the 028 field (Publisher Number), which is repeatable. Publisher numbers can also be provided in the MARC 500 field (General Note), in an unformatted form. Publisher numbers are helpful to distinguish among different editions or versions of a video and are searchable in OCLC and in ILSs via a keyword search or when indexed in the MARC 028 field.

The MARC 028 field has the subfields $a for publisher's number and $b for source of number. Publisher numbers for videos have a first indicator value of 4. The second indicator value for the 028 field can be used to generate a note and/or added entry. A second indicator value of 0 indicates that no note or added entry is generated from the 028 field; all examples in this text have a second indicator value of 0. Miscellaneous numbers, including those that cannot be identified in a specific category, can be recorded in the MARC 500 field General Note, which is repeatable (see Example 4.18).

Information about the origin of the descriptive record (organization responsible for creating the bibliographic record) must be entered in the MARC 040 field along with information about any institution that may have modified the record. The 040 field Cataloging Source is not repeatable. The 040 field is used mainly for records contributed to union databases such as OCLC's WorldCat. Cataloging source is recorded in the MODS element <OriginInfo>.

EXAMPLE 4.18

028 40 LSP 2061 $b DLOB
OR
500 __ "IMMW101 IMMW106" -- Container.

Blu-ray Disc

Blu-ray is an optical disc format jointly developed by the Blu-ray Disc Association (BDA), (which includes Apple, Dell, Hitachi, HP, JVC, LG, Mitsubishi, Panasonic, Pioneer, Philips, Samsung, Sharp, Sony, and TDK) and Thomson.[4] The format was designed to enable recording, rewriting, and playback of high-definition video, and it has five times more storage capacity than a traditional DVD. It is currently one of the predominant video formats collected by libraries, replacing DVD-videos. Blu-ray uses a blue-violet laser that has a shorter wave length than the red laser used in DVDs, allowing for "closer and more precise reading of information on the disc."[5] This capability also facilitates greater data storage in a smaller space. A special player is required to view this type of disc. The codes used in the MARC 007 field and the corresponding MARC 300 field to describe the essential characteristics of Blu-ray discs are shown in Example 4.19.

EXAMPLE 4.19

v	d	blank	m	s	a	i	z	s

007 __ vd msaizs
- v = a video
- d = videodisc
- m = mixed (recorded in color and black & white)
- s = Blu-ray Disc
- a = containing sound on the medium
- i = the sound is on the videodisc
- z = with dimensions not represented in the list of supplied dimensions
- s = in stereo

300 __ 1 BD : $b sd., col. ; $c 4 3/4 in. [*AACR2*]
300 __ 1 Blu-ray Disc : $b sound, color ; $c 12 cm. [*RDA*]

Note: Abbreviations are not used in *RDA* except in certain prescribed cases.

Figure 4.5 shows an image of the container for a popular film distributed on Blu-ray disc, along with publisher information. Note the Blu-ray symbol on the container. Figure 4.6 presents a descriptive record for the

Figure 4.5. Container Image and Publisher Information for *The Bourne Trilogy* Blu-ray Disc

<table>
<tr><td>
</td><td colspan="2">Product Details<ul><li>Actors: Matt Damon, Joan Allen, Julia Stiles, Franka Potente, Chris Cooper</li><li>Format: AC-3, Color, Dolby, Dubbed, Subtitled, Widescreen</li><li>Language: English</li><li>Subtitles: English, French, Spanish</li><li>Aspect Ratio: 2.35:1</li><li>Number of discs: 3</li><li>Rating: PG 13</li><li>Studio: Universal Studios</li><li>DVD Release Date: January 27, 2009</li><li>Run Time: 344 minutes</li></ul></td></tr>
<tr><td colspan="2">Universal Studios presents
Tom Gallop, Matt Damon, Franka Potente, Brian Cox, Chris Cooper, Julia Stiles, Joan Allen, Clive Owen, David Strathairn, Scott Glenn, Albert Finney, Edgar Ramirez. "Bourne Trilogy, The (Film Collections)"
Written by Tony Gilroy produced by Frank Marshall directed by Doug Liman directed by Paul Greengrass
Production Year: 2008</td><td>Technical Specs<ul><li>Blu-ray</li><li>BD-50 Dual-Layer Discs</li><li>Three-Disc Set</li><li>Bonus View (Profile 1.1)</li><li>BD-Live (Profile 2.0)</li></ul></td></tr>
<tr><td>Video Resolution/Codec<ul><li>1080p/VC-1</li><li>480p/i/MPEG-2 (Supplements Only)</li></ul></td><td>Aspect Ratio(s)<ul><li>2.35:1</li></ul></td><td>Audio Formats<ul><li>English DTS-HD Lossless Master Audio 5.1 Surround (48 kHz/24-bit)</li><li>French DTS 5.1 Surround (768 kbps)</li><li>Spanish DTS 5.1 Surround (768 kbps)</li></ul></td></tr>
<tr><td>Subtitles/Captions<ul><li>English SDH</li><li>French Subtitles</li><li>Spanish Subtitles</li></ul></td><td>Supplements<ul><li>Audio Commentaries</li><li>Featurettes</li><li>Deleted Scenes</li></ul></td><td>Exclusive HD Content<ul><li>Picture-in-Picture</li><li>BD-Live</li></ul></td></tr>
</table>

same feature film in the MARC format, and Figure 4.7 (pp. 152–153) presents the record in MODS format.

VHS Videocassette

Figure 4.8 (pp. 153–154) shows a descriptive record for the VHS cassette. The Type of Record code **g** for projected medium and the Bibliographic Level code **m** for monograph are mandatory for this format.

The 008 field includes the system-generated date on which the record was added to the system. The code **p** indicates that the date that follows in Date 1 position is the production or distribution date for the current

(Continued p. 154)

Figure 4.6. MARC Descriptive Record for *The Bourne Trilogy* Blu-ray Disc

Leader 06 Leader 07	Type of record: g [projected medium] Bibliographic level: m [monograph]
007 [videorecordings]	$a v $b d $c [blank; undefined] $d c $e s $f a $g z $h u $i s $a v [video] $b d [videodisc] $c [undefined] $d c [multicolored] $e s [Blu-ray disc] $f a [sound on medium] $g j [videodisc] $h z [other. Dimensions not represented in the list of supplied dimensions.] $i s [stereophonic]
008	Time: 344 Type of material : v [videorecording] Tech: l [live action] Lang: eng Ctry: cau Date: p [because the three feature films were originally produced before 2008] Date 1: 2009
020	[Not available to cataloger.]
028	[Not available to cataloger.]
100	[Not applicable because most DVDs are a cooperative effort of many individuals.]
245 04	The Bourne trilogy $h [videorecording] / $c written by Tony Gilroy ; produced by Frank Marshall; directors, Doug Liman and Paul Greengrass
250	Widescreen version.
260	Los Angeles, CA : $b Universal Studios, $c 2009.
300 __	3 BD (344 min.) : $b sd., col. ; $c 4 3/4 in.
538 __	Blu-ray 50 dual-layer disc. Requires Blu-ray disc player. Audio formats: English DTS-HD Lossless Master Audio 5.1 Surround (48 kHz/24-bit) ; French DTS 5.1 Surround (768 kbps); Spanish DTS 5.1 Surround (768 kbps)
500 __	This is a BD-Live enabled disc.
511 1_	Matt Damon, Joan Allen, Julia Stiles, Franka Potente, Chris Cooper. Also starring Brian Cox, Clive Owen, Karl Urban, David Strathairn, Scott Glenn, Paddy Considine, Édgar Ramírez.
500 __	Aspect ratio 2.35:1; AC3; Dolby. Video resolution: 1080 p/VC-1; 480 p/i/MPEG-2 (Supplements only).
505 0_	The Bourne Identity — The Bourne Supremacy — The Bourne Ultimatum.

(Cont'd.)

Figure 4.6. MARC Descriptive Record for *The Bourne Trilogy* Blu-ray Disc *(Continued)*

650 _0	Feature films.
700 1_	Damon, Matt, $e actor.
700 1_	Allen, Joan, $e actress [Enter a new 700 field for each person recorded in the 511 field. Remember to spell out the term in the $e as required by RDA.]
700 1_	Gilroy, Tony, $e screenwriter.
700 1_	Marshall, Frank, $e producer.
856 42	http://www.dvdfile.com/review/the-bourne-trilogy-bd-58149

Figure 4.7. MODS Descriptive Record for *The Bourne Trilogy* Blu-Ray Disc

```
<titleInfo>
<nonSort>The</nonSort>
<title>Bourne Trilogy<title>
</titleInfo>
<name>
  <name type="personal">
  <namePart>Matt Damon </namePart>
</name>
<name type="personal">
<namePart> Julia Allen </namePart>
</name>

<typeOfResource>moving image </typeOfResource>
<genre authority="marcgt"> videorecording</genre>
<originInfo>
  <place>
  <placeTerm authority="marccountry" type="code">cau
  </placeTerm>
  </place>
  <place> <placeTerm type="text">Burbank, California
  </placeTerm></place>
  <publisher> Universal Studios </publisher>
  <dateIssued>2009</dateIssued>
  <issuance>monographic</issuance>
</originInfo>
<language>
  <languageTerm authority="iso639-2b" type="code">eng
  </languageTerm>
</language>
<physicalDescription/>
  <carriertype> videodisc<carriertype>
  <extent>3 Blu-ray discs (344 min.) : sd., col. ; 12 cm.
  Aspect ratio 2.35:1</extent>

<physicalDescription/>
<version> Widescreen version </version>
<system requirements>English DTS-HD Lossless Master Audio
5.1 Surround (48kHz/24-bit)
Requires Blu-ray disc player. </system requirements>
<content> Bourne Identity--Bourne Supremacy--Bourne
Ultimatum</content>
<abstract>Matt Damon is Jason Bourne, a young man who
tries to find out who he really is after waking up from a
strange accident.</abstract>
<targetAudience> Intended audience: adults</targetAudience>
<note>
  <note type="statement of responsibility">Matt Damon;
  Julia Allen.</note>
<note>Blu-ray 50 dual layer disc.</note>
```

(Cont'd.)

Figure 4.7. MODS Descriptive Record for *The Bourne Trilogy* Blu-Ray Disc *(Continued)*

<note> In English with French and Spanish subtitles </note> <note>Title from container.</note> <note> These feature films were originally produced separately.</note> <note>Also issued separately in the DVD format.</note> <subject authority="lcsh"> <topic> Feature films </topic> </subject>	<recordInfo> <recordContentSource>Rutgers University Libraries. </recordContentSource> <recordCreationDate encoding="marc">100821 </recordCreationDate> <recordIdentifier>4556789</recordIdentifier> </recordInfo> </mods>

Figure 4.8. MARC Descriptive Record for a Videocassette

Leader 06 Leader 07	Record type: g [projected medium] Bibliographic level: m [monograph]
007	v $b f $d c $e b $f a $g h $h o $i u
008	Lang: ita Form of item: v Ctry: ita Desc: a Date type: p Date 1: 1993 Date 2: 1974
040 __	NjR $c NjR
041 0_	ita
245 00	Mussolini ultimo atto $h [videorecording] / $c produced by Enzo Peri ; screenwriter/director, Carlo Lizzani.
260 __	Roma : $b Istituto Luce, $c 1993.
300 __	1 videocassette (128 min.) : $b sd., col. ; $c 1/2 in.
490 0_	Video Club Luce
508 __	Director of photography, Roberto Gerardi ; editor, Franco Fraticelli ; music, Ennio Morricone.
500 __	Originally produced in 1974
538 __	VHS
546 __	In Italian.
511 1_	Rod Steiger, Henry Fonda, Franco Nero, Lisa Gastoni, Lino Capolicchio.
520 __	April 1944 ... Cardinal Schuster intervenes and Mussolini meets with opponents to the Partisan Command. When negotiations break down, Mussolini and his mistress escape to Switzerland disguised as German SS soldiers. He is captured and brought back for punishment.
521 __	"Film per tutti"--Container
600 10	Mussolini, Benito, $d 1883-1945 $v Drama.

(Cont'd.)

Figure 4.8. MARC Descriptive Record for a Videocassette *(Continued)*

650 _0	Motion pictures, Italian.
700 1_	Lizzani, Carlo. $e director $e writer.
700 1_	Steiger, Rod.
700 1_	Nero, Franco.
700 1_	Steiger, Rod, $d 1925-2002.
700 1_	Fonda, Henry, $d 1905-1982.
700 1_	Gastoni, Lisa.
710 2_	Istituto Luce (Italy)

manifestation and that the date differs from the original date of production ("1993") which is inserted in the Date 2 position. Note that the video was "originally produced in 1974." Because the date of the original production and the date of the current distribution differ, the code **p** is used in the fixed field to reflect this difference. Both dates are entered in the "dates" field of the fixed field, but the date of the reproduction is entered in the $c subfield of the MARC 260 field; data in this field refers to the current manifestation of the work. Information about the original date of production was entered in the general note field (MARC 500).

The language code is entered in the MARC 008 fixed field along with other codes required for all formats. In this case "ita" indicates that Italian is the primary language of the film. Information about the language of the film is also entered in the MARC 041 and 546 language fields. The presence of one language in the MARC 041 field indicates that the film is in Italian. The resource does not contain subtitles in another language. The number found on the container is possibly a publisher's number, but because this has not been verified as such, the information is put in this general note field. The 521 field contains, in Italian, the information regarding the recommended or target audience: Film per tutti = a G-rated film.

The VHS tape is no longer used as a video carrier. However, this type of video is included in this chapter because libraries are likely to have this type of resource in their cataloging collections. Although it may be cost-effective to convert important data from VHS to DVD or another current format, libraries that maintain VHS players may decide to keep their videocassettes for as long as the players are available. Example 4.20 lists the codes to use in the MARC 007 and other fields for this type of video.

Streaming Video/Video On Demand

The streaming video hybrid resource is typically described as both a video and an electronic resource. The video characteristics are addressed

EXAMPLE 4.20

Position 00	Category of material: v for "videorecording"
Position 01	SMD: f (videocassette)
Position 02	Undefined; leave blank
Position 03	Color: m (mixed)
Position 04	Videorecording format: b (VHS)
Position 05	Sound on medium or separate: a (sound on medium)
Position 06	Medium for sound: h (videotape)
Position 07	Dimensions: o (1/2 in.)
Position 08	Configuration of playback channels: q (quadraphonic, multichannel, or surround)

v	f	blank	m	b	a	h	o	q

007 __ vf mbahoq
v = a video
f = a cassette
m = mixed; recorded in color and black & white
b = VHS
a = containing sound on the medium
h = the sound is on the videotape
o = with dimensions 1/2 in
q = quadraphonic.

300 1 videocassette (35 min.) : $b sd., b&w and col. ; $c 1/2 in.
538 VHS ; stereo.

in this chapter because the descriptive record for this type of resource must contain two 007 fields: one to reflect the video characteristics and the second for the electronic aspects. The information provided here is based on "Best Practices for Cataloging Streaming Media" prepared by the Cataloging Policy Committee of the Online Audiovisual Catalogers (OLAC); it is available at http://ulib.buffalo.edu/libraries/units/cts/olac/capc/streamingmedia.html.

The OLAC document defines streaming video as that which is transmitted over a network and that may be played immediately without the need to first download an entire file. Content download starts immediately as a datastream, and a temporary file is created via buffering. The file is removed after playback. This process minimizes both the time required to view content online and the required storage space. Additionally, streaming video enables remote users to view live events in real time. Common examples of streaming video are lectures on demand, YouTube videos, and certain types of podcasts.

Note: Streaming video is categorized as an electronic resource for purposes of resource description. The title for a streaming video must be taken from the title screen or homepage of the resource on the Internet. The descriptive record for the streaming video file must also contain a

The OLAC document is currently the only source of information for cataloging streaming video; any documents or guidelines that are published after this book is released will be made available on the companion website for this book at www.neal-schuman.com/describingmedia.

corresponding source of title note, which is mandatory in resource description for electronic resources. Example 4.21 shows a sample 007 field for streaming video, highlighting the essential video aspects that must be recorded.

EXAMPLE 4.21

Position 00 Category of material: v for "video"
Position 01 SMD: z (other)
Position 02 Undefined; leave blank
Position 03 Color: c (multicolored)
Position 04 Videorecording format: z (other)
Position 05 Sound on medium or separate: a (sound on medium)
Position 06 Medium for sound: z (other)
Position 07 Dimensions: n (not applicable)
Position 08 Configuration of playback channels: s (stereo)

v	z	blank	c	z	a	z	n	s

007 __ vz czazns
v = a video
z = in a format not yet defined
c = recorded in color
z = unknown or undefined type
a = containing sound on the medium
z = the sound not coded
n = dimensions not applicable to this format
s = in stereo
300 __ 1 streaming video file (30 min.): $b digital, stereo, sd., col. (*AACR2*)
300 __ 1 online resource (30 min.) : $b digital, stereo, sound, color. (*RDA*)
AND
500 __ Streaming video file

Note that, unlike other remotely accessed electronic resources, OLAC recommends providing duration and other technical details in the MARC 300 field Physical Description for streaming video. Rule 9.5B3 in *AACR2* provides an optional rule for the physical description of electronic resources. Use the term "streaming video file" as an SMD. Record the file's playing time if it is provided or easy to determine (Rule 6.5B2, *AACR2*). *RDA* (3.1.5 and 3.3.1.3) requires the use of "online resource" for all online electronic resources. Information about the specific type of resource, streaming video, is recorded in the "File type" area of the metadata scheme or as a general note in the MARC 500 field, as shown in Example 4.21.

The bottom of Figure 4.9 lists a collection of streaming video files available from the Public Broadcasting Corporation's website (http://www.pbs.org). The production was divided into 11 separate video clips, and each was separately timed.

Figure 4.9. Collection of Streaming Video Files from http://www.pbs.org

Watch LOOKING FOR LINCOLN

Historian Henry Louis Gates Jr.'s quest to piece together Lincoln's complex life takes him from Illinois to Gettysburg to Washington, D.C., and face-to-face with people who live with Lincoln every day – relic hunters, re-enactors, and others for whom the study of Lincoln is a passion. Among those weighing in: Pulitzer Prize winners Doris Kearns Goodwin and Tony Kushner; presidents Bill Clinton and George W. Bush; and Lincoln scholars including Harold Holzer, vice chair of the Abraham Lincoln Bicentennial Commission; Harvard University's president Drew Faust and history professor David Herbert Donald; Yale University history professor David Blight; and Allen Guelzo of Gettysburg College.

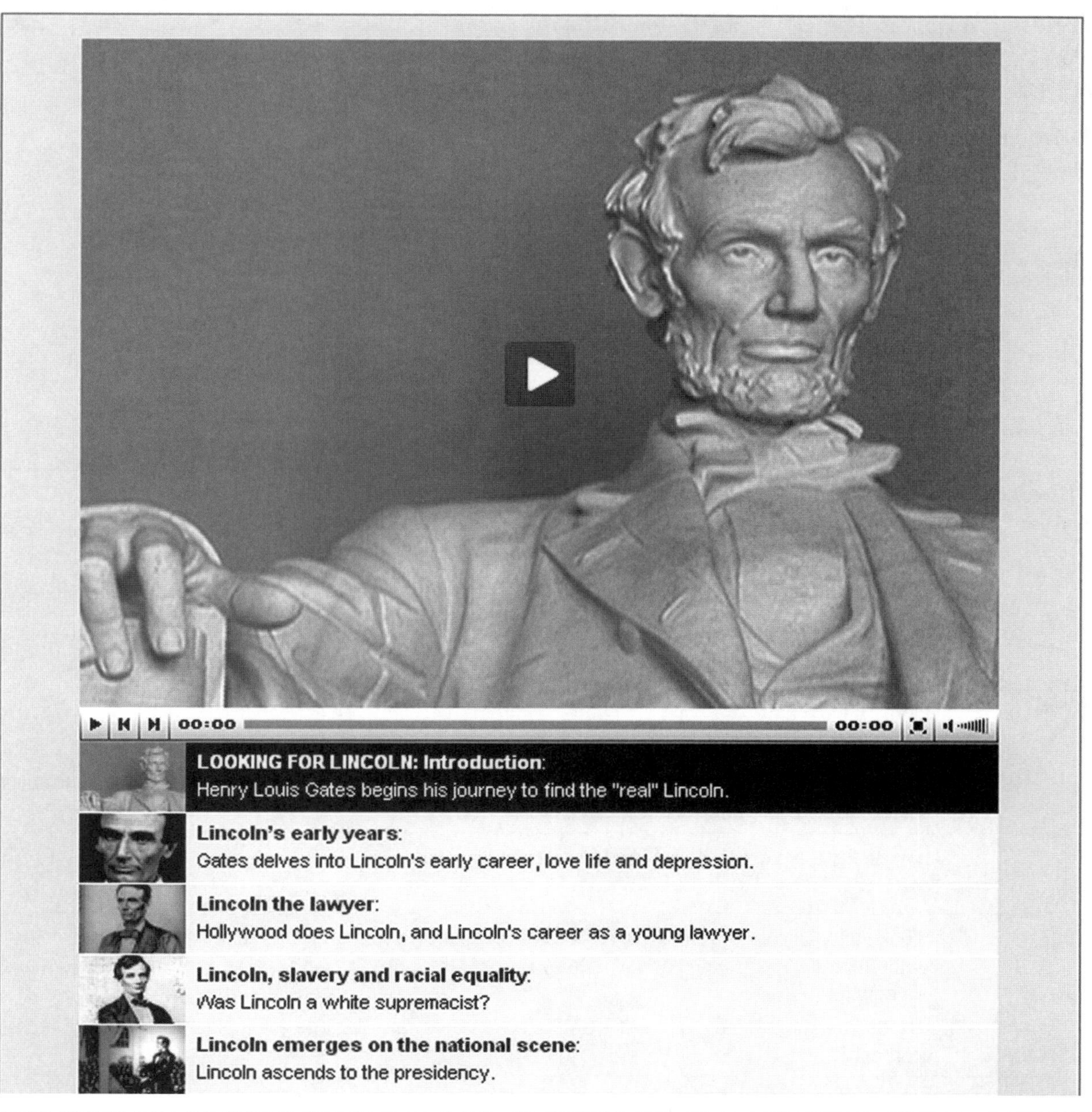

00:00
00:00
LOOKING FOR LINCOLN: Introduction:
Henry Louis Gates begins his journey to find the "real" Lincoln.
Lincoln's early years:
Gates delves into Lincoln's early career, love life and depression.
Lincoln the lawyer:
Hollywood does Lincoln, and Lincoln's career as a young lawyer.
Lincoln, slavery and racial equality:
Was Lincoln a white supremacist?
Lincoln emerges on the national scene:
Lincoln ascends to the presidency.

In the descriptive record for a multipart resource of this type, the URL for the homepage is the preferred locator because each title in the series is listed there. Providing individual access to each segment of the production offers the viewer the advantage of experiencing the production over a period of time. The video clips are a part of a larger website where additional information about Lincoln is available. For this example, the collection of video clips shown in Figure 4.9 is the resource cataloged in Figure 4.10.

Figure 4.10. MARC Descriptive Record for a Collection of Video Clips (Streaming Video)

Leader 06 Leader 07	Type of record: g [projected medium] Bibliographic level: m [(monograph]
006 [Electronic resources]	Form of material : m [electronic resource] Type of computer file: m [combination file-computer characteristics and video characteristics; live action, etc.]
007 [Videorecordings]	$a v $b z $c [blank; undefined] $d m $e z $f a $g [blank] $h [blank] $i [blank] $a v [video] $b z [other. No code defined for streaming video] $c [blank] $d m [mixed: multicolored and black and white] $e z [other] $f a [sound on medium]
007 [Electronic resources]	$a c $b r $d m $e n $f a $a c [electronic resource] $b r [remotely accessed] $d m [mixed] $e n [dimensions (not applicable to streaming video)] $f a [includes sound]
008	Total running time: [The total time for the entire resource must be entered here, if known.] Type of material: v[videorecording] Tech: l [live action] Lang: eng Form of item: s [electronic; "o" may be entered instead of "s" to specify that the resource is an online resource]
020 028	[These fields are generally not used for streaming videos.]
245 00	Looking for Lincoln $h [electronic resource] / $c a film by Kunhardt McGee and Inkwell Films in association with Ark Media ; presented and written by Henry Louis Gates, Jr. ; with special commentary by Doris Kearns Goodwin. [Note: Streaming video requires the GMD electronic resource because a computer is required to access the content.]

(Cont'd.)

Figure 4.10. MARC Descriptive Record for a Collection of Video Clips (Streaming Video) *(Continued)*	
260	New York, NY : $b WNET.org, $c 2009.
300 __	11 streaming video files; [the duration: the sum total of the 11 files should be recorded here when available] $b digital [file type is entered here, if available, followed by information about the sound and the color of the content.] [Note: The $c is omitted because "dimension" is not appropriate for this carrier type.]
538 __	Mode of access: World Wide Web.
538 __	System requirements: Windows Media player and Quicktime software.
511 0_	Narrated by Henry Louis Gates, Jr.; with commentary by Doris Kearns Goodwin. [Chief participants/performers/cast (e.g., narrator, commentator, etc.) are entered in this field.]
500 __	Title from title frame, viewed on March 15, 2009. [Note: If the title is taken from the title frame a separate source of title note is not required. The date viewed is important to establish context for the content.]
505 0_	Introduction (8.02) -- Lincoln's early years (8.45) -- Lincoln the lawyer -- Lincoln, slavery and racial equality (15.13) -- Lincoln emerges on the national scene -- Spreading the gospel of Lincoln -- Lincoln at the beginning of the Civil War -- Presidential perspective -- The Great Emancipator? -- Lincoln and the Civil War -- Assassination and aftermath [The running time for each videoclip may be entered after its title in the contents area when this information is available.]
600 10	Lincoln, Abraham, $d 1809-1865.
650 _0	Slaves $x Emancipation $z United States
655 _0	Documentary films.
700 1_	Gates, Henry Louis. $e screenwriter, $e narrator.
700 1_	Goodwin, Doris Kearns, $e commentator.
710 2_	Kunhardt McGee, $e producer.
710 2_	Inkwell Films, $e producer.
710 2_	PBS (Television)
856 40	http://www.pbs.org/wnet/lookingforlincoln/featured/watch-looking-for-lincoln/290
856 40	http://www.pbs.org/wnet/lookingforlincoln

Laser Videodisc

Laser videodiscs, also known as LD, LaserDiscs, and LV, Laser Vision, have been available since 1978. This format offers several advantages over VHS recordings, including picture and sound quality, special features such as multiple audio channels and still-frame archives (these features are why many publishers have made special editions of films available on this format), and durability. In contrast, some of the drawbacks to this format are high cost, provide playback only and no ability to record, and limited availability.[6] Example 4.22 shows a sample 007 field for a laser videodisc.

EXAMPLE 4.22

Position 00 Category of material: v for "videorecording"
Position 01 SMD: d for "Videodisc"
Position 02 Undefined; leave blank
Position 03 Color: b (black & white)
Position 04 Videorecording format: g (laserdisc)
Position 05 Sound on medium or separate: a (sound on medium)
Position 06 Medium for sound: i (videodisc)
Position 07 Dimensions: z (other)
Position 08 Configuration of playback channels: s (stereo)

v	d	blank	b	g	a	i	z	s

007 __ vdbgaizs
  v = a video
  d = disc
  b = black and white
  g = Laserdisc
  a = containing sound videodisc
  i = sound on videodisc
  z = with dimensions other (not listed)
  s = playback in stereo
300 __ 1 videodisc (104 min.): $b sd., b&w ; $c 12 in.

Note: The dimension of the videodisc is 12 inches. This dimension is not listed in the MARC list of dimensions for position 07. The letter z must be used for "other" than listed.

Physical characteristics are recorded in the appropriate areas of the DC and MODS records. Technical data is recorded in the technical details area of the record, and other details are recorded in the physical description area. Figure 4.11 maps the equivalent areas for the MARC record and two metadata schemes.

Item

Examples of information that is item specific include local notes and information regarding the single representation of the resource. Local and library-specific notes are recorded in the MARC 590 note, reserved in MARC 21 for locally defined practices and information. Typical uses of this note are to indicate copy-specific information, donor information, etc. (see Example 4.23).

Finally, the MARC 856 field provides any available link to online resources and can also include item-specific information related to usage restrictions, availability, etc.; a link to reviews about the work; and

EXAMPLE 4.23

590 __ Media Service's copy dubbed from original motion picture.
590 __ Gift of the Skipworth Family.
590 __ Does not include public performance rights.

Figure 4.11. MARC 007 Fixed Field for Videos and Their Equivalents in DC and MODS

Position	MARC 007	Dublin Core	MODS	Input Requirement (MARC)
00: Category of material	$a v = videorecording	Type	typeOfResource	Mandatory
01: Specific Material Designator	$b DVD	Type	typeOfResource	Mandatory
02: Undefined (BLANK)	n/a	n/a	n/a	n/a
03: Color	$d	format	physicalDescription	Mandatory
04: Format	$e	format	physicalDescription	Required
05: Sound on medium	$f	format	physicalDescription	Required
06: Medium for sound	$g	format	physicalDescription	Required
07: Dimensions	$h	format	physicalDescription	Mandatory
08: Configuration of playback channels	$i	format	physicalDescription	Optional

supplementary information including any other information or links that the cataloger may deem relevant and/or important to the resource discovery experience. According to the "Guidelines for the Use of the 856 Field" available at http://www.loc.gov/marc/856guide.html:

> The data in field 856 may be a Uniform Resource Identifier (URI), which is recorded in subfield $u. The necessary locator information may also be parsed into separate defined subfields. Note that separate subfields for locator data was provided when this field was first established in 1993, but generally, these are seldom used. An access method, or protocol used, is given as a value in the first indicator position (if the access method is email, FTP, remote login (telnet), dial-up, or HTTP) or in subfield $2 (if the access method is anything else). The access method is the first element of a URL. The field may also include a Uniform Resource Name or URN (e.g., a DOI [Digital Object Identifier] or handle).
>
> The $z subfield code in this field is used to provide use restriction information and various other types of information related to the resource referenced in the URL.

See http://www.loc.gov/marc/856guide.html for additional information.

Item information may also include local location information, including the call number and circulation information, so users can determine if the item is available in their library or elsewhere.

Notes

Rule 7.7B10 in *AACR2* provides for a range of notes, both prescribed and recommended, depending on the level of description the cataloger selects. Comprehensive description requires greater detail than minimal level description. Information included in the notes area can include video elements such as sound characteristics, length of file, color, and generation. Notes can be used to provide a variety of supplementary information about the resource, including contents, language, source of title, credits and cast, and features unique to a library's copy of an item.

According to the BIBCO Core Record Standards, some notes are mandatory, if applicable. These include notes pertaining to the source of title (MARC 500), additional formats (MARC 530), system requirements (MARC 538), language peculiarities (MARC 541), "With" notes (MARC 501), summary of contents (MARC 520), and access restriction information (MARC 506). Recent MARC standards updates require the addition of copyright status information (MARC 542). Other note fields are optional but desirable when appropriate, because the goal of "differentiation" is to describe the video so that distinction between resources is obvious to the user.

Notes are provided in the prescribed order for notes as stipulated in *AACR2* and are not arranged in numeric order by MARC field number. However, some online catalogs may arrange MARC fields numerically by default. There is no prescribed order for notes when used in MODS and DC displays.

Information about other formats in which a video has been issued is provided in the MARC 530 field Additional Physical Form Available Note, which is repeatable. Indicator values are not defined for the 530 field. Libraries are making increased use of this field to represent multiple formats in a single bibliographic record (see Example 4.24). For example, libraries that both own a DVD copy of a title and provide access to the streaming version will include in the record for the DVD, an 856 Electronic Location and Access Note to provide a URL and usage information for the streaming version and an additional formats note to describe the additional format. The "additional format available" note is also used to acknowledge when a resource has been issued in another format but not necessarily held by the library.

EXAMPLE 4.24

530 __ Also issued as a motion picture.
530 __ Also available as streaming video.

Notes indicating that the contents of the resource include two distinct works are called "With" notes and include notes for titles that are not the first in a collective title or when a short film or trailer, etc., is included with the motion picture or video. This information is provided in the MARC 500 field General Note, which is repeatable. "With" note information may also be used as the basis for a MARC 740 field Added Entry—Uncontrolled Related/Analytical Title (see Example 4.25). Such notes are entered in the general notes area of the various metadata schemes. The titles represented can be entered as additional titles both to provide access and to differentiate between similar versions of a resource.

EXAMPLE 4.25

500 __ With: Annabelle dances.
740 02 Annabelle dances $h [videorecording].

Note: The second indicator "2" in the 740 field indicates that the title in the entry is contained within the resource described.

Some types of technical notes, while not related to the content of a work, play an important role in distinguishing between different manifestations of a work. Rule 7.7B10 in *AACR2* specifies the type of information that should be recorded in the technical note, such as type of video, recording process (NTSC, PAL, SECAM), other special technical details, and special equipment needs if necessary. NTSC (National Television System Committee) is used for American videos, and PAL (Phase Alternating Line) is often used for European or Asian videos. SECAM (Sequential Color with Memory) is used less frequently and is more likely to be used in France and Eastern Europe. Equipment is normally manufactured to play only one video standard, although instances of equipment capable of playing two standards have been advertised recently.

The technical notes area also contains designated region information. Regions permit manufacturers to produce and market DVDs that may be viewed in a specific geographic area, a standard that was introduced when DVDs became available. There are six geographic regions (1–6). North America is Region 1. Region codes are provided on a label with a globe icon bearing a region number (see Figure 4.12).

In addition, some DVDs may be classified as "Region 0" or "Region all"—categories of DVDs that can be played on any player. Non-regionalized DVDs and Region 0 DVDs do not contain region coding and therefore may or may not include the globe icon. If the icon is included, the word ALL appears.

DVD players are normally manufactured to recognize or accommodate the specifications of a single region. A computer's DVD drive is capable of reading videos for all regions.

DVDs may be single or dual layer, with four different configurations: (1) single-sided, single-layer; (2) double-sided, single-layer; (3) single-sided, dual-layer; and (4) double-sided, dual-layer. This information is

Figure 4.12. Geographic Region Codes

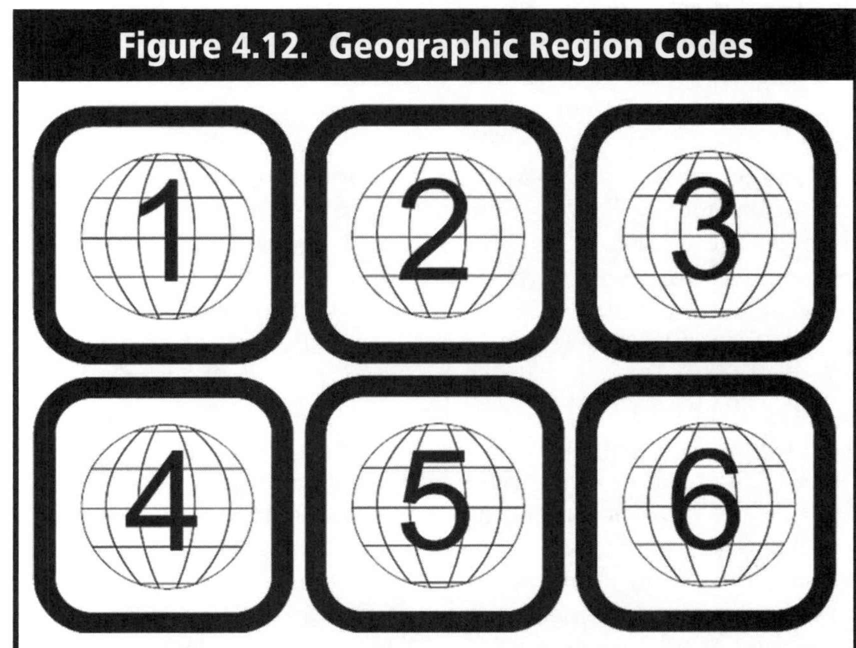

EXAMPLE 4.26

538 __ VHS (NTSC) format.
538 __ DVD, Dolby digital, region 1.
538 __ DVD, NTSC region 0, widescreen.

EXAMPLE 4.27

500 __ This film is "... substantially as it was when it was first released in 1928."
500 __ Originally broadcast as a segment of television program "Caucus New Jersey."
500 __ Originally released as a motion picture in 1996.
500 __ Based upon Batman characters created by Bob Kane and published by DC Comics.
500 __ Based on the novel Dog soldiers, by Robert Stone.
500 __ This is a Blu-ray disc made for Blu-ray disc blue-laser format players and will not play on standard DVD players.

EXAMPLE 4.28

500 __ Videocassette release of the 1978 motion picture.
500 __ A foreign film (France)

provided on the container. Include this information only if it is present, and use the wording as it appears.

A dual-layer DVD has a second physical layer within the disc that permits the disc to store more data than its counterpart, the single-layer DVD. DVD-R, DVD+R, DVD-R DL, and DVD+R DL are types of dual-layer DVDs. All DVD players should have the capacity to play all of these disc types. Variations in the prefix or suffix when describing DVDs generally refer to how data is stored on the disc. Use the MARC 538 field Technical Note for technical details such as recording system and playback equipment (see Example 4.26).

Notes related to the edition and/or publication history of the resource are also recorded in the MARC 500 field General Note area. Rule 7.7136 in *AACR2* requires the inclusion of this information if available as it expands upon and clarifies information in the 250 field Edition Statement (see Example 4.27).

RDA 2.20.7.3 instructs catalogers to "[m]ake notes on details relating to place of publication, publisher or date of publication not recorded in the publication statement element if they are considered important for identification or access." Record this information in the MARC 500 field General Note, which is repeatable (see Example 4.28).

The use of the contents notes ensures that each section of the work is available for resource discovery, which is extremely important when a work embedded in another deserves exposure in its own right. Contents can be as basic as summaries and commentaries or as significant as a list of individual works that are published under a collective title that gives no indication as to the content contained therein.

A summary of the contents is provided in the MARC 520 field, while a listing of the content, which may be formatted or unformatted depending on the cataloger's preference and the perceived needs of the user, is recorded in the MARC 505 field. Formatted contents notes ensure that both title and creator, if applicable, are indexed to provide additional access points for the works contained in the video. Unformatted contents notes are accessible through keyword searches.

Another useful way of exposing the content of a work is to link to the publisher's website where additional information is typically posted. The disadvantage of relying solely on this method is that it may require the user to first locate the "parent" title before the content can be discovered. Placing URLs in the contents area and other prescribed fields allows the user to link directly and effortlessly to the suggested location.

Record information on the contents of the video in the MARC 505 field Formatted Contents Note, which is repeatable. Per Rule 7.7B18 in *AACR2*, statements of responsibility and durations can be included to provide additional information to users. Contents notes in which the various parts of the note are coded are referred to as "enhanced." Enhanced contents notes contain subfield codes that allow for indexing in ILSs. The first indicator for the MARC 505 field has a value of 1 for incomplete contents and a value of 2 for partial contents. The second indicator provides information on content designation and has a value of 0 for enhanced contents and a value of blank for non-enhanced contents notes. The indicators for an enhanced contents note are 00 (a non-enhanced contents note has a single first indicator with a value from 0 to 2, or 8). Detailed information on recording contents is available in *RDA* Chapter 7.

External packaging will often advertise which awards a video has won, information that may be important for libraries with collections that emphasize directors, film genres, cinema studies, etc. Include this information in the MARC 586 field Award Note, which is repeatable (see Example 4.29).

The first indicator value for the 586 field can be used to generate the display constant "Awards." A first indicator value of blank generates the print display, and a value of 8 generates no display. The second indicator value is undefined.

Notes of a very general nature are entered in the MARC 500 field General Note, which is repeatable. Public notes can also be added to the delimiter $z subfield of the 856 field (URL), an accommodation that takes on added importance as more users access resources remotely. Notes are used to identify specific versions or editions of a resource and to specify format and the requirements necessary to view it. Notes also identify usage restrictions and may also indicate the number of simultaneous users permitted (see Example 4.30).

Most videos contain information about the intended audience and/or about the intellectual level of the content. Record this information in the MARC 521 field Target Audience Note, which is repeatable (see Example 4.31). The first indicator value provides an introductory phrase for the MARC 521 field that describes audience or intellectual level of materials. A first indicator value of blank gives the display constant "Audience." A first indicator of 8 is used when the cataloger provides the entire note. Because no display constant is generated, the cataloger needs to provide exactly what is intended for the user. The second indicator value is undefined. For additional information on indicator values for the 521 field, see http://www.loc.gov/marc/bibliographic/bd521.html.

EXAMPLE 4.29

586 __ Winner: National Board of Review, Best Documentary.

586 __ Academy Award Winner 2001, Best documentary short subject.

EXAMPLE 4.30

856 42 $z Related resources available at: $u http://www.ruthieandconnie.com/

856 42 $z Electronic version of index available at: $u http://pbsvideodb.pbs.org/ $z Access restricted to Rutgers University faculty, staff, and students.

EXAMPLE 4.31

521 __ Children under the age of eight.

Note: The public display of the information in the MARC 521 field (shown above) would be as follows: Audience: Children under the age of eight. The example shown below would be displayed without the insertion of "Audience."

521 8_ Intended audience: junior high and high school.

Resource Description (MARC, MODS, FISO) Checklists

The following checklists have been provided as a handy reference guide to the fields and/or areas most frequently used when creating descriptive records for videos. They are intended as guidelines and reminders. Cataloging treatment and choice of access points may vary by library, level of cataloging, and so forth. Always remember that you are the best judge when deciding which fields and/or areas are appropriate to describe the resource you have in hand, *distinctly* and *sufficiently*.

MARC CHECKLIST

For additional information about the MARC fields required by BIBCO (the Monographic Bibliographic Record Program), see http://www.loc.gov/catdir/pcc/bibco/coresr.html.

Leader 06: **Type of Record**: Use **g** for projected medium.

Leader 07: **Bibliographic Level**: Select as appropriate: **m** for monograph, **s** for continuing resource, **i** for integrating resource (including streaming video).

006: Only the first value is coded in this field: **g** for projected medium. This value determines the specific 008 field to be used for the resource. The other values for this type of resource are coded in the 008 field for visual materials.

007: Use for videorecordings.

Example:
$a v $b d $c [blank] $d c $e v $f a $g i $h z $i s.

008: Use for visual materials:
Running time: 216 min.
Type of material: **v** for videorecording
Tech: l
Lang: eng
Date 1: Date of publication
Date 2: Use when multiple dates are available, such as in multipart resources.

Other positions in the MARC 008 field relate to all types of resources and may be coded as required.

020: **ISBN**: Commercially produced videorecordings generally contain an ISBN, which must be entered as it appears on the resource.

028: **Publisher Number**: This normally includes a number and an alphabetic code for the publisher. Enter the alphabetic code in the $b subfield.

100: **Responsible Person** (author, performer): This field is generally not used in resource description for videos, because most videos are a cooperative effort of many contributors rather than the work of a "primary author" or creator. Corporate authorship is possible in selected cases, such as the publication of research activities or organizational policies in descriptions according to AACR2.

245: **Title Information**: Enter the title as it appears on the resource (giving preference to information found on the title and/or credits screen). The "item itself" includes the disc and its label.

246: **Variant Title Information**: Enter the subtitle and/or other significant title by which the resource may be known or identified in the MARC 245 field, subfield $b. Also enter it in the 246 field so that it is indexed and retrievable in a title query.

250: **Edition Statement**: Record statements such as "Collectors' edition" and "Widescreen version" in this field. The edition statement is not repeatable; concatenate as needed.

260: **Publication Details**: $a Place of publication : $b Publisher, and $c date of publication or distribution.

300: **Extent of Item**: Record the number of units that comprise the resource in the first subfield ($a). Also give additional information about the resource, such as color (in subfield $b) and dimensions of the carrier (subfield $c).

400: **Series Statement**: Provide if applicable.

(Cont'd.)

MARC CHECKLIST *(Continued)*

500: **Note Field**: Use for a variety of information, especially information deemed important by the cataloger but for which no MARC field has been specified. This field is also used for the mandatory "Source of title note" for streaming video and for any other resource when the title has been supplied by the cataloger.

505: **Note**: Record the contents of the video here. This is especially useful when there is more than one disc or tape or when more than one movie, episode, etc., is represented.

538: **System Requirements**: This is a mandatory field. Include requirements for video playback and other important technical details.

511: **Note Field**: Use this field to record the names of performers, actors, cast, etc.

508: **Note Field** (credits): Record the names of individuals who have contributed to the production but whose names were not recorded in the statement of responsibility.

520: **Note** (summary): Use to provide a summary of the resource's content.

650 and 655: **Subject and Genre**: Enter subject terms in the 650 field and genre headings in the 655 field.

700: **Additional Responsible Persons**: The names of additional responsible persons such as producers, performers, and/or actors who have been recorded in the descriptive record must be recorded in separate 700 fields.

856: **URL**: Use this field to provide a URL link to additional information, such as reviews and trailers, available on the Internet.

MODS CHECKLIST

For additional information about constructing a descriptive record for videos using MODS, see http://www.loc.gov/standards/mods/v3/mods80700998.xml.

Note: Details specific to videos must be inserted where appropriate to replace those used for motion pictures, as shown in the example on the MODS website.

Example:
Substitute term: "video" for film reel; and the GMD [videorecording] for [motion picture].

<typeOfResource> specifies the type of resource being cataloged; in this case it will be "video."

Example:
<typeOfResource>video</typeOfResource>

<genre> provides information on a style, form, or content expressed in the resource.

Example:
<genre>science fiction </genre>

<identifier> with the attribute " type" is used to provide standard identifiers, such as the ISBN.

Example:
<identifier type="isbn">9783540221814</identifier>

(Cont'd.)

MODS CHECKLIST *(Continued)*

<recordInfo> with the subelement <recordContentSource> with the attribute "authority" is used to provide the code or name of the organization that created or modified the original resource description.

Example:
```
<recordInfo>
  <recordContentSource>Rutgers University Libraries</recordContentSource>
</recordInfo>
```

<languageTerm> has the type="code" and authority="iso639-2b" (several codes may be used in authority; see http://www.loc.gov/standards/mods/v3/mods-userguide-elements.html#language for additional information).

Example:
```
<language>
  <languageTerm type="code" authority="iso639-2b">eng</languageTerm>
</language>
```

<classification> with the attribute "authority" is used to indicate the type of classification scheme used to provide subject access to the resource.

Example:
```
<classification authority="lcc">ML1.S6J65 2005</classification>
```

<name> is used to provide information on the name of a person, organization, or event (conference, meeting, etc.) associated with the resource. This element has a <type> attribute to specify the type of name (personal, corporate, or conference) and an authority attribute (<authority>) to enable catalogers to specify what authoritative source was consulted to provide the authorized form of the name. This element also has the subelement <role>, which is used to specify the role of the named person, corporate body, or conference in relation to the resource.

Example:
```
<name type="personal">
  <role>
    <roleTerm type="text">Performer</roleTerm>
  </role>
<name type="corporate">
  <namePart>Sony Video</namePart>
</name>
```

<titleInfo> is used to convey the title or name of a resource. When the main portion of the title is referenced as core, there is only one core subelement, <title>.

Example:
```
<titleInfo>
<title>Must love dogs</title>
</titleInfo>
```

Use <titleInfo> with the type="alternative" and the subelement <title> to convey title varations.

Example:
```
</titleInfo> <titleInfo type="alternative">
<title>You've got mail</title>
</titleInfo>
```

<originInfo> with the subelement <edition> is used to describe the version or edition of the resource being described.

(Cont'd.)

MODS CHECKLIST *(Continued)*

Example:
```
<originInfo>
   <edition>Widescreen version.</edition>
</originInfo>
```

<originInfo> with the subelement <place> and its subelement <placeTerm> with type="text", the subelement <publisher>, and the subelement <dateIssued> is used to provide information on publication, distribution, etc.

<physicalDescription> with the subelements <form> and <extent> provide descriptive information about the resource. In this text the authoritative source for <form> (used to describe the resource's physical description) is the MARC format.

The subelement <extent> describes the number and types of units that make up a resource.

Example:
```
<physicalDescription>
   <form authority="marcform">DVD-video</form><extent>1</extent>
</physicalDescription>
```

<tableOfContents> may be used for the contents of videos when this information is supplied by the publisher.

Example:
```
<tableOfContents>
Must love dogs--You've got mail.
</tableOfContents>
```

<relatedItem> with the attribute type "series" is used to provide information on the series when appropriate.

Example:
```
<relatedItem type="series">
   <titleInfo>
      <title>Romance</title>
   </titleInfo>
</relatedItem>
```

<note> is used to provide general information about the resource.

Example:
```
<note> Based on the novel by Burt Pine.</note>
```

<subject> may be used with various subelements. Use the attribute type "authority" and the subelement <name> with the attribute "type" (personal, corporate, conference) for names of persons and organizations associated with the resource as subjects. Use the subelement <topic> for topical subjects. The descriptive record should contain at least one subject term.

Example:
```
<subject>
<name type="personal">
<namePart>Burton, Richard Francis</namePart>
<namePart type="termsOfAddress">Sir</namePart>
<namePart type="date">1821-1890</namePart>
</subject>
<subject authority="lcsh">
   <topic> Women abolitionists.</topic>
</subject>
```

FISO CHECKLIST

Having constructed the descriptive record, the cataloger may find it appropriate to review the description based on the *FRBR* principles: *find, identify, select, obtain*:

F—The potential user has to *find* the material.

I—The user should be able to *identify* the resource, distinguishing it from any similar item.

S—The user should be able to retrieve and *select* the material as the appropriate one for a specific purpose or task.

O—The record should help the user to *obtain* the material by giving information about its location and availability and any requirements for and/or conditions of use.

The following questions are helpful in rating the completed product:

- ❑ How easy is it to find this record? Can it be found easily via a library catalog?
- ❑ If a potential user knew only some details about this work, would he or she find it based on the description and access points provided?
- ❑ If the user did not know of this specific manifestation of the work, does any other descriptive record in the catalog suggest the existence of this manifestation: (Hint: Have you used the Other Formats Available note?)
- ❑ Does the record contain information about, or links to, other manifestations of the work?
- ❑ Having reviewed the resource description, how easy is it for the user to identify the work and distinguish it from any other possible expression or manifestation?
- ❑ Does the record include unique resource identifiers (ISBNs and publisher numbers)?

Resources for Catalogers

Crutchfield New Media. 2010. "DVD and Blu-ray Discs: A Closer Look." Crutchfield New Media. Accessed August 4. http://www.crutchfield.com/S-8IdLAXIfDGi/learn/learningcenter/home/dvd_closerlook.html.

DVD Cataloging Guide Update Task Force, Cataloging Policy Committee, and Online Audiovisual Catalogers, Inc. 2010. OLAC. "Guide to Cataloging DVD and Blu-ray Discs Using AACR2R and MARC 21: 2008 Update." Accessed August 4. http://www.olacinc.org/drupal/capc_files/DVD_guide_final.pdf.

DVD Forum Official Website. 2010. "Welcome to DVD Forum." DVD Forum. Accessed August 4. http://www.dvdforum.org/forum.shtml.

Notes

1. American Library Association, Canadian Library Association, and CILIP: Chartered Institute of Library and Information Professionals. 2010. *Resource Description and Access* (Chapter 6.27.1.3). ALA, CLA, and CILIP. Accessed August 1. http://www.rdatoolkit.org.
2. AllforMP3.com. 2010. "What's a Dual-Layer Disc?" (DVD FAQ). Allfor MP3.com. Accessed August 3. http://www.allformp3.com/dvd-faqs/118.htm.
3. Tillet, Barbara. 2004. "What Is *FRBR*? A Conceptual Model for the Bibliographic Universe." Cataloging Distribution Service. http://www.loc.gov/cds/FRBR.html.

4. Blu-ray.com. 2010. "What Is Blu-ray?" Blu-ray.com. Accessed June 11. http://www.blu-ray.com/info.
5. Monaghan, Erin. 2010. "The Difference between DVD and Blu-ray." TopTenReviews. Accessed August 30. http://dvd-players.toptenreviews.com/hd-and-blu-ray/the-difference-between-dvd-and-blu-ray.htm.
6. Herranen, Henrik, and Timm Doolen (compilers). 1995/2007. "LaserDisc FAQ." Blam Entertainment Group. http://www.blam1.com/LaserDisc/FAQ.

Electronic Resources

Overview

The dynamic nature of electronic resources guaranteed that change was inevitable for the nomenclature and rules of description for these resources. As a result, the rules of description for the electronic carrier evolved as the carrier evolved. The proliferation of content delivered via the electronic carrier prompted the revision of Chapter 9 of *AACR2* in 2002 and gave rise to other interim decisions designed to accommodate the description of this evolving resource type.

An electronic resource is defined as "[a] material (data and/or program[s]) encoded for manipulation by a computerized device. This material may require the use of a peripheral device directly connected to a computer (e.g., CD-ROM drive) or a connection to a computer network such as the Internet."[1] The term "electronic resource" has been replaced by "digital resource" and "online resource" in *RDA*, although the definitions remain essentially unchanged. According to *RDA*'s Glossary, "digital resource" applies to any type of resource that requires use of a computer for access, while "online resource" refers to digital resources accessed via connections to a communications network such as the Internet. The term "electronic resource" is used in this chapter, a decision based on the fact that this term has been widely used in libraries for many years.

Dissatisfaction with the limitations of the MARC format led to the emergence of various metadata schemes designed to overcome its perceived shortcomings. In 1997, at approximately the same time that the idea of the Dublin Core (DC) format[2] began to enter the collective consciousness of library professionals, a major change in MARC coding for electronic resources, coding for content instead of carrier, was instituted.[3]

The changes introduced at that time, combined with the publication of the *Draft Interim Guidelines for Cataloging Electronic Resources* in 1997,[4] the subsequent revision of *AACR2* Chapter 9 in 2002, and the completion of the *Functional Requirements for Bibliographic*

IN THIS CHAPTER:

Records (*FRBR*) document,[5] all led to the eventual revision of the entire cataloging code, referred to during the early stages of the revision as *AACRIII*. These changes irrevocably altered the cataloging environment and laid the groundwork for the transition to *RDA*. *RDA* is now the new cataloging code, and MARC co-exists alongside various metadata, the best known of which are the schemes DC and MODS schemes.

The triumph of content over carrier can be considered the bedrock of *RDA*. The publication of the *Draft Interim Guidelines for Cataloging Electronic Resources* established that the groundwork was being laid for the sweeping changes to come with *RDA* in the ways that the bibliographic entity was conceived and described. The following quote from the *Descriptive Cataloging Manual* (Section B19), available at http://www.loc.gov/catdir/cpso/dcmb19_4.html, both suggests and confirms this relationship:

> The interim guidelines establish a common context through the use of entities and concepts derived from an entity analysis technique and based on work done heretofore in LC as part of information modeling and in the more recent work that resulted in an IFLA study Functional Requirements for Bibliographic Records final report: July 1997.[6]

Content is now the overarching focal point and along with media type determines the nature of the cataloging treatment ascribed to each resource type. The emphasis on content also facilitates the "FRBRization"[7] of disparate resources, because FRBR-enabled *software* facilitates the linking of bibliographic records based on related content irrespective of carrier. The FRBR concept is described in detail at http://www.loc.gov/cds/FRBR.html.

Electronic resources can be accessed either directly or remotely, with combined access increasingly being offered by publishers. Combined access requires that, at some time during its use, someone using a direct access resource log on to the Internet to use supplementary or related information.

Electronic resources that are accessed directly are characterized by tangible carriers, such as compact discs, DVDs, and CD-ROMS, on which reside computer software, electronic programs, games, statistical/numerical data, electronic books, maps, etc. Some publishers use flash drives to store accompanying data for printed resources. Based on current trends, it is anticipated that the Blu-ray disc will increasingly be used to store programs and other types of information typically put on CDs and DVDs. The Blu-ray disc is being hailed in some circles as the carrier of the future, because it has a vastly increased storage capacity with no increase in carrier size.

Electronic resources that are accessed remotely include those accessed via the Internet or that reside in cyberspace in the form of webcasts, websites, databases, maps, etc. Computer software, games, statistical/numerical data, and electronic books are now commonplace on the Internet, a scenario that often means that the same work is available in both remote and direct access formats—either separately or in some combination.

The explosion of e-content providers offering full-text content via networked resources and/or the Internet has greatly influenced purchasing decisions in libraries. The array of packages available from vendors demands that libraries reevaluate the ways in which descriptive metadata for electronic resources are added to the online catalog, especially for electronic books (generally called e-books). The emergence of new services and vendors, such as EBL and ebrary (which provide access to electronic book collections), has encouraged libraries to review their policies regarding resource description, because vendors offer full bibliographic records, ready for download into the library's ILS, for the titles that a library leases or purchases. Resource description pertaining to electronic books is discussed in this chapter along with electronic theses and dissertations.

Important Considerations

As we examine the cataloging of electronic resources, a few considerations loom large. More than any other type of resource, the description of electronic resources has been subjected to many changes over the past years, and this is expected to continue as newer carrier types evolve. Subsequently, catalogers who use the MARC format must be vigilant when importing descriptive records from bibliographic utilities and/or online catalogs. Changes and other miscellaneous revisions have resulted in records, currently available in many databases, that are now coded incorrectly or that may contain obsolete terms. For example, one can still find descriptive records that contain the GMD "computer file" rather than the current term "electronic resource" in some online catalogs and/or databases; and this will change yet again because the GMD has been discontinued in *RDA* and libraries will change their policies accordingly.

Changes in the use of the code **m** in the MARC Leader 06 position (Type of Record), introduced in 2004, stipulated that the code be used only for materials that are truly electronic in nature. "Truly electronic" was applied to content that could not be construed as primarily textual. This change means that a large percentage of the websites and databases cataloged as electronic resources and coded **m** for Record type in the Leader 06 position now require the code **a**.

The "new" definition for code **m** (Computer file) further stipulated and clarified that only the following categories of electronic resources should be coded as computer files:

> Computer software (including programs, games and fonts) numeric data, computer-oriented multimedia, online systems or services. For these classes of materials, if there is a significant aspect that causes it to fall into another Leader/06 category, code for that significant aspect (ex. Vector data that is cartographic is not coded as numeric but as cartographic). Other classes of electronic resources are coded for their most significant aspect (whether the item is

Language material, graphic, cartographic material, sound, music, moving image). In case of doubt or if the most significant aspect cannot be determined—consider the item a computer file.[8]

Electronic resources that cannot be categorized as "truly electronic" (which cannot be coded m in the Record type field of the MARC record) require the use of the 006 field for electronic resources to describe the electronic aspects; mandatory for records cataloged in the MARC format. For libraries that contribute records to OCLC, note that OCLC uses the Type of Record field to sort resources by format. The code used for the "Type" of resource determines the codes that must be selected for other fixed field data elements in the MARC record.

Change is constant, and compliance has often been optional or unevenly applied. This has many ramifications for catalogers, who must decide whether to upgrade the incorrectly coded record encountered when using copy from cataloging utilities. The best practice is to apply decisions uniformly and to always carefully review records imported from external sources.

Content versus Carrier

The term "electronic resource" specifies a type of resource delivered via an electronic carrier, which can be tangible or remote. The term "electronic book" refers to textual content realized in digital form (using the remote online vehicle or the compact disc as the carrier). The same content may be available in print using a volume as the carrier and constituting a different manifestation of the resource. Resource description for both manifestations will be almost identical in all areas except those pertaining to the characteristics of the carrier.

Free versus Fee

Several major players have committed to the digitization of books. Google, one of the most famous of these players, has reportedly pledged to digitize every book[9] that enters the public domain. Project Gutenberg was the first major project to digitize text, and the website now contains more than 100,000 books for free download. Today, an increasing number of publishers and vendors provide paid access to digital electronic resources, and this has introduced complicated and restrictive agreements and licenses. The availability of free electronic resources as an option to expensive resources offered through licensing/purchasing options has caused some in the library community to question whether the library should pay vendors for content that may be freely available on the Internet and whether patrons should be required to secure access to free content independent of the library.

Restricted versus Unlimited Access

As previously mentioned, access restrictions typically apply to information for which user licenses are required. This fact, coupled with the permanency of the resource, the frequency of update, and the extent of the content, requires careful decision making related to the availability and affordability of these resources.

Reproduction versus Born Digital

Many electronic resources are reproductions of existing works or works that previously existed in print. The concept of the "born digital" resource is complicated by the need to determine if the resource has been published in another format. The term "born digital" refers to materials that originate in digital form and is generally applied to resources that were first published as digital resources, not online versions of printed resources.[10] The result of this verification can influence description of the online resource.

Single Record versus Multiple Records

When describing an electronic resource that is largely textual, the cataloger must consider the manifestation in hand as possibly related to a printed manifestation, particularly resources bearing a date earlier than 2000. If the existence of a printed version has been verified, the cataloger must make a decision regarding the description of the electronic manifestation or version.

The Library of Congress has issued guidelines for cataloging electronic resources that fall within this category (available at http://www.loc.gov/catdir/cpso/dcmb19_4.html). The guidelines accommodate both the single record and the multiple records options. The single record option requires delineation of the electronic manifestation on the record for the original. This option is preferred by some libraries and is an attractive option largely because it eliminates the need to create another full bibliographic record. If this option is selected, however, the details of the electronic version must be comprehensive enough to allow for positive identification and distinction of the resource. Libraries may find it helpful to adopt a uniform policy after the decision has been made in favor of one option or the other. This is usually not the type of decision that lends itself to a case by case review.

Copyright Issues

Copyright issues regarding electronic resources are still being deliberated, both nationally and internationally. It is important to know what constitutes fair use, because the cataloger and library responsible for making a restricted resource available in violation of copyright laws can be found liable for copyright infringement. Increasingly, rights information is required in resource description, especially for digital resources. The Digital Millennium Copyright Act (DMCA), a summary of which is available at www.copyright.gov/legislation/dmca.pdf, provides guidelines for libraries concerning fair use for educational purposes. Another source of permissions is the Creative Commons, which generally affords more flexibility for copyright holders and the user community. More information about the Creative Commons is available at creativecommons.org.

Networked Resources

All resources offered by a library must be presented in ways that will encourage use without frustration. How the library deals with the dual systems of the ILS and repository in place at many larger institutions is the key to successfully facilitating true access to all resources. With the overabundance of resources available to users, no library can or should aim to provide access to all relevant resources. It is paramount, however, that a library provides access to all of its institutional resources, preferably via a single uncomplicated search strategy. This somewhat elusive goal is of pressing concern to libraries in large universities that typically maintain an integrated library catalog, generally MARC based, that exists in parallel with an institutional repository, generally based on a locally developed metadata scheme or on one of the existing commercial options. We examine the cataloging of networked resources in this chapter.

Electronic resources provide valuable content and cannot be ignored, and the integration of these resources into the online catalog requires advance planning. Answers to the following questions can inform a library's decisions regarding access to electronic resources:

- Who is the typical user for a specific resource?
- Is use of the resource restricted in any way?
- Is access to the content free for all users?
- Has the library paid for the resource with the intention of adding it to its permanent collection?
- What level of description is appropriate for "born digital" resources?
- Does the library own, or should the library own, the necessary equipment required to access or to view the resource? (Issues related to proprietary electronic book readers fall into this category.)
- How stable is the resource? Has the publisher indicated ongoing support for the product? (This applies to online content, particularly websites and electronic books.)
- Do multiple versions of the resource exist? (Multiple versions of the same resource present practical as well as intellectual dilemmas.)
- Is the full content available, or is it an abridged version or summary of a full-text version?
- Should the library consider providing access to electronic resources via a consortium to eliminate the responsibility for maintenance of the cataloging records, particularly URLs?

A valuable source for determining library policy for evaluating and cataloging websites is available at http://www.loc.gov/rr/business/beonline/selectbib.html.

Electronic publishing is a vibrant and dynamic industry that will continue to experience transformations in content delivery. As libraries continue to expand their electronic holdings and as librarians continue to grapple with the description of these resources, the questions and concerns previously posed will resurface for closer scrutiny and new questions will evolve. The key to success, however, lies in always keeping the needs of the users in focus while striving to provide access to information resources, regardless of format. We will examine in detail in this chapter and provide examples of descriptive records for the most common types of electronic resources that one is likely to encounter in the library.

Resource Description

Effective description of an electronic resource requires familiarity with the way in which the specific resource is intended for use. A hybrid electronic resource can include any number of carriers, remote and/or direct or a combination of the two. The carrier's characteristics must be clearly communicated in the resource description so that the user can determine the requirements necessary to view and/or use the resource.

Regardless of the codes and conventions used for data storage, display, and dissemination, the international library community continues to adhere to the core rules of description in *AACR2* and/or *RDA*. While the core rules of description have not been radically altered in *RDA*, they have been rearranged and refocused, with emphasis placed on recording the attributes of works, on collocating various expressions and/or manifestations of a work, and on delineating relationships among entities. The rules are no longer arranged by carrier (gone are the separate chapters on electronic resources, videorecordings, and other carriers); the work and its creator now receive greater prominence. *RDA* has the potential to change the way in which we conceive of the resource and its description, the layout and the terminology we use, and the way in which we examine and express relationships among entities, but the requirement for clear, precise description remains intact.

Catalogers are encouraged to believe that the enhanced descriptive record provides the best service to the user community. Undoubtedly, some catalogers will avoid the MARC format altogether and opt for one of the other metadata schemes, but, irrespective of the conventions used to display the resource description, catalogers should remain conscious of and responsive to user needs and expectations if the library is to remain viable. The description of electronic resources should answer, with the same clarity as for print resources, all of the questions that the user may have when trying to determine the identity and validity of the resource.

It is important to bring out all aspects of the item being described, including its content, its carrier, its publication type and status, and existing bibliographic relationships. In every area of the description, all relevant aspects should be described. As a rule of thumb, the cataloger should follow the more specific rules applying to the item being cataloged whenever they differ from the general rules.[11]

The selection of the core elements of description according to *RDA* reflects a new emphasis on supporting specific-user tasks. Resource description is predicated on the requirement that the user, or potential user, must be able to *find*, *identify*, *select*, and *obtain* the resources that are appropriate for their needs; they must be able to distinguish a specific resource from any other; and they should be made aware of the existence of related resources that may be important to their project or research. These requirements comprise the overarching principle that must guide and inform the creation of each resource description. The core elements are standard for all resource types and highlight the unique aspects of a work that serve to distinguish it from any other. Generally, the most important core elements are also primary access points. The BIBCO website contains a list of core elements for electronic resources, which include, but are not limited to, the title, publication details, source of title note, and system details note.[12] *RDA*, however, stipulates that the resource must be described as fully as necessary for differentiation. Full resource description, which will vary depending on the resource and its carrier, should be the goal for each record the cataloger creates. Regardless of the content and carrier type, the steps leading to a user's selection of a specific resource depend on the cataloger's description of the resource and on information about its precise location.

A well-constructed descriptive record should contain precise, appropriate access points, including the title, alternate title, or subtitle of the resource; the creator, co-creators, and/or any others or entities responsible for the intellectual content of the work; and the appropriate subject terms. Additional access points may include the publisher and unique numeric identifiers assigned to the resource. Access points aid the prospective user in finding, identifying, selecting, and obtaining appropriate resources.

The rules that govern the selection of data for specific access points are governed by *AACR2* and *RDA* and are fairly uniform for the broad spectrum of bibliographic resources. The preferred source of information for all electronic resources is the resource itself—an important change introduced in the latest revision of the *AACR2* rules of description for electronic resources, which can be viewed as evidence that the latest revisions to *AACR2* steadily became more aligned with the precepts of *FRBR* and *RDA*. Another major change gives catalogers the option of recording the extent of the resource when describing remote access electronic resources, hitherto a mandatory requirement restricted to direct access resources.

The discussion, recommendations, and examples that follow demonstrate how the *FRBR* entities are accommodated in MARC and MODS. The MODS schema was selected as representative of the various metadata schemes now available to catalogers. Both the single and multiple record options for resource description are discussed, and resource description reflects the guidelines issued by the Library of Congress's BIBCO Core

Record Standards (available at http://www.loc.gov/catdir/pcc/bibco/core2002.html#27).

Work

Conceiving of the work as a distinct entity (a distinct artistic or intellectual creation) requires the cataloger to distinguish between content and carrier. The cataloger needs to identify, describe, and record details about the creator and others responsible for the creation of the work, the title by which the work is known and identified, the origin of the work, the form and language of its expression and the nature of its contents.

The title is unique in that it is both a preferred access point and the most important element of description. The description of electronic resources, like that of all resources, begins with the accurate identification and transcription of the title. While the title of direct access resources can usually be found on the container and/or carrier and on the title screen or first screen of the resource, the location of the title of remote access resources is less uniform. The title may be given on the homepage or on one of the initial screens of the resource, or, as sometimes happens, the online resource may lack a clearly identifiable title.

The revised rules for description of electronic resources make it clear that the preferred source of information is the *entire resource*. The title should be taken from the title screen of the resource, if there is one, and may also be taken from an HTML header or, in the case of direct access electronic resources, from a label on the container.

As with all resources, it is important to transcribe the title accurately. When an alternate title or information that can be construed as an alternate title is found on the item, access to this alternate title must be provided in the descriptive record. The most important reminder is that one can take the title from anywhere in the entire resource. Title variations require the cataloger to correctly identify the title on the preferred source, and in some cases to use his or her judgment as to the "preferred title," and list the other titles as variant titles in the appropriate record areas.

The fluid nature of electronic resources, particularly those born digital, means that they are subject to changes in appearance, content, and, at times, even title. Such changes have influenced the decision to require a mandatory source of title note (*AACR2* Rule 9.1B2) even when the title is transcribed from the preferred source. The title must be transcribed exactly as it appears on the item, and abbreviations are prohibited unless they appear on the resource (*RDA* Appendix B4). If there is no clear title on the item, the cataloger is instructed to construct a title for the purpose of resource description (*RDA* 2.3.2.11).

The user must be able to verify the title and distinguish it from any other, and the cataloger is required to state exactly where the title was located by giving the accurate URL and the date on which the resource was viewed. Subtitles, alternate titles, and related titles help identify a resource and must be recorded as variant titles, an integral part of the resource description.

FOR MORE INFORMATION

OCLC's input standards for electronic resources: http://www.oclc.org/support/documentation/worldcat/cataloging/electronicresources

MARC format: http://www.loc.gov/marc/bibliographic/ecbdhome.html

Guidelines on the selection of access points, form of name headings, classification numbers, and subject headings are available in Chapter 1 of this manual and in *AACR2* and *RDA*.

FOR MORE INFORMATION

Consult *RDA* Chapter 2 for comprehensive instructions on choosing the preferred source of information.

FOR MORE INFORMATION

Additional information about identifying and recording the title proper and variant titles is available in Chapter 1 and on this book's companion CD.

The title of the work is the most important access point in resource description. However, distinction and/or uniqueness cannot always be based entirely on title variations. Catalogers must seek out and record all elements that make the work in hand distinct or unique and must describe the work in ways that clearly reflect those distinctions.

The creator(s) of the work must also be clearly identified and recorded as preferred access point(s) for the work. Enter the creator as the principal responsible person and in the statement of responsibility, which can also include other individuals or organizations responsible for the content. All names must conform to the established form of name as reflected in an authorized source such as the Library of Congress's Authorities database.

Record the origin of the work in the publication details area of the record, an area of resource description associated with both the expression and the manifestation of the work. Origin information establishes the existence of the work and can be critical in helping to distinguish among versions of a work.

The language of the content and the genre are both important aspects of the work. Although the existence of the work in another language and/or genre signals a different expression of the work, the language of the original work is significant and must always be recorded. Additionally, the resource must be described in the predominant language of the content, using appropriate notes to describe its content and authorized subject terms to enhance access to the work.

Figure 5.1 shows an example of a direct access electronic resource recorded in the MARC format. Leonard Frank is the primary creator of the resource, and his name is recorded in the MARC 100 field and in the $c subfield of the MARC 245 field Statement of Responsibility. This information is recorded in the MODS element <titleInfo> and the DC element <Title>. Additional responsible persons are listed in the MARC 700 and 710 fields, which are used for any co-authors, publishers, etc., who have significant roles in the creation of the work. This information is recorded in the MODS element <name> with the attribute "type" to identify type of name (personal, corporate, or conference) and in the DC element <Contributor>. Rules and guidance for the identification and selection of responsible persons are discussed in detail in Chapter 1.

Enter the preferred title of the work in the MARC 245 field. Record each title variation, as shown in Figure 5.1, in a separate 246 field to maximize access to the resource. The source of title note is mandatory for all electronic resources; record it in the MARC 500 field (e.g., "Title from jewel case insert"). Record the preferred title in the MODS element <titleInfo> and the source of title in the MODS <note>. Catalogers using DC will place the preferred title in the <Title> element and document the source of title in the <Description> element. The source of title note must always refer to the main or preferred title of the resource.

Record the origin of the work in the MARC 260 field (for publication details), the MODS element <originInfo>, and the DC element <Publisher>. The resource illustrated in Figure 5.1 was published in Califon, New Jersey, by the New Jersey Postal History Society in 2004. This

Figure 5.1. Descriptive Record for a Direct Access Electronic Resource

```
001        a2258361
006        m**** ***m* ******
007        co*cg---------
008        041223s2004 njua sb 000*0 eng d
035        (OCoLC)ocm57420456
040        NJR|cNJR
043        n-us-nj
050    4   ML561.8|b.W37 2004
100 1      Frank, Leonard.
245 14     The New Jersey Postal History Society presents the organ manufacturers of Washington, NJ|h[electronic resource] /|cby Len Frank ; from NJPH 2003-2004 in PDF format with album pages from the original collection.
246 30     Organ manufacturers of Washington, NJ
246 1      |iTitle from disc label:|aWashington, NJ organ manufacturers :|bNJPH 2003-4
246 3      NJPH 2003-4
246 1      |iTitle from PDF index page:|aNew Jersey Postal Society presents Washington, NJ, the Organ Capital of the World
246 3      Washington, NJ, the Organ Capital of the World
260        Califon, NJ :|bNew Jersey Postal History Society,|cc2004.
300        1 CD-ROM :|bcol. ;|c4 3/4 in.
500        Title from jewel case insert.
500        "Articles from NJPH / Jean Walton."--Disc label.
500        "April 2004"--disc label.
500        "PDF format"--disc label.
504        Includes bibliographical references.
505 0      Pt. I. -- Daniel F. Beatty -- Pt. II. Cornish & Sons -- Pt. III. Other organ manufacturers in Washington, NJ: Hornbaker ; Carhart & Needham, later Needham & Son ; Alleger ; Alleger, Bowlby & Plotts ; Alleger Acme Organs ; H.W. Alleger ; Bowlby's sons ; Plotts Gem Organs ; Florey Bros. -- Map -- Timeline -- The picture gallery -- Album index: Section 1. Alleger, Bowlby, McMurtrie and Plotts, Carhart & Needham, and Florey Bros ; Section 2. Daniel F. Beatty Organ & Piano Co. ; Section 3. Beethoven Piano Organ ; Section 4. Life of Beatty ; Section 5. Cornish & Son ; Section 6. Organ company trade cards ; Section 7. Clippings and miscellanea.
520        Between 1870 and 1920, Washington, N.J. became known as the Organ Capital of the World. Organ companies used advertising covers in mass marketing to sell directly to the public, making Washington, N.J. the third largest post office in revenues in N.J., after Newark and Jersey City.
538        System requirements: Adobe Acrobat, CD-ROM drive.
596        SPCOL/UA
650  0    Organ (Musical instrument)|xConstruction|zNew Jersey|zWashington.
650  0    Industrialists|zNew Jersey|zWashington.
650  0    Covers (Philately)
650  0    Postal service|zNew Jersey|zWashington|xHistory.
651  0    Washington (N.J.)
700 1     Walton, Jean.
710 2     New Jersey Postal History Society.
730 0     Journal of the New Jersey Postal History Society.|?UNAUTHORIZED
978       jmi
```

resource contains a single year of publication, which is also recorded in the fixed field of the record. When two or more dates are provided on the disc or carrier, catalogers are required to use the date of publication, if present. When it is necessary to record both a publisher and a distributor in subfield $b of the MARC 260 field, and the dates of publication and distribution differ, *ISBD* (Preliminary Consolidated Edition)[13] stipulates that each date must be recorded after its respective body (statement of function) for clarity. Additionally, the MARC 260 field can be repeated as necessary to reflect changes in publishers over time.[14] The MODS element <originInfo> and the DC element <Publisher> can also be repeated as often as necessary. For a review of the rules related to publication details, see www.ifla.org/VII/s13/pubs/isbd3.htm#18d

and the MARC website at http://www.loc.gov/marc/bibliographic/bd260.html.

Record details about the content of the resource in the MARC 505 field Contents Note and in the MARC 520 field Summary (see http://www.loc.gov/marc/856guide.html#other_fields for additional information about the use of URLs in these MARC fields). Record content information in the MODS element <tableOfContents> and in the DC element <Description> with the qualifier "TableOfContents." Notes describing the contents of a resource are required when appropriate. Although providing this information can be detailed and time-consuming, it is highly recommended that catalogers comply especially for multivolume works with distinctive titles so that the individual titles can be indexed in the ILS. URLs have been approved for use in these fields, and some catalogers may opt to include a link to online content information, such as a Table of Contents, when available.

Subject terms indicate content and are useful access points. The example in Figure 5.1 contains topical subjects (MARC 650 fields) as well as geographic subjects (MARC 651). When appropriate, enter genre headings in the MARC 655 field. Provide this type of information in the MODS elements <subject> and <genre> and in the DC element <Subject>.

The MARC fixed field area generally contains the technical information about the resource (i.e., system details), but it also includes selected information about the resource and its content. The MARC 008 field typically contains the code for the country of publication, along with information about the language of the resource and its contents.

The fixed field, shown in Figure 5.2 indicates that the language of the resource is English (Lang = "eng") and that the country of publication is "nju," the code for the state of New Jersey (nj) in the United States of America (u). Only one of the four fixed field positions for Content (Cont) was coded, indicating that the resource contains bibliographical

Figure 5.2. Sample MARC 008 Fixed Field for a Direct Access Electronic Resource

Books		Rec stat	c	Entered	20041223		Replaced	20050318025649.46		
Type	a	ELvl	M	Srce	d	Audn		Ctrl		Lang eng
BLvl	m	Form	s	Conf	0	Biog		MRec		Ctry nju
		Cont	b	GPub		LitF	0	Indx	0	
Desc	a	Ills	a	Fest	0	DtSt	s	Dates	2004 ,	

006	m m
007	c ‡b o ‡d c ‡e g

references ("b"). Detailed information about the contents is placed in the MARC 505 field Contents Note (for this resource content type would be expressed as text in the new field 337 Content Type), in the MODS element <originInfo>, and in the DC element <Language>.

Expression

Edition or version statements generally refer to the content of the work. The version and/or edition statement alerts the user that the work is available in another form, for example, a novel that has been translated into several different languages or content that has been expressed in a different genre. The form of the work and its genre type convey important information about the work and are generally selected from the list of approved types and forms available at http://www.hahnlibrary.net/libraries/formgenre.html.

The concept of "edition" or version is significant for electronic resources because software programs, databases, and so forth, often undergo many updates, typically within a short time period. A particular edition of an electronic resource may require a different operating system, more memory, and other peripherals, differences that are related to specific characteristics of the carrier. Edition statements are not limited to numeric terms, such as "3rd edition." The terms "release," "interactive version," "revision," and others signal a new work rather than a new manifestation. It is important to distinguish between an edition (which invariably includes new or altered content) and a manifestation (which may be referred to as an edition even though the content has not been altered).

Differences in the type and extent of the resource (the physical form in which the work was published) can also signal a new expression or a new version of a work. Generally, the extent (number of pages, size of file, etc.) is another significant indicator of differences related to both the expression and physical manifestation of the work.

Physical differences, such as those pertaining to the carrier, signal a different manifestation of the work and are discussed later in this chapter.

Remote electronic resources (called "online resources" in *RDA*) are considered published resources. The place, publisher, and date of publication must be entered according to *AACR2* or *RDA* guidelines, depending on the authority selected by the cataloger.

The MARC fixed field area in Figure 5.2 shows that the resource is issued as a monograph (BLvl **m**), and the Type of Record code "a" specifies that the material is textual. This field also contains codes for essential elements common to all types of resources, such as codes for year/date of publication (2004), which is a characteristic of both the work and its expression. Other codes indicate the language of the contents (eng) and whether the resource is fiction or nonfiction (LitF "0" = not fiction). The first indication of the language of the resource is given as a fixed field language code. The three-digit language code used in this field is governed by the MARC Codes for Languages (available at http://www.loc.gov/marc/languages/langhome.html). The MARC 041 field must also be used if the resource is multilingual or is a translation. Information pertaining to the language of the resource may also be entered in the MARC 546 field (additional information on the use of the MARC 546 field is available at http://www.loc.gov/marc/bibliographic/bd546 .html). Provide language code information in the MODS elements <language> and <note> and in the DC element <Language>.

Record the title of a related work (parent work or other) in the MARC 730 field when appropriate, including a unifying title that shows the relationship between the resource being described and the resource specified in the MARC 730 field. Record this information in the MODS element <relatedItem> and in the DC element <Title> with the qualifier "Alternative."

Manifestation

Characteristics of the carrier relate to the manifestation of the work and generally include physical and technical details about the carrier and carrier type and any unique numeric identifiers assigned by the publisher (the publisher's number and/or the ISBN). For tangible resources, the numeric or alpha-numeric identifier may be embedded in the disc or etched on a label on the container. For remote access resources, the URL and web address provide a similar point of uniqueness by capturing the specific webpage on which the document is located. For electronic books the Digital Object Identifier (DOI) is another type of unique resource identifier. Notably, for electronic resources found on the Internet, the URL and/or DOI are less constant than embedded numbers and present unique challenges for librarians and researchers related to broken links and changing locations.

Electronic Book: Compact Disc

Figure 5.2 (see p. 184) shows the MARC fixed field area for the descriptive record shown in Figure 5.1 (see p. 183). It is a combined fixed field area in which some 006 and 008 field values are entered along with Leader values and system generated data. The MARC 006, 007, and 008 fields relate mainly to technical details about the resource. These fields complement each other and are represented as a combined fixed field area in some systems, as shown in Figure 5.2. It is important to understand how these fields work with each other. The MARC 006 field is used when additional characteristics of a resource cannot be accommodated in the 008 field, which occurs when a single resource exhibits hybrid qualities or when the resource comprises component parts representing different media types. The MARC 007 field is mandatory in resource descriptions for electronic resources contributed to the OCLC bibliographic utility and recommended but optional for the MARC format. It contains pertinent technical information related to the carrier of the resource (a more detailed explanation of these fields is available at http://www.loc .gov/marc/formatintegration.html).

The form of material code, inserted in the first position of the MARC 006 field, is **m** for electronic resource. This is the only position that must be coded in this field. Because this resource is textual (Type of

Record **a** for textual material), the MARC 006 field for electronic resources must be added to the record to reflect the electronic nature of the resource. The second **m** signals that the contents are mixed or a combination of different types. The ninth position in this field is coded to specify the type of computer file and generally reflects the content of the resource. Some catalogers would have opted to code the ninth position for this resource **d** for document. If the resource does not belong in any of the categories specified in the MARC list of codes for this field, leave this position blank. The codes available for this field are listed at http://www.loc.gov/marc/bibliographic/concise/bd006.html.

The MARC 007 field, as shown in Figure 5.1 (see p. 183), contains **c** in the first position (Position 00), repeating the fact that this resource is electronic. The **o** in the second position (Position 01) signals that the carrier is an optical disc (CD-ROM). Direct access electronic resources on CD or DVD require this code, while remote access resources must be coded **r** in this position. The asterisk in the third position (Position 02) indicates an undefined position in the MARC 007 field. The **c** in the fourth position (Position 03) signals that the resource is multicolored, and the **g** in fifth position (Position 04) represents the dimensions of the CD-ROM (4¾ in.). (Additional details about this field are available at http://www.loc.gov/marc/bibliographic/bd007c.html.) The values provided in the MARC 007 field are recorded in the MODS element <physicalDescription>. Because DC does not specifically accommodate these kinds of characteristics, this information can be provided in the DC element <Description>, which may be used to record a free-text account of a resource.

Authors' Note: Along with changes to coding for computer files (*Draft Interim Guidelines for Cataloging Electronic Resources*, available at http://www.loc.gov/catdir/cpso/dcmb19_4.html), field 007 for computer files was made "mandatory in any record representing an item whose carrier is a computer file."

Other positions in the fixed field are selected based on the type of resource. The MARC 008 values specified for books must be used when describing textual electronic monographs, such as the resource in Figures 5.1 and 5.2 (see pp. 183, 184). This field is not repeatable. This information is recorded in the MODS element <genre>.

Various types of carriers may be used for electronic resources and they are generally categorized as direct or remote access carriers. Access to both types of resources is generally provided in libraries. The most popular direct access electronic resources are published on compact discs.

Authors' Note: In Figure 5.1 (p. 183) the General Material Designation (GMD) is used in the $h subfield of the MARC 245 field. *RDA* has discontinued use of the GMD. However, the term "electronic resource" is used in Figure 5.1 and repeats information found in coded form in the fixed field.

The direct access resource represented in Figures 5.1 and 5.2 (see pp. 183, 184) was not published by a commercial publisher and does not contain an ISBN or other standard numeric identifier. If this information were present, the ISBN would have been entered in the MARC 020 field and the publisher's number in the MARC 028 field. The MARC 024 field is used for "Other Standard Identifier," any other type of number found on the item. This information is provided in the MODS element <identifier> and the DC element <Identifier>.

Example 5.1 shows the MARC fields that have replaced the GMD used in Figure 5.1.

EXAMPLE 5.1

337 __	(Media Type)	$a Computer
338 __	(Carrier Type)	$a Computer disc

It is important to note that the 2004 revision of *AACR2* made the MARC 256 field (for file characteristics) obsolete, although this field will appear in older records. The 2004 revision also provided for the optional use of the MARC 300 field for electronic resources that are accessed remotely. *AACR2* Rule 9.5B3 states, "A new optional rule has been added to permit an extent statement for an electronic resource that is available only by remote access." *RDA* requires the cataloger to record the extent of all resources when available (RDA 3.4.1.3).

QUICK TIP

RDA requires the cataloger to record the extent of electronic resources that mimic textual resources (such as PDF files) in number of pages. For further instructions, see *RDA* Chapter 3.4.1.7.1 and 3.4.1.7.5.

Record information about the number of discs and/or pages that comprise the resource in the MARC 300 field, according to *AACR2* and *RDA* rules for description. Enter the number of pages or discs in subfield $a; use subfield $b to reflect the use of color and/or illustrations in the resource. Record this information in the MODS element <physical Description> and in the DC element <Format> with the qualifier "Extent."

The specific material designation in subfield $a of the MARC 300 field of the descriptive record in Figure 5.1 (see p. 183) reflects the carrier type (CD-ROM). The dimensions of the carrier are recorded in subfield $c of the MARC 300 field (as shown in both Figure 5.1, p. 183, and Example 5.2). The dimension of the carrier is recorded in the MODS element <physicalDescription> and the DC element <Format>. Dimensions will vary depending on the carrier. Most CDs are 4¾ inches.

EXAMPLE 5.2

300 __ 1 CD-ROM : $b col. ; $c 4¾ in.

Electronic Book: Online Resource

Some electronic books are made available via websites as a part of a collection; in such cases it may be more appropriate to describe the website to provide access to all of the electronic books contained therein. The description of the resource would pertain to the website, which is considered an integrating resource (Chapter 6 discusses electronic integrating resources). Figure 5.3 provides the description of a single-issue electronic title in MARC format that was first published on the Internet as a "born digital" resource.

The MARC fixed field indicates that the content of this resource is textual and is issued as a monograph. Electronic books require the code **a** in the MARC Leader 06 position. Because it contains textual content, this resource requires both the MARC 006 and 007 fields (as shown in Figure 5.3). However, as an online resource, the description requires the code **r** in the $b subfield of the MARC 007 field to specify that it is remotely located. The MARC 008 field contains appropriately coded information.

The resource described in Figure 5.3 was published in New York (nyu) in 2005 by the United Nations Department of Public Information. "The United Nations. Secretary-General (1997-2006 : Annan)" was selected as the creator/author of this official publication emanating from the Office of the Secretary-General. The heading in the MARC 110 field was verified in the Library of Congress's Authorities file (available at http://authorities.loc.gov/).

The GMD is included in the MARC 245 field only when required by local cataloging agencies. The following fields appropriately describe the resource as follows:

336 (Content Type): text

337 (Media Type): computer

338 (Carrier Type): online resource

Figure 5.3. Sample Descriptive Record for a Remote Access Book

Leader Positions	Position 06 [Type of record]: a [text] Position 07 [Bibliographic Level]: m [monograph]
006	m d
007	c $b r $d c $e u
008	Lang: eng Form of item: s Ctry: nyu GPub: i SerTy: d Desc: i Date 1: 2005
040	NjR $c NjR $e rda
110 1_	United Nations. Office of the Secretary General.
245 00	In larger freedom : $b towards development, security and human rights for all; report of the Secretary-General.
246 30	Towards development, security and human rights for all
260 __	New York : $b United Nations, Dept. of Public Information, $c 2005.
300 __	31 p. : $b digital, PDF.
336 __ 337 __ 338 __	Text $2 rdacontent Computer $2 rdamedia Online resource $2 rdacarrier
500 __	Title from webpage (viewed on March 9, 2009).
538 __	System requirements: Adobe Acrobat Reader is required to view PDF format.
538 __	Mode of access: World Wide Web.
530 __	Also available in print.
520 __	The Secretary General reports on his view of the requirements and pre-requisites for peace and security among nations
610 20	United Nations.
650 _0	Security, International.
710 2_	United Nations. $b Secretary-General.
776 0_	[This field is used for information linking the user to additional formats to the current resource. Details such as the Library of Congress record number, or OCLC number are entered here when appropriate.]
856 40	http://www.un.org/largerfreedom/index.html

Record publication details in the MARC 260 field, the MODS element <originInfo>, and the DC element <Publisher>. The publication details of the original may be recorded in this field for remotely accessed reproductions of printed texts, and publication details about the reproduction are entered in the MARC 533 field when the *Library of Congress Rule Interpretations* for reproductions is used. In such a case, details about

QUICK TIP

Catalogers using the *Library of Congress Rule Interpretations* (*LCRI*) for reproductions must enter the publication details of the original work in the publication details area. Record publication details about the reproduction in the MARC 533 field, the MODS element <note>, and the DC element <Coverage>.

EXAMPLE 5.3

300 __ 1 online resource (62 pages) ;
$b digital, PDF

<physicalDescription>
<form authority="marcform">
electronic</form>
</physicalDescription>

<Format.Exent>1 online resource (62 pages) : digital, PDF</Format>

300 __ 1 electronic text (62 pages) ;
$b digital, HTML.

Authors' Note: The Draft Interim Guidelines for Cataloging Electronic Resources, available at http://www.loc.gov/catdir/cpso/dcmb19_4.html, states, regarding MARC 538 (System Details Note):

"Do not use this field. Ordinarily, it is not necessary to state explicitly that a browser or other client software is required to access Internet resources, since the protocols necessary should be obvious from the 856 field (e.g., mode of access is http)."

the reproduction are entered in the MODS element <note>, and the DC element <Coverage>.

For all other remote resources, such as born digital resources, record publication details pertinent to the manifestation being cataloged in the MARC 260 field, the MODS element <originInfo>, and the DC element <Publisher>. The resource in Figure 5.3 (see p. xx) was also published in print by the United Nations in New York in 2005, and a MARC 530 note (or the MODS element <note> and DC element <Relation>) in the record confirms the availability of a printed manifestation of the resource. The cataloger was unable to determine which manifestation was published first (the original manifestation), and, in accordance with *AACR2* and *RDA* requirements, the description for the resource in Figure 5.3 was based on the manifestation in hand. Its treatment does not conform to the LCRI for reproductions, because its status as a reproduction is unknown.

The MARC 300 field contains details about the extent of the resource. This field has recently been authorized for use with remote access electronic resources—a mandatory requirement previously restricted to direct access resources. *AACR2*, Rule 9.5C3 (2004 update), instructs catalogers to include the extent of item and other details (i.e., file type) in bibliographic records for remote digital resources. *RDA* requires comprehensive details about the extent of the resource (*RDA* 3.4.1.7.5), entered in the MARC 300 field, as shown in Example 5.3. Record this information in the MODS element <physicalDescription> and in the DC element <Format> with the qualifier "Extent."

The descriptive record in Figure 5.3 (see p. 189) contains the mandatory source of title note in the MARC 500 field—"Title from webpage (viewed on March 9, 2009)"—and the optional MARC 538 field Mode of Access note. The MARC 538 field for Mode of Access is now considered redundant except when access is required by a method other than via the World Wide Web, which is increasingly rare.

However, the cataloger retains the option of using this field, and many catalogers continue to use it for both direct and remote access resources. In Figure 5.3, the requirement that the user's computer must facilitate PDF files is specified in the MARC 300 field, which clearly states PDF as the file format. This single alert is deemed sufficient and satisfies the requirement for notification.

Place a brief annotation about the content of the work in the MARC 520 summary or abstract note field, the MODS element <abstract>, and the DC element <Description> with the qualifier "Abstract." This field is optional, but desirable.

Other fields include the MARC 6XX fields, which contain descriptive subject terms. Each resource should contain at least one subject. In the descriptive record in Figure 5.3, the United Nations was entered as a subject because the content relates to the role of the United Nations. This information is provided in the MODS element <subject> and the DC element <Subject> with the qualifier "LCSH."

For electronic resources, unlike for print resources because they are tangible and can be examined easily, the URL is one of the most important elements of description as it links the user with the resource. The MARC 856 field should always contain a working URL for the resource. This field can also contain public notes pertaining to access restrictions and other relevant information in the $z subfield (see Example 5.4; additional information about the 856 field is available at http://www.loc.gov/marc/856guide.html). Record this information in the MODS element <relatedItem> and in the DC element <Identifier>.

Figure 5.4 shows a MODS descriptive record for the resource illustrated (in MARC format) in Figure 5.3. The ability to select elements based on the importance assigned by the cataloger is one of the attractive features of MODS. MODS follows standard rules of bibliographic description, making it easy for catalogers to transition from MARC to MODS. There are no mandatory elements, and most elements have corresponding subelements that allow for more specificity. For additional details, consult www.loc.gov/standards/mods//mods-outline.html.

The basic elements that comprise a MODS record are listed at the end of this chapter (see "MODS Checklist"). They are required for the distinct description of a resource and generally reflect the same combination of elements found in the MARC record. Differences between the two display formats include that MODS does not require the use of

EXAMPLE 5.4

856 40 $u http://galenet.galegroup.com/servlet/ECCO?c=1&stp=Author&ste=&vrsn=1.0&srchtp=a&d4=0.33&n=10&SU=0LRK&locID=new67449 $z Access from campus or login via Rutgers account.

Figure 5.4. MODS Descriptive Record for the Remote Access Electronic Book Illustrated in Figure 5.3

```
<titleInfo>
  <title>In larger freedom
  <subTitle>Towards development, security and human rights
   for all : report of the Secretary-General.
</title>
<typeOfResource>text</typeOfResource>
<name type="personal">
  <namePart>Annan, Kofi Atta</namePart>
  <affiliation>United Nations. Secretary-General</affiliation>
  <role>
    <roleTerm type="text">author</roleTerm>
    <roleTerm type="code">aut</roleTerm>
  </role>
</name>
<originInfo>
  <place>
    <placeTerm type="code" authority="marccountry">nyu
    </placeTerm>
    <placeTerm type="text">New York, NY </placeTerm>
  </place>
  <publisher>United Nations. Dept. of Public Information
  </publisher>
  <dateCreated>2005</dateCreated>
</originInfo>
<physicalDescription>
  <form authority="marcform">electronic</form>
  <digitalOrigin>born digital</digitalOrigin>
  <internetMediaType>text/html</internetMediaType>
  <extent>33 pages</extent>
  <note> Available in PDF & HTML</note>
</physicalDescription>
<abstract>The Secretary-General reports on his view of t
he requirements for peace and security among nations.
</abstract>
<subject authority="lcsh">
  <topic>Security, International</topic>
</subject>
<location>
  <url>http://www.un.org/largerfreedom/index.html</url>
</location>
```

codes in the bibliographic description of the resource and that the sequence of the elements of description can vary, depending on the choice of the cataloging agency responsible for developing and maintaining specific schemas. Although the use of abbreviations was approved in *AACR2* and in the International Standards for Bibliographic Description (ISBD) and is considered appropriate, most information recorded in the MODS areas is recorded in full form in alignment with the *RDA* requirement prohibiting the use of abbreviations that are not evident on the resource.

Electronic Book: Reproduction

Figure 5.5 shows an image and brief generic resource description for a printed book that was digitized by Project Gutenberg. Figure 5.6 shows a metadata descriptive record for the same resource, and Figure 5.7 shows a MARC descriptive record for the resource. Figure 5.8 demonstrates use of the single record option to describe both the original printed resource and the electronic reproduction of the same record.

Figure 5.5. Online Information for an Electronic Book

Elements of Structural and Systematic Botany

For High Schools and Elementary College Courses

by *Douglas Houghton Campbell*

English, published in 1890

74,464 words (274 pages)

Categories: *Science*, *Nature*

Record 1 shown in Figure 5.9 (p. 195) was retrieved from the Rutgers University Libraries' online catalog for the title described in Figure 5.5. It is a very brief record and does not meet the BIBCO core record standard.[15] Absence of a URL indicates that Rutgers has not provided electronic access to this record for its patrons.

Because this resource is freely available online, the cataloger can enhance the record and provide another option for the user by adding the URL for the web version to the record in the Rutgers online catalog. The following adjustments to the descriptive record are required to accurately reflect the electronic characteristics of its carrier and its Internet location (see Record 2 in Figure 5.9):

- Although the MARC 007 field is required, if applicable, in descriptive records for electronic resources contributed to OCLC (http://www.oclc.org/bibformats/es/0xx/007comp.shtm) it is an optional requirement in the MARC format (http://www.loc.gov/marc/bibliographic/bd007.html). When both print and electronic versions are described in a single record, as shown in Figure 5.9, the cataloger may add the optional MARC 007 field to reflect the electronic aspects of the online resource even though the print version is the primary resource being described.
- A MARC 530 field was added to advertise the availability of another format: Also available on the Internet via Project Gutenberg.
- The URL for the resource was provided in the MARC 856 field.

Figure 5.6. Basic Bibliographic Record for an Electronic Book Using a Metadata Scheme

Elements of Structural and Systematic Botany by Douglas Houghton Campbell	
Bibliographic Record	
Creator	Campbell, Douglas Houghton
Title	Elements of Structural and Systematic Botany For High Schools and Elementary College Courses
Language	English
LoC Class	QK: Science: Botany
Subject	Botany -- Textbooks
EText-No.	20390
Release Date	2007-01-17
Copyright Status	Not copyrighted in the United States. If you live elsewhere check the laws of your country before downloading this e-book.
Base Directory	/files/20390/

Figure 5.7. MARC Descriptive Record for an Electronic Book

Leader 06 Leader 07	a m
007	c [electronic] r [remote access]
008	Type: a BibLvl: m Lang: eng; Date: 1890; Country: mau;
100 1_	Campbell, Douglas Houghton.
245 10	Elements of structural and systematic botany for high schools and elementary college courses / $c Douglas Campbell.
260 __	Boston : $b Ginn., $c 1890.
300 __	274 p.
533 __	$a Electronic reproduction. $b Salt Lake City, Utah: $c Project Gutenberg, $d 2007. $e 1 online resource.
538 __	Available in plain text and PDF version. Adobe Acrobat is required to view the PDF version.
650 _0	Botany.
856 40	http://www.gutenberg.org/etext/20390

Figure 5.8. Single Record Option for Both Print and Electronic Versions of the Same Resource

Leader 06 Leader 07	a m
007	[This field is not used because the description is based on the printed version of the work.]
008	Type: a BibLvl: m Lang: eng; Date: 1890; Country: mau;
100 1_	Campbell, Douglas Houghton.
245 10	Elements of structural and systematic botany for high schools and elementary college courses / $c Douglas Campbell.
260 __	Boston : $b Ginn, $c 1890.
300 __	274 p.
530 __	$a Also available as an electronic resource via World Wide Web $u http://www.gutenberg.org/etext/20390
650 _0	Botany.
856 41	$z Electronic version $u http://www.gutenberg.org/etext/20390

Note: The fixed fields contain only the most important codes for this type of resource. Other codes can be used as appropriate for this format. The GMD is not used in this example because it is not used with printed resources. New 3XX fields, introduced with *RDA*, allow the cataloger to use the 337 and 338 fields to specify media and carrier types for both resources described in this record:

337 (Media Type): $a Unmediated $a Computer
338 (Carrier Type): $a Volume $a Online resource

If this option is used, the cataloger should provide additional descriptive elements for the online resource, such as file type, in the 530 note area.

The resource shown in Figure 5.5 was found on the web at ManyBooks .net. It has also been digitized by Project Gutenberg and is available freely in the public domain. Figure 5.10 shows the MARC descriptive record for the same resource.

The resource description in Figure 5.10 serves only to highlight changes required when describing a reproduction of a work for which a descriptive record of the printed version already exists. Because the library did not own the printed version, the cataloger opted to create a record for the electronic reproduction using the LCRI for *AACR2* Chapter 11, requiring full bibliographic information for the original printed resource and the addition of a MARC 533 field for the reproduction.

The original title of the resource remains intact as it is the same on the reproduction. The MARC Leader 06 and 07 positions and the fixed field information in the 008 field will remain the same as for the printed version, one of the benefits of describing a resource based on its content rather than on the carrier, because the electronic resource is also a textual monograph:

Leader 06: Type of record: **a** for textual material.

Leader 07: Bibliographic level: **m** for monographic.

Figure 5.9. Rutgers University Online Catalog Record for an Electronic Book

Record 1		
Elements of structural and systematic botany for high schools and elementary college courses / Campbell, Douglas Houghton		
Original Record.		
Tag	**Ind.**	**Contents**
980		01209294
035		MRQG020313930-B
100		Campbell, Douglas Houghton.
245	10	Elements of structural and systematic botany for high schools and elementary college courses.
260		Boston,|bGinn.,|c1890.
596		ALEXANDER
Record 2		
Tag	**Ind.**	**Contents**
980 **007**		01209294 **c r**
035		MRQG020313930-B
100	1	Campbell, Douglas Houghton.
245	10	Elements of structural and systematic botany for high schools and elementary college courses
260		Boston,|bGinn.,|c1890.
300		274 p.
530		**Also available via the Internet from Project Gutenberg.**
856	**40**	**|u http://www.gutenberg.org/etext/20390**

Note: Record 2 shows the new fields added (in boldface) to alert the user to the online version of the work. Addition of the 007 field is optional since the descriptive record mainly describes the printed version.

Descriptive details reflect the original printed version, including the publication information in the MARC 260 field and information about the extent and dimensions of the resource in the MARC 300 field.

The MARC 533 note must be added as shown in Figure 5.10. Note that the URL can be included in the $n subfield of the 533 field. The MARC 538 field is added to give system requirements to view the resource.

Finally, to complete the record, the MARC 856 field must be used to provide the URL, which may contain a public note in subfield $z. URL maintenance is a major consideration for libraries that provide access to

Figure 5.10. Single Record Option for Cataloging an Electronic Book Previously Published in Print

007	c [electronic] r [remote access]
008	Type: a BibLvl: m Lang: eng; Date: 1890; Country: mau
100 1_	Campbell, Douglas Houghton.
245 10	Elements of structural and systematic botany for high schools and elementary college courses / $c Douglas Campbell.
260 __	Boston : $b Ginn., $c 1890.
300 __	274 p.
533 __	$a Electronic reproduction. $b Salt Lake City, Utah: $c Project Gutenburg, $d 2007.
538 __	Available in plain text and PDF version. Adobe Acrobat is required to view the PDF version.
650 _0	Botany.
856 40	http://www.gutenberg.org/etext/20390

electronic resources. It is therefore appropriate to prefer URLs that contain link resolvers such as a PURL (persistent URL).

To maintain consistency in the descriptive records provided by electronic publishers, the Library of Congress's Program for Cooperative Cataloging (PCC) has issued guidelines for publishers, which are available at http://www.docstoc.com/docs/855387/PCC-MARC-Record-Guide-for-Monograph-Vendors-Final-Version and www.loc.gov/catdir/pcc/bibco/PN-Mono-charge.pdf. Information for OCLC users is available at http://www.loc.gov/acq/conser/AggNeutMonoFinal.pdf.

Electronic Book: Theses and Dissertations

The manifestation of theses and dissertations as electronic resources, popularly referred to as ETDs, has practically revolutionized the publishing of these resources. Most importantly, a significant number of colleges and universities now require graduating students to submit electronic copies of their works. This format offers some options that were previously not available, including the ability to produce multimedia presentations, the immediacy of access and availability, and the vastly reduced production costs for students and institutions. These advantages have contributed to the ascendancy of electronic theses and dissertations to the level of "preferred format" for all concerned, including the library because physical storage costs have been all but eliminated. However, there are also costs to store information online, such as purchase and maintenance of servers, fees for Handle servers, etc.

The current proliferation of electronic theses and dissertations brings into focus the special concerns about cataloging networked resources. A library may have cataloged the electronic version of the thesis, probably in the MARC format so that it can be accommodated in the MARC-based ILS, while the electronic version may have been described in a metadata format for inclusion in the institutional repository.

Many colleges and universities now maintain dual systems of MARC and some type of metadata scheme, resulting in two distinct descriptive records for the same resource—probably created by two different entities within the organization. Libraries and the communities they serve are still working on solutions that will be cost-effective for both staff and users. Mapping is popular for "cross-walking" metadata schemes such as MODS into the MARC display format and vice versa. However, there are areas of the resource description that are not readily mapped from one scheme to the other. In the interim, the library can ensure that the user has access to both systems. The ILS should provide links to the repository and vice versa. More importantly, federated searching can play an important role in bridging the gap between the two entities. It may also be helpful to ensure that every attempt is made to provide helpful links to major service vendors such as ProQuest/UMI Microfilm because this introduces the user to the broader universe of theses and dissertations. Many libraries also subscribe to databases that provide access to digital theses and dissertations. Also noteworthy is the OCLC research project XT Cat Experimental Thesis Catalog (see http://www.oclc.org/research/projects/etd/default.htm for further information), which is a report on efforts by OCLC researchers to find solutions to the difficulties of maintaining dual systems of MARC and specific other metadata schemes.

Some libraries adhere to the LCRI when describing reproductions. The LCRI for *AACR2* Chapter 11 requires the cataloger to describe electronic theses that are reproductions of theses previously published in print as printed documents with the addition of the MARC 533 field showing details of the reproduction. For more information about resource description for reproductions, consult *AACR2* Chapter 11 (Microforms). *RDA* requires the cataloger to describe the manifestation in hand, which simplifies the description of these resources and allows the cataloger to reference the original document as a related resource.

Born-digital electronic theses and dissertations must be treated in the same manner as any textual electronic resource. Catalogers using the MARC format for display must code the fixed field for the MARC record describing the electronic thesis in the same way as for an electronic book (see the fixed field area in Figure 5.3, p. 189). Details about the degree and degree granting institution must be entered in the MARC 502 field (details about which are available at http://www.loc.gov/marc/bibliographic/bd502.html) (see Example 5.5). The information provided in the MARC 502 is recorded in the MODS element <note> and the DC element <Description>. Figure 5.11 shows the complete resource description for an online thesis.

EXAMPLE 5.5

502 __ $a Thesis (M.A.)--Rutgers University, New Jersey, 1976.

Item

The single exemplar of the work, on a shelf in the library or in cyberspace, constitutes the item. The item may contain peculiarities such as an

Figure 5.11. MARC Resource Description for an Online Thesis (*RDA* Convention)

Leader 06: [Type of record] Leader 07: [Bibliographic level] Descriptive cataloging form:	a [textual resource] m [monograph] ["i" may be used to indicate ISBD compliance]
006 [Electronic resources]	Position 00 m [electronic resource] Position 09 d [document]
007 [Electronic resource] 007 [Microform]	c $b r $d b c [electronic resource] ; r [remote access] ; b [black and white]. h $b e $d a $e m $f b— $g b $h a $i c $j a
008	Lang: eng Form of item: o[online] Type of comp. file: d [document] Ctry: nju Date 1: 1990 Date 2:
040	NjR $c NjR $e rda
100 1_	Furrer, Susan Elizabeth. $e Dissertant
245 12	A phenomenological investigation of drug addiction in women / $c Susan Elizabeth Furrer.
260 __	New Brunswick, New Jersey : $b Rutgers University, $c 1990.
300 __	364 pages.
336 __ 337 __ 338 __	Text $2 rdacontent Computer $2 rdamedia Online resource $2 rdacarrier
502 __*	Thesis (Psy. D)--Rutgers, The State University of New Jersey, Graduate School of Applied and Professional Psychology, 1990.
520 __	This study looks at drug use among women in Newark, New Jersey...
530 __	Also available in microfiche. $b Ann Arbor, Michigan : $c University Microfilms International, $c 2002.
650 _0	Women $x Drugs.
710 2_	Rutgers University. $b Graduate School of Applied and Professional Psychology. $e Degree grantor
856 40	[Note: The URL of the resource must be entered in this field.]

Note: The electronic thesis/dissertation that is not a reproduction is considered a published resource.
*New optional instructions for use of this field are available at http://www.loc.gov/marc/bibliographic/bd502.html.

author's signature or missing pages, details that are generally found in printed resources. The physical location applies to tangible resources such as CDs or DVDs located on the hard drive on a computer in the library or in an external disc drive attached to a computer. Item-specific details and general public notices can also be associated with the URL for online resources when local access restriction notes are included in the MARC 856 field.

Notes

Information that cannot be accommodated in specific named areas and/or fields of the descriptive record is entered in any of the specified or general note areas of MARC, MODS, and DC records. MARC has a variety of numbered note fields that accommodate both specific and free-style notes related to any or all aspects of the work. MODS accommodates notes in a general note area. Catalogers' notes may be entered for any of the *FRBR* entities.

A variety of notes are possible for electronic resources including notes pertaining to contributors, playback requirements, contents, and/or access restrictions. Figure 5.1 (see p. 183) and Example 5.6 show the mandatory source of title note.

EXAMPLE 5.6

500 __ Title from jewel case insert.

Other notes in the descriptive record in Figure 5.1 include the MARC 538 field Systems Detail Note, which is mandatory for direct access resources and is now optional for remote access electronic resources. System requirements information is critical for direct access resources as it stipulates the type of computer equipment and operating system needed to use the resource. This information is entered in the MODS element <note> and the DC element <Relation> with the qualifier "Requires." The MARC 520 field Summary Note and the MARC 505 Contents Note both provide information about the contents of a resource and can be useful if the title does not give an indication of the contents.

Resource Description (MARC, MODS, FISO) Checklists

The following checklists have been provided as a handy reference guide to the fields and/or areas most frequently used when creating descriptive records for electronic resources. They are intended as guidelines and reminders. Cataloging treatment and choice of access points may vary by library, level of cataloging, and so forth. Always remember that you are the best judge when deciding which fields and/or areas are appropriate to describe the resource you have in hand, *distinctly* and *sufficiently*.

MARC CHECKLIST

For additional information about the MARC fields required by BIBCO (the Monographic Bibliographic Record Program), see http://www.loc.gov/catdir/pcc/bibco/coresr.html.

Leader 06: **Type of Record**: Use **a** for textual resource (electronic books) or **s** for electronic resource, depending on the type of resource.

(Cont'd.)

MARC CHECKLIST *(Continued)*

Leader 07: Bibliographic Level: Use **m** for monograph.

006: Only the first value is coded in this field. Select the appropriate 006 field (electronic resources or continuing resources) to represent the form of the material. If the resource is textual use **m** (electronic resource) and if a computer file use **s** (continuing/integrating resources) in Position 00.

007: Use for electronic resources.

Example:
$a c $b r (remote) d (computer disc; unspecified) $c [blank] undefined $d c (color).

008: Use for computer files or continuing resources, as appropriate (consult http://www.loc.gov/marc/bibliographic/bd008c.html). This field must be coded for elements associated with all types of resources:

Lang: eng, or as appropriate.
Date 1: Date of publication
Date 2: Used when multiple dates are available such as in multipart resources.

020: ISBN: If a commercially produced direct access electronic resource has an ISBN, it must be entered as it appears on the resource.

028: **Publisher Number**: This normally includes a number and an alphabetic code for the publisher. Enter the alphabetic code in the $b subfield.

100: **Creator/Author/Performer**: This field must contain information about the "primary author" or creator. Other responsible persons may be entered in 700 fields. Corporate authorship is possible in selected cases, such as the publication of research activities or organizational policies.

245: **Title Information**: Enter the title as it appears on the resource (giving preference to information found on the title screen). The resource, including the disc and its label, is the preferred source of information.

246: **Variant Title Information**: Record the subtitle and/or other significant title by which the resource may be known or identified in the MARC 245 field, subfield $b. Also enter it in the 246 field so that it is indexed and retrievable in a title query.

250: **Edition Statement**: The edition statement is not repeatable; concatenate as needed.

260: **Publication Details**: $a Place of publication : $b Publisher, and $c Date of publication or distribution.

300: **Extent of Item**: Record the number of units that comprise the resource in the first subfield ($a). Also give additional information about the resource such as color (in subfield $b) and size (subfield $c).

400: **Series Statement**: Provide if applicable.

500: **Note Field**: Use for a variety of information, especially information deemed important by the cataloger but for which no MARC field has been specified. This field is also used for the mandatory "Source of title note" for electronic resources and for any other resource when the title has been supplied by the cataloger.

505: **Note**: Record the contents here.

538: **System Requirements**: This is a mandatory field. Include requirements for playback equipment and other pertinent technical details.

520: **Note** (summary): Use to provide a summary of the resource's content.

650 and 655: **Subject and Genre**: Enter subject terms in the 650 field and genre headings in the 655 field.

700: **Added Entry**: Include additional responsible persons in this field.

856: **URL**: Use this field to provide a URL link to supplementary information available on the Internet.

MODS CHECKLIST

For additional information about constructing a descriptive record for electronic resources (specifically, online resources) using MODS, see http://www.loc.gov/standards/mods/v3/mods98801326.xml.

<typeOfResource> is used to specify type of resource being cataloged. Use "text" for textual online resources and "multimedia" for computer/media files.

Example:
```
<typeOfResource>text</typeOfResource>
```

<genre> provides information on a style, form, or content expressed in the resource.

Example:
```
<genre>database</genre>
```

<identifier> with the attribute " type" is used to provide standard identifiers, such as the ISBN.

Example:
```
<identifier type="isbn">9783540221814</identifier>
```

<recordInfo> with the subelement <recordContentSource> with the attribute "authority" is used to provide the code or name of the organization that created or modified the original resource description.

Example:
```
<recordInfo>
   <recordContentSource>Rutgers University Libraries</recordContentSource>
</recordInfo>
```

<languageTerm> with the type="code" and authority="iso639-2b" (several codes may be used in authority; see http://www.loc.gov/standards/mods/v3/mods-userguide-elements.html#language for additional information).

Example:
```
<language>
   <languageTerm type="code" authority="iso639-2b">eng</languageTerm>
</language>
```

<name> is used to provide information on name of a person, organization, or event (conference, meeting, etc.) associated with the resource. This element has a <type> attribute to specify the type of name (personal, corporate, or conference) and an authority attribute (<authority>) to enable catalogers to specify what authoritative source was consulted to provide the authorized form of the name. This element also has a subelement <role> which is used to specify the role of the named person, corporate body, or conference in relation to the resource.

Example:
```
<name type="corporate">
   <role>
      <roleTerm type="text">Creator</roleTerm>
   </role>
<name type="corporate">
   <namePart>Rutgers.</namePart>
</name>
```

<titleInfo> is used to convey the title or name of a resource. When the main portion of the title is referenced as core, there is only one core subelement, <title>.

Example:
```
<titleInfo>
<title>WAAND database</title>
</titleInfo>
```

(Cont'd.)

MODS CHECKLIST *(Continued)*

Use <titleInfo> with the type="alternative" and the subelement <title> to convey title varations.

Example:
```
</titleInfo> <titleInfo type="alternative">
<title >Women Artists Archive National Directory</title>
</titleInfo>
```

<originInfo> with the subelement <edition> is used to describe the version or edition of the resource being described.

Example:
```
<originInfo>
   <edition>7th ed.</edition>
</originInfo>
```

<originInfo> with the subelement <place> and its subelement <placeTerm> with type="text", the subelement <publisher>, and the subelement <dateIssued> is used to provide information on publication, distribution, etc.

<physicalDescription> with the subelements <form> and <extent> provide descriptive information about the resource. In this text the authoritative source for <form> (used to describe the resource's physical description) is the MARC format. The subelement <extent> describes the number and types of units that make up a resource.

Example:
```
<physicalDescription>
   <form authority="marcform">CD-rom</form>    <extent>1</extent>
</physicalDescription>
```

<tableOfContents> is used for the contents of the database when this information is supplied by the publisher. This is more applicable to direct access electronic resources such as CDs.

Example:
```
<tableOfContents>
CD 1: Dictionary of terms. – CD 2: Index of authors.
</tableOfContents>
```

<relatedItem> with the attribute type "series" is used to provide information on the series when appropriate.

Example:
```
<relatedItem type="series">
   <titleInfo>
      <title>Classics Collection</title>
   </titleInfo>
</relatedItem>
```

<note> is used to provide general information about the resource.

Example:
```
<note> Based on the play by William Shakespeare.</note>
```

<subject> with the attribute type "authority" and the subelement <name> with the attribute " type" (personal, corporate, conference) provides names of persons and organizations associated with the resource as subjects. Use the subelement <topic> for topical subject terms. The descriptive record should contain at least one subject term.

Example:
```
<subject authority="lcsh">
   <topic>Women artists</topic>
</subject>
```

FISO CHECKLIST

Having constructed the descriptive record, the cataloger may find it appropriate to review the description based on the FRBR principles: *find, identify, select, obtain*:

F—The potential user has to find the material.

I—The user should be able to identify the resource, distinguishing it from any similar item.

S—The user should be able to retrieve and select the material as the appropriate one for a specific purpose or task.

O—The record should help the user to obtain the material by giving information about its location and availability and any requirements for and/or conditions of use.

The following questions are helpful in rating the completed product:

- ❑ Can a potential user find the resource easily? Appropriate description and an active URL are required to achieve this goal.
- ❑ Has the resource been sufficiently differentiated from any other?
- ❑ How easy is it to identify the resource and select it as different from any other?
- ❑ Can a potential user immediately recognize this resource as being available on the Internet? As requiring Internet access for use? The importance of an active URL cannot be overstated.

Resources for Catalogers

American Library Association, Canadian Library Association, and CILIP: Chartered Institute of Library and Information Professionals. 2010. *Resource Description and Access* (Glossary). ALA, CLA, and CILIP. Accessed August 4. http://www.rdatoolkit.org.

Library of Congress, Business Reference Services. 2010. "BEOnline Bibliographic Elements for Monographic Remote Electronic Resources." Library of Congress. Accessed August 4. http://www.loc.gov/rr/business/beonline/fields.html.

Tillet, Barbara B. 2002. "AACR2's Updates for Electronic Resources: Response of a Multinational Cataloguing Code: A Case Study." http://www.nii.ac.jp/publications/CJK-WS/cjk3-11a.pdf .

Authors' Note: The BEOnline "cheat sheet" template does not include the MARC 300 field, which was authorized for use with description for remotely accessed electronic resources in the *AACR2R* 2004 update.

Notes

1. American Library Association. 1988. *Anglo-American Cataloguing Rules*, 2nd ed., 2005 revision. Chicago: American Library Association.
2. Wikipedia. 2010. "Dublin Core." Wikipedia. Accessed August 4. http://en.wikipedia.org/wiki/Dublin_Core.
3. Library of Congress, Network Development and MARC Standards Office. 1997. "Guidelines for Coding Electronic Resources in Leader 06." Library of Congress. http://www.loc.gov/marc/ldr06guide.html.
4. Library of Congress. 1997. *Draft Interim Guidelines for Cataloging Electronic Resources.* Washington, DC: Library of Congress. http://www.loc.gov/catdir/cpso/dcmb19_4.html.
5. International Federation of Library Associations and Institutions. 2007. *Functional Requirements for Bibliographic Records: Final Report Current Text.* IFLA. http://www.ifla.org/VII/s13/frbr/frbr_current3.htm.

6. Tillett, Barbara. 2004. "What Is FRBR: A Conceptual Model for the Bibliographic Universe." Library of Congress. http://www.loc.gov/cds/downloads/FRBR.PDF.
7. Library of Congress. 1997. *Draft Interim Guidelines for Cataloging Electronic Resources.* Washington, DC: Library of Congress. http://www.loc.gov/catdir/cpso/dcmb19_4.html.
8. Ibid., B19.4.1: Content versus Carrier (Electronic Resources).
9. Toobin, Jeffrey. 2007. "Google's Moon Shot: The Quest for the Universal Library." *The New Yorker*, February 5. http://www.newyorker.com/reporting/2007/02/05/070205fa_fact_toobin.
10. Wikipedia. 2010. "Born Digital." Accessed August 31. http://en.wikipedia.org/wiki/Born-digital#Discrepancies_in_definition.
11. American Library Association, Canadian Library Association, and CILIP: Chartered Institute of Library and Information Professionals. 2010. *Resource Description and Access.* ALA, CLA, and CILIP. Accessed August 11. http://www.rdatoolkit.org.
12. Library of Congress, Program for Cooperative Cataloging. 2010. "Monographic Electronic Resources: BIBCO Core Record Standards." Library of Congress. http://www.loc.gov/catdir/pcc/bibco/coreelectro.html.
13. International Federation of Library Associations and Institutions. 2007. *International Standard Bibliographic Description.* Preliminary consolidated ed., Chapter 4.4.2. IFLA. http://www.ifla.org/publications/international-standard-bibliographic-description.
14. Library of Congress. 2009. "LC/PCC Guidelines for MARC 21 Repeatable 260 Field." Library of Congress. http://www.loc.gov/catdir/cpso/260field.pdf.
15. Library of Congress, Program for Cooperative Cataloging. 2010. "Monographic Electronic Resources: BIBCO Core Record Standards." Library of Congress. http://www.loc.gov/catdir/pcc/bibco/coreelectro.html.

Electronic Integrating Resources

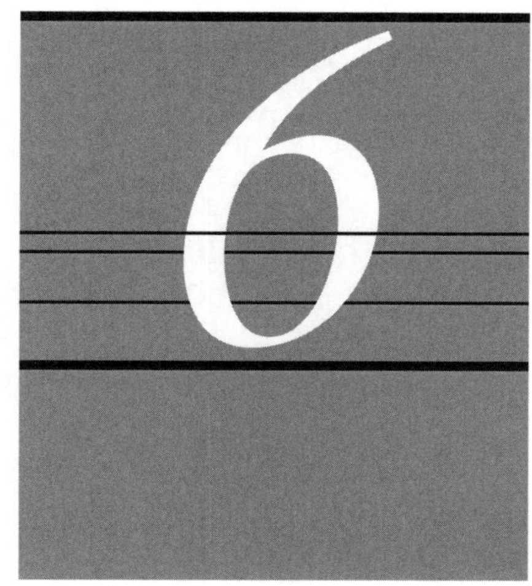

IN THIS CHAPTER:

Overview

Websites and databases comprise a category of resources known as "electronic integrating resources," a category that is uniquely different from any other category examined in this manual because the overall contents of the resources change as new or revised content is integrated. *RDA*'s glossary defines an integrating resource as "A resource that is added to or changed by means of updates that do not remain discrete and are integrated into the whole. An integrating resource may be tangible (e.g., a loose-leaf manual that is updated by means of replacement pages) or intangible (e.g., a Web site that is updated either continuously or on a cyclical basis)."

The ease with which online resources can be updated and the reduced costs realized in online publishing have established the online carrier as a viable, preferred option for many publishers. The deluge of online content has enmeshed libraries in the many challenges associated with making these resources accessible and available to patrons. While there is general agreement on the need to catalog the online databases that libraries have purchased, online resources present a variety of concerns ranging from doubts regarding the stability of the resource to the seemingly impossible challenge of maintaining bibliographic records according to CONSER guidelines for integrating resources,[1] guidelines that require the descriptive record to reflect the current iteration of the resource and to display an active URL.

Should websites be cataloged? This question continues to be a subject of debate within the profession. Although varying in authenticity and significance, websites produced by reputable publishers are generally gateways to a wealth of information and cannot be ignored as valuable information resources. Most websites and databases can be easily accessed by conducting a simple search on the Internet by subject, title, and/or name of the organization responsible for the site and generally fall into three categories:

1. Freely accessible sites available to anyone with an Internet connection
2. Restricted sites available only to authorized users via a URL or password
3. A combination of free and restricted access, where the user can browse the site and access some content, such as abstracts and nonproprietary material, but is denied access to full content or specific types of material unless a password is provided via authorized log-in

Cognizant of the fact that search engine rankings and retrieval can impede access to many worthwhile sites, some libraries provide access to high-quality preselected websites and databases through A–Z lists and/or subject lists, known popularly as "webliographies," that contain hyperlinks to web resources. Increasingly, in the attempt to accommodate networked resources, some libraries operate in a mixed environment, offering webliographies *and* limited, selective access to websites and other online resources via the integrated library system (ILS). Access through the library's ILS has some drawbacks, however, particularly for sites that require a log-on because the URL is frequently linked to the IP address and accessible only from within the library.

Information providers are aware of the difficulties libraries experience in trying to provide access to networked resources (the variety of resources in different formats available via the Internet, the World Wide Web, or computer networks). However, attempts at providing value-added services fall short of offering viable solutions to the inadequacies of service that risk alienating users and potential users.

A review of the recent library literature revealed several experiments aimed at uncovering the "best" path to seamless resource discovery. One of the most encouraging of these seems to be the applicability of the Semantic Web in the library environment.[2]

Federated searching is also gaining in popularity, allowing a single search interface to simplify the first level query. This method was developed in response to a need to search the "deep web," which is not indexed by crawlers and other mechanisms nor searched by traditional search engines such as Google.

A study done by Marist College[3] noted that students were more likely to use the library's catalog after being reassured that Google was one of the databases included in the federated search portal query. Google is relatively unrestricted in the types of resources indexed, and this is reassuring to the user who sees this as an attempt to "cover all the bases." The more sophisticated users become with the Internet, the more reluctant they are to use sources that have been preselected, especially when limited to specific "manageable" formats that can be most readily accommodated in MARC-based library catalogs. The students in the Marist College study reported that they realized the maximum benefits from a query that polled a variety of networked resources to deliver results. The results were presented in a more orderly sequence, the students seemed happier when familiar reputable sources were included in the display, and they confessed to being more satisfied with the federated search results than with results retrieved using Google as the single search portal. This finding seems to suggest that an orderly pathway to selected, high-quality resources, including networked databases and websites, may be what users want and that with an orderly pathway built into the ILSs, libraries may experience increased use of local library catalogs.

What does this mean for catalogers? An orderly pathway, of necessity, assumes that all resources will have been accurately and sufficiently described in ways that facilitate retrieval. Could it be that our success as facilitators of the resource discovery process is linked to the quality of the descriptive metadata we assign to the resources that we "catalog"? Could the answer to interoperability of systems and seamless discovery environments lie chiefly with catalogers (metadata creators/assigners) rather than with systems design professionals and vendors? Those who create and/or assign descriptive metadata must ensure accuracy, appropriateness, and sufficiency of the terms assigned to each resource, regardless of its carrier type.

In the absence of the perfect solution to providing access to online and networked resources, one project that may be offered as a model for some libraries is the Library of Congress's Business Reference Services website (now known as BEOnline Plus and available at http://www.loc .gov//rr/business/beonline), which offers traditional access to resources via the online catalog while simultaneously providing access to networked resources. From a single portal, researchers can access preselected websites that are grouped effectively by title. The titles that comprised the initial project are linked to full-level MARC records, and users are seamlessly directed to the Library of Congress's online catalog, via hyperlink, to view the descriptive record.

Similarly, access to the websites selected for this project from the Library of Congress's online catalog facilitates the traditional method of resource discovery via the URL in the descriptive record, which directs users to the appropriate website, providing another opportunity for discovery to those who use the online catalog. This type of dual access truly facilitates resource discovery by the increased potential for discovery.

Finally, if we support the ideal that content trumps carrier, providing access to appropriate content, regardless of carrier, should be an integral component of our service delivery goals. The fact that a specific resource offers substantive content should be the most important reason to describe it and make it available for use; and websites and databases should be included in this strategy. Consequently, most libraries will be faced with providing access to a small number of highly effective websites and online databases for their patrons, the benefits and advantages of which will vary depending on the type of library, its resources, and the needs of its user community.

Important Considerations

New developments in content delivery are ongoing and require periodic reevaluation of the library's role in providing access to content that it does not own and over which it has no control. Websites and databases are generally not static. This single factor presents several challenges regarding the maintenance of the descriptive record. The following are problem areas and some of the questions that should guide and inform the library's decision to acquire databases and websites.

- **Title**: Titles may vary slightly with each iteration, or the publisher(s) may revert to an earlier version of the title, changes that are minor enough not to warrant a new bibliographic record. However, the title in the resource description must be the title provided on the latest or current iteration. The title history is important and must be maintained in the description, providing access to the resource under any version of the title by which it was or is known.
- **Record maintenance**: Catalogers need to know when to create a new record to replace the existing descriptive record for a website or online database. Substantive changes in format, a different edition and/or edition statement (particularly when the former edition is still available online), and changes in editorial focus, subject matter, and/or content all warrant a new record.[4] When in doubt, catalogers are advised to update the current record to reflect the changes rather than create a duplicate record. Integrating resources are bound by selected conventions unique to the description of continuing resources, and the document "Integrating Resources: a Cataloging Manual" (available at www.loc.gov/catdir/pcc/bibco/irman.pdf) provides instructions. The ALCTS document "Differences Between, Changes Within" (http://www.lita.org/ala/mgrps/divs/alcts/resources/org/cat/differences07.pdf) also provides guidance regarding changes that require the cataloger to create a new record for an integrating resource.
- **Dynamic/inactive URLs**: Dynamic URLs can be troublesome, and inactive URLs impede access to the resources they represent. However, a change in online location does not warrant a new record. Will a "link resolver" or persistent URL be used to ensure consistent access to the resource? How much staff time can be devoted to maintenance of descriptive records for integrating resources? Can the library afford, or rely on, an external service provider for the required maintenance?
- **Content**: How will the library be alerted to changes in the content or other essential elements? Changes in the frequency of updates do not warrant a new record. The frequency of updates should be noted in the descriptive record, which should accurately reflect the current frequency based on the current iteration. The code denoting the frequency of update must also be changed in the relevant fixed field area(s) when appropriate.

In addition, catalogers should be aware of the following facts and caveats about online integrating resources and the carrier type generally associated with them:

- Direct access electronic resources, such as content on CD-ROM and DVDs, are not considered integrating resources even if they are updated periodically. When updated regularly with numbered updates that remain discrete, these are considered continuing resources. Direct access resources can also be considered monographs when no updates to content are planned.
- A website containing digitized objects issued as a collection can be considered a continuing resource if the content is updated with some frequency and if the publisher intends to continue updating the content indefinitely.
- A website that is intended as finite must be categorized as an integrating resource if updates are integrated into the content with some frequency.
- A dictionary on a CD-ROM is considered finite and must be treated as a monograph if updates are not anticipated. Subsequent updates, if provided, would be considered discrete, because it is not possible to integrate the content after the CD has been produced. However, if the same type of dictionary is available online, the content of both the dictionary and the hosting website can be updated easily. This type of online dictionary is integral to the website and therefore must be treated as an integrating resource. *Merriam-Webster Online* is a good example of this type of arrangement (see http://www.merriam-webster.com).

Many online dictionaries and reference resources are available by subscription. Publishers and/or vendors may simultaneously offer identical resources as different packages available through various websites: an emerging challenge that prompted the search for suitable guidelines for aggregator-neutral descriptive records for these resources. The resulting guidelines are published in the CONSER Manual and in the document "Integrating Resources: A Cataloging Manual; Appendix A to the BIBCO Participants' Manual" (available at http://www.loc.gov/catdir/pcc/bibco/irman.pdf). Both publications are highly recommended reading for catalogers charged with providing resource descriptions for the library's online database holdings. To access a summary of the rationale and discussions that preceded the publication of Appendix A, see http://www.loc.gov/acq/conser/ProvNeutforE-IRs-Sept-21-2007.pdf.

Websites that are portals to networked resources are growing in popularity. The idea of providing access to a variety of resources on a specific topic, via a single log-on, has captured the attention of information providers, and the portal continues to grow as a viable means of content delivery. Portals vary in size and mission and can be as unique as a collection of preselected resources on a single subject available as digitized images and/or text or as comprehensive as a collection of databases united via a single search strategy. Providing access to networked resources continues to evolve in different ways and, depending on the library and the needs of its clientele, the simple portal may be all that is

FOR MORE INFORMATION

Although the guidelines offered in this chapter are based on the most current rules available, many changes have occurred and are anticipated for the description of integrating resources. Catalogers are encouraged to visit the companion website to this manual at http://www.neal-schuman.com/describingmedia where changes will be posted periodically. Catalogers may also monitor changes on the *RDA* website (http://www.rdatoolkit.org) and on the MARC website (http://www.loc.gov/marc) to keep abreast of changes to the MARC format.

required to provide an acceptable route to various types of resources on a single topic.

Resource Description

The terms "website" and "database" embody both carrier and content, which for purposes of resource description comprise two distinct areas. Catalogers should become acquainted with and be able to distinguish between elements related to the work (intellectual content) and elements related to the carrier type (online resource: website or database) to gain a comprehensive understanding of this type of resource. Although the term "online resource" as used in this chapter and elsewhere in the library literature embodies both content and carrier, one must never lose sight of the fact that websites and online databases are inextricably linked to a specific carrier type, the online resource. "Integrating" refers to the mode of issuance, a method that allows new content to be integrated, seamlessly, into already existing content. "If the site is updated and the changes are integrated into the resource and the earlier iterations are no longer available, the resource is an integrating resource."[5]

Integrating resources fall into two categories: finite resources and continuing resources. An integrating resource intended as finite will, when its purpose has been completed, contain a recognizable date on which the resource became static. Such a date can generally be found on the first or introductory screen. Continuing integrating resources, intended to be updated indefinitely, are discussed in this chapter.

> **QUICK TIP**
>
> From *AACR2* 12.0Bb: "Base description of an integrating resource, except the beginning date of publication, on the current iteration of that resource."
>
> Information taken from any other source must be enclosed in square brackets. Notes and standard identification numbers can be taken from any iteration and/or any other source.

As with all electronic resources, the preferred source of information for websites and databases is the title screen or source forming part of the resource itself (*RDA* 2.2.2.2–2.2.2.4; *AACR2* 9.0B1). Resource description for websites and databases must be based on the current iteration, with the exception of the publication date, which should reflect the date on which the resource was first published online. The date on which the resource was viewed must also be recorded, which is consistent with *RDA*'s requirement to describe the manifestation in hand.

If the website is a mirror site or if the database is provided as an aggregate resource, the preferred site on which the description is based must be that of the publisher rather than the provider. All information, including the date of publication, must be recorded as it appears on the resource, and the use of abbreviations is forbidden unless they appear on the resource. Although use of abbreviations is approved in *AACR2* and has been accommodated in the MARC format, most information recorded in the MODS elements are spelled out, in alignment with the *RDA* requirement prohibiting the use of abbreviations that are not evident on the resource itself.

Recent guidelines issued by the Library of Congress's Program for Cooperative Cataloging have authorized the use of multiple MARC 260 fields in cases where the publication history of the resource is warranted. Additional information about the use of multiple 260 fields is available at http://www.loc.gov/catdir/cpso/260field.html.

The examples in this chapter illustrate the ways in which the rules of description and access influence the construction of the descriptive record for integrating resources.

Work

A careful look at the website's homepage generally provides clues as to its status. A site that contains a "hot topics" or "new" area suggests that the site is updated periodically and that current content is available to those who click on the provided link. One is also likely to find the date on which the website was last updated at the bottom of the title screen. Although the resource description must be based on the current iteration, certain types of static information, such as related resources, sponsors, and the date of publication as stated in the first version or iteration, can be included.

It can be helpful, before creating the descriptive record, to collocate the essential characteristics of the work and its carrier according to the *FRBR* first level entities of work, expression, manifestation and item. In grouping descriptive elements related to the work (the intellectual or creative content), the preferred title is the single most important descriptive element. If more than one phrase can be construed as the title, the cataloger must select the preferred title (or title proper) and provide access to any and/or all variant titles in the area of the descriptive record designated for variant titles. Although the preferred title is a core element of description, variant titles have not been accorded this status in *RDA* but they must be recorded if useful in distinguishing between similar resources.

The cataloger must next determine the creator of the work, its origin, and its uniqueness. What is the resource about? The subject(s) covered? In what language is it written?

It is sometimes difficult to determine who or what organization is responsible for the creation or publication of a website. Databases generally seem to be better identified. Although there may be a homepage, the information may not be relayed in the standard format to which catalogers have become accustomed. If ownership information is not readily apparent, the cataloger must rely on the publisher's information as indicative of responsibility and ownership. Although the webmaster is identified on most websites, this individual does not generally create the content. The individual or organization that published the content is responsible for the site and must be selected as the preferred creator and recorded in the statement of responsibility. Other persons/organizations that have made significant contributions to the content or creative aspects of the work may be recorded as additional access points, and the appropriate relationship designators should be inserted after their names to specify relationship to the work.

AACR2 Chapter 12 and *RDA* 2.3.2.12.3 (Integrating Resources) instruct catalogers to change the title in the description of the integrating resource to reflect the title in the current iteration whenever there is a title change. On a practical level, this will depend on how often one

QUICK TIP

The date on which the resource was accessed or viewed serves to verify that the resource was indeed active on that date and alerts the user to the possibility that changes in content or other details may have occurred in the lapsed time period between viewings.

EXAMPLE 6.1

500 __ Title from webpage (viewed on March 5, 2007)

<note>Title from webpage last updated Oct. 22, 2009 (viewed Nov. 20, 2009).</note>

<Description>Title from homepage; viewed March 4, 2009.</Description>

retrieves the record and/or on the period of time that elapses between viewings of the website The mandatory note giving the date on which the website was last viewed must also be edited to reflect the latest date of viewing. *RDA* supports this requirement. *RDA* 2.3.4.7.3 provides guidance on recording changes in variant titles.

Enter the preferred title of the work in the MARC 245 field, the MODS <titleInfo> element, and the DC element <Title> exactly as it appears on the resource. Enter all variations of the title, including former titles, in the MARC 246 field (for variant title), the MODS <titleInfo> qualified with the type "alternative," and the DC element <Title> with the qualifier "Alternative" to provide appropriate access by any or all titles by which the resource may be known. Acronyms are valid as preferred titles and may be used when available, as titles can be entered in full form in the notes area of the record. *RDA* supports these instructions, though requiring catalogers to transcribe information as it appears on the resource and omit full stops when in doubt (*RDA* 11.2.2.7).

A source of title note, which includes the date on which the resource was viewed, is mandatory for all electronic resources per *AACR2* Rules 9.7B3 and 12.7B3; *RDA* supports this requirement (*RDA* 2.20.2.3). Enter this note in the MARC 500 field, the MODS element <note>, and the DC element <Description> (see Example 6.1).

Record the beginning date of publication or a range of dates for a finite integrating resource in the MARC 362 field. Provide this information in the MODS element <note> qualified with the type "date/sequential designation" and in the DC element <Description>.

A brief summary of the contents is recommended in the MARC 520 note, as this information is generally quite helpful to the user. The summary is an unformatted note and can also be provided in the MODS element <abstract> and the DC element <Description> with the qualifier "Abstract."

Other relevant MARC fields in which elements of the work are recorded include the MARC 6XX fields for subject access and genre headings, examples of which include "website," "database," and "directories." This information is recorded in the MODS element <subject>, with the subelement <genre> inserted when genre headings are applied. Subject and genre terms are provided in the DC element <Subject> with the qualifier "LCSH." Further information on the use of genre headings and subjects is available at http://www.loc.gov/marc/bibliographic/bd6xx.html; and an extensive listing of genre terms is available at http://www.loc.gov/marc/relators/relasour.html#rela655.

Record the names of contributors and other responsible parties who have contributed to the creation of the resource, including publishers when considered important, in the MARC 7XX fields, the MODS element <name>, and the DC element <Contributor>. Use the appropriate relator codes (such as "editor" and "author") in conjunction with the preferred form of the name to establish the relationship between the contributor and the resource. The MARC 776 field may be used to record related resources in accordance with the MARC format guidelines for this field. Related resources are described using the MODS element <relatedItem> and the DC element <Relation>.

The next step is to establish the bibliographic level of the resource. Is the resource monographic or serial in nature? Generally, for websites and online databases, the bibliographic level is based on whether the content is meant to be changed and/or updated with some frequency. If the changes are integrated into the content and are not discrete changes, the website is considered an integrating resource and coded **i** for integrating resource in the MARC Leader 07 position: Bibliographic Level, which expresses the mode of issuance in alphabetic code. The mode of issuance, the way in which the publisher has published or intends to publish the resource, whether as a single issue or continuing resource, must be established early on in the descriptive process as this level influences other aspects of the description.

Some websites will be considered electronic files because the electronic characteristics take predominance over the textual characteristics. Consider a website that is interactive, containing mixed media such as sound and video, as an electronic file, which must be coded **m** for content that is mainly electronic. Similarly, a database that is interactive, requiring a search engine to retrieve data contained both within the database and from the Internet, is considered electronic and will be coded **m** in the Leader 06 position. When the nature of the website cannot be determined or when in doubt, use **m** for the Type of Record code. Integrating resources most likely to be coded **a** (for content that is primarily textual) in this position are online catalogs, textual databases, and organizational and personal websites and portals.

Expression

Websites are generally unique, but they can appear in different versions when published in two or more languages. A website that exists in mirror versions can be published and/or maintained in different parts of a country or in different countries and will require separate descriptive records for each location under the following circumstances:

- Different URLs
- Content uniquely related to a specific geographic area

Note that although some websites offer automatic translation and/or currency conversion geared to the country of access (often requiring the user to indicate preference by clicking on the image of a national flag), the identical URL is generally used to gain access to the website regardless of the country or region of the world from which access is being sought. Similarly, a website's homepage can mimic a portal that enables the user to access the site in various languages. In such cases, a single descriptive record is sufficient provided that users are informed about the options available for access.

Although uncommon, a website or database can exist in several expressions or manifestations, and it is important for the cataloger to distinguish among them. A website can comprise individual works or may contain additional content that may or may not exist in similar manifestations of the site. The URL is generally a reliable indicator of difference. Answers to the following questions can help the cataloger to determine whether a website or database is a manifestation of another or a related resource:

- Is the content of both resources textual?
- Who is responsible for making the website or database publicly available? The same publisher?
- When was the resource published? Where and in what language?
- Has the existence of other versions been noted on the site?
- Have the contents of the site been expressed in any other form or genre (such as the play *Hamlet*, which exists in several online versions)?

These details will help the cataloger to determine whether a single descriptive record is sufficient and/or whether the existence of related resources must be recorded in the description.

The work must be described in the predominant language of its content and the appropriate language code must be entered in the MARC fixed field (http://www.loc.gov/marc/bibliographic/bd008a.html). If two or more languages are associated with the resource, catalogers are instructed to use the MARC 041 field, the MODS element <language>, and the DC element <Language> to reflect the different languages. In addition, information about the language(s) used on the website or database is recorded in the MARC 546 field, the MODS element <note> with the type "language," and the DC element <Language> when clarification is needed or if the cataloger wishes to emphasize the language.

A variant title note can also be entered for the foreign language title in the MARC 246 field with the appropriate indicator to identify it as a parallel title, as shown in Example 6.2. Record variant title notes in the MODS element <titleInfo> with the attribute type "translated" and in the DC element <Title> with the qualifier "Alternative."

QUICK TIP

If the website is available in more than one language and a separate URL is required to access content in a specific language, provide separate URLs for each language represented. The $z subfield of the MARC 856 field should contain a publicly accessible note that specifies the appropriate language. Enter this information in the MODS element <relatedItem> and the DC element <Identifier>, both of which can be repeated as often as needed.

EXAMPLE 6.2

246 11 Naciones Unidas son su mondo
856 41 $u http://www.un.org/es/ $z Spanish language version.

The United Nations' website is a good example of a multilingual website offering individual URLs for each of the six official languages of the United Nations. Figure 6.1 shows the website's homepage, where the multilingual display prompts the user to select a language portal to enter the site. Users can also switch to any of the five languages from within any of the language portals, an important factor in the decision to create one descriptive record for this multilingual website.

The descriptive record for this website requires notes indicating that the content of the website is available in five languages. The addition of individual MARC 856 fields in which the URL directs the user to a specific language is both appropriate and convenient for the user.

The MARC fixed fields 006, 007, and 008 complement each other and are represented as a combined fixed field area in some systems. It is important to understand how these fields work with each other. The 006 field is used when additional characteristics of a resource cannot be accommodated in the 008 field. This generally occurs when a single resource exhibits hybrid qualities (websites and databases fall into this category) or when the resource comprises component parts representing

Figure 6.1. United Nations' Homepage with a Multilingual Display to Select a Language Portal

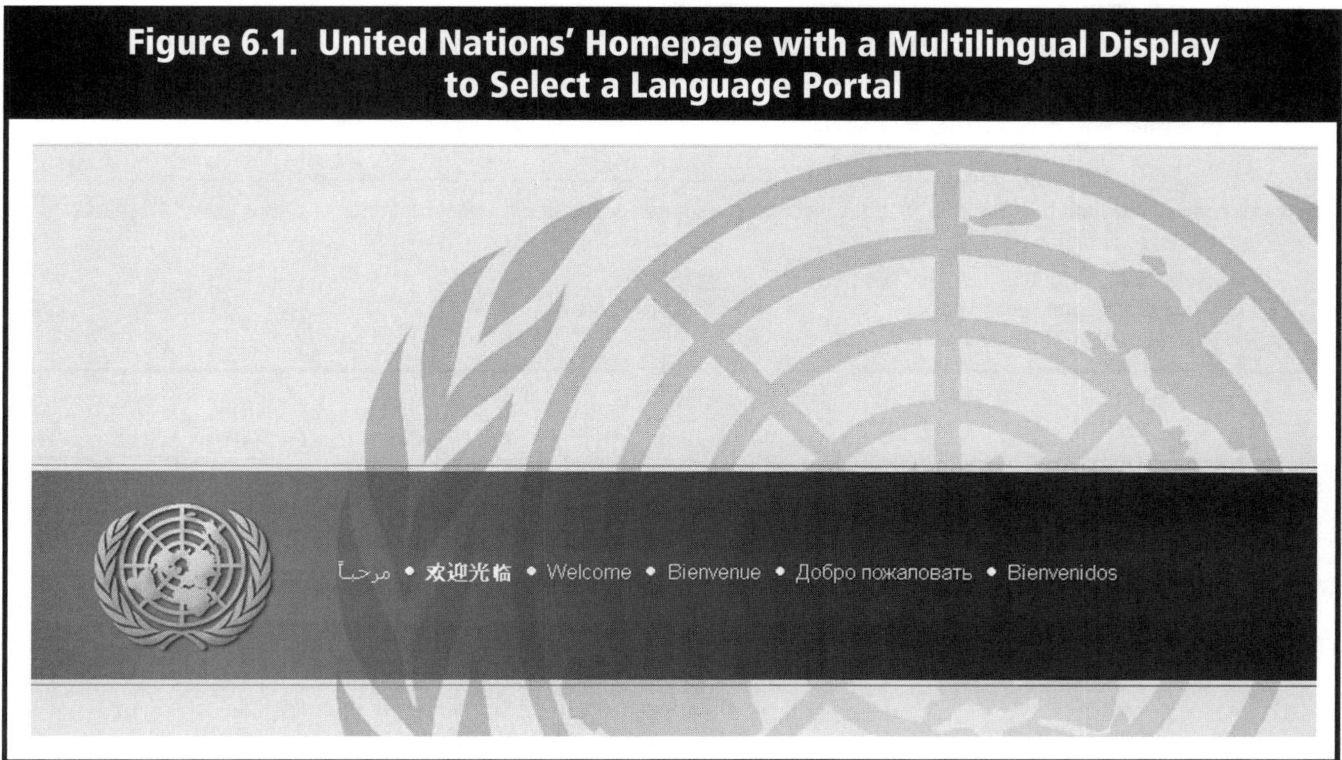

different media types. Detailed information about the use of these fields is available at http://www.loc.gov/marc/formatintegration.html.

The form of material code is inserted in the first position of the 006 field, the only position that must be coded in this field. Choice of the appropriate 006 field depends on the code selected for the Type of Record (Leader 06). If the code for Type of Record is **a** for textual material, the MARC 006 field for electronic resources must be used to reflect the electronic nature of the resource (see the example provided in Figure 6.2). All other characteristics of the resource must be coded in the MARC 008 field for continuing/integrating resources. However, it is customary to find records where positions 06 and 09 have also been coded in the MARC 006 field when the cataloger has determined that such codes are warranted because specific characteristics of the resource cannot be adequately expressed in the MARC 008 field. Instructions for the use of the MARC 006 field are available at http://www.loc.gov/marc/bibliographic/bd006.html.

Position 00 is coded **m** for electronic resource. When used appropriately, as shown in Figure 6.2, position 06 (form of item, which is also position 23 in the MARC 008 field) must be coded **o** to specify that the type of resource is an online resource or service. Position 09 (type of computer file) may be coded **d** for document or **m** for mixed types, as appropriate.

Alternately, when the value **m** is used as the Type of Record code, indicating that the resource is an electronic resource, the MARC 006 field for continuing resources, which is also used for integrating resources,

Figure 6.2. MARC 006 Fixed Field for Electronic Resources

Position 00: m	Position 01–04: undefined	Position 06: o	Position 09: m

The coded information in the 006 field for electronic resources illustrates the most popular positions coded to reflect characteristics of online resources:

m = electronic resource
o = online (remotely accessed)
m = combination of file types

must be used to reflect the serial or continuing nature of the resource (see Figure 6.3).

Position 00 is coded **s** for continuing/integrating resource. The code **d** (updating database) or **w** (updating website) may be entered in Position 04 of the MARC 006 field for continuing resources, which is equivalent to position 21 in the MARC 008 field. When used, Position 06 (form of item) requires the code **o** for online resource or **q** for direct electronic. Code **s** may be used if preferred by the cataloger. For databases or websites coded **a** in the Type of Record field signifying that the content is largely textual, the 006 field for continuing resources may also be required if the resource is an integrating resource (see Figure 6.3).

The other positions are coded in the MARC 008 field because the 006 and 008 fields complement each other. While it is customary to see 006 as a separate MARC field, it can be combined with other fixed field elements in some ILSs. For detailed information about the codes for these fields, consult http://www.loc.gov/marc/bibliographic/bd006.html.

The 008 field values for continuing resources are used for websites and databases that are continuing integrating resources. This field accommodates additional resource-specific details, and the values in this field, from positions 18 to 34, are identical to those in the 006 field positions 1 to 17. All positions identified for the 006 field, with the exception of

Figure 6.3. MARC 006 Field for Continuing Integrating Resources

Position 00 Form of material: s	Position 01 Frequency: k or u	Position 02 Regularity: r or u	Position 03 Undefined	Position 04 Type of integrating resource: d or w	Position 06 Form of item: s, o, or q	Position 017 Entry convention: 2

The coded information in the 006 field for continuing/integrating resources illustrates the positions most commonly coded to reflect the characteristics of an online integrating resource:

s = continuing/integrating resource
k = continuously updated; u = frequency of update unknown or less than daily
r = regularly updated; u = unknown
d = updating database; w = updating website.
s = electronic; o = online; q = direct electronic
2 = integrating entry

the first position, must be entered in the 008 field unless the required position in the 008 field has been coded for a component resource. The 008 field contains elements related to both the expression and manifestation of a resource. This type of information is recorded in the MODS element <genre>. The most important 008 positions that must be coded in the resource description for websites and databases are as follows:

- Frequency of update (continuously updated sites require code **k**; all other frequencies require this position be left blank)
- Regularity
- Type of continuing resource
- Form of item (currently **o** for online and **q** for direct access; **s** for electronic resources may still be used in this position)
- Entry convention (formerly known as Latest/Successive Entry)

For Entry Convention, the value "2" is currently required for all integrating resources to specify that the resource description was based on the latest (current) iteration and that the resource is an integrating resource.

Manifestation

The resources discussed in this chapter belong to a single carrier type: online resources. Characteristics of the carrier generally relate to the manifestation of the work and include physical and technical details about the carrier and carrier type and unique numeric identifiers generally assigned by the publisher.

For catalogers using MARC, the MARC 007 fixed field for electronic resources is mandatory for all electronic resources and accommodates information related to the manifestation of the work. The first position of this field reflects the category of material and is coded **c** for electronic resources (dependent on the use of a computer for access). The next character in the 007 field is determined by the individual carrier (as indicated by the specific material designator). The code **r** is used for integrating resources that are remotely accessed. These two positions are mandatory for core level cataloging, and the most common values in these positions for websites and online databases are **c** for electronic resources and **r** for remotely accessed. Additional details about the 007 field are available at http://www.loc.gov/marc/bibliographic/bd007c.html.

The following elements, though not an integral part of the work, facilitate retrieval of the resource and allow for immediate machine manipulation of specific segments of the record. In the MARC format, technical details appear at the beginning of the descriptive record. Taken together, the Leader (06 and 07 positions) and fixed fields (006, 007, 008) accommodate technical information about the resource and its carrier in coded alphabetic form. The code in the Leader 06 position (Record Type) determines the appropriate values for the codes in the MARC 006, 007, and 008 fields.

Figure 6.4 illustrates a sample MARC fixed field showing the most important fields for integrating resources. This is a combination fixed

FOR MORE INFORMATION

OCLC guidelines for field 007 are available at http://www.oclc.org/bibformats/en/0XX/field007table.shtm.

Figure 6.4. Combined MARC Fixed Fields Showing Frequently Coded Fields for Integrating Resources

Type:	a	ELvl:	[blank]	Form:	o	Lang:	eng	Ctry:	nyu
Blvl:	i	Form:	s	Freq:	k	Regl:	r	Date 1:	2009
Desc:	a	S/L:	2	Type:	d	DtTy:	c	Date 2:	9999

Leader 06: Type: textual

Leader 07: Blvl: bibliographic level: i = integrating resource

Note: The leader field positions 06 and 07 are not identified as leader positions in the combined fixed field. They are coded as Type and Blvl, respectively.

Common 008 field positions used for all types of resources:

Ctry: country of publication

Lang: language

ELvl: This is left blank for full-level resource description.

Desc: description convention: a = according to AACR2

Date type: publication status: c = currently published.

Date 1 and **Date 2:** Complete as appropriate.

Common 008 field positions used for continuing resources:

Form of item: o = online; s = electronic resource

Frequency of update: [code only if stated] k=continuously updated.

Regularity: r = regular

Type [of continuing/integrating resource] d = updating database; w = updating website

S/L [entry convention]: 2 [All integrating resources are coded 2 in this position.]

[Positions 18-34 in the 008 field relate to specific types of resources.]

QUICK TIP

In descriptive records for nonprint resources, a General Material Designation (GMD) has been used as an early alert for the user and to facilitate indexing. When required by cataloging utilities, the GMD is inserted in the delimiter $h subfield of the title (MARC 245) and is enclosed in square brackets. The term used for all online resources is "electronic resource."

The terms GMD and SMD were never authorized for use with the various metadata schemes that accommodate relevant data in appropriately designated areas. The SMD "website" or "database" is used in the $a subfield of the MARC 300 field, when required.

RDA 3.1.5 has authorized the use of "online resource" as the carrier type for all online resources.

field, containing some MARC 006 and 008 values, as reflected in OCLC MARC records. This field contains characteristics that are applicable to all resource types, such as codes for the language of the resource, the place, and the year of publication and codes indicating whether the resource is a government publication. For detailed information about the input requirements for the OCLC fixed field, see http://www.oclc.org/us/en/bibformats/en/fixedfield/default.htm.

Additional details about the carrier are recorded in the MARC 300 field describing the extent of resource and in the MARC 337 (Media Type) and 338 (Carrier Type) fields. The Specific Material Designation (SMD) is generally found in the MARC 300 field, subfield delimiter $a when used. The extent of the resource is entered in this field, which is optional for electronic resources per *AACR2* but is required for description according to *RDA* 3.4.1.7.5 for resources that are complete and when extent can be determined and easily recorded. The extent of a resource is an important distinguishing element, and *RDA* has authorized additional details in this field, including file size and/or number of databases, when such information is readily available. Provide details about the extent of the resource in the MODS element <physical

Description> with the subelement <extent> and in the DC element <Format> with the qualifier "Extent." Information that cannot be accommodated in specific fields can be entered in a general note.

Figure 6.5 presents an overview of the bibliographic elements relevant to describing both websites and databases using the MARC display format.

Figure 6.5. Bibliographic Elements for Describing Websites and Databases in the MARC Format

007	"c" [computer resource] and "r"[remotely located] should be assigned for all websites and databases.
Leader 06 and Leader 07	Code per MARC guidelines for Leader 06 and 07. Available at http://www.loc.gov/marc/bibliographic/bdleader.html
006	Code for electronic resources.
007	This field is required for all electronic resources.
008	Code for continuing resources.
020	ISBN: This is not applicable for websites.
040	Code for the library creating the descriptive record (applies to original cataloging only).
043	Supply as required.
050	This is an optional field.
1XX	Main entries: While the 100 field is not normally used when cataloging websites (the site is usually the cooperative effort of many individuals), the 110 field for responsible corporate body is used when appropriate. Example: membership directories and corporate websites
240	Use if appropriate; may be appropriate in resource description for databases.
245	Title: This must be taken from the website itself, preferably from the title screen. For databases, this must be taken from the title screen or the website itself.
246	Variant title: This is any other possible titles by which the site is known or a title that was formerly used for the website. This is also used when the website title varies from the title on another version of the resource. Example: 246 1 $i HTML title: $a————————
250	Edition statement: Supply as required; information may also specify version.
260 $a	Place of publication.
260 $b	Publisher.
260 $c	Publication date: Select a date that represents publication or production of the item described. If no such date is present, use the latest copyright date or any approximate date in the website entered in square brackets with a question mark. Example: [2000?-]). Assume all remote-access resources to be published.

(Cont'd.)

Figure 6.5. Bibliographic Elements for Describing Websites and Databases in the MARC Format *(Continued)*

300	This field is optional for electronic resources, though required when described according to RDA. The cataloger may use either of the following: 1 website; or 1 electronic database; or 1 online resource (the terminology required by RDA).
490	Series: Use as required.
500	"Title from [. . .] as viewed on [date]" — note: This note is mandatory.
500	Other notes in this area can include people or organizations associated with the site, such as sponsors.
520	Summary: Give a brief, objective, generic summary of the content unless another part of the description provides enough information.
530	Other physical forms available note: Use when there are multiple formats available.
538	Mode of access: World Wide Web.
6XX	Subject headings: Use or propose as needed; use form/genre subdivisions as appropriate.
7XX	Personal and corporate added entries: Use as necessary; create authority records as needed.
730	Added entry: Uniform title: Use as needed for title added entries.
770	Related site or related material associated with the website.
856	Electronic location: Use for all remote resources.

QUICK TIP

In older records, the MARC 256 field usually contains the computer file characteristics. However, the *AACR2* update included several major changes to Chapter 9, and the 256 field was made obsolete at that time. In the same update, the 300 field was authorized for optional use to record the extent of remote access electronic resources.

Refer to the latest documentation from the Library of Congress for additional information about the publication area. The publication "Integrating Resources: A Cataloging Manual, Appendix to the BIBCO Participants' Manual" is available at http://www.loc.gov/catdir/pcc/bibco/irman.pdf. Relevant information is also available from the International Federation of Library Associations and Museums (IFLA) in its document International Standard Bibliographic Description (ISBD): Preliminary Consolidated Edition, available at http://www.ifla.org/files/cataloguing/isbd/isbd-cons_2007-en.pdf.

Websites

Integrating resources are considered to be published, and publication data must be recorded according to *AACR2* and *RDA*. The MARC 260 field in which this data is recorded can be repeated as necessary to accommodate publication history, a recently approved option that is especially useful for providing important data about continuing and/or integrating resources. The nature of integrating websites often means that information about the publisher can vary while the site is active and available on the Internet. The publication details area should always contain current information as reflected in the current iteration of the website or database. The publication history is important and must be recorded to provide continuity and to reflect ownership. The MARC 260 field may be repeated to reflect changes in publisher. Field indicator values are used to specify whether the publisher named in the 260 field is the current publisher or an intervening publisher. The MODS <originInfo> element and the DC element <Publisher> can be repeated as necessary. Enter more detailed information regarding the publication history in the general notes area in the MARC 500 field, the MODS <note> element, and the DC element <Description> when required. See http://www.loc.gov/marc/bibliographic/bd260 .html for further details. Publication details can also be provided in the MODS element <originInfo> and the DC element <Publisher>. There may be several different dates on a website, including a copyright date; catalogers are required to use the date of publication when available.

Figure 6.6 provides a good example of a corporate website that contains both static and changing information. The sections titled "News & Events" and "Calendar of Events" denote areas wherein the content is expected to change, not necessarily daily, but frequently. The section "Our Campuses" contains information that will be largely static (information about admissions policies, the university, and the mission of serving New Jersey).

Note: The contents of the website illustrated in Figure 6.6 are mainly textual, containing images that are static. Information at the bottom of the webpage supplies the copyright date, contact information, and the name of the owner of the website. There is also a section for questions,

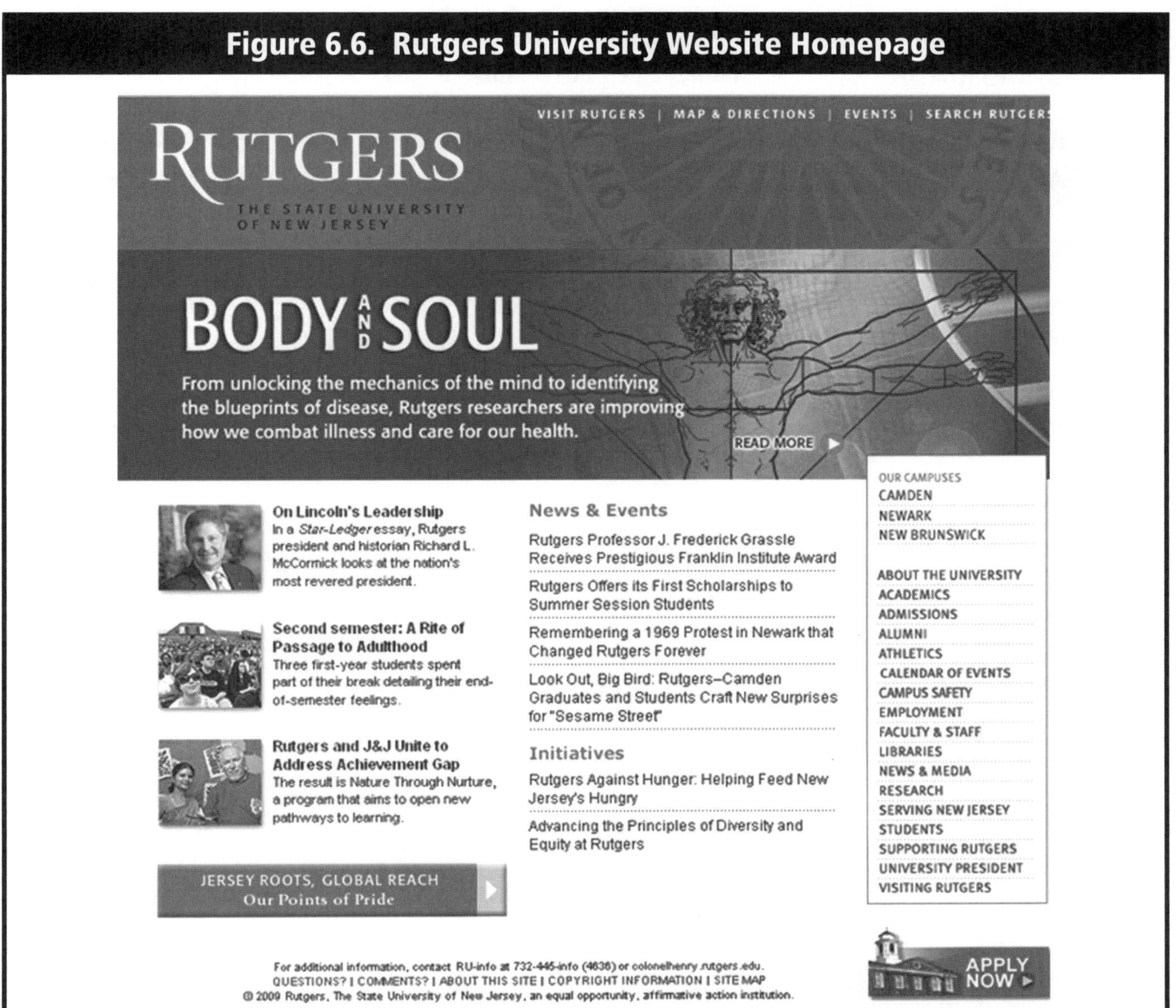

Figure 6.6. Rutgers University Website Homepage

EXAMPLE 6.3

300 __ 1 Web site. [(*AACR2*])

300 __ 1 online resource (32 pages) : $b color illustrations. [*RDA*]

<physicalDescription>
<extent>1 web site</extent>
</physicalDescription> [*AACR2*]

<physicalDescription>
<extent>1 online resource (32 pages) : color illustrations</extent>
</physicalDescription> [*RDA*]

comments, and a site map. Figure 6.7 shows a descriptive MARC record for this website.

Recording the extent of the resource (entered in the MARC 300 field, the MODS element <physicalDescription> with the subelement <extent>, and the DC element <Format>) is currently optional for online electronic resources described according to *AACR2*. It is required for description done according to *RDA*. Recent practice reflects its use, as shown in Example 6.3.

The MARC fields that have replaced the GMD require the use of authorized terms for content, media, and carrier types, as provided in the tables 3.1 and 3.3.1.3 in *RDA* Chapter 3. Although information related to these categories can be repeated in other areas of the bibliographic record, such as in the MARC 008 field and in the general fixed field area, the additional 3XX fields are required for MARC records based on *RDA* rules for description. Record the appropriate term in the delimiter $a subfield and the source list or thesaurus from which the term was extracted in the delimiter $2 subfield.

Figure 6.7. MARC Descriptive Record for the Rutgers University Website

Leader 06 Leader 07	a: Textual material. i : Integrating resource.
006 [Electronic resources]	m [electronic resource]
007	c [electronic resource] r [remotely accessed]
008 [combined 006 for continuing resources & 008 field]	Lang: eng Form of item: s Ctry: nju S/L 2 SerTy: w Desc: a Freq: u Reg: u Date 1: 199? Date 2: 9999
110 2_	Rutgers University.
245 00	Rutgers $h [electronic resource] : $b The State University of New Jersey.
260 __	New Brunswick, N.J. : $b Rutgers,
300 __	1 updating website.
500 __	Title from homepage (viewed, February 20, 2009).
520 __	The main website of the university. This web portal contains general information about the departments, faculty, programs, admission requirements and events at the university. Contains links to the various departments and divisions within the university.
538 __	Mode of access: World Wide Web.
610 10	Rutgers University.
856 40	$u http://www.rutgers.edu

The terms in the $2 subfield in Example 6.4 are pending approval by the various cataloging agencies. The terms can be repeated in separate $a subfields or in separate 3XX fields. Generally, the *RDA* guideline is flexible and allows the terms, if they are from the same source (such as "rdacontent"), to be inserted in the same field, separated by repeating the subfield "a."

Other fields that are appropriate for integrating resources include the following:

- Use the MARC 310 field to indicate the frequency with which a website or database is updated. The field is mandatory if this information is published on the resource. (The frequency is also coded in the 008 field of the MARC record.) Record this information in the MODS element <originInfo> with the subelement <frequency> and in the DC element <Accrual Periodicity>.
- Use the MARC 362 field to record the beginning date of publication or, for a finite or static integrating resource, a range of dates. Record this information in the MODS element <note> qualified with the type "date/sequential designation" and in the DC element <Description>.

EXAMPLE 6.4

336 __ Content type $a Text $a images $2 rdacontent
337 __ Media type $a computer $2 rdamedia
338 __ Carrier type $a online resource $2 rdacarrier.

Databases

Figure 6.8 demonstrates the type of website that can be considered a portal or database. In most cases, it may be more appropriate to provide separate descriptive records for important sections of the website, such as the webpage or site for a specific project or a popular research department. The image in Figure 6.8 was captured from the Rutgers University website for a specific project within the university and is the homepage for the project.

The website illustrated is primarily a directory of resources. It operates in the traditional sense of a directory in that archives located throughout the United States are indexed and are easily retrievable via a simple search. The search retrieves information about the specific archive queried and provides the URL for the archive's website, if available. Additional information such as news and information about upcoming events is included and new information is added periodically, as evidenced by a request for archives to submit information to the site owner. This is considered a textual updating website and is described as such in the example MARC and MODS descriptive records in Figures 6.9 and 6.10.

Resource description for online databases mirrors that of websites because they are both considered electronic integrating resources. The cataloger must first determine whether the resource is a database established by the publisher, an aggregator database, or a website, a necessary distinction that the descriptive record should reflect. Aggregator databases are collections of electronic journals made available simultaneously by different vendors. The contents of these databases are considered continuing resources with discreet updates and are therefore beyond the scope of this chapter. Integrating resources and continuing resources share some

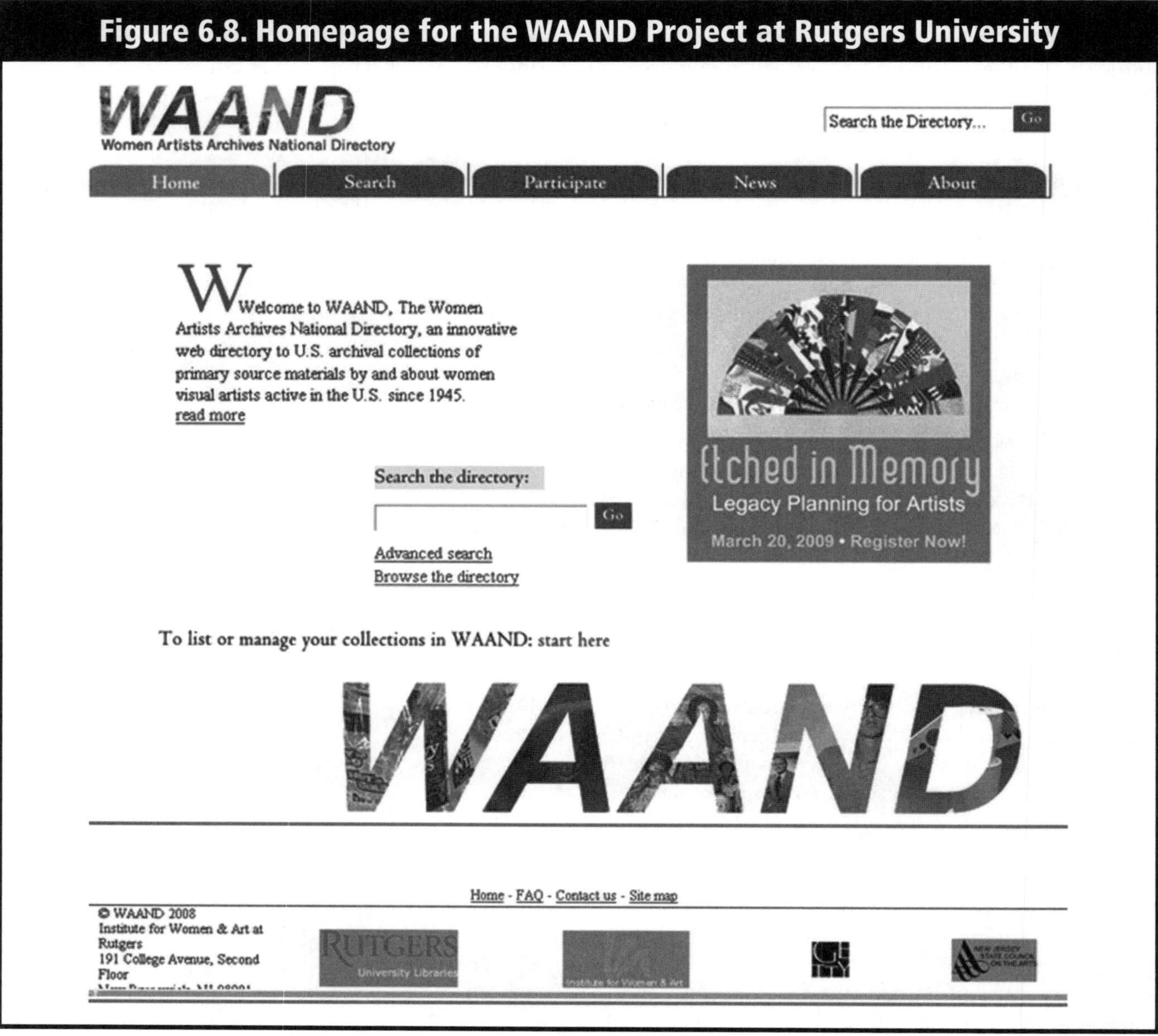

Figure 6.8. Homepage for the WAAND Project at Rutgers University

common characteristics and descriptive elements, thus providing distinct advantages for the cataloger who understands and is familiar with cataloging requirements for both types of resources.

Publication details may present the most important area in which databases require special considerations not accorded to websites. The database may be the online equivalent of a resource that exists in the printed form. Moreover, a print resource is generally static and may be updated by discrete updates, while the online version may contain additional information and features not available in the printed version. *RDA* is clear in its requirement for description of both manifestations of this type of resource and requires catalogers to "record the elements describing the carrier as they apply to the manifestation being described"—

Figure 6.9. MARC Descriptive Record for the WAAND Website

Leader 06 Leader 07 Leader 18	Type of record: a Bib Level: i Desc: a
006	m [electronic resource]
007	c r
008	Lang: eng Form of item: s [electronic resource] Ctry: nju S/L: 2 [integrated resource] SerTy: d[updating database] Nature of work: r [directory] Freq: u Reg: u Date 1: 2007 Date 2: 9999
110 1_	Rutgers University. $b Institute for Women and Art.
245 00	WAAND $h [electronic resource] : $b Women Artists Archives National Directory / $c Institute for Women and Art at Rutgers.
246 13	Women Artists Archives National Directory
300 __	1 website.
500 __	Title from homepage (viewed February 20, 2009).
500 __	WAAND's initial development (2005-06) was funded by a grant from The Getty Foundation.
538 __	Mode of access: World Wide Web.
520 __	"An innovative web directory to U.S. archival collections of primary source materials by and about women visual artists active in the U.S. since 1945" -- Website.
650 _0 655 _0	Women artists $z United States $v Directories. Directories
710 1_	$b Institute for Women's Leadership. $b Institute for Women and Art.
710 1_	Rutgers University. $b Institute for Women and Art.
856 40	$u http://waand.rutgers.edu/

in this case, the online resource (*RDA* 3.1.2). This is important for integrating databases for which a print version may be available, or that were available as printed volumes in the past, as it affords the cataloger flexibility in the resource description that is unhampered by the limits of a tangible printed resource. The rule further stipulates that other available formats of the resource must be referenced and refers catalogers to *RDA* 27.1 and 24.4, both of which provide instructions for recording related manifestations.

In the absence of an existing print version of the database content, the cataloger is required to describe the resource at hand by recording the publisher information according to *AACR2* or *RDA*. If the cataloger has knowledge of another manifestation, the MARC 530 field (for

```
<titleInfo>
  <title>WAAND</title>
  <titleInfo type="alternative">
    <title>Women Artists Archives National Directory
    </title>
</titleInfo>
<typeOfResource>software, multimedia</typeOfResource>
<name type="corporate">
  <namePart>Rutgers University</namePart>
  <namePart>Institute for Women and Art</namePart>
  <role>
    <roleTerm type="text">creator</roleTerm>
  </role>
</name>
<language>
  <languageTerm type="code" authority="iso639-2b">
  eng</languageTerm>
</language>
<genre authority="marcgt">directory</genre>
<originInfo>
  <place>
    <placeTerm type="code" authority="marccountry">
    nju</placeTerm>
    <placeTerm type="text"> New Brunswick, N.J.
    </placeTerm>
  </place>
  <publisher>Rutgers University. Institute for Women and
  Art</publisher>
  <dateCreated>2006</dateCreated>
  </originInfo>
<typeOfResource>software, multimedia
</typeOfResource>
<abstract>WAAND is a directory of women artists' archives
in the United States. Contains basic information about
museums across the United States. Includes information such
as address and type of museum and extent of holdings.
</abstract>
<tableOfContents> Repository Directory -- Collections --
Entity (artist or artists' organization) Database.
</tableOfContents>
<note>WAAND's initial development (2005-06) was funded
by a grant from The Getty Foundation. WAAND consists of
three linked databases: a Repository Directory, Collections,
and an Entity (artist or artists' organization) Database.
</note>
<subject authority="lcsh">
  <topic>Women artists</topic>
  <geographic>United States</geographic>
</subject>
<location>
  <url>http://waand.rutgers.edu</url>
</location>
```

additional formats) is used to record information about the availability of another format. Information about other manifestations is provided in the MODS element <note> with the type attribute "additional physical form" and in the DC element <Description> with the qualifier <HasFormat>.

The following examples illustrate the changing nature of databases. *Note*: Some of the examples are no longer available on the Internet as they were selected during the first quarter of 2009. They are included here to demonstrate why catalogers are required to use only the current iteration of an integrating resource. We encourage you to visit the websites and databases to see what changes may be required to the descriptive records in these examples if you were to describe them after you have read this chapter.

Figure 6.11 presents an earlier version of the Black Drama website in which the publisher advised, in a posted notice on the website, that this image and link will be available on the Internet until March 1, 2009. Having encountered such a notice, a cataloger may decide to wait until after the website has been relocated to create the descriptive record or, alternatively, may describe the database despite the information posted and allow users to be automatically redirected (by the URL-switching feature promised by the publisher) to the correct site after the posted date of the move. The database shown in Figure 6.11 provides a good example of the dynamic nature of integrating databases and websites.

The descriptive record for the database pictured in Figure 6.11 should contain the following, as shown in Figure 6.12:

- The Leader field Record Type is coded **a** for primarily textual material.
- The Leader field Bibliographic Level is coded **i** for integrating resource.

Figure 6.11. Black Drama Database Homepage

An earlier version of the Black Drama website; this image and link will be available on the Internet until March 1, 2009.

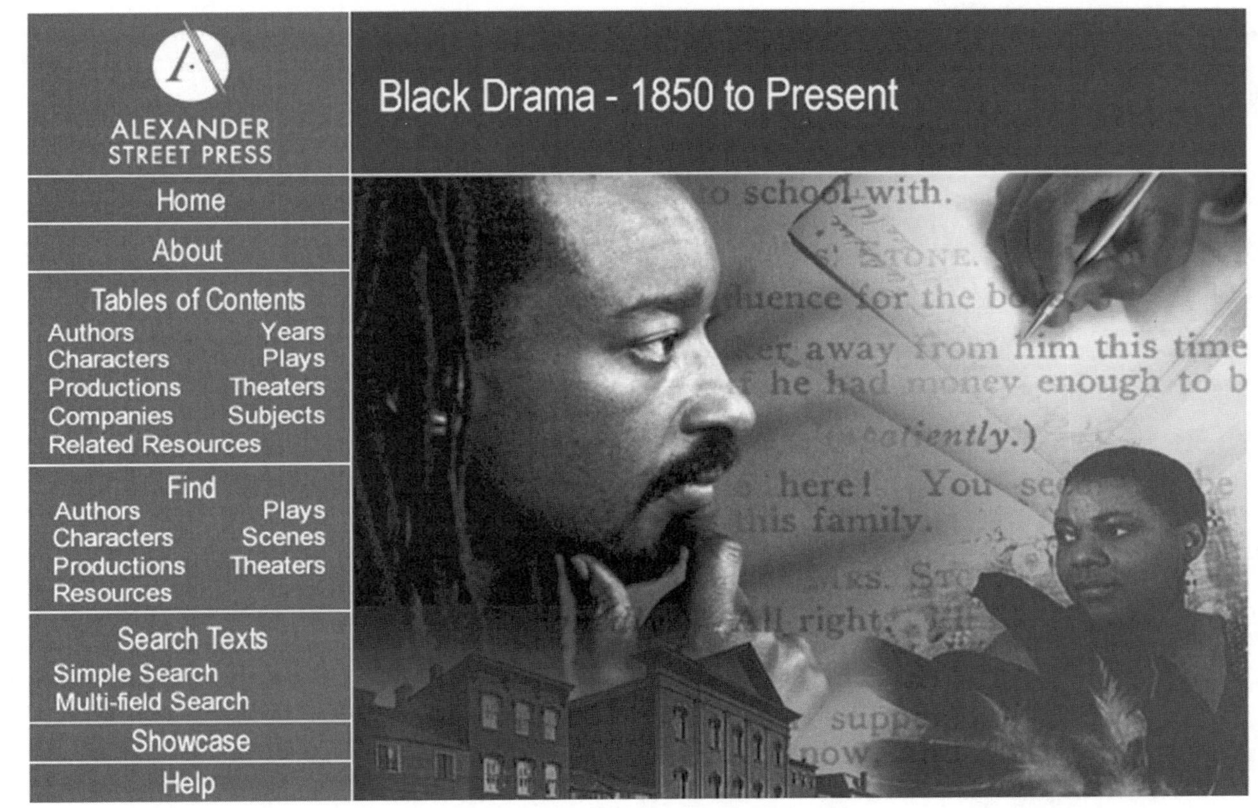

Figure 6.12. MARC Descriptive Record for the Black Drama Integrating Database

Leader 06 Leader 07	[Record type]: a [text] [Bibliographic level]: i [integrating resource]
006 [electronic resource]	m d
007 [electronic resource]	c $b r $d c $e n $f u
008	Lang: eng Form of item: s Ctry: vau S/L 2 SerTy: d Desc: a Freq: u Reg: u Date 1: 2001 Date 2: 9999
245 00	Black drama $h [electronic resource] : $b 1850 - present
260 __	[Chicago] : $b Alexander Street Press, $c 2001-
300 [required by RDA]	1 updating database
500 __	Title from title screen (viewed February 20, 2009).
538 __	Mode of access: World Wide Web
506 __	Access restricted to subscribers.
500 __	Produced in collaboration with the University of Chicago.
516 __	Text file.
520 __	The database contains approximately 1200 plays by 201 playwrights.
650 _0	Drama $x Black authors.
650 _0	Drama $x Black authors $v Databases.
655 _0	Electronic reference sources.
710 2_	Alexander Street Press.
710 2_	University of Chicago.
856 40	$u http://www.alexanderstreet2.com/BLDRLive

- The continuing resources fixed field values are used in the combined fixed field area (containing the Leader, 006, and 008 field values).
- The 006 field values include S/L **2** for integrating resource; frequency is **u** for unknown; type of continuing resource (SrTp) is **d** for updating database.
- The 008 fixed field values include coded data for the language of the resource (eng: English); form of item, which is **s** for electronic; and date of publication.
- The 006 field for electronic resources has been added: form of material is **m** for computer resource; type of computer file

is **d** for database and may also be coded **m** for combination files.

- The 007 field (mandatory) indicates that the resource is **c**, electronic; **r**, remotely accessed; **n**, not applicable; and **u**, unknown.
- The database was created sometime in 2001 but was viewed on February 20, 2009, according to the mandatory 500 field for source of title note.
- The 506 field note informs that "Access is restricted to subscribers." This information is not repeated in the MARC 856 field. The cataloger had the option of putting this information in the $z of the 856 field of the record.
- Note the use of form headings in the subject fields ($v Databases).
- Also note the use of the 655 genre heading "Electronic reference sources."

The descriptive record in Rutgers University's ILS (see Figure 6.13) contains information that differs from the descriptive record in Figure 6.12:

Figure 6.13. Rutgers University Online Descriptive Record for the Black Drama Database

```
000:      : ai a c
001:      : a1705257
007:      : cr cn
008:      : 020425c20019999ilu dss 0 2eng d
035:      : (NIC)4247915
035:      : (OCoLC)ocm49876412
040:      : VXW|cVXW|dNIC|dNjR
245: 00   : Black drama, 1850 to present|h[electronic resource].
246: 30   : Black drama
260:      : [Chicago] :|bAlexander Street Press,|c2001-
500:      : "The plays...have been selected using leading bibliographies and with the editorial advice of James V.
            Hatch, a leading expert in this area."--Introductory screen
500:      : Produced in collaboration with the University of Chicago.
506:      : Access restricted to subscribing institutions.
516:      : Documents available in HTML format.
538:      : System requirements: Netscape Navigator Version 1.2 or higher or Microsoft Explore 2.0 or higher.
500:      : Title from introductory screen (viewed Jul. 25, 2008).
520:      : Contains approximately 1200 plays by 201 playwrights, together with detailed, fielded information on
            related productions, theaters, production companies, and more. The database also includes selected
            playbills, production photographs and other ephemera related to the plays.
650: 0    : American drama|xAfrican American authors.
650: 0    : African Americans|xDrama.
650: 0    : African American theater.
650: 0    : Black theater.
650: 0    : Drama|xBlack authors.
650: 0    : Blacks|xDrama.
710: 2    : Alexander Street Press.
710: 2    : University of Chicago.
856: 40   : |uhttp://bldr.alexanderstreet.com|zAccess restricted to Rutgers University faculty, staff, and
            students.
```

- The data for the Leader fields is contained in the 000 field (the Leader field in Sirsi's Unicorn).
- The 007 field contains the same values except for the optional positions 03 (**c** for multicolored) and 04 (**n** for dimensions not applicable). The first two positions of the 007 field are required for core level cataloging.
- The 516 field specifies that the format is HTML (a useful piece of information).
- The slight variation in the 246 title is accounted for in the 500 note for this record, which states that the title was viewed on July 25, 2008.

Figure 6.14 shows an image of a newer version of the website for the Black Drama database as viewed on February 20, 2009. This is the version to which users were directed when they accessed the earlier version shown in Figure 6.11. The URL is different and the homepage looks

Figure 6.14. The New Version of the Black Drama Database

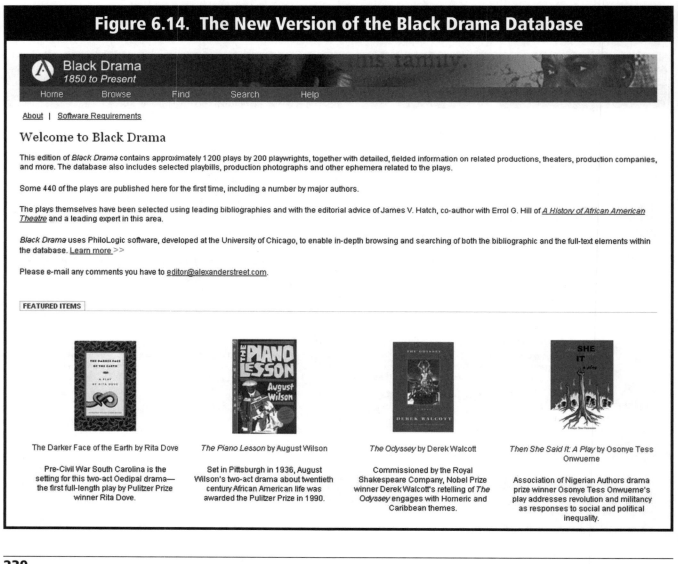

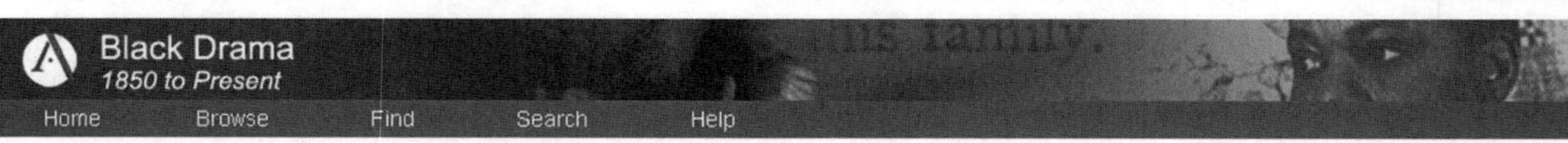

About | Software Requirements

Welcome to Black Drama

This edition of *Black Drama* contains approximately 1200 plays by 200 playwrights, together with detailed, fielded information on related productions, theaters, production companies, and more. The database also includes selected playbills, production photographs and other ephemera related to the plays.

Some 440 of the plays are published here for the first time, including a number by major authors.

The plays themselves have been selected using leading bibliographies and with the editorial advice of James V. Hatch, co-author with Errol G. Hill of *A History of African American Theatre* and a leading expert in this area.

Black Drama uses PhiloLogic software, developed at the University of Chicago, to enable in-depth browsing and searching of both the bibliographic and the full-text elements within the database. Learn more >>

Please e-mail any comments you have to editor@alexanderstreet.com.

FEATURED ITEMS

The Darker Face of the Earth by Rita Dove

Pre-Civil War South Carolina is the setting for this two-act Oedipal drama—the first full-length play by Pulitzer Prize winner Rita Dove.

The Piano Lesson by August Wilson

Set in Pittsburgh in 1936, August Wilson's two-act drama about twentieth century African American life was awarded the Pulitzer Prize in 1990.

The Odyssey by Derek Walcott

Commissioned by the Royal Shakespeare Company, Nobel Prize winner Derek Walcott's retelling of *The Odyssey* engages with Homeric and Caribbean themes.

Then She Said It: A Play by Osonye Tess Onwueme

Association of Nigerian Authors drama prize winner Osonye Tess Onwueme's play addresses revolution and militancy as responses to social and political inequality.

different, but the title is the same. The changes in the URL and in the appearance of the homepage do not justify a new record.

A change of title is not always considered a major change for online resources. However, a change of title accompanied by other changes, such as a change of focus, is considered a major change and a new record is required in such cases.

Figure 6.15 shows a revised descriptive record, which includes the changes required to reflect the new iteration, the new URL. Figure 6.16 shows the resource description using MODS.

FOR MORE INFORMATION

The ALCTS document *Differences Between, Changes Within: Guidelines on When to Create a New Record* can help clarify when a new record must be added for integrating resources.

Figure 6.15. Sample MARC Record for the New Version of the Black Drama Database

Leader 06 Leader 07	[Record type]: a [Bibliographic level]: i [integrating resource]
006	m d
007	c $b r $d c $e n $f u
008	Lang: eng Form of item: s Ctry: vau S/L 2; SerTy: d Desc: a Freq: u Reg: u Date 1: 2001 Date 2: 9999
245 00	Black drama $h [electronic resource] : $b 1850 - present
260 __	[Chicago] : $b Alexander Street Press, $c 2001-
300 [optional]	1 updating database
506 __	Access restricted to subscribers.
500 __	Produced in collaboration with the University of Chicago.
520 __	The database contains approximately 1200 plays by two hundred playwrights.
538 __	Mode of access: World Wide Web
538 __	"Black Drama is optimized to operate with Netscape Navigator Version 1.2 or higher or Microsoft Explorer 7.0 or higher" --Website.
500 __ **[New info.]**	Title from title screen (viewed March 1, 2009).
516 __ [type of computer file]	Text file
650 _0	Drama $x Black authors.
650 _0	Drama $x Black authors $v Databases.
655 _0	Electronic reference sources.
710 2_	Alexander Street Press.
710 2_	University of Chicago.
856 40 **[New URL]**	$u http://solomon.bldr.alexanderstreet.com

Figure 6.16. Abbreviated MODS Record for the New Black Drama Database

Descriptive Area	
Title (and subelements):	Black drama. 1850 - present
Type of resource:	Integrating database.
Name (responsible agency):	Alexander Street Press.
Genre:	Database
Origin info (place, publisher, date): Issuance:	[Chicago] Alexander Street Press. 2001-
Physical description (form, extent, Internet media type, digital origin, etc.):	1 updating database.
Abstract:	The database contains approximately 1200 plays by two hundred playwrights.
Table of contents:	Not applicable.
Note:	Access restricted to subscribers.
Subject:	Drama -- Black authors.
Classification:	[Insert when appropriate.]
Identifier (hdl):	[Insert when appropriate.]
Physical location:	http://solomon.bldr.alexanderstreet.com

Networked Resources

The ability to provide simultaneous access to information on CD-ROMs hosted on a remote server was one of the earliest models of providing access to networked resources. This method of content delivery invariably required the user to visit the library to use an on-site workstation. This type of connection still exists in some libraries, but the remote server has been largely replaced by the Internet, and the possibilities and types of resources have multiplied.

Users are now more likely to access information from almost any location within or outside of the library via a link in the descriptive record through which access to the desired resource is secured. It is customary to find resources that were first offered as networked CD-ROMS now being offered as electronic resources. And, it is not unusual to find resources whose earlier issues, formerly available only on networked CDs, are available both on CD and on the Internet. Experiments in linking, tagging, and metadata application[6] are closing in on the ability to offer the user seamless access to a wide variety of resources using as few interactions as possible. The Internet continues to exert a revolutionary effect on content delivery and constantly reveals new ways of delivering content. Most importantly, the variety of resource types now being networked was not possible in the networked database environment. A number of institutions are exploring the ability to link images and datasets to bibliographic data, albeit in a variety of ways.

The ability to link disparate yet related resources is the hallmark of networked resources. The retrieval of these resources depends on the skillful use of controlled vocabularies. Prerequisite to providing access to networked resources is the accurate description of the content of the resource and the assignment of appropriate subject terms. Today, resource description for networked resources may be as simple as describing a website or online database.

New Jersey Digital Highway is an example of a portal providing access to networked resources (see Figure 6.17), and ToxNet is an example of a portal to networked databases (see Figure 6.18). There are no unique requirements for the description of portals. Portals are essentially websites and are treated in the same way (see Figure 6.19).

Item

The item represents a single exemplar of the resource. Because online resources are remotely located and are not tangible resources, item-specific information will generally be limited to local notes regarding

Figure 6.17. New Jersey Digital Highway Portal

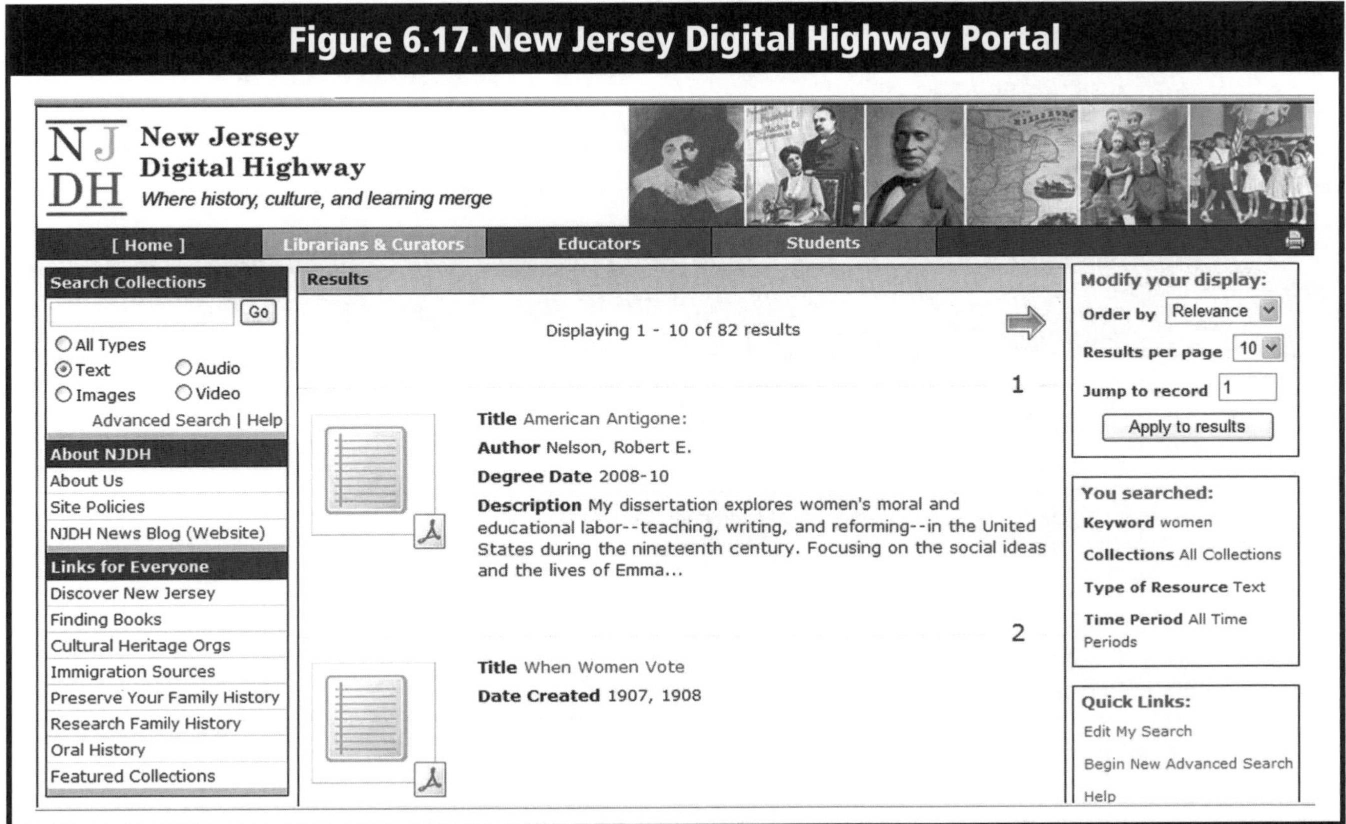

Figure 6.18. ToxNet Portal

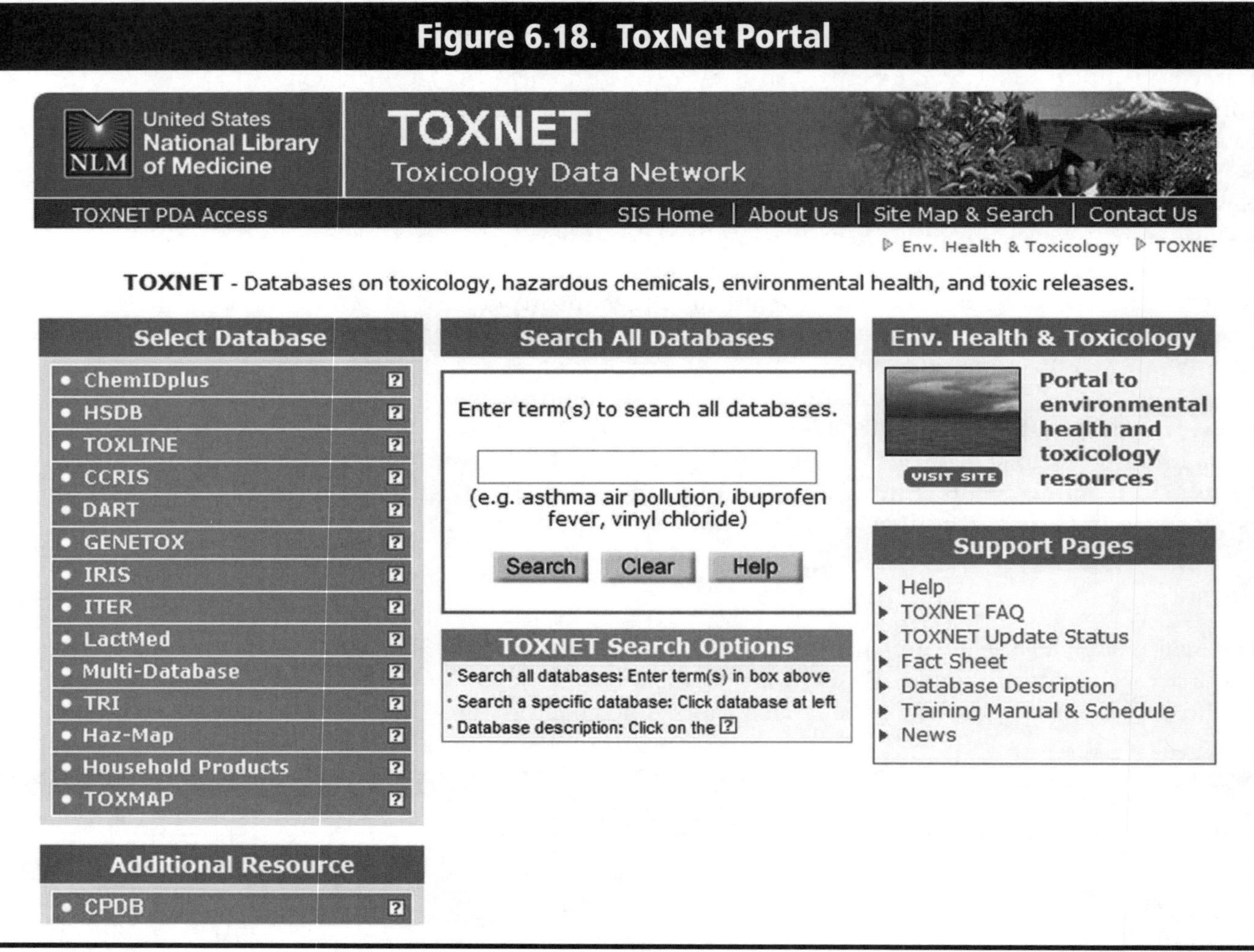

Figure 6.19. MARC Descriptive Record for the ToxNet Networked Portal Using *RDA*

Leader 06 Leader 07 Leader 18	Type of record: a Bib Level: i Desc: i [ISBD]
006	m[electronic resource] d [database] f [bibliographies]
007	c r cn
008	Lang: eng Form of item: s [electronic resource] Ctry: mdu S/L: 2 [integrated resource]; SerTy: d [updating database] Nature of work: d [database] Freq: u Reg: u Date 1: 2000 Date 2: 9999
040	NjR $c NjR $e rda

(Cont'd.)

Figure 6.19. MARC Descriptive Record for the ToxNet Networked Portal Using *RDA (Continued)*

110 2_	National Library of Medicine (U.S.). $b Specialized Information Services Division.
245 10	TOXNET : $b toxicology data network /$c National Library of Medicine.
246 30	Toxicology data network
260 __	Bethesda, MD : $b U.S. National Library of Medicine, $c 2000-
300 __	1 online resource.
336 __ 337 __ 338 __	text $a images $2 rdacontent computer $2 rdamedia online resource $2 rdacarrier
310 __	[Frequency should only be stated when it can be determined. This is left blank because, based on information on the website, individual databases are updated at different intervals.]
538 __	Mode of access: World Wide Web.
500 __	Title from home page (viewed June 21, 2010).
550 __	Issued by the Division of Specialized Information Services of the National Library of Medicine, the National Institutes of Health and the Department of Health & Human Services.
520 __	A collection of "databases on toxicology, hazardous chemicals, environmental health, and toxic releases" -- Homepage.
500 __	A training manual for the TOXNET database is available online at: sis.nlm.nih.gov/enviro/toxnetmanual012009.pdf
650 _0 655 _0	Toxicology $v Databases. Databases
710 2_	National Institutes of Health (U.S.)
710 1_	United States. $b Dept. of Health and Human Services
787 0_ related resource	$t TOXNET and beyond. Using the National Library of Medicine's Environmental Health and Toxicology portal.
856 40	$u http://toxnet.nlm.nih.gov/

access restriction. The specific notes related to the item include access restrictions and copy-specific notes.

The contents of the MARC 506 field Restrictions on Access Note can also be included as a public note in the subfield $z of the 856 field. As noted previously, the MODS element <accessCondition> qualified with the type attribute "restrictionsOnAccess" and the DC element <Rights> with the qualifier "AccessRights" also contain information about restrictions on access (see Example 6.5).

The MARC 856 field contains the URL for the website or online database. A URL is also provided in the MODS element <identifier>

EXAMPLE 6.5

506 __ $a Registration required for access to some sections of this Web site.

<accessCondition type=restrictions OnAccess>Subscription required for access.</accessCondition>

<Rights.AccessRights>Subscription and registration required for access.</Rights>

with the type attribute "doi" (Digital Object Identifier) and in the DC element <Identifier>. The URL should be tested for accuracy and currency before the record is loaded into the library's ILS. A good rule of thumb is to explore the concept of the persistent URL, which ensures that the link always points to the desired resource. When using the MARC 856 field, note that the indicators are selected based on the type of online resource it retrieves. The first indicator indicates the type of resource (1 = FTP; 4 = HTTP). The second indicator is used to indicate the version, when applicable. Delimiter $z of the 856 field contains notes that the cataloger wants to display in the public catalog. For additional information about the MARC 856 field, consult http://www.loc.gov/marc/856guide.html.

Notes

Both *AACR2* and *RDA* require the cataloger to use the notes area to record information that is deemed important but for which no descriptive field or element has been specified. Record information in the latter category in the MARC 500 general note field, which is repeatable, in the MODS element <note>, and in the DC element <Description> (both of which are also repeatable as needed).

A variety of notes is possible for online integrating resources, including notes on contributors, contents, and/or access restrictions, all of which benefit users. The source of title note (recorded in the MARC 500 field) is mandatory and must include the date on which the website was viewed. The 516 field can be used to specify the type of database, information that is also entered in coded form in the MARC 008 fixed field, the MODS element <note>, and the DC element <Description> (see Example 6.6). Use the MARC 506 field, the MODS element <accessCondition> qualified with the type attribute "restrictionsOnAccess," and the DC element <Rights> with the qualifier "AccessRights" to provide information about restrictions on access. Many institutions provide this information only in the 856 field and do not include a 506 field in their descriptive records.

EXAMPLE 6.6

516 __ $a A searchable database.
506 1_ $a Registration required to access the contents of this database.
506 1_ $a Access restricted to subscribers.

<note>Electronic journal.</note>

<note type= "restrictionsOnAccess"> Access restricted to authorized users and institutions.</note>

<Description>Electronic program and data</Description>

<Rights.AccessRights>Access is restricted to users affiliated with the licensed institutions.</Rights>

One of the most frequently used prescribed note fields is the MARC 538 System Details Note. Correspondingly, the MODS element <note> qualified with the attribute type "system details" and the DC element <Relation> with the qualifier "Requires" are used. System information, while obvious and optional, is usually recorded as shown in Example 6.7.

EXAMPLE 6.7

538 __ $a Mode of access: World Wide Web.

<note type="system details">Mode of access: Internet from the EIA web site. Previously available as of 9/26/01: http://www.eia.doe.gov/cneaf/alternate/page/datatables.html.</note>

<Relation.Requires>Mode of access: Internet from the FDA web site.</Relation>

The Library of Congress recently expressed its support for the *RDA* viewpoint that a mode of access note is necessary only when the method required to access the resource is not readily apparent to the user.

Resource Description (MARC, MODS, FISO) Checklists

The following checklists have been provided as a handy reference guide to the fields and/or areas most frequently used when creating descriptive records for electronic integrating resources. They are intended as guidelines and reminders. Cataloging treatment and choice of access points may vary by library, level of cataloging, and so forth. Always remember that you are the best judge when deciding which fields and/or areas are appropriate to describe the resource you have in hand, *distinctly* and *sufficiently*.

MARC CHECKLIST

For additional information about the MARC fields required by BIBCO (the Monographic Bibliographic Record Program), see http://www.loc.gov/catdir/pcc/bibco/coresr.html.

Leader 06: **Type of Record**: Code **a** for textual.

Leader 07: **Bibliographic Level**: Code **i** for integrating resource.

006: Use for electronic resources that are integrating resources. The first position is generally coded **m** for content that is electronic. The fourth position is the code **d** for databases. Other values are coded in the 008 field for continuing resources.

007: Use for electronic resources (optional but desirable in MARC; mandatory in OCLC).

Example:
$a c (electronic resource) $b r (remote) d (computer disc; unspecified) $c [blank] undefined $d c (color).

008: Use for continuing resources and integrating resources. Code frequency and regularity here in addition to other general attributes, such as Lang, a three-letter MARC code; Date 1, date of publication; and Date 2, used when multiple dates are available, such as in multipart resources. Consult http://www.loc.gov/marc/bibliographic/bd008c.html for additional information.

100: **Creator**: Websites and databases are generally a collaborative effort and as such are entered under the title in most cases. Nevertheless, corporate authorship is preferred in selected cases, such as when describing a corporate website or the publication of a research activities database.

245: **Title Information**: Enter the title as it appears on the resource (giving preference to information found on the title screen). In the absence of a recognizable title screen, the entire resource can be considered the preferred source of information.

246: **Variant Title Information**: Enter the subtitle and/or other significant title by which the resource may be known or identified in the MARC 245 field, subfield $b.

250: **Edition Statement**: This is generally not indicated for websites and online databases because the descriptive record is edited to reflect the current iteration (version) of the site.

260: **Publication Detail**: Websites and databases are published resources. Subfields $a (place of publication), $b (publisher), and $c (date of publication or distribution) are required if available. In the absence of the required information, the cataloger may supply a suitable phrase, such as: [place of publication unknown].

300: **Extent of Item**: Record the number of units that comprise the resource in the first subfield ($a). Also give additional information about the resource, such as color (in subfield $b) and size (subfield $c).

400: **Series Statement**: Provide if applicable, especially for databases.

500: **Note Field**: Use for a variety of information, especially information deemed important by the cataloger but for which no MARC field has been specified. This field is also used for the mandatory "Source of title note" for electronic resources and for any other resource when the title has been supplied by the cataloger.

505: **Note**: Record the contents in this field.

(Cont'd.)

MARC CHECKLIST *(Continued)*

538: **System Requirements**: This is a mandatory field. Include requirements for playback equipment and other pertinent technical details regarding use of the resource.

520: **Note (summary)**: Use to provide a summary of the resource's content.

650 and 655: **Subject and Genre**: Enter subjects terms in the 650 field and genre headings in the 655 field.

700: **Added Entry**: Include additional responsible persons here.

856: **URL**: Use this field to provide a URL link to supplementary information available on the Internet.

MODS CHECKLIST

For additional information about constructing a descriptive record for electronic integrating resources (specifically, online resources) using MODS, see http://www.loc.gov/standards/mods/v3/mods98801326.xml.

<typeOfResource> Use to specify type of resource being cataloged; in this case it will be "electronic resource."

Example:

```
<typeOfResource>electronic resource</typeOfResource>
```

<genre> provides information on a style, form, or content expressed in the resource.

Example:

```
<genre>database</genre>
```

<identifier> with the attribute " type" is used to provide standard identifiers, such as the ISBN.

Example:

```
<identifier type="isbn">9783540221814</identifier>
```

<subject> may be used with various subelements, including the subelement <genre>. However, prefer to use <genre> as the main element.

Example:

```
<genre authority="marcgt">
  <genre>dictionary</genre>
```

<recordInfo> with the subelement <recordContentSource> with the attribute "authority" is used to provide the code or name of the organization that created or modified the original resource description.

Example:

```
<recordInfo>
  <recordContentSource>Rutgers University Libraries</recordContentSource>
</recordInfo>
```

<languageTerm> with the type="code" and authority="iso639-2b" (several codes may be used in authority; see http://www.loc.gov/standards/mods/v3/mods-userguide-elements.html#language for additional information).

Example:

```
<language>
  <languageTerm type="code" authority="iso639-2b">eng</languageTerm>
</language>
```

(Cont'd.)

MODS CHECKLIST *(Continued)*

<name> is used to provide information on name of a person, organization, or event (conference, meeting, etc.) associated with the resource. This element has a <type> attribute to specify the type of name (personal, corporate, or conference) and an authority attribute (<authority>) to enable catalogers to specify what authoritative source was consulted to provide the authorized form of the name. This element also has a subelement <role> which is used to specify the role of the named person, corporate body, or conference in relation to the resource.

Example:
```
<name type="corporate">
  <role>
    <roleTerm type="text">Creator</roleTerm>
  </role>
<name type="corporate">
  <namePart>Rutgers.</namePart>
</name>
```

<titleInfo> is used to convey the title or name of a resource. When the main portion of the title is referenced as core, there is only one core subelement, <title>.

Example:
```
<titleInfo>
<title>WAAND database</title>
</titleInfo>
```

Use <titleInfo> with the type="alternative" and the subelement <title> to convey title varations.

Example:
```
</titleInfo> <titleInfo type="alternative">
<title >Women Artists Archive National Directory</title>
</titleInfo>
```

<originInfo> with the subelement <edition> is used to describe the version or edition of the resource being described.

Example:
```
<originInfo>
  <edition>7th ed.</edition>
</originInfo>
```

<originInfo> with the subelement <place> and its subelement <placeTerm> with type="text", the subelement <publisher>, and the subelement <dateIssued> is used to provide information on publication, distribution, etc.

<physicalDescription> with the subelements <form> and <extent> provide descriptive information about the resource. In this text the authoritative source for <form> (used to describe the resource's physical description) is the MARC format. The subelement <extent> describes the number and types of units that make up a resource.

Example:
```
<physicalDescription>
  <form authority="marcform">
  <form>CD-rom</form>
  <extent>1</extent>
</physicalDescription>
```

(Cont'd.)

MODS CHECKLIST *(Continued)*

<tableOfContents> is used for the contents of the database when this information is supplied by the publisher. This is more applicable to direct access electronic resources such as CDs.

Example:
<tableOfContents>
CD 1: Dictionary of terms. – CD 2: Index of authors.
</tableOfContents>

<relatedItem> with the attribute type "series" is used to provide information on the series when appropriate.

Example:
<relatedItem type="series">
  <titleInfo>
    <title>Classics Collection</title>
  </titleInfo>
</relatedItem>

<note> is used to provide general information about the resource.

Example:
<note> Based on the play by William Shakespeare.</note>

<subject> with the attribute type "authority" and the subelement <name> with the attribute "type" (personal, corporate, conference) is used for names of persons and organizations associated with the resource as subjects. Use the subelement <topic> for topical subjects. The descriptive record should contain at least one subject term.

Example:
<subject authority="lcsh">
<topic>Mirrors in art</topic>
</subject>

FISO CHECKLIST

Having constructed the descriptive record, the cataloger may find it appropriate to review the description based on the *FRBR* principles: *find*, *identify*, *select*, *obtain*:

F—The potential user has to *find* the material.
I—The user should be able to *identify* the resource, distinguishing it from any similar item.
S—The user should be able to retrieve and *select* the material as the appropriate one for a specific purpose or task.
O—The record should help the user to *obtain* the material by giving information about its location and availability and any requirements for and/or conditions of use.

The following questions are helpful in rating the completed product:

- ❑ Does the finished description conform to the *FRBR* principles?
- ❑ Can a potential user find the resource easily? Appropriate description and an active URL are required to achieve this goal.
- ❑ Has the resource been sufficiently differentiated for any other?
- ❑ How easy is it to identify the resource and select it as different from any other?
- ❑ Can a potential user immediately recognize this resource as being available on the Internet? As requiring Internet access for use? The importance of an active URL cannot be overstated.

Resources for Catalogers

American Library Association, Canadian Library Association, and CILIP: Chartered Institute of Library and Information Professionals. 2010. *Resource Description and Access.* ALA, CLA, and CILIP. Accessed June 11. http://www.rdatoolkit.org/constituencyreview.

Library of Congress, Network Development and MARC Standards Office. 1997. "Guidelines for Coding Electronic Resources in Leader 06." Library of Congress. http://www.loc.gov/marc/ldr06guide.html.

Program for Cooperative Cataloging. 2010. *Integrating Resources: A Cataloging Manual: Appendix A to the BIBCO Participants' Manual and Module 35 of the CONSER Cataloging Manual.* 2010 revision. Library of Congress. http://www.loc.gov/catdir/pcc/bibco/irman.pdf.

Weitz, Jay. 2006. "Cataloging Electronic Resources: OCLC-MARC Coding Guidelines." OCLC. http://www.oclc.org/support/documentation/worldcat/cataloging/electronicresources.

Notes

1. Program for Cooperative Cataloging. 2010. *Integrating Resources: A Cataloging Manual: Appendix A to the BIBCO Participants' Manual and Module 35 of the CONSER Cataloging Manual.* 2010 revision. Library of Congress. http://www.loc.gov/catdir/pcc/bibco/irman.pdf.
2. Greenberg, Jane. 2007. "Advancing the Semantic Web via Library Functions." In *Knitting the Semantic Web*, edited by Jane Greenberg and Eva Mendez, 203–226. Binghamton, NY: Haworth Press.
3. Newton, Verne W., and Kathryn Silberger. 2007. "Out-Googling Google: Federated Searching and the Single Search Box." Presented at the 13th Annual Meeting of the ACRL, March 31. http://library.marist.edu/ACRL/Foxhunt_demo.html.
4. American Library Association, Canadian Library Association, and CILIP: Chartered Institute of Library and Information Professionals. 2010. *Resource Description and Access.* ALA, CLA, and CILIP. Accessed August 11. http://www.rdatoolkit.org.
5. Ibid.
6. Brand, Amy, and Kristen Fisher. 2010. "Linking Evolved: The Future of Online Research." *Research Information.* Online journal. Europa Science. Accessed June 14. http://www.researchinformation.info/rispring03linking.html.

Microforms

Overview

Microforms have been a fundamental part of library collections for many decades. From its earliest appearance in libraries, this format enabled access to large collections that were no longer available in print; to aged, fragile print material generally microfilmed for preservation; and to older runs of serials or other large collections that could not be housed as easily if available in print.

Today, while microforms still offer the same advantages, the format has been partly replaced by digitization and electronic storage techniques for most types of resources, especially because the newer technology has enhanced accessibility options and content display. It is also quite common for some resources to be produced both in microform and digitally, a development that has influenced the description of both types of formats. However, there are some compelling reasons why microforms show no sign of imminent demise:

- Although the U.S. Government Printing Office (GPO) has published its plan to move toward a fully digital environment "to deliver Federal information products and services from a flexible digital platform,"[1] the U.S. government, both federal and state, has been a major microform publisher and, though to a lesser extent, continues to supply older documents on microform to many libraries in the depository program. Frequently, documents are published both in print and in microform, requiring libraries to make choices regarding resource description and the display of such records. Options include the single record approach, in which a single record contains information about both formats, or the multiple records approach, which utilizes individual format-specific records.
- Many foreign governments, quasi-governmental international bodies, and major international organizations such as the United Nations continue to publish documents in microform.

- The digital divide has meant that some countries around the globe do not have reliable access to the Internet and will therefore continue to rely on traditional media such as print and microform.
- The durability of digital content has not been thoroughly tested and certified.
- Perpetual availability of U.S. government documents continues to be questioned, as the "disappearance" of digital documents has caused some measure of alarm among certain researchers.[2]

The apparent reluctance to abandon the familiar microforms seems to echo support for a statement issued by the Kodak Corporation in response to a survey by the British Library in 2007. Kodak, through its spokesperson, acknowledged that although use of microfilm and microfiche as information distribution formats has declined, "microfilm continues to be a viable archive medium."[3] This statement also supports recent articles in the library literature that seem to second-guess current efforts at digital preservation.[4] Newer types of material, such as polyester microfilm, and the most recent advances in computer-output microfilm have reinforced microforms as viable carriers. The search continues for the best preservation method amid a lack of consensus and ongoing debate over the durability of digital carriers.

Many of the major research libraries own large microform collections that have been cataloged as part of the National Register of Microform Masters (NRMM) Retrospective Conversion Project.[5] In addition, the Association of Research Libraries (ARL) has endorsed digitization as an acceptable preservation format,[6] suggesting that microforms and digital formats are expected to coexist for a very long time.

The NRMM Retrospective Conversion Project is a major cataloging project through which bibliographic records for preservation microfilm masters owned by member libraries were added to the OCLC database.[7] Catalogers can download and edit these records for local use by making the necessary changes to reflect service or general use microform copy. If the cataloger's library does not own the preservation copy, information about the service copy must be added to the descriptive record to alert users to its availability, because the preservation copy is not for general use. In MARC, a separate 007 fixed field coded for the service copy, must be added to the descriptive record. Similarly, when the participating library owns both master and service copies, a single descriptive record will contain two 007 fields, one for each generation of microform owned. The first 007 field represents the generation on which the descriptive record is based, and the second describes the service copy. It is not unusual to find different combinations or a single descriptive record containing information about the preservation master, the printing master, and the service copy in separate 007 fields, an occurrence that is possible only when the three generations of microform were generated from a single filming operation.

What is a microform? How is this category of resource defined for the purpose of description and access?

- *RDA* (Glossary) defines the microform as "media used to store reduced-size images not readable to the human eye, designed for use with a device such as a microfilm or microfiche reader. Includes both transparent and opaque micrographic media."
- *AACR2* (Appendix D-5) defines a microform as "[a] generic term for any medium, transparent or opaque, bearing micro-images." A microfiche is defined as "[a] sheet of film bearing a number of micro-images in a two-dimensional array," while microfilm is defined as "[a] length of film bearing a number of micro-images in linear array."

These definitions are important because they establish the microform as a tangible carrier used for both original publications (documents that were never published in any other form) and reproductions of documents and/or other types of resources that were originally published in the same or another format. While it may be customary to think of microforms as reproductions (the majority of microforms found in libraries generally are reproductions), the term "reproduction" does not appear in either definition.

It is immediately apparent that *RDA*, in keeping with the general trend toward specificity and sufficiency, has a more precise definition of a microform than *AACR2*, specifying that the images are meant to be read by a microfilm or microfiche reader. Conceiving the microform as carrier is critical to its description and treatment, especially because the current cataloging rules that govern the description of this type of resource have been subjected to different and conflicting interpretations.

In *RDA*, as in *AACR2*, the microform is aptly defined as "media." *RDA* also defines the carrier as "A physical medium in which data, sound, images, etc., are stored"—the vehicle through which a work (content) is made manifest. By extension, the definition of a microform is unambiguous and leaves no room for interpretation. The microform is both medium and carrier, and the subsequent reorientation required of catalogers unaccustomed to this interpretation has important ramifications for the description of this type of resource.

The types of microform carriers most commonly found in libraries are microfiche, available in single sheets, and microfilm, available on reels. Microfilm and microfiche were discovered to be important, durable "carriers" many years ago, and their use as carriers is likely to continue for the indefinite future. Although their portability as a resource is hampered by their requirement for bulky readers, users who need access to resources that are available only in this format readily adapt to this seeming disadvantage. The availability of hand-held portable microfiche readers (see Figure 7.1) may have an unimaginable impact on the future utility of the microfiche; and the newer microfiche and microfilm desktop readers are trimmer and more compact than those of several years ago.

Figure 7.1. Handheld Portable Microfiche Reader

Important Considerations

The microform tradition dates back to the early nineteenth century and the format continues to be universally accepted as an archival format with "a life expectancy of five hundred years."[8] Some microform characteristics of note:

- Whether used as a preferred carrier for purposes of preservation or convenience, the microform is still regarded as a viable option for many publishers and information managers.
- The microform carrier is not used only for reproductions. However, when used as such the cataloger must decide whether the work in hand is an *exact* copy of an existing or previously existing resource and describe it appropriately.
- It is important to note that the Library of Congress, in the issue of its Rule Interpretations for Chapter 11 (Microforms), Rule Interpretation 11.1, elected to disregard the *AACR2* rules governing the cataloging of reproductions, facsimiles, and copies. Catalogers adhering to Library of Congress Rule Interpretations (LCRI) must describe reproductions on microform carriers in terms of the original resource, giving details about the reproduction as a note.[9]
- The policy adopted by the Library of Congress was approved by OCLC as the preferred method for describing microform reproductions. Libraries that contribute cataloging to OCLC must follow the LCRI for reproductions.
- The decision whether to adopt the LC policy or to follow the rules outlined by *AACR2* and *RDA* will most likely be determined by internal library policy.
- Libraries that have purchased specific microform collections may have the option to also obtain MARC records for the collections. Bibliographic records for microform sets are available through OCLC, providing additional options and possible solutions for detailed description of resources available on microfiche or microfilm.

QUICK TIP

Reproductions on microform can be described as manifested, according to the rules of description for facsimiles, photocopies, and other reproductions as provided in *RDA* (where the microform is considered a carrier) and in *AACR2*, Chapter 11, "Microforms."

Although resource description for printed textual resources is not covered in this manual, the description of the resource, regardless of its media type, takes precedence over the characteristics of its carrier. Whether its carrier is a volume or a microform, a textual resource is described according to the rules specified for textual resources. The microform is essentially a carrier on which original documents or copies (reproductions of original documents) are stored. Specific carrier characteristics are the only distinguishing features that aid in the identification of different manifestations of a textual resource and, as such, must be sufficient and accurate. Many of the resources issued on microform are single issue monographs, such as theses and dissertations. Though a well-defined category with some unique requirements, theses and dissertations are treated as any other textual publication.

Finally, the description of a resource on microform may require a URL to direct the user to additional online content, such as a description of a large collection, content notes, and finding aids. The advantage to finding aids located on the Internet is that they can be indexed and/or updated as needed, and serendipitous discovery, via the finding aid, may lead users to the microfiche collection, wherever housed.

The most common types of microforms found in libraries are discussed in this chapter. Although many serial publications are issued in microform, such as census documents and newspapers, the discussions and examples in this chapter are limited to resource description for monographic publications on microform. Microopaques and aperture cards are not included in this discussion.

Resource Description

Work

As defined in the *RDA* Glossary, each work is a "distinct intellectual or artistic creation," and the core elements that serve to distinguish between similar works are standard, irrespective of carrier. One of the hallmarks of *RDA* is its emphasis on sufficiency and differentiation both of which are essential to resource discovery and often require a detailed or comprehensive description of the resource.

As discussed in Chapter 1 of this manual, a resource is described primarily in terms of its creator, the title by which it is represented, additional responsible persons associated with the creation of the work, its origin (place and publisher), and its content. *RDA*, in its list of core elements of description (*RDA* 1.3), gives catalogers the option of providing as little or as much information about a resource as deemed necessary for the type of resource and for differentiation among similar resources. In its general guidelines for resource description, *RDA* 2.2.2.1 instructs catalogers as follows:

> When choosing a preferred source of information, treat both the storage medium (e.g., paper, tape, or film) and any housing (e.g., a cassette or cartridge) that is an integral part of the resource as part of the resource itself. Treat accompanying material as part of the resource itself when describing the resource as a whole using a comprehensive description.

This comprehensive instruction designates the storage medium as the preferred source of information and allows catalogers to use information that is visible to the naked eye. Resources in microform cannot be physically separated from their carrier. Accordingly, *RDA* 2.2.2.2 states that the preferred source of descriptive data for microforms is the title page or title sheet, but it provides alternative instructions that allow the cataloger to use any eye-readable information, such as found on a label on

FOR MORE INFORMATION

Comprehensive resource description is discussed in *RDA* Chapter 1.5.2.

Authors' Note: The description of the microform resource will depend on whether the resource is an original or a reproduction and on whether the cataloger uses *AACR2* or *RDA* or LCRI for microform reproductions.

the microform carrier, as the preferred source. *AACR2* Rule 11.0B1 stipulates that the title must be taken from the chief source of information, which, for microforms, is the title frame.

The microform resource should yield all information required for sufficient, accurate resource description, including information about the origin of the work, the individual or organization responsible for its creation, and the date on which it was made publicly available. If important information is lacking from the preferred source, or when creating comprehensive description, the cataloger may treat accompanying material as part of the resource itself or refer to appropriate reference sources (*RDA* 2.2.2.1 and 2.2.4).

The creator of the work maintains primary responsibility for its content and is the preferred access point for the work. When several individuals have collaborated on the creation of a resource, the co-creators receive equal prominence as preferred access points. The old rule of three (*AACR*: choice of main entry) does not apply for works described according to *RDA*, which gives the cataloger the option of recording only the first named responsible person in the statement of responsibility or of recording all responsible persons associated with the work if their role is significant and/or merits mention. The cataloger can also use an all-embracing phrase such as "and three others" when acknowledging the collaboration of others in the creation of the work. The authorized form of name must be used as an access point, and the addition of a relator term is recommended to specify the role or relationship of the person to the work.

How is the work represented to the potential user? What is the title of the work? Are there any variant or different titles by which the work is or was known? A preferred title must be established when a resource contains or may be known by more than one title. The stipulation that the preferred title can be the title used in reference sources[10] is particularly valuable for works reproduced on microform, because the titles of some earlier imprints reproduced in this format may be difficult to verify in the absence of original copies. *RDA* also contains specific guidelines regarding the selection of preferred titles for resources published before and after the year 1500.[11]

A single compiler has been identified for the resource shown in Figure 7.2. "Edith Brayer" is not the creator of the work, but, as the compiler, she is entered as a responsible person in the MARC 700 field. "Anne S. Korteweg," who authored the accompanying resource, is listed as an additional responsible person. The names of responsible persons can also be recorded in MODS as shown in Example 7.1.

EXAMPLE 7.1

```
<name type="personal">
  <role>
    <roleTerm type="text">compiler
    </roleTerm>
  </role>
```

Three titles are associated with the work described in Figure 7.2, and, after having selected the preferred title, the two variant titles were entered in separate MARC 246 fields. Title information is recorded in MODS as shown in Example 7.2.

EXAMPLE 7.2

```
<titleInfo>
  <title>Catalogue of French-language
  medieval manuscripts in the
  Koninklijke Bibliotheek</title>
</titleInfo>
```

Use <titleInfo> with the type= "alternative" and the subelement <title> to record variant titles.

The date of publication recorded for the microform depends on whether the cataloger describes the manifestation in hand or, as required by the LCRI for Chapter 11, the original resource. The resource described in Figure 7.2 is a reproduction on microfiche of the

Figure 7.2. MARC Descriptive Record for a Resource on Microfiche Using *AACR2*

Leader 06 Leader 07	a [textual] m [monographic, single issue]
006 field [additional material characteristics] [Only one position must be entered for this field.]	Form of material: a [language material] [This information may be entered in the fixed field (008) for some systems such as OCLC.]
007 [Microform]	h $b e $d a $e m $f b—- $g b $h a $i c $j a [h = microform; e = microfiche; a = positive; m = 11x15 cm; b = normal reduction; b = black & white; a = silver halide; c = service copy; a = safety base]
008 [for all formats]	Lang: fre Form of item: b [microfiche] Ctry: ne Date Date type: s Date 1: 2003 Date 2: [not applicable for this resource which is a monograph with a single date type.]
040 __	NjR $c NjR
041 __	fre $g eng [This field indicates that the language of the primary content is French. Note that "fre" is used as the code in the 008 field. Subfield $g in this field stipulates that the language of the accompanying material is in English.]
245 00	Catalogue of French-language medieval manuscripts in the Koninklijke Bibliotheek and Meermanno-Westreenianum Museum, the Hague on microfiche $h [microform] / $c compiled by Edith Brayer ; with a printed guide and introduction by Anne S. Korteweg.
246 13	$i Title on guide: $a Guide to the Catalogue of the French-language medieval manuscripts in the Koninklijke Bibliotheek and Meermanno-Westreenianum Museum, the Hague on microfiche
246 13	$i Fiche header: $a IRHT catalogue of French-language medieval manuscripts
260 __	Amsterdam : $b Moran Micropublications, $c 2003, c2002.
300 __	18 microfiches (silver positive) ; $c 11 x 15 cm. + $e 1 guide (89 p. ; 30 cm.) [RDA requires the actual extent of the resource (number of pages) if known.]
500 __	"MMP102"--Fiche header.
520 __	[Since the title gives a specific description of the contents, a summary is not necessary here.]
530 __	Also available on microfilm reels.
534 __	$n Original manuscript prepared in 1954 & 1956 by Edith Brayer and issued by the Institut de Recherche et d'Histoire des Textes; Paris.
538 __	Requires the use of a microfiche reader.

(Cont'd.)

Figure 7.2. MARC Descriptive Record for a Resource on Microfiche Using *AACR2* (Continued)

546 __	The guide is written in English; the manuscripts on the microfiche are written in French.
610 20	Koninklijke Bibliotheek (Netherlands).
610 20	Rijksmuseum Meermanno-Westreenianum.
650 _0	French language $v Manuscripts.
700 1_	Korteweg, A. S.
700 1_	Brayer, Edith.
856 48	$u http://www.kb.nl/manuscripts/ $z Guide also available online.

original unpublished manuscript, and as such the date of publication in the MARC 260 field reflects the date on which the microfiche was published.

The MARC 546 field language note specifies that the summaries contained in the resource are in French, as does the code "fre" in the 008 field. The language of the resource is recorded in MODS as shown in Example 7.3.

EXAMPLE 7.3

```
<language>
  <languageTerm type="code"
  authority="iso639-2b">fre
  </languageTerm>
</language>
```

The descriptive record in Figure 7.3 describes a different manifestation of the resource in Figure 7.2, and the descriptive record in Figure 7.4 shows the MODS display for the same resource.

Figure 7.3. MARC Descriptive Record for a Resource on Microfilm Reels Using *AACR2*

Leader 06 Leader 07	a [textual] m [monographic, single issue]
006 field	Form of material: a [language material] Form of item: a [microfilm]
007 [microform]	$a h $b d $d a $e f $f b--- $g b $h u $i c $j a [h = microform; d = microfilm reels; a = positive; f = 35mm; b = normal reduction; b = black & white; u = unknown emulsion; c = service copy; a = safety base]
008	Lang: fre Form of material: a Ctry: ne Desc: a Date Type: s Date 1: 2002 Date 2:
041 __	$a fre $g eng [The code in this field indicates that the language of the primary content is French. Note that "fre" is used as the code in the 008 field. Subcode $g in this field stipulates that the language of the accompanying material is in English.]

(Cont'd.)

Figure 7.3. MARC Descriptive Record for a Resource on Microfilm Reels Using *AACR2* *(Continued)*

245 00	Catalogue of French-language medieval manuscripts in the Koninklijke Bibliotheek and Meermanno-Westreenianum Museum, the Hague $h [microform] / $c compiled by Edith Brayer ; with a printed guide and introduction by Anne S. Korteweg.
246 13	$i Title on guide: $a Guide to the Catalogue of the French-language medieval manuscripts in the Koninklijke Bibliotheek and Meermanno-Westreenianum Museum, the Hague
246 13	$i Film header: $a IRHT catalogue of French-language medieval manuscripts
260 __	Amsterdam : $b Moran Micropublications, $c 2002.
300 __	3 microfilm reels (positive) $b black and white + $e 1 guide (89 p. ; 30 cm.)
520 __	[Since the title gives a specific description of the contents, a summary is not necessary here.]
534 __	$p Original manuscript prepared in 1954 & 1956 by Edith Brayer and issued by the Institut de Recherche et d'Histoire des Textes; Paris.
530 __	Also available on microfiche.
538 __	Requires the use of a microfilm reader.
610 20	Koninklijke Bibliotheek (Netherlands).
610 20	Rijksmuseum Meermanno-Westreenianum.
650 _0	French language $v Manuscripts.
700 1_	Korteweg, A. S.
700 1_	Brayer, Edith.

Figure 7.4. MODS Resource Description for Microfilm Reels Using *AACR2*

titleInfo:	Catalogue of French-language medieval manuscripts in the Koninklijke Bibliotheek Meermanno-Westreenianum Museum, the Hague on microfiche IRHT catalogue of French-language medieval manuscripts
name: [Responsible person(s)]	Edith Brayer, compiler Anne S. Korteweg, writer.
typeofResource:	Microfiche sheets.
publicationDetails: place: publisher: date:	 Amsterdam Moran Micropublications 2002.

(Cont'd.)

Figure 7.4. MODS Resource Description for Microfilm Reels Using *AACR2 (Continued)*	
extent:	18 microfiches (silver positive) 11 x 15 cm. 1 guide (89 p. ; 30 cm.)
note:	"MMP102"--Fiche header. Requires the use of a microfiche reader.
abstract:	[Since the title gives a specific description of the contents, a summary is not necessary here.]
originInfo:	[Input details about the library or agency responsible for creating the bibliographic description.]
place: creator:	Netherlands. Koninklijke Bibliotheek.
subjectTerm:	Manuscripts. Illuminated manuscripts. Middle Ages.
language:	French
note:	Service copy.

Expression

Relevant questions related to the expression of the work include the following:

- In what form has the work been expressed? What genre is used?
- Is the work textual or numerical?
- Does it contain cartographic material?
- In what language is the content?
- Is the resource a monograph or continuing resource?

Generally, the expression of the work relates to its content and is not associated with any specific type of carrier. Variant editions, differences in language used, and slight variations in content (such as abridged versions) are indicative of a different expression of a work.

Manifestation

Differences in descriptive elements for identical works generally relate to the manifestation and the specific characteristics of the carrier. As important elements of distinction, these must be accurately recorded in the resource description.

Most microfiche and microfilm contain unique publisher numbers located on the container or on the resource itself. If present, this numerical identifier must be recorded in the MARC 028 field. Documents issued by the U.S. Government Printing Office generally contain a GPO item number in lieu of an ISBN, which must be entered in the MARC 074 field reserved for these numbers. The abbreviation "MF" can be enclosed in parentheses following the number to indicate that the item is a microform, as shown in Example 7.4.

EXAMPLE 7.4

074 __ 563-44 (MF)

To describe a microform carrier fully and sufficiently, catalogers must be acquainted with the following carrier-specific characteristics:

- **Generation**: Microforms are described in relation to three specific outputs: archival/preservation, master, and service copies. Of what generation is the copy in hand? Is it the archival master copy of the original resource? Or the printing master used to produce service copies? Archival masters should not be used to generate copies, and notification of the availability of the printing master alerts other libraries to the existence of a supply source for copies. Enter information pertaining to generation in the MARC 007 field and in the areas of the metadata record reserved for technical data about the resource.
- **Material used in the manufacture of the carrier**: This presents another important element of distinction between similar microform resources. Silver halide is the preferred base for film and has the LE (life expectancy) rating of 500 years. Although acetate bases are no longer used for commercial purposes, this type of material may be found in older microfilm.
- **Reduction ratio**: The microform carrier accommodates reduced-size images, and the ratio of the reduction in relation to the original affects the quality of the reproduction. Normal reproduction is between 1/16 and 1/30 the size of the original, and any other reduction ratio must be specified as low or high reduction ratio. Record ratios in the MARC 007 fixed field and in the physical details area in other metadata schemes.
- **Polarity of the reproduced images**: Polarity is reflected as positive or negative. Positive images manifest as dark on clear or white background, while the opposite is true for negative images.
- **Emulsion**: Microfilm is coated with an emulsion. Generally diazo has been used from 1983 onward; silver halide was used pre-1977.
- **Production**: Microfiche is generally produced in 11 × 15 cm sheets, which accommodate seven rows of 14 pages of text. Microfilm is generally produced on 35 mm film.

Information related to the microfiche or microfilm carrier is generally given on the resource itself or within accompanying material and is recorded in the MARC 007 and 300 fields of the descriptive record, fields that are required whether the microform is a reproduction or an original. A volume is considered an unmediated carrier and as such does not require a MARC 007 field, which is mandatory for nonprint resources, although a little used option allows catalogers to code two positions in the 007 field specifying that the resource is textual. For additional information on the use of the 007 field for textual/printed resources, see http://www.loc.gov/marc/bibliographic/bd007t.html.

The appropriate carrier type for the microform must be selected from the following authorized carrier types: microfiche, microfiche cassette, microfilm cartridge, microfilm cassette, microfilm reel, microfilm slip, microopaque. The relationship, if any, between the work (manifested as a microform) and any other manifestation of the work must be established and documented. This is important whether the other existing manifestation is an equivalent manifestation, as represented by the phrase "reproduced as," or a related manifestation, which may be preceded by the phrase "also available as." Elements of description must also include information about the extent of the work, any numerical identification present on the carrier, version, technique, etc.

Record the extent of the resource in the MARC 300 field and, to comply with *RDA* instructions, include the actual pagination. *RDA* guidelines require detailed pagination for microforms, in alignment with various metadata schemes in which the extent of the resource is entered in the physical description area. *RDA*, nevertheless, advises against including details for incomplete resources or when unsure about the exact extent of the resource (*RDA* 3.4.1.10).

> **QUICK TIP**
>
> **RDA 3.4.1.7.4 Microfiche**
>
> "If the format of the resource parallels a print, manuscript, or graphic counterpart, specify the number of subunits by applying the instructions for extent of cartographic resources (see **3.4.3**), notated music (see **3.4.3**), still images (see **3.4.4**), and/or text (see **3.4.5**), as appropriate."

Theses and Dissertations

Theses and dissertations are not carriers but instead represent a category of resources generally found on microforms. They are included here to illustrate the types of microform carriers that have been used for these resources. The examples in this section showcase the descriptive records for a thesis reproduced on microfilm and a photocopied version of the same work.

The form in which the work was issued influences the choice of descriptive elements, and the category of resources known as "theses and dissertations" can be used to illustrate this because these resources must include information about the institution granting the degree. The MARC 502 field is unique to this type of resource, and information such as the institution granting the degree, the year, and the type of degree is entered in this field. Additionally, theses and dissertations are not considered published resources and the omission of all publication details, with the exception of the year of submission/issue, presents another area in which the type of resource influences its description.

Cognizant of the fact that many libraries comply with the LCRI 11.1 requirement (available at http://www.itsmarc.com/crs/LCRI0012.htm) to describe the original resource, the description in Figure 7.5 adheres to LCRI 11.1 by describing the original manuscript.

The form of item field contains the code **r** to indicate that the resource is a reproduction. The date area contains two dates, the most recent being the date of the photocopy reproduction. The date in the MARC 260 field represents the date of the original manuscript, the date on which the thesis was submitted to the degree-granting institution. When the original is described in the descriptive record, information

Figure 7.5. Resource Description for the Photocopy Reproduction of a Thesis According to LCRI for Reproductions

Leader 06 Leader 07	a [textual] m [monograph]
007	[Not mandatory for the print photocopy, though the code "t" may be used in the first position, signifying that the resource contains " text."]
008 [includes combined 006 and other fixed field values]	Lang: eng Form of item: r [regular print reproduction] Ctry: nju Desc: a Type of Date: r [includes date of reproduction] Date 1: 2002 Date 2: 1990 Gov. Pub: 0
040 __	NjR $c NjR
100 1_	Furrer, Susan Elizabeth.
245 12	A phenomenological investigation of drug addiction in women / $c Susan Elizabeth Furrer.
260 __	$c 1990.
300 __	364 p.
502 __	Thesis (Psy. D)--Rutgers University. Graduate School of Applied and Professional Psychology, 1990.
520 __	[An abstract may be entered here.]
533 __	Photocopy. $b Ann Arbor, Mich. : $c University Microfilms International, $d 2002. $e 20 cm.
650 _0	Women $x Drug use.
710 2_	Rutgers University. $b Graduate School of Applied and Professional Psychology.

about the reproduction (the photocopy in this case) is entered in the MARC 533 field. LCRI 11.1 requires the cataloger to record details about the reproduction in the specific note field or area reserved for reproduction notes, such as the MARC 533 field Reproduction Note:

> Give in a single note (in the MARC 533 field) all other details relating to the reproduction and its publication/availability. Include in the note the following bibliographic data in the order listed:
>
> Specific material designation of the microform (the appropriate carrier type as specified in *RDA* 3.3.1.3);
>
> Place and name of the agency responsible for the reproduction;
>
> Date of the reproduction;
>
> Physical description of the microform;
>
> Series statement of the reproduction (if applicable);
>
> Notes relating to the reproduction (if applicable).

Catalogers who submit records to OCLC have the option of using the OCLC-MARC 539 field for technical characteristics that are generally recorded in the $7 subfield of the MARC 533 field.

Alternatively, when the manifestation is a reproduction and is described as such, the description must contain, in the note area of the record, information about the original, preceded by a statement such as "microfilm reproduction of" to alert the user to the relationship between the resource being described and the original document. The MARC 534 field can be used to record information about the original resource, including date of publication and general description, when the reproduction has been described as the manifestation in hand. For further information about the MARC 534 field and its various subfields, see http://www.loc.gov/marc/bibliographic/bd534.html.

The descriptive record in Figure 7.6 represents the printed resource as the original manifestation, with the addition of details for the microfiche reproduction in a MARC 533 note. According to the LCRI for Chapter 11 (Microforms), describe the original resource in all fields except the form of item (**r** for regular print reproduction or, in this case, **b** for microfiche) and the 533 note. The genre type "thesis" is mentioned in the MARC 502 note and entered in the MODS record as shown in Example 7.5. Genre may also be entered in the MARC 655 field.

EXAMPLE 7.5

<genre>thesis</genre>

QUICK TIP

LCRI 11.1 requires the cataloger to describe the original resource in all fields except the form of item (**r** for regular print reproduction, or, in this case, **b** for microfiche) and the MARC 533 note. *RDA* guidelines for resource description require description of the manifestation in hand, in this case, the microform.

The existence of an electronic manifestation of the resource requires the addition of two essential fields. These fields are the 007 field, which is mandatory for electronic resources, and the 856 field, which contains the URL to direct the user to the resource located on the Internet.

Some catalogers may prefer to create separate descriptive records for each carrier type, as recommended by the Library of Congress. However, many libraries use the combined approach shown in Figure 7.6 (displayed in MARC format) for descriptive records in their local catalogs, although separate records can be used when submitted to a cataloging utility.

Additional information about describing the content of theses and dissertations can be found in *RDA* 7.9. The MARC code list for content type is available at http://www.loc.gov/standards/valuelist/marccontent.html.

Reproduction on Microform

The reproduction illustrated in Figure 7.7 is displayed in the MARC format and adheres to *AACR2* and *RDA* guidelines requiring the description of the manifestation in hand. The microform reproduction (on microfilm reels) is described in all fields of the record except in a general note where the details of the original are recorded.

The Library of Congress in its Rule Interpretations for Chapter 11 gives a fitting definition of a reproduction:

> A reproduction is a manifestation that replicates an item (or a group of items) or another manifestation (e.g., a reprint with no changes) that is intended to function as a substitute. The reproduction may be in a different physical format from the original. Reproduction is generally a mechanical rather than an intellectual process. The physical characteristics of the reproduction such as

Figure 7.6. Resource Description for the Microfiche Reproduction of a Thesis

Type of record: Bibliographic level:	Leader 06 : a Leader 07: m
007 [for microforms]	h $b e $d a $e m $f b— $g b $h a $i c $j a
007 [for electronic resources (optional in this case because the microform resource is the one being described)]	c $b r $d b c [electronic resource] r [remote location] b [represented in black and white]. [It is possible to code for the source of the online file, if known. For additional information about the use of this field consult: http://www.loc.gov/marc/bibliographic/bd007c.html.]
008	Lang: eng Form of item: b [microfiche] Ctry: Desc: a Date type: r [contains date of reproduction in Date 1] Date 1: 1991 Date 2: 1990
100 1_	Furrer, Susan Elizabeth.
245 12	A phenomenological investigation of drug addiction in women $h [microform] / $c Susan Elizabeth Furrer.
260 __	$c 1990.
300 __	364 p.
502 __	Thesis (Psy. D)--Rutgers University. Graduate School of Applied and Professional Psychology, 1990.
530 __ [This field must be used to indicate that the resource is available in another format, when applicable.]	Also available on the Internet.
533 __	Microfiche. $b Ann Arbor, Mich. : $c University Microfilms International, $d 1991. $e 1 microfiche; 20 cm.
650 _0	Women $x Drug use.
710 1_	Rutgers University. $b Graduate School of Applied and Professional Psychology.
856 40	[The URL must be added here to provide access to the online version, if appropriate.]

> color, image resolution, or sound fidelity are influenced by the particular process used to create it, and therefore may differ from those of the original. Reproductions are usually made for such reasons as the original's limited availability, remote location, poor condition, high cost, or restricted utility.

The resource illustrated in Figure 7.8 (displayed in the MARC format) is a reprint of a microfilm first published in 1984. This is not a reproduction of an original resource in a different format. Because this resource is categorized as a reprint, the details of the reprint are entered in all areas of the record except for the general note area, which contains

Figure 7.7. Resource Description for a Microfilm Reproduction Using *ACCR2* and *RDA*	
Leader 06 Leader 07 Leader 18	[Type of record]: a [Bibliographic level]: m [Cataloging convention]: i [ISBD]
007 [Microforms]	h $b d $d a $e m $f b--- $g b $h a $i c $j u
008	Lang: eng Form of item: h Ctry: ctu Desc: a DatType: r Date 1: 2009 Date 2: 1999
020 [for guide]	0842042008
040 __	NjR $c NjR $e rda
245 00	Slavery miscellaneous manuscripts collection.
260 __	Woodbridge, Ct. : $b Primary Source Media, $c [2009?]
300 __	3 microfilm reels ; 35 mm. + $e 1 guide (5 leaves ; $c 22 cm.)
336 __ 337 __ 338 __	Text $2 rdacontent Microform $2 rdamedia Microfilm reels $2 rdacarrier
500 __	Accompanying printed guide has title: Slavery miscellaneous manuscripts collection: guide to the Scholarly Resources microfilm edition, from the holdings of Manuscripts and Archives, Yale University.
500 __	Microfilmed by Yale University Photographic Services in 1983.
500 __	First published by Scholarly Resources, Inc., 1999.
538 __	Requires the use of a microfilm reader.
650 _0	Slavery $z United States $x History $v Sources.
710 1_	Yale University. $b Dept. of Manuscripts and Archives.
710 2_	Primary Source Media (Firm).

information about the original. For more information about this rule, consult *AACR2* 1.11A and 1.11C.

Technical details about the carrier were recorded in the MARC 007 field, and the MARC 776 field contains information about a related resource. Since the resource was reduced 12 times smaller than the original, below what is considered the normal reduction ratio, the actual reduction ratio has been recorded in the general note area (MARC 500).

Per Rule 11.7B10 of *AACR2*, reduction ratio must be provided when it differs from the standard range, which is 16× to 30×. *RDA* 3.15.1.3 supports this requirement. Accompanying material, if present, must be recorded in subfield $e of the MARC 300 field.

Figure 7.8. Resource Description for a Microform Reprint Using *AACR2* and *RDA*

AACR2	
Type of record: Bibliographic level:	Leader 06: a Leader 07: m
007	h $b d $d a $e f $f b012 $g b $h a $i c $j a [Note: $f indicates a low reduction ratio of 12x. This information is repeated in a general 500 note to alert the user.]
008	Lang: eng Form of item: h Ctry: ctu Desc: a DateType: r (reprint/reissue) Date 1: 2009 (reissue) Date 2: 1984 (original)
024 8_ [unidentified standard number found on resource]	$a1002-B (MF)
040 __	NjR $c NjR
100 1_	Buxton, Thomas Fowell, $c Sir, $d 1786-1845.
245 14	The papers of Sir Thomas Fowell Buxton, 1786-1845 $h [microform]
246 13	$i Typescript title page title: $a Papers of Sir Thomas Fowell Buxton, 1786-1845, abolitionist and reformer, in Rhodes House Library, Oxford
260 __	Woodbridge, CT : $b Primary Source Media, $c [2009?]
300 __	17 microfilm reels ; $c 35 mm. + $e 1 guide ([6] leaves ; 28 cm)
500 __	Low reduction ratio.
500 __	Reprint of : "The papers of Sir Thomas Fowell Buxton, 1786-1845" published on microfilm in 1984.
500 __	"This microform edition first published by Harvester Press Microform Publications Ltd, Brighton in 1984" — Guide
500 __	Includes on reel 1 of microfilm: Calendar of the papers of Sir Thomas Fowell Buxton, 1786-1845 / by Patricia M. Pugh.
538 __	Requires the use of a microfilm reader.
600 1_	Buxton, Thomas Fowell, $c Sir, $d 1786-1845.
650 _0	Slavery $z Great Britain $x Anti-slavery movement $x History $v Sources.
700 12	Pugh, P.M. $t Calendar of the papers of Sir Thomas Fowell Buxton, 1786-1845. $f 1980.

(Cont'd.)

Figure 7.8. Resource Description for a Microform Reprint Using to *AACR2* and *RDA (Continued)*

AACR2 (Cont'd.)	
710 2_	Rhodes House Library.
710 2_	Rhodes House Library. $t Calendar of the papers of Sir Thomas Fowell Buxton, 1786-1845.
RDA	
Type of record: Bibliographic level:	Leader 06: a Leader 07: m
007	h $b d $d a $e f $f b012 $g b $h a $i c $j a [Note: $f indicates a low reduction ratio of 12x. This information is repeated in a general 500 note to alert the user.]
008	Lang: eng Form of item: h Ctry: ctu Desc: a Date Type: r (reprint/reissue) Date 1: 2009 (reissue) Date 2: 1984 (original)
024 __	$a1002-B (MF)
040 __	NjR $c NjR $e rda
100 1_	Buxton, Thomas Fowell, $c Sir, $d 1786-1845, $e author $2 rda.
245 14	The papers of Sir Thomas Fowell Buxton, 1786-1845.
246 13	$i Typescript title page title: $a Papers of Sir Thomas Fowell Buxton, 1786-1845, abolitionist and reformer, in Rhodes House Library, Oxford
260 __	Woodbridge, CT : $b Primary Source Media, $c [2009?]
336 __ [Content] 337 __ [Media] 338 __ [Carrier]	Text $2 rdacontent Microform $2 rdamedia Microfilm $2 rdacarrier
300 __	17 microfilm reels [insert number of pages, if known]; $c 35 mm. + $e 1 guide([6] leaves) ; $c 28 cm.
500 __	Low reduction ratio.
500 __	Reprint of "The papers of Sir Thomas Fowell Buxton, 1786-1845" published in 1984.
500 __	"This microform edition first published by Harvester Press Microform Publications Ltd, Brighton in 1984" -- Guide
500 __	Includes on reel 1 of microfilm: Calendar of the papers of Sir Thomas Fowell Buxton, 1786-1845 / by Patricia M. Pugh. London : Swift Printers, 1980. (List & Index special series; v. 13)

(Cont'd.)

Figure 7.8. Resource Description for a Microform Reprint Using to *AACR2* and *RDA* (Continued)

RDA (Cont'd.)	
538	Requires the use of a microfilm reader.
600 1_	Buxton, Thomas Fowell, $c Sir, $d 1786-1845.
650 _0	Slavery $z Great Britain $x Anti-slavery movement $x History $v Sources.
700 12	Pugh, P.M. $t Calendar of the papers of Sir Thomas Fowell Buxton, 1786-1845. $f 1980.
710 2_	Rhodes House Library.

The type of date code in the fixed field area is **r** for a reprint/reissue. This is a reprint, on microfilm, of a resource published in 1984 on microfilm.

Although it is appropriate to list the SMD (microfiche or microfilm) without specifying the exact number of fiche or film in the MARC 300 field, as shown in Figure 7.8, *RDA* requires the use of pagination for microfiche or film that is textual and contains paging, as shown in Example 7.6.

Per *RDA* 3.5.1.3, "Unless instructed otherwise, record dimensions in centimeters to the next whole centimeter up, using the metric symbol cm." *Note*: "cm." is a symbol, not the abbreviation of centimeter. The dimensions given for the microfilm reels in our example refer to the film, 35 mm. For additional information on constructing the MARC 300 field, see http://www.loc.gov/marc/bibliographic/bd300.html.

Related resources are entered in the MARC 530 and 776 fields as shown in Example 7.7. For additional information about the 776 field, see http://www.loc.gov/marc/bibliographic/bd776.html. *RDA* Chapter 3 also includes detailed information related to the description of the carrier and the extent of the resource.

EXAMPLE 7.6

300 __ 3 microfiche (1 score (118 pages))

300 __ 18 microfiches (245 p.) $b silver nitrate ; $c 11 x 15 cm. + $e 1 guide (89 p. ; 30 cm.)

In MODS, the subelement <extent> contains the number and types of units that make up a resource.

EXAMPLE 7.7

530 __ Also available in print

AND

776 1_ $t [title of resource] $z [ISBN]

Item

The resource must be described in terms of the unique identifiers relating to the single item, its identifying number, shelving location, and availability. Item information for related resources, such as finding aids, that may be available on the Internet require an active URL.

A related item is defined as an item related to the resource being described (e.g., an item used as the basis for a microform reproduction). Information about the related item must also be included in the resource description in the appropriate field (776 for MARC records). A related item can also be represented by the series statement indicating that the resource is a part of a series. This information is displayed in MODS as shown in Example 7.8.

EXAMPLE 7.8

```
<relatedItem> [used with type of attribute]
  <relatedItem type="series">
    <titleInfo>
      <title>Collection africaine</title>
    </titleInfo>
</relatedItem>
```

EXAMPLE 7.9

<typeOfResource>textual
</typeOfResource>

EXAMPLE 7.10

<recordInfo>
<recordContentSource>Rutgers University Libraries
</recordContentSource>
</recordInfo>

The resource illustrated in Figure 7.9 (in MARC format) is a microform in the Rutgers University library. With regard to the addition of a MARC 538 system requirements note, the record in Figure 7.9 incorporates the following *RDA* guideline:

> **RDA 3.20.1.3 Recording Equipment and System Requirements**
> Record any equipment and/or system requirements beyond what is normal and obvious for the type of carrier or type of file.

Because the carrier is microfiche, it is normal and obvious that a microfiche reader will be required to use this resource. However, the cataloger can state this requirement at his or her discretion (see Figure 7.8).

The resource was not published originally on microfiche, and all descriptive elements pertain to the original resource. The existence of an online version of the resource is noted in the MARC 530 field, and the MARC 856 field contains the appropriate URL.

Figure 7.10 shows a thesis that was published originally on microfiche, and the description pertains to the manifestation in hand. The content type can be displayed in the MODS format as shown in Example 7.9. The library responsible for creating the descriptive record is identified in the MARC 040 field and can be displayed in the MODS record as shown in Example 7.10.

Notes

Various types of notes are appropriate for resources on microform carriers. Some types of notes relate to the work itself, such as the source of title, language, summary, and contents notes. Others are more appropriate to the expression and/or manifestation of a work:

- Notes pertaining to the original (when the reproduction has been described) and vice versa
- Edition history
- Type of equipment required to use the resource and system requirements
- Reduction ratio

Descriptive records for microforms can also contain local notes pertaining to specific copies or to access restrictions. Notes pertaining to the library or organization responsible for producing and/or owning the archival or printing copy can be added to the MARC 533 or 500 field, depending on whether the original or reproduction is being described, and in the appropriate areas of the various metadata schemes.

Resource Description (MARC, MODS, FISO) Checklists

The following checklists have been provided as a handy reference guide to the fields and/or areas most frequently used when creating descriptive

Figure 7.9. Resource Description for the Microfiche Reproduction of a Thesis, with the Addition of Descriptive Information for the Electronic Format of the Same Resource

Leader 06 Leader 07 Leader 18	a m a [described according to AACR2 or similar code]
006 [electronic resources]	m [electronic resource]
007 [microforms]	h $b e $d a $e m $f b—- $g b $h a $i c $j a
007 [electronic resources]	c $b r $d b [c = electronic resource; r = remote location; b = represented in black and white. It is possible to code for the source of the online file, if known. For additional information about the use of this field consult: http://www.loc.gov/marc/bibliographic/bd007c.html.]
008	Lang: eng Form of item: b [microfiche] Ctry: Date type: r [contains date of reproduction (in Date 1)] Date 1: 1991 Date 2: 1990
040 __	NjR $c NjR
100 1_	Furrer, Susan Elizabeth.
245 12	A phenomenological investigation of drug addiction in women $h [microform] / $c Susan Elizabeth Furrer.
260 __	$c 1990.
300 __	364 p.
502 __	Thesis (Psy. D)--Rutgers University. Graduate School of Applied and Professional Psychology, 1990.
530 __ [This field must be used to indicate that the resource is available in another format.]	Also available on the Internet.
533 __	Microfiche. $b Ann Arbor, Mich. : $c University Microfilms International, $d 1991. $e 20 cm.
650 _0	Women $x Drug use.
710 1_	Rutgers University. $b Graduate School of Applied and Professional Psychology.
856 40	[The URL must be added here to provide access to the online version.]

records for microform resources. They are intended as guidelines and reminders. Cataloging treatment and choice of access points may vary by library, level of cataloging, and so forth. Always remember that you are the best judge when deciding which fields and/or areas are appropriate to describe the resource you have in hand, *distinctly* and *sufficiently*.

Figure 7.10. Descriptive Record (*RDA*) for a Thesis Published Originally on Microfiche with Information about the Online Manifestation of the Same Resource

Leader 06 Leader 07 Leader 18	[Type of record] a [Bibliographic level] : m [Descriptive convention]: a [described according to an AACR-like code: RDA]
007 [microforms]	h $b e $d a $e m $f b--- $g b $h a $i c $j a
007 [electronic resources (optional in this case because the microform resource is the one being described)]	c $b r $d b [c = electronic resource; r = remote location; b = represented in black and white. It is possible to code for the source of the online file, if known. For additional information about this field consult, http://www.loc.gov/marc/bibliographic/bd007c.html.]
008 [includes some 006 codes]	Lang: eng Form of item: b [microfiche] Date type: s [contains a single publication date (in Date 1)] Date 1: 1991 Date 2: xxxx
040 __	NjR $c NjR $e rda (described according to RDA)
100 1_	Michaels, Elizabeth. $e author
245 12	An investigation of drug addiction in women / $c Elizabeth Michaels.
260 __	$c 1991.
300 __	436 p.
336 __ 337 __ 338 __	Text $2 rdacontent Microform $a Computer $2 rdamedia Microfiche $a Online resource $2 rdacarrier
502 __	Thesis (Psy. D)--Rutgers University. Graduate School of Applied and Professional Psychology, 1991.
530 __ [This field must be used to indicate that the resource is available in another format.]	Also available on the Internet.
504 __	Includes bibliographical references.
650 _0	Women $x Drug use.
710 1_	Rutgers University. $b Graduate School of Applied and Professional Psychology.
856 40	[The active URL must be added here to provide access to the online version.]

MARC CHECKLIST

For additional information about the MARC fields required by BIBCO (the Monographic Bibliographic Record Program), see http://www.loc.gov/catdir/pcc/bibco/coresr.html.

Leader 06: **Type of Record**: Code **a** for textual material. Other codes appropriate for resources on microform are **e** for cartographic material and **c** for notated music, as maps and musical scores are often published on microforms.

Leader 07: **Bibliographic Level**: Code **m** for monographic or **s** for serial.

GMD: When used in subfield $h of the MARC 245 field, use "microform." *Note*: The GMD has been replaced by three fields: MARC 336 (Content Type), 337 (Media Type), and 338 (Carrier Type). For microforms the media type is "microform." The content type will vary depending on the content of the work; the carrier types for the resources in this chapter are restricted to "microfiche" and "microfilm".

SMD: Use this in the $a subfield of the MARC 300 field: microfiche, microfilm.

006: Enter additional physical characteristics about the resource that cannot be accommodated in the 800 field.

007: Record characteristics of the microform carrier here. BIBCO core level cataloging requires the following positions to be coded (see http://www.loc.gov/marc/bibliographic/bd007h.html for additional information about the valid codes for this field):

- **Position 00**: Category of material (**h** for all microforms)
- **Position 01**: Special material designator (**d** for microfilm on a reel; **e** for microfiche)
- **Position 03**: Positive/negative aspects of the microform
- **Position 04**: Dimensions (**Microfilm**: a = 8 mm.; d = 16 mm.; f = 35 mm.; g = 70 mm.; h = 105 mm. **Microfiche**: l = 3 x 5 in. or 8 x 13 cm.; m = 4 x 6 in. or 11 x 15 cm.; o = 6 x 9 in. or 16 x 23 cm.)
- **Position 05**: Reduction ratio (**b** for normal reduction)
- **Positions 06, 07, 08**: Additional information about the reduction ratio or tape configuration (entered in the $f subfield)
- **Position 09**: Color
- **Position 10**: Emulsion
- **Position 11**: Generation (most commercial copies of microfiche are service copies and are coded **c**)
- **Position 12**: Base material of film

008: This field contains general information about the work as specified in the instructions for this field at http://www.loc.gov/marc/bibliographic/bd008m.html.

028: **Numerical Identifiers/Publisher Number**: Most microfiche and microfilm contain a unique publisher number, generally found on the container, which is recorded in the MARC 028 field. Other optional numerical fields to include in the descriptive record when warranted and appropriate are the geographic area code (MARC 043) and the language code (MARC 041).

100/110: **Author/Creator**: Enter the person or organization credited with the chief responsibility for the existence of the resource. The authorized form of the name must be used.

245: Enter the preferred title. (Record variant titles in separate MARC 246 fields)

260: **Place, Publisher, and Date of Publication**: Take this information from the preferred source (generally the first title frame) or from information visible to the naked eye (generally found elsewhere on the item itself; such as the container or carrier).

(Cont'd.)

MARC CHECKLIST *(Continued)*

300: **Extent of Resource**: Record the number of units that comprise the resource, if known. Optionally, the number of frames can be stated in parentheses. *RDA* requires exact paging in this field, if available.

336 (Content Type): This will depend on the content of the resource, which for microforms is generally textual, images, or a combination of the two.

337 (Media Type): Microform is used here.

338 (Carrier Type): Use microfilm or microfiche, as appropriate.

490: **Series**: Microfiche and microfilm resources often comprise large sets and/or series. Record the title of the series in this field and repeat it in the 830 field, according to PCC guidelines for series entry (see http://www.loc.gov/catdir/pcc/Field440.pdf).

5XX: **Notes**: Record the URL of an equivalent manifestation in the MARC 530 field, if appropriate, as well as in the 856 field. The 500 field is also used for notes about content, other formats, and the original resource.

6XX: **Subject Terms**: Each descriptive record should contain at least one subject term.

7XX: These fields contain the names of persons or organizations who have contributed to the creation of the work. Those who have made minor contributions are not recorded as additional responsible persons.

776: This can be used in conjunction with the MARC 530 field note to accommodate information about related resources.

830 _0: The established form of the series contained in the MARC 490 field is entered here.

856: Record the URL for remotely located supplementary resources, such as finding aids. A cataloger may also want to provide a URL for the online version of the resource, when available. The URL is required when appropriate.

MODS CHECKLIST

For additional information about constructing a descriptive record for textual resources on microform using MODS, see http://www.loc.gov/standards/mods/v3/mods99042030.xml.

<typeOfResource> is used to specify the type of resource being cataloged, in this case "text."

Example:

```
<typeOfResource>text</typeOfResource>
```

<genre> provides information on a style, form, or content expressed in the resource.

Example:

```
<genre>biography</genre>
```

<identifier> with the attribute " type" is used to provide standard identifiers, such as the ISBN.

Example:

```
<identifier type="isbn">9783540221814</identifier>
```

<recordInfo> with the subelement <recordContentSource> with the attribute "authority" is used to provide the code or name of the organization that created or modified the original resource description.

Example:

```
<recordInfo>
   <recordContentSource>Rutgers University Libraries</recordContentSource>
</recordInfo>
```

(Cont'd.)

MODS CHECKLIST *(Continued)*

<languageTerm> with the type="code" and authority="iso639-2b" (several codes may be used in authority; see http://www.loc.gov/standards/mods/v3/mods-userguide-elements.html#language for additional information).

Example:

```
<language>
   <languageTerm type="code" authority="iso639-2b">eng</languageTerm>
</language>
```

<name> is used to provide information on name of a person, organization, or event (conference, meeting, etc.) associated with the resource. This element has a <type> attribute to specify the type of name (personal, corporate, or conference) and an authority attribute (<authority>) to enable catalogers to specify what authoritative source was consulted to provide the authorized form of the name. This element also has a subelement <role> that is used to specify the role of the named person, corporate body, or conference in relation to the resource.

Example:

```
<name type="personal">
   <role>
      <roleTerm type="text">Creator</roleTerm>
   </role>
<name type="personal">
   <namePart>Charles Maxwell </namePart>
</name>
```

<titleInfo> is used to convey the title or name of a resource. When the main portion of the title is referenced as core, there is only one core subelement, <title>.

Example:

```
<titleInfo>
<title>Papers of Charles Maxwell</title>
</titleInfo>
```

Use <titleInfo> with the type="alternative" and the subelement <title> to convey title varations.

Example:

```
<titleInfo><titleInfo type="alternative">
<title>Charles Maxwell</title>
</titleInfo>
```

<originInfo> with the subelement <edition> is used to describe the version or edition of the resource being described.

Example:

```
<originInfo>
   <edition>7th ed.</edition>
</originInfo>
```

<originInfo> with the subelement <place> and its subelement <placeTerm> with type="text", the subelement <publisher>, and the subelement <dateIssued> is used to provide information on publication, distribution, etc.

<physicalDescription> with the subelements <form> and <extent> provide descriptive information about the resource. In this text the authoritative source for <form> (used to describe the resource's physical description) is the MARC format. The subelement <extent> describes the number and types of units that make up a resource.

Example:

```
<physicalDescription>
   <form authority="marcform">microform</form>
   <extent>1</extent>
</physicalDescription>
```

(Cont'd.)

MODS CHECKLIST *(Continued)*

<tableOfContents> is used for the contents of the microform when this information is supplied by the publisher.

Example:

```
<tableOfContents>
1: The war years: 1946-1950. –2: Postscript: 1951-1977.
</tableOfContents>
```

<relatedItem> with the attribute type "series" is used to provide information on the series when appropriate.

Example:

```
<relatedItem type="series">
  <titleInfo>
    <title>Historical Biographies</title>
  </titleInfo>
</relatedItem>
```

<note> is used to provide general information about the resource.

Example:

```
<note> Written by the author assisted by James Laper.</note>
```

<subject> with the attribute type "authority" and the subelement <name> with the attribute "type" (personal, corporate, conference) provides names of persons and organizations associated with the resource as subjects. Use the subelement <topic> for topical subjects. The descriptive record should contain at least one subject term.

Example:

```
<subject authority="lcsh">
  <topic>Politicians</topic>
</subject>
```

FISO CHECKLIST

Having constructed the descriptive record, the cataloger may find it appropriate to review the description based on the *FRBR* principles: *find*, *identify*, *select*, *obtain*:

F—The potential user has to *find* the material.

I—The user should be able to *identify* the resource, distinguishing it from any similar item.

S—The user should be able to retrieve and *select* the material as the appropriate one for a specific purpose or task.

O—The record should help the user to *obtain* the material by giving information about its location and availability and any requirements for and/or conditions of use.

The following questions are helpful in rating the completed product:

- ❑ Can a potential user find the resource easily? Appropriate description and an active URL, when appropriate, are required to achieve this goal.
- ❑ Has the resource been sufficiently differentiated from any other?
- ❑ How easy is it to identify the resource?
- ❑ Can a user readily distinguish between the original and the microform reproduction of the same work? Information in the additional formats available note must be specific and accurate.
- ❑ Can a potential user immediately recognize this resource as a microform that requires use of specific equipment?

Resources for Catalogers

Digital Library Federation. 2007. *Registry of Digital Masters Record Creation Guidelines.* Digital Library Federation. http://www.diglib.org/collections/reg/DigRegGuide200705.htm#_Toc165952452.

Gwinn, Nancy E., and Lisa L. Fox, eds., for the Association of Research Libraries. 1996. *Preservation Microfilming: A Guide for Librarians and Archivists.* 2nd ed. Chicago: American Library Association and Association of Research Libraries.

Library of Congress. 2010. "Reconsidering the Cataloging Treatment of Reproductions." Library of Congress. April 29. http://www.loc.gov/acq/conser/reproductions.pdf (accessed August 31, 2010).

Notes

1. U.S. Government Printing Office. 2004. "A Strategic Vision for the 21st Century." U.S. Government Printing Office. December 1. http://www.gpo.gov/pdfs/congressional/04strategicplan.pdf.
2. Sproles, Claudene, and Angel Clemens. 2009. "Permanent Electronic Access to Government Information: A Study of Federal, State and Local Documents." *Electronic Journal of Academic and Special Librarianship* 10, no. 2 (Summer). http://southernlibrarianship.icaap.org/content/v10n02/sproles_c01.html.
3. Negus, Paul. 2008. "The Future of Microfilm." Approved Business. September 25. http://www.approvedbusiness.co.uk/ViewArticle_1539.aspx.
4. Tennant, Roy. 2009. "Whither Digital Preservation?" *Tennant: Digital Libraries* (blog). LibraryJournal.com. January 19. http://blog.libraryjournal.com/tennantdigitallibraries/2009/01/19/whither-digital-preservation.
5. Association of Research Libraries. 2007. "National Register of Microform Masters (NRMM) Retrospective Conversion Project." Association of Research Libraries. Last modified March 20. http://www.arl.org/preserv/presresources/Microform_masters.shtml.
6. Association of Research Libraries. 2004. "ARL Endorses Digitization as an Acceptable Preservation Reformatting Option." Association of Research Libraries. Last modified September 13, 2007. http://www.arl.org/news/pr/digitization.shtml.
7. OCLC, Online Computer Library Center. 2010. "Connexion: A Full Service Online Cataloging Tool." OCLC. Accessed August 30. http://www.oclc.org/connexion/.
8. Graphic Communications Group. 2010. "Kodak Reliable Image Tip #50." Eastman Kodak Company. Accessed June 14. http://graphics.kodak.com/docimaging/uploadedFiles/techTip50.pdf.
9. Its.MARC.com. 2010. "LCRI: 11. Microforms." The Library Corporation. Accessed June 14. http://www.itsmarc.com/crs/LCRI0012.htm.
10. American Library Association, Canadian Library Association, and CILIP: Chartered Institute of Library and Information Professionals. 2010. *Resource Description and Access* (Chapter 2.2.4). Accessed August 14. http://www.rdatoolkit.org.
11. Ibid., Chapter 3.1.2.

Multimedia Kits and Mixed Materials

Overview

Kits are unique resources primarily because there is no standard container and the composition of each kit is likely to be different. Today's kit may contain electronic resources, printed and/or visual resources, as well as instructions for logging on to the Internet for additional or supplementary material. Older kits (published before the mid-1990s) are likely to contain outdated media and/or media types that have either become obsolete or have waned in popularity. Also, a cataloger may choose to designate as a "kit" any collection of resources meant to be used together, primarily for instructional purposes, whether or not the term appears on the item.

A random review of cataloging practices regarding kits and mixed materials revealed that the description of kits has been subject to various practices and interpretations. A further complication is that it is sometimes difficult to determine whether the resource being cataloged is indeed a kit, as defined by *AACR2*; whether the resource should be described as having accompanying material; or whether the resource is simply a collection of miscellaneous objects and/or resources, published or unpublished works, not intended as a unit.

It is important to distinguish between a resource that is a kit and resources that comprise a collection or a resource consisting of a main component and one or more pieces of accompanying material. This determination influences the description of the resource. *AACR2* defines a kit as "an item containing two or more categories of material, no one of which is identifiable as the predominant constituent of the item; also designated 'multimedia item.'"[1] This categorization of a kit as "an item" reinforces the concept that the components of a kit are intended as the "whole" resource. According to *AACR2*'s definition, a kit can also be "a single-medium package of textual material." *RDA* provides no definition for a kit in its Glossary but instead offers instructions for describing resources issued in more than one part or containing many components, none of which is the main component.[2] The term "kit" is

IN THIS CHAPTER:

rarely used in *RDA*, and the guidelines applicable to this type of resource are the same as those for multipart monographs, because the kit is considered a monograph and its component parts may have been previously published, separately and/or at different times.

A collection, as defined in the *RDA* Glossary, is "a group of resources assembled by a person, family or corporate body from a variety of sources." As defined in the glossary of *AACR2*, a collection is "1. Three or more independent work or parts of works by one author published together. 2. Two or more independent works or parts of works by more than one author published together and not written for the same occasion or for the publication in hand." The cataloger may also encounter a resource that comprises a predominant component accompanied by a supplementary resource that is required for a comprehensive understanding of the work. Therefore, the cataloger must determine if the resource in hand is a kit, a collection, or a resource that includes one or more pieces of accompanying material. This determination must be made before attempting to create a descriptive record.

Important Considerations

Each kit will likely present its own unique challenges for description, and the cataloger must remain wary of misrepresenting a resource. Resources that describe themselves as online interactive kits or online toolkits do not necessarily conform to the definition of a kit.[3] Kits are categorized as visual materials, whereas the online interactive kit must be described as an online resource. As is increasingly common today, the library may create special interest or special purpose "kits" out of independently published resources (the popular "Book Club kit" is a good example of this trend), and local practice for describing such kits varies. Deciding whether the kit was commercially published or locally produced and determining the creator's purpose for the kit will assist the cataloger in representing the resource adequately, enhancing the potential for discovery by the precise category of users for whom it was intended. Information about the purpose and target audience for the resource can be taken from the components themselves or from any reliable source.

Before describing the kit, a few preliminary steps, such as identifying the primary components and their media and carrier types, will steer the cataloger in the right direction. It is often helpful to first mentally or physically sort the components into media types, as this brings the associated carriers into focus and will help to ensure that each component is described adequately. The media type describes the medium used to publish or display content and can be auditory, visual (video, projected medium, film, etc.), or unmediated (printed or visual material for which no equipment is required for use). Carrier types relate to the specific "vehicle" or "conduit" through which the media is distributed, such as audio CDs, filmstrips, and DVD-videos.

AACR2 Chapter 1.0H2 requires catalogers to base description on the first component in the kit that provides the most information about the entire resource. If the item being described consists of two or more separate physical parts, catalogers are advised to "Treat a container that is the unifying element as the chief source of information if it furnishes a collective title and the items themselves and their labels do not."[4] In such a case a source of title note is required (*AACR2* Chapter 8.7B3). In addition, *AACR2* stipulates that if information is not available from the chief or preferred source, a component that provides the most information about the entire resource, then it must be taken from the following sources in this order of preference: "The container (box or frame): the accompanying textual material (e.g., manuals, leaflets) or other sources."

A number of rules in *RDA* apply to the description of kits:

- *RDA* 2.1.2.1 stipulates that the source of information for resource description must be "appropriate to the mode of issuance."
- *RDA* 2.1.2.2 instructs catalogers to take descriptive information from a source that identifies the resource as an integrated whole.
- *RDA* 2.1.2.3 (Resource issued in more than one part) instructs catalogers to prefer a source of information identifying the resource as a whole and in 2.1.2.3 (d) stipulates the following: "Otherwise, treat the sources identifying the individual parts as a collective source of information for the resource as a whole."
- Additional guidelines in *RDA* 2.2.2.1 stipulate that catalogers should "treat a container such as a box in which a game or kit is issued as part of the resource itself," a directive that designates the container as an integral part of the resource bearing equal weight with any other component as a preferred source of information.

The core elements of description must be identified and recorded in keeping with those identified in *RDA* 1.3 and in the BIBCO Core Record Standards for Graphic Material (available at http://www.loc.gov/catdir/pcc/bibco/coregm.html). For additional information on the identification of preferred sources for descriptive information, refer to Chapter 1 of this manual and to *RDA* Chapter 2.

Resource Description

Kit descriptions must accurately reflect all essential characteristics of its components. Catalogers are advised to choose the level of resource description based on the anticipated needs of the user community and the purpose of the catalog.

RDA Chapter 3 provides three options for resource description, each of which contains the core elements for kit resources. Comprehensive description is the fullest level of description (*RDA* 3.1.4.3), and catalogers are instructed as follows: "When preparing a comprehensive description for a resource consisting of more than one carrier, apply whichever of the methods described under 3.1.4.1, 3.1.4.2, or 3.1.4.3 is appropriate to the nature of the resource and the purpose of the description."[5]

Comprehensive resource description ensures that the appropriate details for each component are recorded, especially because some components may require the use of specialized equipment, and allows the cataloger to designate and describe the relationship/relevance of the components to the entire resource and to any other related resource, if appropriate. Recording the core elements provides adequate description, and many core elements are also preferred access points. Nevertheless, catalogers are encouraged to describe the resource fully, as comprehensive description enhances the potential for resource discovery.

Work

The description of kits, like that of all resources, begins with the accurate identification and transcription of the title. Commercially published kits are likely to have a single unifying title. For kits that lack a readily identifiable title, the title can be taken from anywhere on or within the entire resource. If variations in the title are found dispersed throughout the resource, the cataloger is required to use judgment as to the "preferred title" and to list the other title(s) as variant titles in the appropriate area of the record.

RDA (6.2.2.3-6.2.2.7) requires the cataloger to select the title that represents the work accurately, further stipulating that the title designated as the preferred title should be, in order of preference, "the title most frequently found in resources embodying the work in its original language, the title found in reference sources, or the title most frequently found in resources listing the work." *RDA* 2.3.1.2 contains additional guidelines regarding the selection of the preferred title. The title must be transcribed exactly as it appears on the item, including punctuation. Abbreviations are prohibited unless they appear on the resource. Other titles found in resources embodying the work or in reference sources should be recorded as variant titles.[6] The title proper and earlier or later variant titles are core elements of description.

In the absence of a readily identifiable title, or when there are several possible titles, the cataloger must use judgment when selecting the preferred title. If there is no clear title on the item, the cataloger is allowed to construct a title for the purpose of cataloging the item. In such a case, *AACR2* Rule 1.7B3 (1998) requires the cataloger to create a note stating that the title was constructed by or selected by the cataloger. A note is also required to state the source of the title when it was selected from a source other than the preferred sources of information. *RDA* 2.3.2.2 supports this requirement. Enter the title in the MARC 245 field, the MODS element <title>, and the DC element <title>. The source of title note can be entered as shown in Example 8.1.

Kits may be created by a team or may comprise disparate resources published independently and at different times. Whether a collaborative venture or a variety of resources assembled to be used together, this type of arrangement generally results in the selection of a unifying title as the preferred access point for the resource. Additional access points are required for authors and creators of individual components that have

EXAMPLE 8.1

500 __ Title supplied by cataloger.
500 __ Title from accompanying teacher's guide.

```
<titleInfo>
  <title>Title supplied by cataloger
  </title>
</titleInfo>

<Description>Title from supplemental materials</Description>
```

been published separately or that are significant and/or that can be used independently. When a single individual or a corporate entity can be credited with creation of the kit, the cataloger is required to enter the kit under the creator as the preferred access point and to record this information in the statement of responsibility. Separately published components that are included in a kit may represent different manifestations of original works, especially if an identification number, such as an ISBN or publisher's number, has been affixed to the piece. This type of information must be recorded in the descriptive record as instructed in *RDA* 19.2: "If the resource being described contains two or more independent works by different persons, families, or corporate bodies, record the persons, families, and corporate bodies associated with each of the works in the aggregate resource as instructed under 19.2–19.3." *AACR2* and *RDA* have different requirements regarding the selection of the creator and the recording of the statement of responsibility:

- *AACR2* requires the cataloger to choose the creator who bears primary responsibility for the creation of the resource and to enter this person as the "main entry" for author. This person is often the first named person in the statement of responsibility. Additional responsible persons, who may be recorded in the statement of responsibility and who may bear equal responsibility, are treated as added entries.
- *RDA* requires only that the cataloger record the person credited with principal responsibility for creating the work, or the first named responsible person, in the statement of responsibility. However, optionally, the cataloger can record all responsible persons in the statement of responsibility. Because the cataloger is not required to designate a "main entry," all creators who share equal responsibility for the work can be recorded as responsible persons.

These guidelines are illustrated in Example 8.2.

Names omitted from the statement of responsibility can be added in a general note when appropriate. If no person or organization is specifically named in the statement of responsibility, the cataloger is instructed to record a general statement of responsibility as found on the item (*RDA* 2.4.1.9) (see Example 8.3).

When used as access points, the preferred name of the creator and/or responsible persons or organizations must be recorded in accordance with established authorities such as the Library of Congress's Authority File and other recognized authorities such as the Virtual International Authority File (http://viaf.org). The cataloger can also add the appropriate relationship term to the name to specify relationship of the person to the resource. Relationship terms (known popularly as "relator terms") are listed in *RDA* Appendix I.

Record additional responsible persons, including publishers deemed to have made a significant contribution to the creation of the resource, in the MARC 700 field Added Entry—Personal Name. Record additional responsible persons in the MODS element <name> with the qualifiers

EXAMPLE 8.2

245 10 Daisy chain / $c John Berry [and three others] (*RDA*)

245 10 Daisy chain / $c John Berry, Mary Brown, Lar Shriner, Judith James. (*RDA* optional)

245 10 Daisy chain / $c John Berry... et al. (*AACR2*)

EXAMPLE 8.3

245 00 [title] / $c by two ladies in New Jersey.

<name type> and <role>. Use the DC element <Contributor> for this purpose.

Language is a core element of resource description. The title of the resource must be recorded in the language in which it appears on the preferred source of information, and the resource must be cataloged in the predominant language of its content if it contains more than one language.[7] In MARC, record a three-letter code representing the main language of the resource in the language code area of the MARC 008 fixed field. The three-digit language code is governed by the MARC Codes for Languages (available at http://www.loc.gov/marc/languages/langhome.html). If the kit contains multilingual components or versions of text in several languages or is a translation, the MARC 041 field is required to reflect this, as shown in Example 8.4.

EXAMPLE 8.4

Fixed field language code: fre (French)
041 __ fre $a ita $a ger
The kit contains components in the three languages listed in the 041 field.

A note can also be created in the MARC 546 field. Additional information is available at http://www.loc.gov/marc/bibliographic/bd546.html.

Other important elements of description include the detailed listing of the components of the kit, the content or subject matter, and the target audience. When the components are of various media and carrier types, a good rule of thumb is to enter a separate 006 field for each component to provide specific characteristics not readily accommodated in the MARC 008 field. The example in Figure 8.1 (see p. 277) does not contain a MARC 006 field because the required information was entered in the MARC 008 field.

FOR MORE INFORMATION

OCLC provides a chart that outlines and highlights the relationship between the MARC 006 and 008 fields. The chart is available at http://www.oclc.org/bibformats/en/fixedfield/008006summary.shtm.

Approved subject terms, based on thesauri such as the *Library of Congress Subject Headings*,[8] provide additional access points for the resource and are entered in the MARC 6XX fields; in the MODS element <subject>, which can be further refined with the subelements <topic>, <geographic>, <titleInfo>, and <name>; and in the DC element <Element> with the qualifier "lcsh."

Kit Containing VHS Cassette and Volumes

The title was selected as the preferred access point for the kit illustrated in Figure 8.1. The kit was prepared and published by the Center for Substance Abuse Treatment, National Institutes of Health, and this name is entered as an additional access point. However, one of the components, the videocassette, was published by AARP and the Hazelden Foundation in 1996, information that was clearly stated in the description and on the component. Both AARP and Hazelden have been selected as additional access points.

The enhanced contents notes in Figure 8.1 describe the components in terms of carrier type, title, and extent, and the brief summary explains the purpose of the kit. Because English is the only language used, there is no need for an additional language note in the MARC 546 field. The language of the kit is recorded in the MARC 008 fixed field area.

Kit Containing CD and Volumes

Figure 8.2 shows the components of a kit. Figures 8.3 and 8.4, respectively, illustrate its corresponding MARC and MODS resource descriptions.

Figure 8.1. MARC Resource Description for a Kit Containing a VHS Cassette Using *RDA*

Leader 06 Leader 07	o = kit m = monograph
007 [sound recordings (VHS tape)]	$a v $b f $c [undefined] $d m $e b $f a $g h $h o $i u
008 [visual materials; includes information specific to kits]	Lang: eng [English] Form of item: [blank. None of the provided codes for this field is appropriate.] Ctry: mdu [Maryland, United States] Govt. Pub: f [federal government document] Type of visual material: b [kit] Date type: m [multiple dates] Date 1: 1996 Date 2: 2003 [dates on the components range from 1996 to 2003]
040 [Cataloging library code and code for description convention (*RDA*)]	NjR $c NjR $e rda
245 00 [Title] [$h subfield was omitted, in accordance with *RDA*.]	Get connected! linking older adults with medication, alcohol and mental health resources / $c Center for Substance Abuse Treatment, National Institutes of Health.
246 13 [Variant title]	Linking older adults with medication, alcohol, and mental health resources
260 __ [Publication information]	Rockville, Maryland : $b Center for Substance Abuse Treatment, Substance Abuse and Mental Health Services Administration, $c 1996-2003.
300 __ [Extent]	1 3-ring binder (Program Coordinator's guide), 2 booklets, 3 pamphlets, 1 VHS videocassette (26 min.) ; $c in container (27 x 33 x 6 cm.).
336 __ [Content type] 336 __	Text $2 rdacontent Two-dimensional moving image $2 rdacontent
337 __ [Media type] 337 __	Unmediated media $2 rdamedia Video $2 rdamedia
338 __ [Carrier type] 338 __	Volumes $2 rdacarrier Videocassette $2 rdacarrier
490 1_ [Series]	DHHS publication ; $v no. (SMA) 03-3824
500 __ [General note]	Videocassette published in 1996 by AARP and Hazelden.
505 00 [Enhanced contents]	$g Binder $t Substance abuse among older adults : a guide for social service providers, 2000 $g (68 p. ; 28 cm.) -- $t Promoting older adult health : aging network partnerships to address medication, alcohol, and mental health problems, 2002 $g (124 p. ; 28 cm.) -- $t How to talk to an older person who has a problem with alcohol or medications $g (12 p. ; 22 cm.) -- $t Good mental health is ageless, 2001 $g (6 p. : col. ill. ; 23 x 10 cm.) -- $t Aging, medicines and alcohol, 2001 $g (6 p. : col. ill. ; 23 x 10 cm.) -- $g Videocassette, $t It can happen to anyone : problems with alcohol and medication among older adults, $g c1996 (26 min. : sd., col. ; 1/2 in.).

(Cont'd.)

Figure 8.1. MARC Resource Description for a Kit Containing a VHS Cassette Using *RDA (Continued)*	
520 __ [Summary]	Kit of materials to be used by service providers and care givers to help older adults in trouble with drug and/or alcohol abuse.
511 0_ [Performer/narrator]	Videocassette; narrated by Edward Asner.
530 __ [Additional format available]	This kit is also available with a DVD videodisc instead of a videocassette.
650 _0 [Authorized subject (Library of Congress heading; preferred access point)]	Older people $x Mental health services $z United States.
710 1_ [Additional responsible person/organization (additional access point)]	United States. $b Administration on Aging.
710 1_	United States. $b Substance Abuse and Mental Health Services Administration.
710 2_	Hazelden Foundation.
710 2_	AARP (Organization).
700 1_	Asner, Edward, $e narrator.
830 0_ [Preferred series]	DHHS publication ; $v no. (SMA) 03-3824
856 4_ [URL]	$u http://www.samhsa.gov/Aging/docs/GetConnectedToolkit.pdf $z Program Coordinator's guide.
Note: The fixed fields contain only the most important codes for this type of resource. Other codes can be used as appropriate for this format.	

The kit's contents are listed on the container as follows:

- 2 workbooks
- 6 chapter books
- 8 Hooked on Phonics storybooks
- 4 audio CDs
- 2 progress posters to track learning success
- 1 set of fun stickers for kids
- 1 parents' guide
- 7 flash card sets

Grouping the contents of kits according to media and carrier type can help the cataloger to describe this resource sufficiently.

Use the MARC 007 field to code the essential characteristics or attributes of the audio disc components. Used in conjunction with the

Figure 8.2. Contents of a Kit Containing CDs and Print Volumes

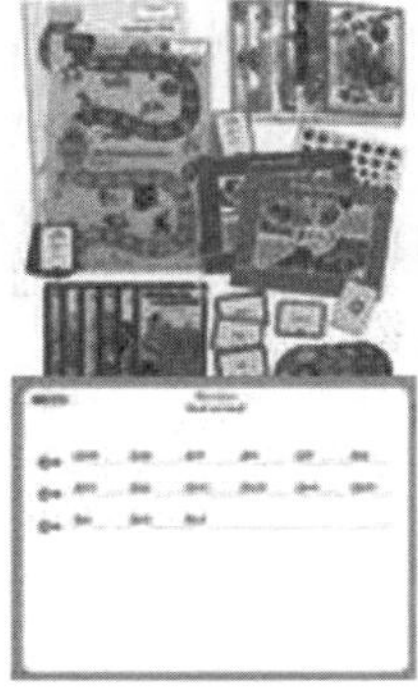
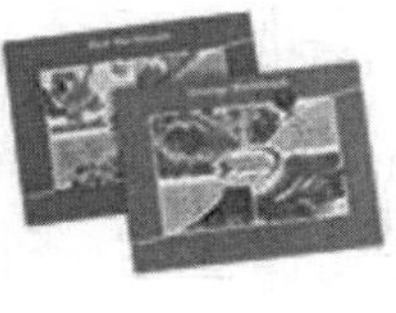

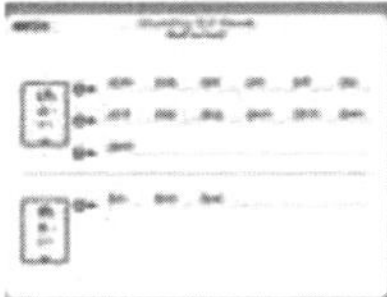

Figure 8.3. MARC Resource Description for a Kit Containing CDs and Volumes

Leader 06 [Type of record] Leader 07 [Bibliographic level]	o [kit] m [monograph]
006 [Position 00]	i [non-musical sound recording]
007 [For sound recordings]	$a s $b d $c [undefined] $d f $e s $f [blank] $g g $h [blank] $m e $n [blank]
008 [Combined 006 for visual materials]	Lang: eng Form of item: [blank; none of supplied codes are applicable] Ctry: us Type: b [kit] Target audience: b [primary grades] Date 1: 2005 Date 2: Running time: nnn [not applicable to the entire resource]
020	9781887942560 (pbk. : 1-2) [It is recommended that the cataloger record the ISBNs for each book in this kit to provide important access points.]

(Cont'd.)

Figure 8.3. MARC Resource Description for a Kit Containing CDs and Volumes *(Continued)*	
028 12 028 12 028 12 028 12	12252 $b HOP (Red Disc 1) 12253 $b HOP (Red Disc 2) 12352 $b HOP (Orange Disc 1) 12353 $b HOP (Orange Disc 2)
040 __	[Reserved for the symbol of inputting library and description convention code.]
050 _4	[Reserved for the call number.]
245 00	Hooked on phonics $p First grade : $b learn to read
246 30 [portion of title]	Learn to read
260 [per *RDA]*	[Undetermined place] $b Hop LLC, $c p2005.
300 __	2 workbooks, 6 chapter books, 7 Hooked on Phonics books, 2 progress posters (45 cm x 28 cm), 7 sets of flashcards ; $c in container (32 x 24 x 6 cm)
300 __	4 audio discs (digital) ; $c 12 cm.
336 __ [Content type]	Audio $a text $2 rdacontent
337 __ [Media type]	Audio disc $a unmediated $2 rdamedia
338 __ [Carrier type]	computer disc $a volume $a other $2 rdacarrier
505 00 [The enhanced contents note provides additional access to the individual titles in the kit and their respective authors.]	$g Hop chapter level 2, book 1. $t Detective dog and the lost rabbit / $r Leslie McGuire -- $g Hop chapter level 2, book 2. $t Detective dog and the ghost / $r Leslie McGuire ; -- $g Hop chapter level 2, book 3. $t Picnic at Black Rock / $r Leslie McGuire. [Cataloger may include the titles and authors of all of the books included in the kit. The structure of the enhanced contents note provides access to the titles and authors listed after the appropriate subfield codes.]
520 __	This kit is made up of color-coded material designed to help first grade children learn to read. The orange-coded workbooks introduce sounds that come at the beginning of words, while the red workbooks showcase sounds that come at the end of words.
538 __	Requires a CD player.
650 _0	Reading $x Phonetic method $v Audio-visual aids.
710 1_	HOP, LLC.
856 42	[Enter the URL that directs a user to supplementary material on the Internet in this field, if available.]

006 and 300 fields, the 007 field represents the extent of the resource and its technical elements. Because the kit in Figure 8.2 contains audio as well as textual components, it is appropriate to use two MARC 300 fields. In Figure 8.3, the first MARC 300 field contains all of the textual components. The second MARC 300 field contains the number of discs

Figure 8.4. Basic MODS Descriptive Record for a Kit Containing CDs and Print Volumes

titleInfo: subTitle:	Hooked on phonics ; first grade Learn to read
typeOfResource: typeOfResource:	Textual material Visual material
name:	
recordInfo/description Standard:	
genre:	
originInfo: place: publisher: date:	United States. HOP, LLC 2005
physicalDescription: [form, extent, Internet media type, digital origin, etc.]	Kit contains: 2 workbooks, 6 chapter books, 8 Hooked on Phonics(®) storybooks, 4 audio CDs, 2 progress posters to track learning success, 1 set of fun stickers kids love, 1 Parent's guide, and 7 flash card sets.
abstract:	This kit is made up of color-coded material designed to help first grade children learn to read. The orange-coded workbooks introduce sounds that come at the beginning of words, while the red workbooks showcase sounds that come at the end of words.
contents:	Hop chapter level 2, book 1. Detective dog and the lost rabbit by Leslie McGuire -- Hop chapter level 2, book 2. Detective dog and the ghost by Leslie McGuire -- Hop chapter level 2, book 3. Picnic at Black Rock by Leslie McGuire.
note: [artistic and/or technical credits]	Compiled and published by HOP, LLC.
subject:	Reading -- Phonetic method -- Audio-visual aids.
classification:	Use as required.
identifiers (hdl):	12252 HOP (Red Disc 1) 12253 HOP (Red Disc 2) 12352 HOP (Orange Disc 1) 12353 HOP (Orange Disc 2) [ISBNs are also recorded in this field.]
relatedName:	HOP, LLC
carriers:	Volumes CDs
physicalLocation:	Not applicable.

QUICK TIP

If the CD is a computer disc containing files or text rather than audio, the 007 field for computer files is required.

in subfield $a. The presence of color and/or illustrations would be given in subfield $b and the actual dimensions of the item in subfield $c, which for audio CDs is 4¾ inches (12 cm.).

Record the media and carrier types in the MARC fields 337 and 338, respectively. Use of $b instead of $a in these fields is reserved for coded data describing content. Delimiter $2 is used to record the source of the term. As shown in Figure 8.3, the $a subfield can be repeated to enter more than one type of media, content, or carrier in a single field. For additional information on use of these fields, consult http://www.loc.gov/marc/changes-rda-336.html.

Kit Containing Microfilm

A kit containing microfilm components requires very specific description related to the carrier. Microforms (microfiche and microfilms) are generally language material/textual and do not require a 006 field, although coding the microfilm or microfiche as language material in the first position of this field is acceptable. Figure 8.5 shows the carrier characteristics for a microfilm reel. The specific material designation provides details about the specific type of resource. For a microform carrier whose specific carrier type is microfilm, **d** (microfilm reels) is used. For additional details, consult http://www.loc.gov/marc/bibliographic/bd007c.html.

Record information about the number of rolls or sheets in the $a subfield of the MARC 300 field, and record the presence of color and/or illustrations in the component resource in subfield $b. The dimensions of the item will vary depending on the carrier; record these in subfield $c. Example 8.5 shows typical 300 fields for direct access resources in microform.

EXAMPLE 8.5

300 __ 3 reels : $b black and white ; $c 35mm. [*AACR2*]

300 __ 4 microfiche sheets : $b negative ; $c 11 x 15 cm. [*AACR2*]

Expression

The presence of an edition or version statement that is applicable to the whole kit rather than to any single component generally signals a new expression or manifestation of the kit and must be recorded. Edition statements pertaining to individual components in the kit must be recorded in the general notes area if deemed important.

Figure 8.5. Generic MARC 007 Field for a Microfilm Reel

Position 00	Position 01	Position 02	Position 03	Position 04	Position 05	Positions 06–08	Position 09	Position 10	Position 11	Position 12
Category of material	Specific Material Designation	Undefined	Positive/ negative	Dimensions	Reduction ratio	Additional ratio values	Color	Emulsion	Generation	Base
h	d	Blank	a	f	b		b	Blank	c	Blank
Microform	Microfilm reel		Positive	35 mm	Normal	Use as needed	Black and white	No attempt to code	Service copy	No attempt to code

When appropriate, information about the edition or version is provided in the MARC 250 field. Edition statements are recorded in the MODS element <edition> and in the DC element <relation> with the qualifier <isVersionof> to specify the relationship of the current resource to another bearing the same title. Additional information on the use of the relation element in DC is available at http://dublincore.org/2008/01/14/dcelements.rdf#relation.

Enter the appropriate country code for the origin of the resource in the MARC fixed field area. The country codes are listed at http://www.loc.gov/marc/countries/cou_home.html.

Enter details about the publication, such as the name of the publisher and date and place of publication, in the MARC 260 field. Enter this information in the MODS element <originInfo> qualified by the subelements <place>, <publisher>, and <copyrightDate>. For DC, enter this information as <dcterm> <Publisher>, and use the label <date> for the date information recorded in the YYYY-MM-DD format.

Components of the kit can contain different dates of publication, but a single date is preferred, when available, if it applies to the kit as a whole. Kits are treated as multipart single issue (monographic) publications, and, in the absence of a single date of publication, the rules that apply to multipart monographic sets are applied. As illustrated in Figure 8.1 (p. 277), the "Date type" area of the MARC 008 fixed field contains the code **m** (for multiple dates), and "Date 1" and "Date 2" respectively contain the dates of the first and last published component. The MARC 008 fixed field also contains codes for language of content, place, and year of publication, as well as other elements related to the description of visual materials. The MARC 500 General Note field can additionally be used to identify the components listed in the date fields.

Publication details are generally specified for the kit as a whole, except when a significant individual component has been published by a different entity (as illustrated in Figure 8.1, p. 277). *RDA* 2.8–2.9 provides detailed instructions for selecting and entering the names of publishers and distributors and for selecting and recording dates of publication. Additional information about the MARC 260 field is available at http://www.loc.gov/marc/bibliographic/bd260.html.

QUICK TIP

Depending on the specific ILS, the MARC 008 fixed field elements are located in the fixed field area of the record along with the Leader fixed field elements. In addition, some values in the Leader field are system supplied.

QUICK TIP

In the absence of a known publisher, the distributor or manufacturer must be recorded, if known. Likewise, in the absence of a publication date, the date of manufacture and/or the copyright date must be recorded, if present.

Manifestation

A reissued kit containing components in a language different from the original represents a new manifestation of the resource. Similarly, content reissued on or through different carriers constitutes different manifestations of a resource. The kit in Figure 8.1 (see pp. 277–278) was reissued with a DVD disc instead of the VHS tape, and this other manifestation was noted in the MARC 530 field (for other available formats). The version with the DVD requires a different record.

The MARC 007 field specifies the category of material and includes the specific material designation. Coding for the 007 field indicates that the item is a kit, which is defined in MARC 21 Format for Bibliographic

Data as "a mixture of various components issued as a unit and intended primarily for instructional purposes. No one component is identifiable as the predominant component of the kit."

Developments in the MARC format, including the creation of separate 007 fields for different types of resources, accommodate and encourage the use of separate 007 fields for the various components of a kit. Because the kit described in Figure 8.1 contains only two carrier types, one of which is unmediated, the record contains a single 007 field that represents characteristics for the VHS tape. *RDA* description is reflected in the addition of the MARC fields 336, 337, and 338, respectively, for content, media, and carrier types.

The extent of the resource is one of the most important areas in the description of kits. All characteristics of the components should be clearly represented in this area, including information about individual carriers. *RDA* offers the option of describing as many carrier types as comprise the resource and in Chapter 3, Section 1.4.1, specifies that both the carrier type and the extent must be recorded; both are core elements (*RDA* 1.3). The cataloger has the option of describing the extent of the resource in general terms or in a detailed description, including basic information and additional characteristics. Alternatively, the following options are provided:

> If the resource being described consists of more than one carrier type, record only
>
> a) The carrier type that applies to the predominant part of the resource (if there is a predominant part)
>
> or
>
> b) The carrier types that apply to the most substantial parts of the resource (including the predominant part, if there is one) using one or more of the terms listed.[9]

By definition, kits do not contain any predominant part, and as such each component should be described fully. The cataloger has the option of recording the dimensions of each carrier type, the dimensions of the most substantial component, or the dimensions of the container only.

AACR2 provides the option of using a single field to describe the extent of the resource as a whole or using multiple fields, one for each media type that comprises the kit. Details about the composition of a kit are important, especially in the school library setting. The ability to record content, media, and carrier types in separate fields, as introduced in *RDA,* makes it easier to identify and record a kit's different components. Carrier type is repeated in the MARC 300 field (the SMD) along with details about the extent of the resource. The description of the kit in Figure 8.1 (see pp. 277–278) is comprehensive and contains details about the carriers and extent of the resource both in the 300 field and in the enhanced contents notes. The MARC fields for content, media, and carrier type (336, 337, and 338) were included according to *RDA* requirements.

Record the extent of the component resource (number of pages, discs, etc.) in subfield $a of the MARC 300 field. Subfield $b accommodates

FOR MORE INFORMATION

See *RDA* Chapter 3 for additional details related to describing the extent of a resource.

QUICK TIP

A descriptive record prepared according to *RDA* requirements must be coded to reflect that it conforms to *RDA*. The approved code is entered in the 040 field, as shown in Figure 8.1, p. 277.

information about the presence of color and/or illustrations in the resource. Record the actual dimensions of the components in subfield $c of the MARC 300 field if applicable; recording only the dimensions of the container is appropriate for kits containing several components (see Example 8.6).

If the kit contains numerous pieces, the cataloger is not expected to count or to list each specific piece. Example 8.7 illustrates a condensed 300 field constructed according to *RDA* guidelines.

A typical MARC 300 field for a kit containing a CD component (a direct access electronic resource) is shown in Example 8.8, described according to *AACR2* guidelines. The following 3XX fields demonstrate the use of the *RDA*-required MARC fields:

300 __ 1 computer disc, 2 volumes and 23 flash cards ; $c in container (21 × 38 × 6 cm.).

336 __ text $a two dimensional moving images $2 rdacontent

337 __ unmediated $a computer $2 rdamedia

338 __ volume $a computer disc $a other $2 rdacarrier

The kit illustrated in Figure 8.1 is also available with a DVD instead of a VHS tape. The carrier type is the only difference noted, but the description must be changed in the following fields:

MARC 007 field must reflect coding for the DVD-video

MARC 338 Carrier Type (DVD video)

Dimensions (12 cm)

SMD (DVD-video)

Notes pertaining to the DVD can include "Use of a DVD player required" in the MARC 538 field.

The description area in the MODS record accommodates the detailed description of disparate resources in a single area of the record: MODS element <physicalDescription> modified by the subelements <form> and <extent>. Information about the extent of the resource is recorded in the DC element <Format> with the qualifier <Extent> (see Example 8.9).

A commercially published kit may contain a unique numeric identifier assigned by the publisher (publisher number and/or the ISBN) and printed on the container or on one or more components. Enter the ISBN in the MARC 020 field, which is repeatable when more than one number is found on the resource. Enter the publisher number in the MARC 028 field, and use the 024 MARC field Other Standard Identifier to record any other type of number found on the item. Record numerical identification in the MODS element <identifier>, qualified by identifier type (ISBN, matrix number, music publisher number, etc.), and in the DC element <Identifier> (see Example 8.10).

The kit illustrated in Figure 8.1 contains only a DHHS publication number, which is part of an established series. Enter series in the MARC 490 and 830 fields.

EXAMPLE 8.6

300 __ 1 3-ring binder (Program Coordinator's guide), 2 booklets, 3 pamphlets, 1 VHS videocassette (26 min.) ; $c in container (27 x 33 x 15 cm.).

EXAMPLE 8.7

300 __ 26 various pieces ; $c in container (21 x 38 x 6 cm.).

EXAMPLE 8.8

300 __ 1 CD, 4 posters (12 x 12 cm), 14 flash cards, 1 teacher's manual ; $c in container (21 x 38 x 6 cm). [*AACR2*]

EXAMPLE 8.9

```
<physicalDescription>
   <form authority="marcform">print
   </form>
<physicalDescription>
   <extent>75 minutes</extent>
</physicalDescription>
<Format>
<Extent>2 sheets</Extent>
</Format>
```

FOR MORE INFORMATION

RDA requires expanded description when recording the extent of a resource. *RDA* Chapter 3 provides additional information regarding the description of carriers and recording the extent of resources using both comprehensive and analytic description.

EXAMPLE 8.10

```
024 __ 1 720229912723
<identifier type="music publisher">
821TRN Music Publisher</identifier>
<Identifier> 077779548125</Identifier>
```

EXAMPLE 8.11

856 42 $u http://www.samhsa.gov/Aging/docs/GetConnectedToolkit.pdf $z Program Coordinator's guide.

<identifier type="url">http://www.samhsa.gov/Aging/docs/GetConnectedToolkit.pdf </identifier>

<Identifier>http://opac.newsbank.com/select/evans/41774</Identifier>

QUICK TIP

AACR2 and MARC standards, as well as some local cataloging authorities, require the GMD for descriptive records. The GMD may also be required for records added to OCLC, as it continues to serve as an early "media/carrier type" alert for users. When required, the GMD for this type of resource is "kit."

The kit may include a URL or web address to direct a user to supplementary or publisher information available on the Internet. Enter the URL in the MARC 856 field, the MODS element <location>, and the DC element <Identifier> (see Example 8.11). As shown in Figure 8.1, the URL links the user to the online copy of the Program Coordinator's guide.

Item

The kit is considered a unit and as such represents a single resource. Information pertaining to the item refers to the resource as a whole. As with other resource types, item-specific peculiarities may be recorded in the item details area of the descriptive record.

URLs are increasingly being included to direct users to supplementary or related materials, and this is an area where local practices apply to the item-level description. A cataloger may also consider it worthwhile to provide a URL for the publisher of the resource. The MARC 856 field is used to record URLs for publisher and/or other supplementary resources on the Internet when appropriate. Additional information about the MARC 856 field is available at http://www.loc.gov/marc/856guide.html.

Notes

No specific note fields are unique to kits, but notes enable the cataloger to record additional resource-specific information. The general note area is used for information that is deemed important but for which there is no specific MARC field or metadata element. Catalogers are encouraged to take advantage of the notes area to highlight and record important information that the user may find useful. Such notes include creators, playback requirements, contents, access restrictions, age/grade level requirements, etc.

In addition, because of the nature of the resource, individual components may represent media types, such as electronic resources, for which specific note fields are mandatory. A kit containing electronic resources requires detailed information about system requirements, including type of computer equipment and operating system and/or necessary playback equipment. Enter these details in the MARC 538 note field and the appropriate areas in the MODS or DC records.

Other notes that may be used when describing kits include, in random order, the following:

- General notes pertaining to the source of the title and any other notes deemed appropriate by the cataloger are included in the MARC 500 field and in the general notes areas in MODS and DC.
- A general note is recommended when any significant component of the kit is a reproduction of an existing work. Information about the original can be included in the general note and in the MARC 775 field Other Edition Entry. The details of a single

component that is a reproduction can be recorded as shown in Example 8.12.

- Title access to a significant component of the kit is included when appropriate.
- Additional information about the resource may also be added in the MARC 776 field Additional Physical Form Entry.
- Access restriction notes and parent advisories are important, depending on the specific situation. Such notes can be recorded in a MARC 506 field or as a public note in the subfield $z of the MARC 856 field.
- One or more components of the kit may be available in another format. When this is known, record the availability in the MARC 530 field (see Example 8.13). The MARC 530 note field was used in Figure 8.1 (see pp. 277–278) to alert users to the availability of another manifestation of the kit, one containing a DVD instead of a VHS tape.
- Content notes largely depend on the cataloger's judgment, particularly because providing this information can be time-consuming. Nevertheless, it is highly recommended that catalogers use these fields when appropriate and especially when information can aid the resource discovery experience. Also note that the addition of a URL has been approved for use in the MARC 505 Contents and 520 Summary fields. Additional information about appropriate placement of URLs is available at http://www.loc.gov/marc/856guide.html#other_fields.

EXAMPLE 8.12

500 __ The booklet entitled "Blue dog" is a photocopy of the original resource published by John Publishers in 1996.

EXAMPLE 8.13

530 __ Kit also available with DVD-video disc.

QUICK TIP

Numbered note fields are specific to the MARC format only. For MODS the note element can be used with appropriate subelements to specify the type of note.

This chapter demonstrates the diverse nature of kits. A kit can comprise a variety of components, and the overarching concern is that each component be described in a manner that is consistent with its media and carrier types. When approached methodically, the description of kits becomes less challenging for catalogers, who may initially feel overwhelmed when confronted with a box of miscellaneous "pieces." Identifying the components that comprise the kit and grouping them into media and carrier types deconstructs the kit into a resource that can be managed and described easily.

Resource Description (MARC, MODS, FISO) Checklists

The following checklists have been provided as a handy reference guide to the fields and/or areas most frequently used when creating descriptive records for kits and multimedia resources. They are intended as guidelines and reminders. Cataloging treatment and choice of access points may vary by library, level of cataloging, and so forth. Always remember that you are the best judge when deciding which fields and/or areas are appropriate to describe the resource you have in hand, *distinctly* and *sufficiently*.

MARC CHECKLIST

For additional information about the MARC fields required by BIBCO (the Monographic Bibliographic Record Program), see http://www.loc.gov/catdir/pcc/bibco/coresr.html.

Leader 06: **Type of Record**: Use **o** for kit.

Leader 07: **Bibliographic Level**: Use **m** for monograph. Kits are categorized as monographic.

006: Use for additional characteristics of the resource not accommodated in the MARC 008 field. Additional 006 fields may be required if the kit contains components such as maps, CDs, and other special types of resources.

007: Use for specific media and carrier characteristics. A kit containing components such as video, sound recordings, cartographic materials, and microfilm/microfiche requires a separate 007 field for each media type. A good rule of thumb is to enter a separate 007 field for each component of the kit except for printed and unmediated components.

008: This field is required for details about the resource as a whole. Position 23, used to code the form of item in other formats, is not available in the MARC 008 field for visual materials, because a single form of an item is not appropriate for a resource composed of multimedia components.

010–02X: Unique numeric identifiers are considered core elements of resource description. Include publisher-assigned numbers and other numbers unique to the resource. Record the ISBN in the MARC 020 field.

1XX: **Creator/Responsible Person**: Enter the primary person or organization responsible for the creation of the kit. All names must conform to the established form of name in the Library of Congress's Authorities database (available at http://authorities.loc.gov).

245: Enter the preferred title in this field. This must be the unifying title for the kit as a whole unit.

260: **Publication Details**: Record the place of publication and the publisher information according to *RDA* or *AACR2*: [$a Place of publication: $b Publisher, $c date of publication].

300: **Physical Description**: Extent of resource: Multiple 300 fields can be used to accommodate a variety of components. For a list of approved carrier types for kits, consult MARC's website (http://www.loc.gov/marc/bibliographic/bd007g.html). Terms are categorized for projected and/or nonprojected graphics. *RDA* Chapter 3 contains a list of the approved carrier types.

336, 337, 338: These fields accommodate information formerly entered as the GMD in the $h subfield of the MARC 245 field (see http://www.loc.gov/marc/formatchanges-RDA.html for additional details about these fields):

336 (Content Type): $a text $a two-dimensional images $a moving images

337 (Media Type): $a unmediated $a graphic $a visual

338 (Carrier Type): $a volume $a other $a DVD-video.

5XX: Various types of notes may be used in the description of kits. There are no mandatory notes, except for those required when the cataloger has supplied the title or has selected a title that is not readily identifiable on any component of the kit.

650: At least one subject term is required.

700 and 710: List additional responsible parties in these fields; they are required if appropriate.

856: Record the URL for remotely located supplementary resources. A cataloger may also want to provide a URL for the publisher of the resource, as this may prove useful to users. Additional information on the MARC 856 field is available at http://www.loc.gov/marc/856guide.html. The URL is required if appropriate.

MODS CHECKLIST

For additional information about constructing a descriptive record for kits using MODS, see http://www.loc.gov/standards/mods/v3/mods80700998.xml.

<typeOfResource> is used to specify type of resource being cataloged, in this case "kit."

Example:
```
<typeOfResource>kit</typeOfResource>
```

<genre> provides information on a style, form, or content expressed in the resource.

Example:
```
<genre> science project </genre>
```

<identifier> with the attribute " type" is used to provide standard identifiers, such as the ISBN.

Example:
```
<identifier type="isbn">9783540221814</identifier>
```

<recordInfo> with the subelement <recordContentSource> with the attribute "authority" is used to provide the code or name of the organization that created or modified the original resource description.

Example:
```
<recordInfo>
  <recordContentSource>Rutgers University Libraries</recordContentSource>
</recordInfo>
```

<languageTerm> with the type="code" and authority="iso639-2b" (several codes may be used in authority; see http://www.loc.gov/standards/mods/v3/mods-userguide-elements.html#language for additional information).

Example:
```
<language>
  <languageTerm type="code" authority="iso639-2b">eng</languageTerm>
</language>
```

<classification> with the attribute "authority" is used to indicate the type of classification scheme used to provide subject access to the resource.

Example:
```
<classification authority="lcc">L50.S6J65 2005</classification>
```

<name> is used to provide information on name of a person, organization, or event (conference, meeting, etc.) associated with the resource. This element has a <type> attribute to specify the type of name (personal, corporate, or conference) and an authority attribute (<authority>) to enable catalogers to specify what authoritative source was consulted to provide the authorized form of the name. This element also has a subelement <role> which is used to specify the role of the named person, corporate body, or conference in relation to the resource.

Example:
```
<name type="personal">
  <role>
    <roleTerm type="text">Creator</roleTerm>
  </role>
<name type="corporate">
  <namePart>Sony Video</namePart>
</name>
```

(Cont'd.)

MODS CHECKLIST *(Continued)*

<titleInfo> is used to convey the title or name of a resource. When the main portion of the title is referenced as core, there is only one core subelement, <title>.

Example:
```
<titleInfo>
<title>Science fair kit</title>
</titleInfo>
```

Use <titleInfo> with the type="alternative" and the subelement <title> to convey title varations.

Example:
```
</titleInfo><titleInfo type="alternative">
<title>Creating waterfalls</title>
</titleInfo>
```

<originInfo> with the subelement <edition> is used to describe the version or edition of the resource being described.

Example:
```
<originInfo>
   <edition>2nd edition</edition>
</originInfo>
```

<originInfo> with the subelement <place> and its subelement <placeTerm> with type="text", the subelement <publisher>, and the subelement <dateIssued> is used to provide information on publication, distribution, etc.

<physicalDescription> with the subelements <form> and <extent> provide descriptive information about the resource. In this text the authoritative source for <form> (used to describe the resource's physical description) is the MARC format. The subelement <extent> describes the number and types of units that make up a resource.

Example:
```
<physicalDescription>
   <form authority="marcform">DVD-video</form>  <extent>1</extent>
</physicalDescription>
```

<tableOfContents> is used for the contents of sound recordings when this information is supplied by the publisher.

Example:
```
<tableOfContents>
Creating waterfalls -- Using green materials for your project -- Making colored grass.
</tableOfContents>
```

<relatedItem> with the attribute type "series" is used to provide information on the series when appropriate.

Example:
```
<relatedItem type="series">
   <titleInfo>
      <title>Science Fairs</title>
   </titleInfo>
</relatedItem>
```

<note> is used to provide general information about the resource.

Example:
```
<note> Recommended for Grades 2 and 3.</note>
```

(Cont'd.)

MODS CHECKLIST *(Continued)*

<subject> with the attribute type "authority" and the subelement <name> with the attribute "type" (personal, corporate, conference) provides information on the primary topics of the resource. The descriptive record should contain at least one subject term.

Example:

```
<subject>
<name type="topic">
</subject>
<name type="corporate">
   <namePart> Sony Video.</namePart>
</name>
```

FISO CHECKLIST

Having constructed the descriptive record, the cataloger may find it appropriate to review the description based on the *FRBR* principles: *find*, *identify*, *select*, *obtain*:

F—The potential user has to *find* the material.
I—The user should be able to *identify* the resource, distinguishing it from any similar item.
S—The user should be able to retrieve and *select* the material as the appropriate one for a specific purpose or task.
O—The record should help the user to *obtain* the material by giving information about its location and availability and any requirements for and/or conditions of use.

The following questions are helpful in rating the completed product:

- ❑ Does the description represent the resource accurately? Comprehensive resource description can be time-consuming, but it is worth the effort.
- ❑ Have all possible access points been made available?
- ❑ Have all variant titles been recorded?
- ❑ Have the names of creators, contributors, and other access points been verified in established authority databases?
- ❑ Does the description make it quite clear to the user that specialized equipment is required to access specific components of the resource?
- ❑ Can any component benefit from additional exposure (such as being given title access or an explanatory note)?

Resources for Catalogers

International Federation of Library Associations and Institutions. 2010. *Functional Requirements for Bibliographic Records.* IFLA. Accessed June 4. http://archive.ifla.org/VII/s13/frbr.

Library of Congress, Network Development and MARC Standards Office. 2002. "MARC 21 Format for Bibliographic Data: 007: Physical Description Fixed Field—General Information." Library of Congress. http://www.loc.gov/marc/bibliographic/bd007.html.

Library of Congress, Network Development and MARC Standards Office. 2009. "MARC 21 Format Changes to Accommodate *RDA* (Draft)." Library of Congress. http://www.loc.gov/marc/formatchanges-RDA.html.

OCLC Research. 2010. "VIAF: Virtual International Authority File." OCLC. Accessed June 4. http://viaf.org.

Notes

1. American Library Association. 1998. *Anglo-American Cataloguing Rules.* 2nd ed. rev. (Appendix D-4). Chicago: American Library Association.
2. American Library Association, Canadian Library Association, and CILIP: Chartered Institute of Library and Information Professionals. 2010. *Resource Description and Access* (Chapter 2.2.2–2.2.4). ALA, CLA, and CILIP. Accessed August 24. http://www.rdatoolkit.org.
3. Ibid., Glossary.
4. American Library Association. 1998. *Anglo-American Cataloguing Rules.* 2nd ed. rev. (8:3). Chicago: American Library Association.
5. American Library Association, Canadian Library Association, and CILIP: Chartered Institute of Library and Information Professionals. 2010. *Resource Description and Access* (Chapter 3.1.4.1). ALA, CLA, and CILIP. Accessed August 24. http://www.rdatoolkit.org.
6. Ibid., Chapter 2.3.6 (Variant titles).
7. Ibid., Chapter 1.4.
8. Library of Congress. 2008. *Library of Congress Subject Headings*, 31st ed. Washington, DC: Library of Congress.
9. American Library Association, Canadian Library Association, and CILIP: Chartered Institute of Library and Information Professionals. 2010. *Resource Description and Access* (Chapter 3.3.1.2). ALA, CLA, and CILIP. Accessed August 24. http://www.rdatoolkit.org.

Index

Page numbers followed by the letter "i" indicate illustrations, which includes checklists, figures, and sidebars.

D

E

F

G

I

N

O

P

R

S

V

W

X

About the Authors

Mary Beth Weber has been head of Central Technical Services at Rutgers University Libraries since 2008. She has served in a number of positions at Rutgers, including Head of Cataloging and Metadata Services for four years and Special Formats Catalog Librarian and the Head of the Copy Cataloging Section. Weber earned an MLS from Clarion University of Pennsylvania and a bachelor's in English and art history from Michigan State University. She is the editor of the *ALCTS Newsletter Online* and serves as an ex-officio member of the ALCTS Board of Directors. Weber has also served as chair of the following ALCTS groups: Audiovisual Committee, Copy Cataloging Discussion Group (now an interest group), and Computer Files Discussion Group (now Electronic Resources Interest Group). She also serves as the Essays and Opinions Editor for the international electronic journal *LIBRES*. Weber served as an associate editor on the *LIBRES* editorial board in 1993–2008 and has been the Essays and Opinions Editor since 2008. She has served as an ex-officio member of the *Library Resources and Technical Services* (*LRTS*) editorial board since 2005.

Fay Angela Austin, MLS, CSM, is currently Head of the Monographs Cataloging and Database Management Section within Central Technical Services at Rutgers University Libraries in Piscataway, New Jersey, a position she has held since 2005. Prior to her appointment at Rutgers, Austin was President of Phoenix Information Services, a library technical services consulting company, for thirteen years. Prior to that, she was employed as Manager of Technical Services at the U.S. Department of the Interior libraries and the Goddard Library at NASA, Greenbelt, Maryland. Austin has more than thirty years of experience in technical services as a cataloger, trainer, and manager. She has served on the boards of the Special Libraries Association (New Jersey Chapter) and the United Nations Association (New Jersey Division) and remains active on the IFLA President's Working Group on the World Information Society.